THE PERFECT GIFT

PHILANTHROPIC AND NONPROFIT STUDIES

Dwight F. Burlingame and David C. Hammack, general editors

THE PERFECT GIFT

The Philanthropic Imagination in Poetry and Prose

EDITED BY AMY A. KASS

INDIANA University Press

Bloomington & Indianapolis

This book is a publication of

Indiana University Press
601 North Morton Street
Bloomington, Indiana 47404-3797 USA

http://iupress.indiana.edu

Telephone orders   800-842-6796
Fax orders   812-855-7931
Orders by email   iuporder@indiana.edu

© 2002 by Amy A. Kass

All rights reserved

Manufactured in the United States of America

Library of Congress Cataloging-in-Publication Data

The perfect gift: the philanthropic imagination in poetry and prose /
edited by Amy A. Kass.
    p. cm. — (Philanthropic and Nonprofit studies)
Includes index.
    ISBN 0-253-34131-0 (alk. paper) — ISBN 0-253-21542-0 (pbk. : alk.
paper)
    1. Generosity—Literary collections. 2. Conduct of life—Literary
collections. I. Kass, Amy A. II. Series.
    PN6071.G42 P47 2002
    808.8'0355—dc21

                                         2002000410

3 4 5 07 06 05 04

Published with the generous support of
Barbara E. and Karl R. Zimmer
and the Project on Civic Reflection
at Valparaiso University,
with funding from Lilly Endowment, Inc.

CONTENTS

Introduction   1

PART I. WHY SHOULD I GIVE?

1. Genesis 4, The Offering of Cain   13
2. Aristotle, *Nichomachean Ethics:* "Generosity, Extravagance, and Stinginess"   15
3. Alexis de Tocqueville, *Democracy in America:* Freedom and Utility   21
4. George Eliot, *Romola:* "An Arresting Voice"   34
5. O. Henry, "Two Thanksgiving Day Gentlemen"   42
6. C. S. Lewis, "Charity"   47
7. P. G. Wodehouse, "Jeeves Takes Charge"   57
8. William F. May, "The Prayers of Thanksgiving"   75
9. Barry Schwartz, "The Social Psychology of the Gift"   77
10. Clifford Orwin, "Princess Diana and Mother Teresa: Compassion and Christian Charity"   88
11. Elizabeth M. Lynn and D. Susan Wisely, "Toward a Fourth Philanthropic Response: American Philanthropy and Its Public"   102

PART II. HOW SHOULD I GIVE?

1. Matthew 25:1–46, Three Parables   115
2. Homer, *The Odyssey:* The Meeting of Nausikaa and Odysseus   119
3. Moses Maimonides, *Laws Concerning Gifts to the Poor:* "The Book of Seeds"   125
4. Sarah Orne Jewett, "The Spur of the Moment"   127
5. Isaac Peretz, "Motl Prince"   135
6. Jane Addams, "Charitable Effort"   140
7. O. Henry, "The Chair of Philanthromathematics"   155
8. Edith Wharton, "The Rembrandt"   161
9. Rudyard Kipling, "The Record of Badalia Herodsfoot"   174
10. Sylvia Warner, "A Work of Art"   191
11. John Reed, "Another Case of Ingratitude"   197
12. Gwendolyn Brooks, "The Lovers of the Poor"   200

PART III. TO WHOM OR FOR WHAT SHOULD I GIVE?

1. Genesis 25:19–34; 27–28:9, Parents and Children:
   The Case of Jacob and Esau   207

2. Matthew 25:14–30, The Parable of the Talents   213

3. William Shakespeare, *Timon of Athens,* Act I, Scene 1   215

4. William H. McGuffey, "True and False Philanthropy"   227

5. Andrew Carnegie, "The Gospel of Wealth"   230

6. Henri Barbusse, "The Eleventh"   245

7. Stephen Leacock, "Mr. Plumter, B.A., Revisits the Old Shop"   249

8. Stephen Crane, "The Men in the Storm"   261

9. Leon R. Kass, "Charity and the Confines of Compassion"   267

PART IV. WHAT SHOULD I GIVE?

1. Luke 15:11–32, The Parable of the Prodigal Son   283

2. Alexis de Tocqueville, *Democracy in America:*
   "Appendix U," The Pioneer Woman   285

3. Sholom Aleichem, "Epilogue: Reb Yozifl and the Contractor"   289

4. Rabindranath Tagore, "Gift"   295

5. O. Henry, "The Gift of the Magi"   298

6. Robert Frost, "The Death of the Hired Man"   303

7. Dorothy Parker, "Song of the Shirt, 1941"   308

8. John O'Hara, "Memorial Fund"   315

9. Eudora Welty, "Lily Daw and the Three Ladies"   319

10. Lewis Hyde, "Some Food We Could Not Eat"   328

11. Mitch Albom, *Tuesdays with Morrie:*
    "The Eighth Tuesday: We Talk About Money"   336

PART V. CAN GIVING BE TAUGHT?

1. Aristotle, *Nichomachean Ethics:*
   "Moral Virtue as the Result of Habits"   345

2. Benjamin Franklin, *The Autobiography of Benjamin Franklin:*
   Practice Makes Perfect?   348

3. Woodrow Wilson, "Princeton for the Nation's Service"   356

4. Pierre Mac Orlan, "The Philanthropist"   369

5. Kenneth E. Kirk, Worship, Humility and Service   372

6. Stephen Vincent Benet, "The Bishop's Beggar"   378

7. Edward Holmes, "Town Office"   395

8. His Holiness the XIV Dalai Lama, "Giving and Receiving:
   A Practical Way of Directing Love and Compassion"   399

9. Elizabeth M. Lynn and D. Susan Wisely, "Only Reflect:
   A Philanthropic Education for Our Time"   409

Acknowledgments   416

Author and Subject Index   419

THE PERFECT GIFT

Introduction

To the ancient Greeks, Hermes, the divine messenger, was known as the "Swift Appearer." It was his habit to alight, suddenly and without warning, next to someone who was walking along the road. The tidings Hermes delivered at such moments invariably made the recipient pause, take stock, and change his direction, both physically and psychically. Often these miraculous moments were accompanied by great gifts—for example, a sudden acquisition of enormous wealth. Hence, Hermes was also widely known as the "Great Windfall." But Hermes was also connected to sudden misfortunes and great downfalls, including the "downfall" of death. In both stories and paintings, he is depicted as a person's principal escort to the house of Hades. Thus, the "gifts" of Hermes could lead people both to greater and richer life and also to death. Mindful of the double-edged character of any wondrous moment, the Greeks understood that great misfortune may lurk in the shadow of great good fortune. They knew that a great windfall can cause a great downfall, and that gifts are equally conducive to benefit and harm, to joy and sorrow.

Few of us believe in Hermes these days—perhaps because we don't recognize him when he comes. Yet the principal insights embodied in this mythical figure are still available to us. Imagine yourself suddenly in receipt of a great fortune. Would you not be moved to pause, take stock, and ponder the direction of your life? What would you do with the money? Would you keep most of it for yourself? How would you change the way you live? Would you give some of it away? If so, to whom or for what?

Or imagine yourself suddenly appointed to the board of a major philanthropic foundation—or, better yet, thanks to a great windfall, starting a philanthropic foundation of your own. Toward what goals would you aim your philanthropy? Relief of the homeless, the poor, and the infirm? General improvement of life through such things as parks, museums, or libraries? Advancement of individual achievement, for example, through endowing scholarships or professorships? Social reform? Political advocacy? How would you decide? Could you be sure in advance that the changes you contemplated making with your windfall would be for the better and not for the worse?

But, you may be thinking, this is idle speculation. Very few of us ever win the lottery or inherit millions. Few of us ever have the opportunity to make the sorts of big choices that great wealth allows. True enough. Nevertheless, each of us must face, sooner or later, the very same issues that Hermes compelled our ancient forebears to confront: Where am I headed? Am I on the right road?

What and whom do I care most about? However meager our fortunes, most of us sooner or later will write a will, at which time we must take stock and decide what is to become of our property. If you do not want your assets to be buried with you, what do you plan to do with them? To whom—to what—might you bequeath them? On what basis will you decide? What do you hope to achieve with your gifts?

Such questions arise not only as we anticipate the end of our lives. Everyday life provides multiple occasions to deliberate about the same kinds of issues. Start small—say, with your best friend's birthday party last Saturday night. Did you take her a gift? What was it? What considerations guided your choice of gift? How much did you spend? As much as you did on the gift you gave your sister the week before? Or, recall what happened in church last Sunday: When the basket came around, did you make a contribution? How much? How did you decide? Or again: What was your reaction to last night's news? When you saw the suffering on the faces of the people whose homes were destroyed by the hurricane, did you send money? Food? Clothing? When you heard about the fire in the house down the block, did you run over to offer your neighbors a bed for the night? When you learned of the local school's lack of resources, did you donate those books you will probably never look at again? What about that old computer?

Another moment's reflection reminds us that money and property are not the only things we are able to give. We also have time, energy, and attention to spend, as well as our native talents and acquired skills. We not only give goods; we also give service. For this reason, our opportunities to give and to serve are virtually unlimited. Think again about your friends and relations: Have you telephoned your best friend recently just to say hello? How about your sister? Did you visit Aunt Sophie when she was in the hospital? Have you visited your aging grandfather recently? Go back to church for a moment: When you were asked to volunteer a couple of hours to bake for the church social or paint houses for the needy, did you do so? Why or why not? Or revisit last night's news: Did the report of the fire in your neighborhood move you to offer to baby-sit the children of your stricken neighbor? Did news of the plight of the local school move you to volunteer to tutor? To offer music or art lessons? To teach the children how to use a computer?

Everyday life sometimes ceases to be ordinary, as when great disaster strikes a community. When the World Trade Center in New York was destroyed on September 11, 2001, were you moved to send money or to donate blood? Did you send food or volunteer to cook meals for the rescue workers? Did you write or call to comfort the widows or the orphans that you knew? In the aftermath, how did you respond to the sight of firefighters entering the burning towers or to the stories of heroic rescuers? Has the memory of September 11th affected your philanthropic practices in your ongoing everyday life?

The numerous occasions in life that invite us to give and to serve prompt us to think about and to demonstrate what it is that matters to us. Whether we give time, talent, or treasure, whether our gift be great or small, and whatever our culture or religion, we cannot escape the fact that we are born into human communities and are therefore obliged, time and again, to consider what we can offer. Whatever road we travel, we inevitably encounter Hermes on the way. More important, we inevitably have the opportunity to *be* Hermes: to provide a gift or to perform a service, however small, that can make a difference, for better or for worse. We can choose or refuse to be philanthropic. We can give and serve well or poorly. But we cannot choose whether or not to have such choices.

This anthology has been prepared on the assumption that we are all, willy-nilly, called upon to give and to serve—that we are all, in the root sense of the term, philanthropists. In current usage, the term "philanthropy" is generally restricted to those who give large sums of money, be they individual donors or incorporated foundations. But "philanthropy" (from the Greek *philanthropia*) literally means love of human beings, practical goodwill toward human beings in general. Hence, "philanthropic" describes the disposition to promote the happiness and well-being of one's fellows. Starting from this understanding, the readings collected here are intended to address the fundamental concerns of each of us as philanthropists, present and future—as human beings who seek to promote the well-being of others. The readings lead us to some basic issues of giving and serving that we all must ponder if we are to wield our philanthropic powers well. Taken seriously, such basic thinking should improve the practical decisions we will make, privately or publicly, and these decisions will in turn affect the vitality of the organizations and communities of which we are a part. But the first purpose of this volume is to help each of us become more thoughtful about our own activities as givers and servers. This volume aims, in short, at cultivating and enlightening our philanthropic imagination.

By concentrating our attention on giving as a fundamental human activity, I do not mean to slight the institutional forms and socioeconomic aspects of philanthropy. On the contrary, I merely mean to emphasize that, whatever the social context, whatever the size or nature of the gift, there are always individual human beings who choose to give and to serve, and who therefore necessarily encounter, explicitly or tacitly, certain enduring questions about giving. The reader will find here no specific practical advice about how much to give and to whom, or about how to establish a philanthropic trust fund or to maximize its yield. Such particularities can be addressed only case by case and by the prudent person on the spot, to whom the specific facts of the case will usually be clear enough. What is rarely clear enough—and what is therefore at the heart of this anthology—is the grounds of our own judgments about why, how, to whom, and what we should give. Caught up in the particulars, we seldom make clear to ourselves the standards that guide us as givers or the expectations we have of our recipients.

In the belief that clearer and deeper understanding of such standards and expectations will improve our philanthropic judgments, I have organized this anthology in a way that might best bring these matters to light. There are five parts, each of which is organized around a basic question about giving: "Why should I give?" "How should I give?" "To whom should I give?" "What should I give?" and "Can giving be taught?" Many of the readings address more than one of these basic questions, and the placement of each reading in one part rather than another may in some cases seem to be arbitrary. The assignment of selections to the different parts is, in fact, based primarily on my desire to demonstrate, by juxtaposition of readings, the complexity of the issues that each of the basic questions invites us to consider.

For example, each of the readings collected in Part I raises the basic question "Why should I give?" but responds to that question in very different ways. These readings turn our attention to different, oftentimes competing, underlying motives and/or overarching principles or purposes that seed the philanthropic landscape. One reading invites reflection on the moral meaning of being a neighbor, another on the meaning of generosity, another on the meaning of charity, and yet another on compassion. Some spur us to think about giving in relation to liberty, both personal and political; others focus on its relation to the aspiration to nobility, gentlemanliness, and saintliness. One directs our attention to the ethics of gratitude, inviting us to ponder whether we human beings are primordially givers or receivers, or whether we can be the one without being the other. Still another discusses the social psychology of giving, that is, giving in relation to personal self-definition. Some of the readings provide arguments, while others tell stories, inviting us to ponder not only why particular givers and servants do what they do, but also, more generally, how giving and serving might differ.

In Part II, the basic question becomes not why but "How should I give?" Readings included here explore the tone or manner—the "spirit"—of giving. Should we, for example, act mercifully and spare judgment? Should we act prudently and compassionately? What if the two conflict? Some of the texts direct our attention to the various temptations of giving (for example, to be overbearing or condescending) and receiving (for example, to be manipulative and hypocritical), as well as offer insights into what we might do to keep giving and receiving honest. Should we, for example, give gifts anonymously? Still other readings address the specific means we use to achieve our ends. May we use shady means if our philanthropic ends are unquestionably good? What about the age-old problem of using "tainted money"—money acquired unscrupulously or from morally dubious sources, but now capable of doing some good in the world?

In Part III, we turn our attention to the recipient of giving, asking, "To whom or for what should I give?" Some of the readings included here invite reflection on whether parents should privilege one child over another in allocating their inheritance, or, more generally, on whether one should give to those who have already shown promise—or, better, accomplishment—rather than to those who might one day do so. Other readings prompt us to think about the sorts of institutions that we might want to support or serve, as well as whether such institutions ought to be local, national, or global. In one way or another, however, almost all of the readings collected in this part pointedly invite us to ponder what makes a recipient "worthy" or "deserving," as well as whether desert and merit should matter at all.

Part IV focuses attention on the gift itself, asking, "What should I give?" Here you will find stories and poems about the things we give, for better or worse. Some readings, either by direct prescription or by poetic depiction, indicate what are the best gifts to give, provoking us to agree or disagree. Others dramatically reveal the power of a particular gift, prompting us to try to articulate why it works or why it is apt. Still others invite us to reflect on how to assess the worth of a gift, as well as whether an ordinarily good gift is a good gift from *this* giver or for *this* recipient.

Up until its final part, this anthology assumes that readers are already disposed to be philanthropic and aims at illuminating the judgments or articulating the standards that implicitly guide us. But, as we are well aware, many of us, young and old, are not (yet) philanthropic. Many of us regularly make decisions about giving, but in the negative: we choose not to give. Yet one of the goals of philanthropy is to induce others to be philanthropic as well, most especially our own children or our close friends. Indeed, it may well be true that the chief mark of successful philanthropists is that they have made others desire to imitate them. How, then, to teach others to give of their time, treasure, and talent, and to want to do so wisely and well? Part V is devoted to this question. In keeping with my emphasis on the deeds of individuals, I have included some readings on the psychic seeds of the philanthropic disposition, and others on the kinds of education that can help make these seeds grow. I conclude with a selection that discusses how explicit discussion of readings such as those collected in this volume can function to enrich the philanthropic imaginations of people currently gathered together in giving and serving.

When we ponder fundamental questions of the sort raised here, we often get our most valuable help from fundamental texts. Accordingly, most of the readings collected in this anthology are excerpted from "classic" texts, written by major thinkers and writers: poets such as Homer and Shakespeare; philosophers such as Aristotle and Maimonides; novelists such as George Eliot and Edith Wharton; social theorists such as Alexis de Tocqueville and Jane Addams; short-story writers such as Sholom Aleichem, O. Henry, Rudyard Kipling, and Eudora

Welty. These texts have been chosen not because they are part of a canon, or because they represent a particular position or portion of humanity, but because they are especially effective in posing basic questions and offering alternative answers. In addition, imaginative literature—more than half of the selections included here—encourages us to identify and think with characters who are making the sorts of decisions each of us is called upon to make in real life. Whatever their historical or cultural origins, the best poets and storytellers enable us to experience human life in all its complexity and profundity, often providing access and insights not otherwise available to us.

In nearly thirty years of teaching college students, I have found readings such as those collected here to be the best companions for thought and the richest materials for enlarging the students' horizons, stimulating their imaginations, and challenging their intellectual complacencies. But I also have some strong evidence for the value of using this approach with philanthropists. It comes from a recent series of projects designed to support and invigorate civic leadership, all of them generously supported by the Lilly Endowment. The first of these projects, the "Tocqueville Seminars for Civic Leadership" at the University of Chicago, sponsored seminars in five different states for key staff members, trustees, and volunteers of selected non-profit organizations in philanthropy, education, the arts, social service, health care, and law. A second effort, the "Project on Civic Reflection" at Valparaiso University, has developed seminars in the state of Indiana for groups of individual givers, for boards and staffs of neighborhood associations, for coalitions of community leaders, and for chambers of commerce. A third project, administered by the Federation of State Humanities Councils and titled "The Art of Association," is currently developing reading programs for boards of state humanities councils, in the hope that these organizations will in turn develop reading programs for their own communities' civic leaders.

In each project, seminars have been established in the belief that giving and serving can be made more thoughtful and effective through collegial discussion of relevant and important texts. We have assumed, to paraphrase Tocqueville, that civic "feelings and ideas can be renewed, the heart enlarged, and the understanding developed" by such discussion. According to reports from the seminar participants, this is exactly what has happened to them. They have come to see more clearly the meaning and purpose of their own activities. They have been moved to consider ways of improving their practices and their institutions. And they have found, in the texts represented here, a more nuanced and imaginative "vocabulary of attention" for the complex problems of civic leadership than had previously been available to them. Many of the selections in this volume were originally chosen for or by the seminar participants. The sparks they ignited in actual discussion were, at least in part, the grounds for their inclusion here.

As any teacher knows, and as our seminar experience has confirmed, even good books generally do not teach themselves. We are frequently lazy readers who pass off what is puzzling or unfamiliar, and (even worse) who fail to see the depth in what is, by contrast, familiar and congenial. Moreover, when a subject is especially close to us or when a text challenges the way we live, our prejudices often get in the way of understanding, blinding us to crucial subtleties and nuances and, even more important, to the hard questions it invites us to ask ourselves. Accordingly, in arranging this anthology, I have introduced each selection with some observations and questions designed to make for more active and discerning reading. In some cases, where I thought it would be helpful, I have taken a decidedly didactic tone, asking the reader to approach the text with certain questions and concerns in mind. I have done this with mixed feelings, not wishing to get between author and reader, nor wishing to imperil your understanding of texts written by subtler and greater minds by imposing my own limited understanding and personal concerns. I encourage you to use the introductions if you find them helpful, but to treat them with the proverbial grain of salt.

As with any anthology, readers are free to pick and choose what they will. I heartily encourage you to do just that. In spirit and purpose, as stressed above, this anthology is not a one-size-fits-all reader. Its purpose is to help *you* cultivate *your own* way of giving and to find *your own* reasons for doing so. Yet I do make one request: Wherever you happen to alight, try to pause . . . slow down . . . and use the occasion to take stock of the road you are traveling. Try on Hermes' winged sandals and let your imagination soar. Perhaps you will find a better, and more philanthropic, way.

PART ONE

Why Should I Give?

PART I: TABLE OF CONTENTS

Genesis 4, The Offering of Cain

Aristotle, *Nichomachean Ethics:* "Generosity, Extravagance, and Stinginess"

Alexis de Tocqueville, *Democracy in America:* Freedom and Utility

George Eliot, *Romola:* "An Arresting Voice"

O. Henry, "Two Thanksgiving Day Gentlemen"

C. S. Lewis, "Charity"

P. G. Wodehouse, "Jeeves Takes Charge"

William F. May, "The Prayers of Thanksgiving"

Barry Schwartz, "The Social Psychology of the Gift"

Clifford Orwin, "Princess Diana and Mother Teresa:
Compassion and Christian Charity"

Elizabeth M. Lynn and D. Susan Wisely, "Toward a Fourth Philanthropic
Response: American Philanthropy and Its Public"

I.1

The Offering of Cain

Genesis 4

The first recorded example of gift-giving in the Bible occurs in the story of the first human family, when Cain, the first man born of woman, brings an offering unto the Lord. This story is also the source of the famous question "Am I my brother's keeper?," an affirmative answer to which has long served as a fundamental principle of philanthropic giving. Curiously, however, Cain, the primordial gift-giver, denies with word and fratricidal deed that he is his brother's keeper. Is there a way to connect these facts? What were Cain's motives for bringing his offering? Do his shame and anger when the gift is not accepted shed retrospective light on his motives as gift-giver? What is the connection between his frustrated desire to please God with gifts and his fratricidal deed? What, in fact, would it mean to be one's brother's keeper? Is there some link between a proper disposition toward God and a willingness to care for one's brother? Does the spirit of brotherhood and the philanthropic disposition require reverence for the divine?

4 1 AND Adam knew Eve his wife; and she conceived, and bare Cain, and said, I have gotten a man from the LORD.

2 And she again bare his brother Abel. And Abel was a keeper of sheep, but Cain was a tiller of the ground.

3 And in process of time it came to pass, that Cain brought of the fruit of the ground an offering unto the LORD.

4 And Abel, he also brought of the firstlings of his flock and of the fat thereof. And the LORD had respect unto Abel and to his offering:

5 But unto Cain and to his offering he had not respect. And Cain was very wroth, and his countenance fell.

6 And the LORD said unto Cain, Why art thou wroth? and why is thy countenance fallen?

7 If thou doest well, shalt thou not be accepted? and if thou doest not well, sin lieth at the door. And unto thee *shall* be his desire, and thou shalt rule over him.

From *The Holy Bible,* King James version (New York: American Bible Company).

8   And Cain talked with Abel his brother: and it came to pass, when they were in the field, that Cain rose up against Abel his brother, and slew him.

9   ⁋ And the LORD said unto Cain, Where *is* Abel thy brother? And he said, I know not: *Am* I my brother's keeper?

10   And he said, What hast thou done? the voice of thy brother's blood crieth unto me from the ground.

11   And now *art* thou cursed from the earth, which hath opened her mouth to receive thy brother's blood from thy hand;

12   When thou tillest the ground, it shall not henceforth yield unto thee her strength; a fugitive and a vagabond shalt thou be in the earth.

13   And Cain said unto the LORD, My punishment *is* greater than I can bear.

14   Behold, thou hast driven me out this day from the face of the earth; and from thy face shall I be hid; and I shall be a fugitive and a vagabond in the earth; and it shall come to pass, *that* every one that findeth me shall slay me.

15   And the LORD said unto him, Therefore whosoever slayeth Cain, vengeance shall be taken on him sevenfold. And the LORD set a mark upon Cain, lest any finding him should kill him.

16   ⁋ And Cain went out from the presence of the LORD, and dwelt in the land of Nod, on the east of Eden.

17   And Cain knew his wife; and she conceived, and bare Enoch: and he builded a city, and called the name of the city, after the name of his son, Enoch.

18   And unto Enoch was born Irad: and Irad begat Mehujael: and Mehujael begat Methusael: and Methusael begat Lamech.

19   ⁋ And Lamech took unto him two wives: the name of the one *was* Adah, and the name of the other Zillah.

20   And Adah bare Jabal: he was the father of such as dwell in tents, and *of such as have* cattle.

21   And his brother's name *was* Jubal: he was the father of all such as handle the harp and organ.

22   And Zillah, she also bare Tubal-cain, an instructor of every artificer in brass and iron: and the sister of Tubal-cain *was* Naamah.

23   And Lamech said unto his wives, Adah and Zillah, Here my voice; ye wives of Lamech, hearken unto my speech: for I have slain a man to my wounding, and a young man to my hurt.

24   If Cain shall be avenged sevenfold, truly Lamech seventy and sevenfold.

25   ⁋ And Adam knew his wife again; and she bare a son, and called his name Seth: For God, *said she,* hath appointed me another seed instead of Abel, whom Cain slew.

26   And to Seth, to him also there was born a son; and he called his name Enos: then began men to call upon the name of the LORD.

I.2

Nichomachean Ethics:
"Generosity, Extravagance, and Stinginess"

Aristotle

Thanks to our biblical heritage, when most of us think about ethics or morality, we think mainly in terms of what we should or should not do—"thou shalts" and "thou shalt nots." As Americans, we may think as well in terms of rights and duties, or as modernists, in terms of values and beliefs. For the ancient Greek philosopher Aristotle (384–322 B.C.), ethical discourse has another focus: his crucial distinction is between virtue (or "excellence," in Greek *arete*) and vice. The good human being is a person of virtuous character. Ethical human beings are those who comport themselves virtuously (or excellently), especially with respect to their desires and temptations. Such people, Aristotle explains, have acquired, with practice and over time, the "habit of choosing well," that is, of making the right choices, which choices he adds, always lie in the "mean (or median), relative to us." That is to say, people of moral virtue always know and choose the just-right-thing (the fitting thing, the "mean") for them (not for you) to do, depending on their circumstances, internal and external. (Hence, the choice is relative to the chooser or "relative to us.") Yet Aristotle emphasizes that such people always choose as the practically wise or prudent person—the person of comprehensive virtue—would choose. Appropriate or fitting choice is relative, then, but the standard is not. If, for example, you are a young person but you happen to have a broken leg, it would not be appropriate for you—or for anyone else in your circumstances—to get up and offer a frail old woman a seat on the bus. It would be appropriate, however, for a young person—any young person—of sound body to do so.

The present selection focuses on Aristotle's analysis of one particular virtue, generosity, which, he argues, governs the desire to give (and receive) material goods. Aristotle does not tell us—not here, not anywhere in his *Ethics*—what we should or should not do or, in this case, give. But by carefully distinguishing excessive giving ("extravagance") from insufficient giving ("stinginess"), and each of these extremes from the "mean," "generosity," he equips us to recognize what giving well is. Aristotle focuses his attention on deeds, but he is not indifferent to motives. Generous deeds, he argues, like all virtuous actions, are "noble" (or "beautiful," in Greek *kalon*) and are performed "for the sake of the noble." Accordingly, a generous person will give the "right thing," at the "right time," in the "right way," to the "right person," and especially for the right reason. Such a person is moved not by personal gain, gratitude, or obligation, or

Nichomachean Ethics: Aristotle by Ostwald, © Reprinted by permission of Pearson Education, Inc., Upper Saddle River, N.J., pp. 83–89.

by any of the other motives or purposes that often prompt giving, but rather by the recognition that it is noble or beautiful to give. In giving well, people display their nobility. What does this mean? What might such giving actually look like? What would be the proper response of a recipient of gifts from Aristotle's generous person? Is Aristotle's view of generosity possible to achieve? Is it desirable? Is there a difference between generosity and charity? Though Aristotle explicitly restricts his discussion of generosity to the giving of material goods or wealth, is it also applicable to the giving of other things, such as time or talent?

Next in order let us discuss generosity. It seems to be the mean in the sphere of material goods. A man is praised as generous neither for what he does on the battlefield, nor in situations in which a person is praised as self-controlled, nor again in the making of judicial decisions. He is praised in matters involving the giving and taking of material goods, more particularly the giving. By "material goods" we understand everything whose value is measured in money.

There also exists in matters involving material goods extravagance and stinginess as excesses and deficiencies. We attach the label of stinginess always to those who are more intent on material goods than they should be; the term "extravagance," on the other hand, is sometimes used with wider implications, when we call moral weaklings and people who spend their money in indulging themselves "extravagant." They have so many vices all at once that they are regarded as the most worthless of all. But that is not proper usage; for "extravagant" denotes a person who has only one bad quality, namely, that of wasting his property. A man ruined by his own doing is a hopeless case indeed; wasting one's property seems to be a kind of self-destruction, since property provides the means for living. This is, therefore, the sense in which we understand "extravagance."

Things meant for use can be used well and badly, and wealth is a useful thing. Now, any particular object is put to the best use by a man who possesses the virtue proper to that object. Accordingly, wealth will be put to best use by him who possesses the excellence proper to material goods, and that is the generous man. Use, we think, consists in spending and giving material goods, while taking and keeping them is more properly called "possession." Therefore, a generous man is characterized rather by giving to the right people than by taking from the right and not taking from the wrong sources. For excellence consists in doing good rather than in having good done to one, and in performing noble actions rather than in not performing base ones. It is fairly obvious that giving implies doing good and acting nobly, and that taking implies having good done to one and not acting basely. Furthermore, we show gratitude to him who gives, not to him who does not take, and, what is more, we praise him. Also, it is easier not to take than to give, for people are less liable to give away what belongs to them than not to take what is another's. Moreover, givers are called "generous," whereas those who do not take are rather praised for their honesty and justice, not their generosity, and takers are not likely to be praised. Generous men are perhaps loved more than any other people who are loved for their excellence, for they are helpful, and their helpfulness consists in giving.

Virtuous actions are noble and are performed because they are noble. Accordingly, a generous man, too, will give—and give in the correct manner—because that is noble. He will give to the right people, the right amount, at the right time, and do everything else that is implied in correct giving. Moreover, it will give him pleasure to do so, or (at least) no pain; for to act in conformity with virtue is pleasant or painless, but certainly not painful. If he gives to the wrong people or for the wrong motive, and not because it is noble to give, he will not be called generous but something else. (The same applies to a man who finds giving) painful. He would prefer material goods to noble action, and that is not what marks a man as generous. Nor will a generous man take from the wrong source; that kind of taking is not characteristic of a man who holds material goods in low esteem. He is not likely to make requests, either: a person who does good is not one to accept good turns lightly. But he will take from the right source, from his own possessions, for example, not because it is noble to do so, but because it is necessary in order to have (something) to give. He will not, however, be careless of his personal possessions, since he wishes to use them as a means of helping others. He will not give to anybody and everybody, so that he may have (something) to give to the right people at the right time and where it is noble to do so. Still, a generous man has a strong tendency to go to such excess in giving that he leaves too little for himself; for not to look out for himself is typical of a generous person.

We speak of generosity relative to a person's property. For a generous act does not depend on the amount given, but on the characteristic of the giver, and this makes him give relative to his property. In other words, it is quite possible that a man who gives less is more generous, if his gift comes from smaller resources. Those who have not accumulated their own property but have inherited it are thought to be more generous, not only because they never experienced want, but also because everyone has a greater love for what he has produced himself, as do parents and poets. A generous man does not easily get rich, inasmuch as he is not a taker or a keeper, but an openhanded spender who values material goods not for their own sake but for the sake of giving. That is also why fortune is blamed when the most worthy individuals are the least wealthy. And not without reason: one cannot have material goods or anything else without devoting care to getting them.

Still, (a generous man) will not give to the wrong people, at the wrong time, and so forth; for if he did, his actions would no longer be dictated by generosity, and if he spent his money on the wrong things, he would have none to spend on the right ones. For as we have said, a man is generous who spends relative to his property and on the right objects; he who (spends) to excess is extravagant. Therefore, we do not call tyrants or absolute monarchs extravagant, for, it seems, the amounts they give and spend cannot very well be in excess of the amounts they possess.

Now, since generosity is the mean in giving and taking material goods, a generous person will give and spend the right amounts on the right objects, in small and great matters alike, and he will derive pleasure from doing so. Also, he will take the right amounts from the right sources. For since the virtue is a mean both in giving and in taking, he will do both in the proper manner: honest taking goes with honest giving, and any other kind of taking is contrary to it. Now, the practices that belong together are found in the same individual, while contrary practices obviously are not. If he should happen to spend his money in a manner other than proper and noble, he will feel pain, but moderately and in the right way; for it is a mark of virtue or excellence to feel pleasure and pain at the right objects and in the right way. Moreover, a generous man is easy to get along with in business matters, for he can be taken advantage of, since he sets no store by material goods and since he feels more vexation at not having made a proper expenditure, than pain at having made a wrong one . . .

Here, too, an extravagant man goes completely wrong: he feels neither pleasure nor pain at the right objects and in the right manner. This will become more apparent as we go on. We have stated that extravagance and stinginess are excesses and deficiencies in two respects, i.e., in giving and in taking, for we classify spending with giving. Extravagance is an excess in giving without taking, but it falls short in taking. Stinginess, on the other hand, is a deficiency in giving and an excess in taking, but only in small matters.

Now, these two aspects of extravagance do not usually go together. For it is not easy for a person to give to all and take from none. Private individuals soon exhaust their property by giving, and it is of private individuals that we think (when we say that a person) is extravagant. Still, a man who is extravagant in both senses is thought to be considerably superior to a stingy man: age and poverty easily cure him, and he can attain the median state. He has the qualities requisite for a generous man: he gives and does not take, though he does neither rightly and well. If he were to acquire this practice by habit or by changing in some other way, he would be generous: he will then give to the right people and will not take from the wrong source. That is why he is not regarded as bad in character, for excess in giving and in not taking marks a man as foolish, but not as wicked or ignoble. A man who is extravagant in this fashion seems to be far superior to a stingy person for the reasons mentioned, and also because he is helpful to many people, while a stingy man helps nobody, not even himself.

However, most extravagant people, as we have pointed out, also take from the wrong sources and are, in this respect, stingy. They tend to take because they want to spend, but they are unable to do so with an open hand, since their own resources are soon exhausted. As a result, they are compelled to provide means from elsewhere. At the same time, their indifference to what is noble makes them take indiscriminately from any and every source. They have an appetite for giving, no matter how or from what source. For that reason, their gifts are not even generous. Their gifts are not noble, they are not given because it is noble to give, and they are not given in the right way. On the contrary, persons of this sort sometimes make wealthy those who ought to be poor; they would give nothing to people of respectable character but much to those who flatter them or provide them with other kinds of pleasure. Hence, most of them are also self-indulgent: they are easy spenders and squander their money to indulge themselves. They incline toward pleasure, since their lives are not oriented toward what is noble.

This is what an extravagant man will develop into if left unschooled, but if he receives proper care he may attain the median, the right state. But stinginess is incurable and more deeply ingrained in men than extravagance, for we can see that old age and any kind of disability can make men stingy. Most people love to hang on to material goods rather than to give them away. Moreover, stinginess reaches far and takes many forms, for there seem to be many kinds of it.

There are two aspects to stinginess: deficiency in giving and excess in taking. This means that it is not found in its entirety in all men, but is sometimes divided, so that some exceed in taking while others fall short in giving. Names such as "miser," "niggard," "penny-pincher," are all used of people who fall short in giving but do not covet or wish to take what belongs to another. Some are motivated by a sense of honesty and have scruples against acting basely—for there are those who seem (or, at any rate, profess) to keep what they have in order to avoid being compelled to do something base. Here belongs the skinflint and everyone like him who gets his name from his excessive reluctance to give anything. Some do not touch another man's property through fear, in the belief that it is not easy to take what belongs to another while at the same time preventing others from taking what belongs to oneself. Accordingly, they are satisfied neither to take nor to give.

Still others exceed in taking in that they take anything from any source; such, for example, are those who follow occupations not fit for free men, such as pimps and all their ilk, and usurers who lend small sums at high interest. All these people take from the wrong sources and more than they should. What they have in common is clearly the motive of profiteering, for they all endure notoriety for the sake of profit, and small profit at that. But those who take the wrong things from the wrong source on a large scale, such as tyrants who sack cities and plunder temples, are not called "stingy" or "mean" but "wicked," "impious," and "unjust." However, gamblers and highwaymen are classified as stingy and mean, for they are profiteers in that both ply their trade and endure notoriety for the sake of profit, the one taking the greatest risks to get booty, and the other to make a profit at the expense of his friends to whom he ought to give. Now, since both wish to gain profit from the wrong sources, they are profiteers, and all such ways of taking are stingy and mean.

It is with good reason that stinginess is said to be the opposite of generosity. For not only is it a greater evil than extravagance, but people are more prone to go wrong in following it than in following extravagance as we have described it. So much for generosity and the vices opposed to it.

I.3

Democracy in America:
Freedom and Utility

Alexis de Tocqueville

In the early 1830s, the French aristocrat and social theorist Alexis de Tocqueville (1805–1859) traveled to the United States, where he was struck by the condition of equality and its effects on everyday life. He observed our political institutions and social mores, and, through interviews with city-dwellers and frontiersmen, sought to ascertain the passions, morals, beliefs, goals, and intellectual habits that informed our ways. Notwithstanding the lapse of time and our greatly changed socioeconomic conditions, Tocqueville's analysis, recorded in his magisterial *Democracy in America,* is still regarded by many as the most penetrating extant account of the democratic ethos in general and of American democracy in particular.

Tocqueville rightly assumed that the march of equality was inevitable, both in the United States and abroad, but he thought it possible to shape and channel its effects. "Within the wide verge of the circle," he notes, "men are powerful and free; we cannot determine whether conditions will or will not be equal, we can determine whether equality will lead to wretchedness or to greatness, to slavery or to freedom." Tocqueville especially commends the American "habit" of forming voluntary associations—what we call "non-profit organizations"—as an important bulwark against tyranny. He is well aware that such civic service does not consciously spring from or aim at anything very lofty or noble. He reports having met many Americans who were moved to help their neighbors for seemingly disinterested reasons, but he emphasizes the fact that no one acknowledges such motives. They give credit, instead, to their fundamentally utilitarian philosophy, which he refers to as the "doctrine of self-interest properly understood." Tocqueville's primary reason for praising the habit of association—to safeguard and promote political freedom—seems, then, at least at first glance, to be at odds with our own motives for associating—to safeguard and promote our own personal interests.

The three excerpts in this selection—on political associations, civil associations, and the doctrine of self-interest properly understood—invite careful scrutiny, both taken separately and in relation to each other. Is Tocqueville right to suggest that our habit of association is especially conducive to the preservation of freedom? Is the habit laudable apart from the actual associations in which it eventuates? Should we regard

Pages 513–517, 525–528 from *Democracy in America* by Alexis de Tocqueville. Edited by J. P. Mayer and Max Lerner. Translated by George Lawrence. English translation copyright © 1965 by Harper & Row, Publishers, Inc. Reprinted by permission of HarperCollins Publishers Inc.

ourselves as philanthropic if we stand to gain from our own philanthropy or, more to the point, if we are moved from the outset by what is in it for us? Is political freedom well served if we are either unaware of or indifferent to the fact that we are preserving it?

POLITICAL ASSOCIATION IN THE UNITED STATES

... [T]his powerful instrument of action [i.e., association] has been applied to more varied aims in America than anywhere else in the world.

Apart from permanent associations such as townships, cities, and counties created by law, there are a quantity of others whose existence and growth are solely due to the initiative of individuals.

The inhabitant of the United States learns from birth that he must rely on himself to combat the ills and trials of life; he is restless and defiant in his outlook toward the authority of society and appeals to its power only when he cannot do without it. The beginnings of this attitude first appear at school, where the children, even in their games, submit to rules settled by themselves and punish offenses which they have defined themselves. The same attitude turns up again in all the affairs of social life. If some obstacle blocks the public road halting the circulation of traffic, the neighbors at once form a deliberative body; this improvised assembly produces an executive authority which remedies the trouble before anyone has thought of the possibility of some previously constituted authority beyond that of those concerned. Where enjoyment is concerned, people associate to make festivities grander and more orderly. Finally, associations are formed to combat exclusively moral troubles: intemperance is fought in common. Public security, trade and industry, and morals and religion all provide the aims for associations in the United States. There is no end which the human will despairs of attaining by the free action of the collective powers of individuals.

Later I shall have occasion to speak of the effects of association on civil life. For the moment I must stick to the world of politics.

The right of association being recognized, citizens can use it in different ways. An association simply consists in the public and formal support of specific doctrines by a certain number of individuals who have undertaken to cooperate in a stated way in order to make these doctrines prevail. Thus the right of association can almost be identified with freedom to write, but already associations are more powerful than the press. When some view is represented by an association, it must take clearer and more precise shape. It counts its supporters and involves them in its cause; these supporters get to know one another, and numbers increase zeal. An association unites the energies of divergent minds and vigorously directs them toward a clearly indicated goal.

Freedom of assembly marks the second stage in the use made of the right of association. When a political association is allowed to form centers of action at certain important places in the country, its activity becomes greater and its influence more widespread. There men meet, active measures are planned, and opinions are expressed with that strength and warmth which the written word can never attain.

But the final stage is the use of association in the sphere of politics. The supporters of an agreed view may meet in electoral colleges and appoint mandatories to represent them in a central assembly. That is, properly speaking, the application of the representative system to one party.

So, in the first of these cases, men sharing one opinion are held together by a purely intellectual tie; in the second case, they meet together in small assemblies representing only a fraction of the party; finally, in the third case, they form something like a separate nation within the nation and a government within the government. Their mandatories, like those of the majority, represent by themselves all the collective power of their supporters, and, like them in this too, they appear as national representatives with all the moral prestige derived therefrom. It is true that, unlike the others, they have no right to make laws, but they do have the power to attack existing laws and to formulate, by anticipation, laws which should take the place of the present ones.

Imagine some people not perfectly accustomed to the use of freedom, or one in which profound political passions are seething. Suppose that, besides the majority that makes the laws, there is a minority which only deliberates and which gets laws ready for adoption; I cannot help but think that then public order would be exposed to great risks.

There is certainly a great gap between proving that one law is in itself better than another and establishing that it ought to be substituted for it. But where trained minds may still see a wide gap, the hasty imagination of the crowd may be unaware of this. Moreover, there are times when the nation is divided into two almost equal parties, each claiming to represent the majority. If, besides the ruling power, another power is established with almost equal moral authority, can one suppose that in the long run it will just talk and not act?

Will it always stop short in front of the metaphysical consideration that the object of associations is to direct opinions and not to constrain them, and to give advice about the law but not to make it?

The more I observe the main effects of a free press, the more convinced am I that, in the modern world, freedom of the press is the principal and, so to say, the constitutive element in freedom. A nation bent on remaining free is therefore right to insist, at whatever cost, on respect for this freedom. But *unlimited* freedom of association must not be entirely identified with freedom to write. The former is both less necessary and more dangerous than the latter. A nation may set limits there without ceasing to be its own master; indeed, in order to remain its own master, it is sometimes necessary to do so.

In America there is no limit to freedom of association for political ends.

One example will show better than anything I could say just how far it is tolerated.

One remembers how excited the Americans were by the free-trade-tariff controversy. Not opinions only, but very powerful material interests stood to gain or lose by a tariff. The North thought that some of its prosperity was due thereto, while the South blamed it for almost all its woes. One may say that over a long period the tariff question gave rise to the only political passions disturbing the Union.

In 1831, when the quarrel was most envenomed, an obscure citizen of Massachusetts thought of suggesting through the newspapers that all opponents of the tariff should send deputies to Philadelphia to concert together measures to make trade free. Thanks to the invention of printing, this suggestion passed in but a few days from Maine to New Orleans. The opponents of the tariff took it up ardently. They assembled from all sides and appointed deputies. Most of the latter were known men, and some of them had risen to celebrity. South Carolina, which was later to take up arms in this cause, sent sixty-three people as its delegates. On October 1, 1831, the assembly, which in American fashion styled itself a convention, was constituted at Philadelphia; it counted more than two hundred members. The discussions were public, and from the very first day it took on an altogether legislative character; discussion covered the extent of the powers of Congress, theories of free trade, and finally the various provisions of the tariff. After ten days the assembly broke up, having issued an address to the American people. In that address it declared first that Congress had not the right to impose a tariff and that the existing tariff was unconstitutional, and second that it was against the interest of any people, in particular the American people, that trade should not be free.

It must be admitted that unlimited freedom of association in the political sphere has not yet produced in America the fatal results that one might anticipate from it elsewhere. The right of association is of English origin and always existed in America. Use of this right is now an accepted part of customs and of mores.

In our own day freedom of association has become a necessary guarantee against the tyranny of the majority. In the United States, once a party has become predominant, all public power passes into its hands; its close supporters occupy all offices and have control of all organized forces. The most distinguished men of the opposite party, unable to cross the barrier keeping them from power, must be able to establish themselves outside it; the minority must use the whole of its moral authority to oppose the physical power oppressing it. Thus the one danger has to be balanced against a more formidable one.

The omnipotence of the majority seems to me such a danger to the American republics that the dangerous expedient used to curb it is actually something good.

Here I would repeat something which I have put in other words when speaking of municipal freedom: no countries need associations more—to prevent either despotism of parties or the arbitrary rule of a prince—than those with a democratic social state. In aristocratic nations secondary bodies form natural associations which hold abuses of power in check. In countries where such associations do not exist, if private people did not artificially and temporarily create something like them, I see no other dike to hold back tyranny of whatever sort, and a great nation might with impunity be oppressed by some tiny faction or by a single man.

The meeting of a great political convention (for conventions are of all kinds), though it may often be a necessary measure, is always, even in America, a serious event and one that good patriots cannot envisage without alarm.

That came out clearly during the convention of 1831, when all the men of distinction taking part therein tried to moderate its language and limit its objective. Probably the convention of 1831 did greatly influence the attitude of the malcontents and prepared them for the open revolt of 1832 against the commercial laws of the Union.

One must not shut one's eyes to the fact that unlimited freedom of association for political ends is, of all forms of liberty, the last that a nation can sustain. While it may not actually lead it into anarchy, it does constantly bring it to the verge thereof. But this form of freedom, howsoever dangerous, does provide guarantees in one direction; in countries where associations are free, secret societies are unknown. There are factions in America, but no conspirators.

Concerning the different ways in which the right of association is understood in Europe and in America, and the different uses made of it.

The most natural right of man, after that of acting on his own, is that of combining his efforts with those of his fellows and acting together. Therefore the right of association seems to me by nature almost as inalienable as individual liberty. Short of attacking society itself, no lawgiver can wish to abolish it. However, though for some nations freedom to unite is purely beneficial and a source of prosperity, there are other nations who pervert it by their excesses and turn a fount of life into a cause of destruction. So I think it will be thoroughly useful both for governments and for political parties if I make a comparison between the different ways in which associations are used in those nations that understand what freedom is and in those where this freedom turns into license.

Most Europeans still regard association as a weapon of war to be hastily improvised and used at once on the field of battle.

An association may be formed for the purpose of discussion, but everybody's mind is preoccupied by the thought of impending action. An association is an army; talk is needed to count numbers and build up courage, but after that they march against the enemy. Its members regard legal measures as possible means, but they are never the only possible means of success.

The right of association is not understood like that in the United States. In America the citizens who form the minority associate in the first place to show their numbers and to lessen the moral authority of the majority, and secondly, by stimulating competition, to discover the arguments most likely to make an impression on the majority, for they always hope to draw the majority over to their side and then to exercise power in its name.

Political associations in the United States are therefore peaceful in their objects and legal in the means used; and when they say that they only wish to prevail legally, in general they are telling the truth.

There are several reasons for this difference between the Americans and ourselves. In Europe there are parties differing so much from the majority that they can never hope to win its support, and yet these parties believe themselves strong enough to struggle against it on their own. When such a party forms an association it intends not to convince but to fight. In America those whose opinions make a wide gap between them and the majority can do nothing to oppose its power; all others hope to win it over.

So the exercise of the right of association becomes dangerous when great parties see no possibility of becoming the majority. In a country like the United States, where differences of view are only matters of nuance, the right of association can remain, so to say, without limits.

It is our inexperience of liberty in action which still leads us to regard freedom of association as no more than a right to make war on the government. The first idea which comes into a party's mind, as into that of an individual, when it gains some strength is that of violence; the thought of persuasion only comes later, for it is born of experience.

The English, though the divisions between them are so deep, seldom abuse the right of associations, because they have had long experience of it.

Furthermore, we have such a passionate taste for war that there is no enterprise so reckless or dangerous to the state, but it is thought glorious to die for it with arms in one's hand.

But perhaps universal suffrage is the most powerful of all the elements tending to moderate the violence of political associations in the United States. In a country with universal suffrage the majority is never in doubt, because no party can reasonably claim to represent those who have not voted at all. Therefore associations know, and everyone knows, that they do not represent the majority. The very fact of their existence proves this, for if they did represent the majority, they themselves would change the law instead of demanding reforms.

Thereby the moral strength of the government they attack is greatly increased and their own correspondingly weakened.

Almost all associations in Europe believe or claim that they represent the wishes of the majority. This belief or claim greatly increases their strength and wonderfully serves to legitimize their acts. For what is more excusable than violence to bring about the triumph of the oppressed cause of right?

Thus in the immense complication of human laws it sometimes comes about that extreme freedom corrects the abuse of freedom, and extreme democracy forestalls the dangers of democracy.

In Europe associations regard themselves in a way as the legislature and executive council of the nation which cannot raise its own voice; starting from this conception, they act and they command. In America, where everyone sees that they represent only a minority in the nation, they talk and petition.

The means used by associations in Europe are in accord with the aim proposed.

The main aim of these associations being to act and not to talk, to fight and not to convince, there is naturally nothing civilian about their organization, and indeed military ways and maxims are introduced therein; one also finds them centralizing control of their forces as much as they can and placing the whole authority in very few hands.

Members of these associations answer to a word of command like soldiers on active service; they profess the dogma of passive obedience, or rather, by the single act of uniting, have made a complete sacrifice of their judgment and free will; hence within associations, there often prevails a tyranny more intolerant than that exercised over society in the name of the government they attack.

This greatly diminishes their moral strength. They lose the sacred character belonging to the struggle of the oppressed against the oppressor. For how can a man claim that he wants to be free when in certain cases he consents servilely to obey some of his fellow men, yielding up his will and submitting his very thoughts to them?

The Americans too have provided a form of government within their associations, but it is, if I may put it so, a civil government. There is a place for individual independence there; as in society, all the members are advancing at the same time toward the same goal, but they are not obliged to follow exactly the same path. There has been no sacrifice of will or of reason, but rather will and reason are applied to bring success to a common enterprise.

ON THE USE WHICH THE AMERICANS MAKE OF ASSOCIATIONS IN CIVIL LIFE

... [H]ere I am only concerned with those associations in civil life which have no political object.

In the United States, political associations are only one small part of the immense number of different types of associations found there.

Americans of all ages, all stations in life, and all types of disposition are forever forming associations. There are not only commercial and industrial associations in which all take part, but others of a thousand different types—religious, moral, serious, futile, very general and very limited, immensely large and very minute. Americans combine to give fêtes, found seminaries, build churches, distribute books, and send missionaries to the antipodes. Hospitals, prisons, and schools take shape in that way. Finally, if they want to proclaim a truth or propagate some feeling by the encouragement of a great example, they form an association. In every case, at the head of any new undertaking, where in France you would find the government or in England some territorial magnate, in the United States you are sure to find an association.

I have come across several types of association in America of which, I confess, I had not previously the slightest conception, and I have often admired the extreme skill they show in proposing a common object for the exertions of very many and in inducing them voluntarily to pursue it.

Since that time I have traveled in England, a country from which the Americans took some of their laws and many of their customs, but it seemed to me that the principle of association was not used nearly so constantly or so adroitly there.

A single Englishman will often carry through some great undertaking, whereas Americans form associations for no matter how small a matter. Clearly the former regard association as a powerful means of action, but the latter seem to think of it as the only one.

Thus the most democratic country in the world now is that in which men have in our time carried to the highest perfection the art of pursuing in common the objects of common desires and have applied this new technique to the greatest number of purposes. Is that just an accident or is there really some necessary connection between associations and equality?

In aristocratic societies, while there is a multitude of individuals who can do nothing on their own, there is also a small number of very rich and powerful men, each of whom can carry out great undertakings on his own.

In aristocratic societies men have no need to unite for action, since they are held firmly together.

Every rich and powerful citizen is in practice the head of a permanent and enforced association composed of all those whom he makes help in the execution of his designs.

But among democratic peoples all the citizens are independent and weak. They can do hardly anything for themselves, and none of them is in a position to force his fellows to help him. They would all therefore find themselves helpless if they did not learn to help each other voluntarily.

If the inhabitants of democratic countries had neither the right nor the taste for uniting for political objects, their independence would run great risks, but they could keep both their wealth and their knowledge for a long time. But if they did not learn some habits of acting together in the affairs of daily life, civilization itself would be in peril. A people in which individuals had lost the power of carrying through great enterprises by themselves, without acquiring the faculty of doing them together, would soon fall back into barbarism.

Unhappily, the same social conditions that render associations so necessary to democratic nations also make their formation more difficult there than elsewhere.

When several aristocrats want to form an association, they can easily do so. As each of them carries great weight in society, a very small number of associates may be enough. So, being few, it is easy to get to know and understand one another and agree on rules.

But that is not so easy in democratic nations, where, if the association is to have any power, the associates must be very numerous.

I know that many of my contemporaries are not the least embarrassed by this difficulty. They claim that as the citizens become weaker and more helpless, the government must become proportionately more skillful and active, so that society should do what is no longer possible for individuals. They think that answers the whole problem, but I think they are mistaken.

A government could take the place of some of the largest associations in America, and some particular states of the Union have already attempted that. But what political power could ever carry on the vast multitude of lesser undertakings which associations daily enable American citizens to control?

It is easy to see the time coming in which men will be less and less able to produce, by each alone, the commonest bare necessities of life. The tasks of government must therefore perpetually increase, and its efforts to cope with them must spread its net ever wider. The more government takes the place of associations, the more will individuals lose the idea of forming associations and need the government to come to their help. That is a vicious circle of cause and effect. Must the public administration cope with every industrial undertaking beyond the competence of one individual citizen? And if ultimately, as a result of the minute subdivision of landed property, the land itself is so infinitely parceled out that it can only be cultivated by associations of laborers, must the head of the government leave the helm of state to guide the plow?

The morals and intelligence of a democratic people would be in as much danger as its commerce and industry if ever a government wholly usurped the place of private associations.

Feelings and ideas are renewed, the heart enlarged, and the understanding developed only by the reciprocal action of men one upon another.

I have shown how these influences are reduced almost to nothing in democratic countries; they must therefore be artificially created, and only associations can do that.

When aristocrats adopt a new idea or conceive a new sentiment, they lend it something of the conspicuous station they themselves occupy, and so the mass is bound to take notice of them, and they easily influence the minds and hearts of all around.

In democratic countries only the governing power is naturally in a position so to act, but it is easy to see that its action is always inadequate and often dangerous.

A government, by itself, is equally incapable of refreshing the circulation of feelings and ideas among a great people, as it is of controlling every industrial undertaking. Once it leaves the sphere of politics to launch out on this new track, it will, even without intending this, exercise an intolerable tyranny. For a government can only dictate precise rules. It imposes the sentiments and ideas which it favors, and it is never easy to tell the difference between its advice and its commands.

Things will be even worse if the government supposes that its real interest is to prevent the circulation of ideas. It will then stand motionless and let the weight of its deliberate somnolence lie heavy on all.

It is therefore necessary that it should not act alone.

Among democratic peoples associations must take the place of the powerful private persons whom equality of conditions has eliminated.

As soon as several Americans have conceived a sentiment or an idea that they want to produce before the world, they seek each other out, and when found, they unite. Thenceforth they are no longer isolated individuals, but a power conspicuous from the distance whose actions serve as an example; when it speaks, men listen.

The first time that I heard in America that one hundred thousand men had publicly promised never to drink alcoholic liquor, I thought it more of a joke than a serious matter and for the moment did not see why these very abstemious citizens could not content themselves with drinking water by their own firesides.

In the end I came to understand that these hundred thousand Americans, frightened by the progress of drunkenness around them, wanted to support sobriety by their patronage. They were acting in just the same way as some great territorial magnate who dresses very plainly to encourage a contempt of luxury among simple citizens. One may fancy that if they had lived in France each of these hundred thousand would have made individual representations to the government asking it to supervise all the public houses throughout the realm.

Nothing, in my view, more deserves attention than the intellectual and moral associations in America. American political and industrial associations easily catch our eyes, but the others tend not to be noticed. And even if we do notice them we tend to misunderstand them, hardly ever having seen anything similar before. However, we should recognize that the latter are as necessary as the former to the American people; perhaps more so.

In democratic countries knowledge of how to combine is the mother of all other forms of knowledge; on its progress depends that of all the others.

Among laws controlling human societies there is one more precise and clearer, it seems to me, than all the others. If men are to remain civilized or to become civilized, the art of association must develop and improve among them at the same speed as equality of conditions spreads.

HOW THE AMERICANS COMBAT INDIVIDUALISM BY THE DOCTRINE OF SELF-INTEREST PROPERLY UNDERSTOOD

When the world was under the control of a few rich and powerful men, they liked to entertain a sublime conception of the duties of man. It gratified them to make out that it is a glorious thing to forget oneself and that one should do good without self-interest, as God himself does. That was the official doctrine of morality at that time.

I doubt whether men were better in times of aristocracy than at other times, but certainly they talked continually about the beauties of virtue. Only in secret did they study its utility. But since imagination has been taking less lofty flights, and every man's thoughts are centered on himself, moralists take fright at this idea of sacrifice and no longer venture to suggest it for consideration. So they are reduced to inquiring whether it is not to the individual advantage of each to work for the good of all, and when they have found one of those points where private advantage does meet and coincide with the general interest, they eagerly call attention thereto. Thus what was an isolated observation becomes a general doctrine, and in the end one comes to believe that one sees that by serving his fellows man serves himself and that doing good is to his private advantage.

I have already shown elsewhere in several places in this book how the inhabitants of the United States almost always know how to combine their own advantage with that of their fellow citizens. What I want to point out now is the general theory which helps them to this result.

In the United States there is hardly any talk of the beauty of virtue. But they maintain that virtue is useful and prove it every day. American moralists do not pretend that one must sacrifice himself for his fellows because it is a fine thing to do so. But they boldly assert that such sacrifice is as necessary for the man who makes it as for the beneficiaries.

They have seen that in their time and place the forces driving man in on himself are irresistible, and despairing of holding such forces back, they only consider how to control them.

They therefore do not raise objections to men pursuing their interests, but they do all they can to prove that it is in each man's interest to be good.

I do not want to follow their arguments in detail here, as that would lead too far from my subject. It is enough for my purpose to note that they have convinced their fellow citizens.

Montaigne said long ago: "If I did not follow the straight road for the sake of its straightness, I should follow it having found by experience that, all things considered, it is the happiest and the most convenient."

So the doctrine of self-interest properly understood is not new, but it is among the Americans of our time that it has come to be universally accepted. It has become popular. One finds it at the root of all actions. It is interwoven in all they say. You hear it as much from the poor as from the rich.

The version of this doctrine current in Europe is much grosser but at the same time less widespread and, especially, less advertised. Every day men profess a zeal they no longer feel.

The Americans, on the other hand, enjoy explaining almost every act of their lives on the principle of self-interest properly understood. It gives them pleasure to point out how an enlightened self-love continually leads them to help one another and disposes them freely to give part of their time and wealth for the good of the state. I think that in this they often do themselves less than justice, for sometimes in the United States, as elsewhere, one sees people carried away by the disinterested, spontaneous impulses natural to man. But the Americans are hardly prepared to admit that they do give way to emotions of this sort. They prefer to give the credit to their philosophy rather than to themselves.

I might drop the argument at this point without attempting to pass judgment on what I have described. The extreme difficulty of the subject would be my excuse. But I do not want to plead that. I would rather that my readers, seeing clearly what I mean, refuse to agree with me than that I should leave them in suspense.

Self-interest properly understood is not at all a sublime doctrine, but it is clear and definite. It does not attempt to reach great aims, but it does, without too much trouble, achieve all it sets out to do. Being within the scope of everybody's understanding, everyone grasps it and has no trouble in bearing it in mind. It is wonderfully agreeable to human weaknesses, and so easily wins great sway. It has no difficulty in keeping its power, for it turns private interest against itself and uses the same goad which excites them to direct passions.

The doctrine of self-interest properly understood does not inspire great sacrifices, but every day it prompts some small ones; by itself it cannot make a man virtuous, but its discipline shapes a lot of orderly, temperate, moderate, careful, and self-controlled citizens. If it does not lead the will directly to virtue, it establishes habits which unconsciously turn it that way.

If the doctrine of self-interest properly understood ever came to dominate all thought about morality, no doubt extraordinary virtues would be rarer. But I think that gross depravity would also be less common. Such teaching may stop some men from rising far above the common level of humanity, but many of those who fall below this standard grasp it and are restrained by it. Some individuals it lowers, but mankind it raises.

I am not afraid to say that the doctrine of self-interest properly understood appears to me the best suited of all philosophical theories to the wants of men in our time and that I see it as their strongest remaining guarantee against themselves. Contemporary moralists therefore should give most of their attention to it. Though they may well think it incomplete, they must nonetheless adopt it as necessary.

I do not think, by and large, that there is more egoism among us than in America; the only difference is that there it is enlightened, while here it is not. Every American has the sense to sacrifice some of his private interests to save the rest. We want to keep, and often lose, the lot.

I see around nothing but people bent publicly on proving, by word and deed, that what is useful is never wrong. Is there no chance of finding some who will make the public understand that what is right may be useful?

No power on earth can prevent increasing equality from turning men's minds to look for the useful or disposing each citizen to get wrapped up in himself.

One must therefore expect that private interest will more than ever become the chief if not the only driving force behind all behavior. But we have yet to see how each man will interpret his private interest.

If citizens, attaining equality, were to remain ignorant and coarse, it would be difficult to foresee any limit to the stupid excesses into which their selfishness might lead them, and no one could foretell into what shameful troubles they might plunge themselves for fear of sacrificing some of their own well-being for the prosperity of their fellow men.

I do not think that the doctrine of self-interest as preached in America is in all respects self-evident. But it does contain many truths so clear that for men to see them it is enough to educate them. Hence it is all-important for them to be educated, for the age of blind sacrifice and instinctive virtues is already long past, and I see a time approaching in which freedom, public peace, and social stability will not be able to last without education.

I.4

Romola: "An Arresting Voice"

George Eliot

English Victorian novelist and essayist George Eliot, née Mary Ann Evans (1819–1880), is especially well known for developing the method of psychological analysis so characteristic of modern fiction. Her novel *Romola,* the source of this selection, gives evidence of her prodigious gifts and insight. Set in Florence during the tumultuous years at the end of the fifteenth century, its plot is closely informed by the campaign against corruption and sensuality led by the charismatic Dominican friar Fra Girolamo Savonarola. (The Medicis and all other lovers of humanistic classicism were his prime targets.)

Eliot's central character, the young, beautiful, intelligent, and well-educated Romola, is caught in the middle of the war. Educated in the classics by her blind scholar-father, Bardo, Romola serves diligently and devotedly as his amanuensis. To no one's surprise, when she falls in love and marries, it is to a man with scholarly aptitudes and interests similar to hers, one who she assumes will be as devoted to her father as she is. But Tito Melema's ambition and lack of scruples, which he conceals before winning Romola, eventually show themselves. In time, he becomes unfaithful not only to Romola and her father but to Florence as well.

After her father's death, Tito's treachery becomes unbearable, and Romola, in defiance of both civic and religious law, decides to leave him and try to make a new life for herself elsewhere. Alone and in disguise, she sets out to find Cassandra Fidele, the best-educated woman of her time, in order to learn how she might support herself. But on the road she encounters Savonarola, who persuades her to forgo her quest for independence and scholarship, to return to her husband and city, and to embrace, instead, a life of service and self-renunciation. Their conversation is the subject of this selection. One can choose marriage, Savonarola argues, but one cannot choose what it means to be a wife; one can choose a place to live, but one cannot choose what it means to be a neighbor. Duties are given, not chosen. He persuades Romola not only to give up her desire for independence but also to denounce the life devoted to scholarship and learning as a snare and delusion. Why does Romola so readily agree? Had she lived in a time less fraught with hostility and more hospitable to women's education, talents, and possibilities, do you think Savonarola would have succeeded in persuading her? Has he persuaded you?

When Romola sat down on the stone under the cypress, all things conspired to give her the sense of freedom and solitude: her escape from the accustomed walls and streets; the widening distance from her husband, who was by this time riding toward Siena, while every hour would take her farther the opposite way; the morning stillness; the great dip of ground on the roadside making a gulf between her and the sombre calm of the mountains. For the first time in her life she felt alone in the presence of the earth and sky, with no human presence interposing and making a law for her.

Suddenly a voice close to her said,—

"You are Romola de' Bardi, the wife of Tito Melema."

She knew the voice: it had vibrated through her more than once before; and because she knew it, she did not turn round or look up. She sat shaken by awe, and yet inwardly rebelling against the awe. It was one of those black-skirted monks who was daring to speak to her, and interfere with her privacy: that was all. And yet she was shaken, as if that destiny which men thought of as a sceptred deity had come to her, and grasped her with fingers of flesh.

"You are fleeing from Florence in disguise. I have a command from God to stop you. You are not permitted to flee."

Romola's anger at the intrusion mounted higher at these imperative words. She would not turn round to look at the speaker, whose examining gaze she resented. Sitting quite motionless, she said,—

"What right have you to speak to me, or to hinder me?"

"The right of a messenger. You have put on a religious garb, and you have no religious purpose. You have sought the garb as a disguise. But you were not suffered to pass me without being discerned. It was declared to me who you were: it is declared to me that you are seeking to escape from the lot God has laid upon you. You wish your true name and your true place in life to be hidden, that you may choose for yourself a new name and a new place, and have no rule but your own will. And I have a command to call you back. My daughter, you must return to your place."

Romola's mind rose in stronger rebellion with every sentence. She was the more determined not to show any sign of submission, because the consciousness of being inwardly shaken made her dread lest she should fall into irresolution. She spoke with more irritation than before.

"I will not return. I acknowledge no right of priests and monks to interfere with my actions. You have no power over me."

"I know—I know you have been brought up in scorn of obedience. But it is not the poor monk who claims to interfere with you: it is the truth that commands you. And you cannot escape it. Either you must obey it, and it will lead you; or you must disobey it, and it will hang on you with the weight of a chain which you will drag forever. But you will obey it, my daughter. Your old servant will return to you with the mules; my companion is gone to fetch him; and you will go back to Florence."

She started up with anger in her eyes, and faced the speaker. It was Fra Girolamo: she knew that well enough before. She was nearly as tall as he was, and their faces were almost on a level. She had started up with defiant words ready to burst from her lips, but they fell back again without utterance. She had met Fra Girolamo's calm glance, and the impression from it was so new to her that her anger sank ashamed as something irrelevant.

There was nothing transcendent in Savonarola's face. It was not beautiful. It was strong-featured, and owed all its refinement to habits of mind and rigid discipline of the body. The source of the impression his glance produced on Romola was the sense it conveyed to her of interest in her and care for her apart from any personal feeling. It was the first time she had encountered a gaze in which simple human fellowship expressed itself as a strongly felt bond. Such a glance is half the vocation of the priest or spiritual guide of men, and Romola felt it impossible again to question his authority to speak to her. She stood silent, looking at him. And he spoke again.

"You assert your freedom proudly, my daughter. But who is so base as the debtor that thinks himself free?"

There was a sting in those words, and Romola's countenance changed as if a subtle pale flash had gone over it.

"And you are flying from your debts: the debt of a Florentine woman; the debt of a wife. You are turning your back on the lot that has been appointed for you—you are going to choose another. But can man or woman choose duties? No more than they can choose their birthplace or their father and mother. My daughter, you are fleeing from the presence of God into the wilderness."

As the anger melted from Romola's mind, it had given place to a new presentiment of the strength there might be in submission, if this man, at whom she was beginning to look with a vague reverence, had some valid law to show her. But no—it was impossible; he could not know what determined her. Yet she could not again simply refuse to be guided; she was constrained to plead; and in her new need to be reverent while she resisted, the title which she had never given him before came to her lips without forethought.

"My father, you cannot know the reasons which compel me to go. None can know them but myself. None can judge for me. I have been driven by great sorrow. I am resolved to go."

"I know enough, my daughter: my mind has been so far illuminated concerning you, that I know enough. You are not happy in your married life; but I am not a confessor, and I seek to know nothing that should be reserved for the seal of confession. I have a Divine warrant to stop you, which does not depend on such knowledge. You were warned by a message from heaven, delivered in my presence,—you were warned before marriage, when you might still have lawfully chosen to be free from the marriage-bond. But you chose the bond; and in wilfully breaking it—I speak to you as a pagan, if the holy mystery of matrimony is not sacred to you—you are breaking a pledge. Of what wrongs will you complain, my daughter, when you yourself are committing one of the greatest wrongs a woman and a citizen can be guilty of,—withdrawing in secrecy and disguise from a pledge which you have given in the face of God and your fellow-men? Of what wrongs will you complain, when you yourself are breaking the simplest law that lies at the foundation of the trust which binds man to man,—faithfulness to the spoken word? This, then, is the wisdom you have gained by scorning the mysteries of the Church?—not to see the bare duty of integrity, where the Church would have taught you to see, not integrity only, but religion."

The blood had rushed to Romola's face, and she shrank as if she had been stricken. "I would not have put on a disguise," she began; but she could not go on,—she was too much shaken by the suggestion in the Frate's words of a possible affinity between her own conduct and Tito's.

"And to break that pledge you fly from Florence: Florence, where there are the only men and women in the world to whom you owe the debt of a fellow-citizen."

"I should never have quitted Florence," said Romola, tremulously, "as long as there was any hope of my fulfilling a duty to my father there."

"And do you own no tie but that of a child to her father in the flesh? Your life has been spent in blindness, my daughter. You have lived with those who sit on a hill aloof, and look down on the life of their fellow-men. I know their vain discourse. It is of what has been in the times which they fill with their own fancied wisdom, while they scorn God's work in the present. And doubtless you were taught how there were pagan women who felt what it was to live for the Republic; yet you have never felt that you, a Florentine woman, should live for Florence. If your own people are wearing a yoke, will you slip from under it, instead of struggling with them to lighten it? There is hunger and misery in our streets, yet you say, 'I care not; I have my own sorrows; I will go away, if peradventure I can ease them.' The servants of God are struggling after a law of justice, peace, and charity, that the hundred thousand citizens among whom you were born may be governed righteously; but you think no more of this than if you were a bird, that may spread its wings and fly whither it will in search of food to its liking. And yet you have scorned the teaching of the Church, my daughter. As if you, a wilful wanderer, following your own blind choice, were not below the humblest Florentine woman who stretches forth her hands with her own people, and craves a blessing for them; and feels a close sisterhood with the neighbor who kneels beside her and is not of her own blood; and thinks of the mighty purpose that God has for Florence; and waits and endures because the promised work is great, and she feels herself little."

"I was not going away to ease and self-indulgence," said Romola, raising her head again, with a prompting to vindicate herself. "I was going away to hardship. I expect no joy: it is gone from my life."

"You are seeking your own will, my daughter. You are seeking some good other than the law you are bound to obey. But how will you find good? It is not a thing of choice: it is a river that flows from the foot of the Invisible Throne, and flows by the path of obedience. I say again, man cannot choose his duties. You may choose to forsake your duties, and choose not to have the sorrow they bring. But you will go forth; and what will you find, my daughter? Sorrow without duty—bitter herbs, and no bread with them."

"But if you knew," said Romola, clasping her hands and pressing them tight, as she looked pleadingly at Fra Girolamo; "if you knew what it was to me,—how impossible it seemed to me to bear it."

"My daughter," he said, pointing to the cord round Romola's neck, "you carry something within your mantle; draw it forth, and look at it."

Romola gave a slight start, but her impulse now was to do just what Savonarola told her. Her self-doubt was grappled by a stronger will and a stronger conviction than her own. She drew forth the crucifix. Still pointing towards it, he said,—

"There, my daughter, is the image of a Supreme Offering, made by Supreme Love, because the need of man was great."

He paused, and she held the crucifix trembling,—trembling under a sudden impression of the wide distance between her present and her past self. What a length of road she had traveled through since she first took that crucifix from the Frate's hands! Had life as many secrets before her still as it had for her then, in her young blindness? It was a thought that helped all other subduing influences; and at the sound of Fra Girolamo's voice again, Romola, with a quick involuntary movement, pressed the crucifix against her mantle and looked at him with more submission than before.

"Conform your life to that image, my daughter; make your sorrow an offering: and when the fire of Divine charity burns within you, and you behold the need of your fellow-men by the light of that flame, you will not call your offering great. You have carried yourself proudly, as one who held herself not of common blood or of common thoughts; but you have been as one unborn to the true life of man. What! you say your love for your father no longer tells you to stay in Florence? Then, since that tie is snapped, you are without a law, without religion: you are no better than a beast of the field when she is robbed of her young. If the yearning of a fleshly love is gone, you are without love, without obligation. See, then, my daughter, how you are below the life of the believer who worships that image of the Supreme Offering, and feels the glow of a common life with the lost multitude for whom that offering was made, and beholds the history of the world as the history of a great redemption in which he is himself a fellow-worker, in his own place and among his own people! If you held that faith, my beloved daughter, you would not be a wanderer flying from suffering, and blindly seeking the good of a freedom which is lawlessness. You would feel that Florence was the home of your soul as well as your birthplace, because you would see the work that was given you to do there. If you forsake your place, who will fill it? You ought to be in your place now, helping in the great work by which God will purify Florence, and raise it to be the guide of the nations. What! the earth is full of iniquity—full of groans—the light is still struggling with a mighty darkness, and you say, 'I cannot bear my bonds; I will burst them asunder; I will go where no man claims me'? My daughter, every bond of your life is a debt: the right lies in the payment of that debt; it can lie nowhere else. In vain will you wander over the earth; you will be wandering forever away from the right."

Romola was inwardly struggling with strong forces: that immense personal influence of Savonarola, which came from the energy of his emotions and beliefs; and her consciousness, surmounting all prejudice, that his words implied a higher law than any she had yet obeyed. But the resisting thoughts were not yet overborne.

"How, then, could Dino* be right? He broke ties. He forsook his place."

"That was a special vocation. He was constrained to depart, else he could not have attained the higher life. It would have been stifled within him."

"And I too," said Romola, raising her hands to her brow, and speaking in a tone of anguish, as if she were being dragged to some torture. "Father, you may be wrong."

"Ask your conscience, my daughter. You have no vocation such as your brother had. You are a wife. You seek to break your ties in self-will and anger, not because the higher life calls upon you to renounce them. The higher life begins for us, my daughter, when we renounce our own will to bow before a Divine law. That seems hard to you. It is the portal of wisdom, and freedom, and blessedness. And the symbol of it hangs before you. That wisdom is the religion of the Cross. And you stand aloof from it: you are a pagan; you have been taught to say, 'I am as the wise men who lived before the time when the Jew of Nazareth was crucified.' And that is your wisdom! To be as the dead whose eyes are closed, and whose ear is deaf to the work of God that has been since their time. What has your dead wisdom done for you, my daughter? It has left you without a heart for the neighbors among whom you dwell, without care for the great work by which Florence is to be regenerated and the world made holy; it has left you without a share in the Divine life which quenches the sense of suffering Self in the ardors of an ever-growing love. And now, when the sword has pierced your soul, you say, 'I will go away; I cannot bear my sorrow.' And you think nothing of the sorrow and the wrong that are within the walls of the city where you dwell: you would leave your place empty, when it ought to be filled with your pity and your labor. If there is wickedness in the streets, your steps should shine with the

---

*Dino is Romola's brother, who, much earlier, had abandoned his home to join the church.

light of purity; if there is a cry of anguish, you, my daughter, because you know the meaning of the cry, should be there to still it. My beloved daughter, sorrow has come to teach you a new worship: the sign of it hangs before you."

Romola's mind was still torn by conflict. She foresaw that she should obey Savonarola and go back: his words had come to her as if they were an interpretation of that revulsion from self-satisfied ease, and of that new fellowship with suffering, which had already been awakened in her. His arresting voice had brought a new condition into her life, which made it seem impossible to her that she could go on her way as if she had not heard it; yet she shrank as one who sees the path she must take, but sees, too, that the hot lava lies there. And the instinctive shrinking from a return to her husband brought doubts. She turned away her eyes from Fra Girolamo, and stood for a minute or two with her hands hanging clasped before her, like a statue. At last she spoke, as if the words were being wrung from her, still looking on the ground.

"My husband . . . he is not . . . my love is gone!"

"My daughter, there is the bond of a higher love. Marriage is not carnal only, made for selfish delight. See what that thought leads you to! It leads you to wander away in a false garb from all the obligations of your place and name. That would not have been, if you had learned that it is a sacramental vow, from which none but God can release you. My daughter, your life is not as a grain of sand, to be blown by the winds; it is a thing of flesh and blood, that dies if it be sundered. Your husband is not a malefactor?"

Romola started. "Heaven forbid! No; I accuse him of nothing."

"I did not suppose he was a malefactor. I meant, that if he were a malefactor, your place would be in the prison beside him. My daughter, if the cross comes to you as a wife, you must carry it as a wife. You may say, 'I will forsake my husband,' but you cannot cease to be a wife."

"Yet if—oh, how could I bear—" Romola had involuntarily begun to say something which she sought to banish from her mind again.

"Make your marriage-sorrows an offering too, my daughter: an offering to the great work by which sin and sorrow are being made to cease. The end is sure, and is already beginning. Here in Florence it is beginning, and the eyes of faith behold it. And it may be our blessedness to die for it: to die daily by the crucifixion of our selfish will,—to die at last by laying our bodies on the altar. My daughter, you are a child of Florence; fulfil the duties of that great inheritance. Live for Florence,—for your own people, whom God is preparing to bless the earth. Bear the anguish and the smart. The iron is sharp—I know, I know—it rends the tender flesh. The draught is bitterness on the lips. But there is rapture in the cup,—there is the vision which makes all life below it dross forever. Come, my daughter, come back to your place!"

While Savonarola spoke with growing intensity, his arms tightly folded before him still, as they had been from the first, but his face alight as from an inward flame, Romola felt herself surrounded and possessed by the glow of his passionate faith. The chill doubts all melted away; she was subdued by the sense of something unspeakably great to which she was being called by a strong being who roused a new strength within herself. In a voice that was like a low, prayerful cry, she said,—

"Father, I will be guided. Teach me! I will go back."

Almost unconsciously she sank on her knees. Savonarola stretched out his hands over her; but feeling would no longer pass through the channel of speech, and he was silent.

I.5

"Two Thanksgiving Day Gentlemen"

O. Henry

There are occasions when the impulse to give seems especially acute.
Consider, for example, Thanksgiving Day. Not by accident do so many of
us remember the needy on this particular day. But why do we do so?
And, moreover, why are those to whom we give so ready and willing, especially on this holiday, to accept our gifts? Through this short story,
American writer O. Henry (pseudonym of William Sydney Porter [1862–
1910]) invites us to reflect on the why and wherefore of traditions of
giving.

Stuffy Pete is a homeless man. Every Thanksgiving for the last nine
years, he has been summoned from his bench in New York City's Union
Square by an old gentleman who takes him to a restaurant, orders up a
sumptuous dinner, and sits idly by as Stuffy eats it. This year, however, as
Stuffy is making his way to his park bench, "two old ladies of ancient
family" stop him, invite him into their home, and serve him a meal even
more sumptuous than his traditional fare. By the time he reaches his old
familiar bench and the old gentleman shows up, he is already stuffed to
the gills. What happens thereafter raises most poignantly the deepest
questions about giving and receiving. Who is the real "gentleman," and
who the philanthropist, in the story? Are his deeds beneficent? admirable? foolish? noble? Are the traditions reported herein praiseworthy?
In general, is the American "liturgical" calendar, which so prominently
features Thanksgiving, as conducive as it appears to be to true philanthropic effort?

There is one day that is ours. There is one day when all we Americans who are
not self-made go back to the old home to eat saleratus biscuits and marvel how
much nearer to the porch the old pump looks than it used to. Bless the day.
President Roosevelt gives it to us. We hear some talk of the Puritans, but don't
just remember who they were. Bet we can lick 'em, anyhow, if they try to land
again. Plymouth Rocks? Well, that sounds more familiar. Lots of us have had to
come down to hens since the Turkey Trust got its work in. But somebody in
Washington is leaking out advance information to 'em about these Thanksgiving proclamations.

From *The Complete Works of O. Henry* (Garden City, N.Y.: Doubleday & Co., 1953).

The big city east of the cranberry bogs has made Thanksgiving Day an institution. The last Thursday in November is the only day in the year on which it recognizes the part of America lying across the ferries. It is the one day that is purely American. Yes, a day of celebration, exclusively American.

And now for the story which is to prove to you that we have traditions on this side of the ocean that are becoming older at a much rapider rate than those of England are—thanks to our git-up and enterprise.

Stuffy Pete took his seat on the third bench to the right as you enter Union Square from the east, at the walk opposite the fountain. Every Thanksgiving Day for nine years he had taken his seat there promptly at one o'clock. For every time he had done so things had happened to him—Charles Dickensy things that swelled his waistcoat above his heart, and equally on the other side.

But today Stuffy Pete's appearance at the annual trysting place seemed to have been rather the result of habit than of the yearly hunger which, as the philanthropists seem to think, afflicts the poor at such extended intervals.

Certainly Pete was not hungry. He had just come from a feast that had left him of his powers barely those of respiration and locomotion. His eyes were like two pale gooseberries firmly imbedded in a swollen and gravy-smeared mask of putty. His breath came in short wheezes; a senatorial roll of adipose tissue denied a fashionable set to this upturned coat collar. Buttons that had been sewed upon his clothes by kind Salvation fingers a week before flew like popcorn, strewing the earth around him. Ragged he was, with a split shirt front open to the wishbone; but the November breeze, carrying fine snowflakes, brought him only a grateful coolness. For Stuffy Pete was overcharged with the caloric produced by a super-bountiful dinner, beginning with oysters and ending with plum pudding, and including (it seemed to him) all the roast turkey and baked potatoes and chicken salad and squash pie and ice cream in the world. Wherefore he sat, gorged, and gazed upon the world with after-dinner contempt.

The meal had been an unexpected one. He was passing a red-brick mansion near the beginning of Fifth Avenue, in which lived two old ladies of ancient family and a reverence for traditions. They even denied the existence of New York and believed that Thanksgiving Day was declared solely for Washington Square. One of their traditional habits was to station a servant at the postern gate with orders to admit the first hungry wayfarer that came along after the hour of noon had struck, and banquet him to a finish. Stuffy Pete happened to pass by on his way to the park, and the seneschals gathered him in and upheld the custom of the castle.

After Stuffy Pete had gazed straight before him for ten minutes he was conscious of a desire for a more varied field of vision. With a tremendous effort he moved his head slowly to the left. And then his eyes bulged out fearfully, and his breath ceased, and the rough-shod ends of his short legs wriggled and rustled on the gravel.

For the Old Gentleman was coming across Fourth Avenue toward his bench.

Every Thanksgiving Day for nine years the Old Gentleman had come there and found Stuffy Pete on his bench. That was a thing that the Old Gentleman was trying to make a tradition of. Every Thanksgiving Day for nine years he had found Stuffy there, and had led him to a restaurant and watched him eat a big dinner. They do those things in England unconsciously. But this is a young country, and nine years is not so bad. The Old Gentleman was a staunch American patriot, and considered himself a pioneer in American tradition. In order to become picturesque we must keep on doing one thing for a long time without ever letting it get away from us. Something like collecting the weekly dimes in industrial insurance. Or cleaning the streets.

The Old Gentleman moved, straight and stately, toward the Institution that he was rearing. Truly, the annual feeding of Stuffy Pete was nothing national in its character, such as the Magna Carta or jam for breakfast was in England. But it was a step. It was almost feudal. It showed, at least, that a Custom was not impossible to New Y—ahem!—America.

The Old Gentleman was thin and tall and sixty. He was dressed all in black, and wore the old-fashioned kind of glasses that won't stay on our nose. His hair was whiter and thinner than it had been last year, and he seemed to make more use of his big, knobby cane with the crooked handle.

As his established benefactor came up Stuffy wheezed and shuddered like some woman's over-fat pug when a street dog bristles up at him. He would have flown, but all the skill of Santos-Dumont could not have separated him from his bench. Well had the myrmidons of the two old ladies done their work.

"Good morning," said the Old Gentleman. "I am glad to perceive that the vicissitudes of another year have spared you to move in health about the beautiful world. For that blessing alone this day of thanksgiving is well proclaimed to each of us. If you will come with me, my man, I will provide you with a dinner that should make your physical being accord with the mental."

That is what the Old Gentleman said every time. Every Thanksgiving Day for nine years. The words themselves almost formed an Institution. Nothing could be compared with them except the Declaration of Independence. Always before they had been music in Stuffy's ears. But now he looked up at the Old Gentleman's face with tearful agony in his own. The fine snow almost sizzled when it fell upon his perspiring brow. But the Old Gentleman shivered a little and turned his back to the wind.

Stuffy had always wondered why the Old Gentleman spoke his speech rather sadly. He did not know that it was because he was wishing every time that he had a son to succeed him. A son who would come there after he was gone—a son who would stand proud and strong before some subsequent Stuffy, and say, "In memory of my father." Then it would be an institution.

But the Old Gentleman had no relatives. He lived in rented rooms in one of the decayed old family brownstone mansions in one of the quiet streets east of the park. In the winter he raised fuchsias in a little conservatory the size of a steamer trunk. In the spring he walked in the Easter parade. In the summer he lived at a farmhouse in the New Jersey hills, and sat in a wicker armchair, speaking of a butterfly, the ornithoptera amphrisius, that he hoped to find some day. In the autumn he fed Stuffy a dinner. These were the Old Gentleman's occupations.

Stuffy Pete looked up at him for a half minute, stewing and helpless in his own self-pity. The Old Gentleman's eyes were bright with the giving-pleasure. His face was getting more lined each year, but his little black necktie was in as jaunty a bow as ever, and his linen was beautiful and white, and his gray mustache was curled gracefully at the ends. And then Stuffy made a noise that sounded like peas bubbling in a pot. Speech was not intended; and as the Old Gentleman had heard the sounds nine times before, he rightly construed them into Stuffy's old formula of acceptance.

"Thankee, sir. I'll go with ye, and much obliged. I'm very hungry, sir."

The coma of repletion had not prevented from entering Stuffy's mind the conviction that he was the basis of an Institution. His Thanks-giving appetite was not his own; it belonged by all the sacred rights of established custom, if not by the actual Statute of Limitations, to this kind old gentleman who had preempted it. True, America is free; but in order to establish tradition some one must be a repetend—a repeating decimal. The heroes are not all heroes of steel and gold. See one here that wielded only weapons of iron, badly silvered, and tin.

The Old Gentleman led his annual protégé southward to the restaurant, and to the table where the feast had always occurred. They were recognized.

"Here comes de old guy," said a waiter, "dat blows dat same bum to a meal every Thanksgiving."

The Old Gentleman sat across the table glowing like a smoked pearl at his cornerstone of future ancient Tradition. The waiters heaped the table with holiday food—and Stuffy, with a sigh that was mistaken for hunger's expression, raised knife and fork and carved for himself a crown of imperishable bay.

No more valiant hero ever fought his way through the ranks of an enemy. Turkey, chops, soups, vegetables, pies, disappeared before him as fast as they could be served. Gorged nearly to the uttermost when he entered the restaurant, the smell of food had almost caused him to lose his honor as a gentleman, but he rallied like a true knight. He saw the look of beneficent happiness on the Old Gentleman's face—a happier look than even the fuchsias and the ornithoptera amphrisius had ever brought to it—and he had not the heart to see it wane.

In an hour Stuffy leaned back with a battle won.

"Thankee kindly, sir," he puffed like a leaky steampipe; "thankee kindly for a hearty meal."

Then he arose heavily with glazed eyes and started toward the kitchen. A waiter turned him about like a top, and pointed him toward the door. The Old Gentleman carefully counted out $1.30 in silver change, leaving three nickels for the waiter.

They parted as they did each year at the door, the Old Gentleman going south, Stuffy north.

Around the first corner Stuffy turned, and stood for one minute. Then he seemed to puff out his rags as an owl puffs out his feathers, and fell to the sidewalk like a sunstricken horse.

When the ambulance came the young surgeon and the driver cursed softly at his weight. There was no smell of whiskey to justify a transfer to the patrol wagon, so Stuffy and his two dinners went to the hospital. There they stretched him on a bed and began to test him for strange diseases, with the hope of getting a chance at some problem with the bare steel.

And lo! an hour later another ambulance brought the Old Gentleman. And they laid him on another bed and spoke of appendicitis, for he looked good for the bill.

But pretty soon one of the young doctors met one of the young nurses whose eyes he liked, and stopped to chat with her about the cases.

"That nice old gentleman over there, now," he said, "you wouldn't think that was a case of almost starvation. Proud old family, I guess. He told me he hadn't eaten a thing for three days."

I.6

"Charity"

C. S. Lewis

In *The Four Loves,* the prolific English novelist, essayist, and Christian humanist C. S. Lewis (1898–1963) discusses four fundamental species of human loving: Affection, Friendship, Eros, and Charity. The last chapter, from which this selection is excerpted, contrasts the first three loves, each of which is rooted in our natural need for or attraction to one another (hence, referred to by Lewis as "Need-love"), with the last, which is rooted in Divine or "Gift" love. Unlike "Need-love," Lewis argues, "Gift-love" is "wholly disinterested and desires what is simply best for the beloved"; it is also that which enables us to love what is not naturally lovable (e.g., lepers, enemies, etc.), as well as to feed and clothe perfect strangers. "That such a Gift-love comes by Grace and should be called Charity, everyone will agree," Lewis asserts. But, he adds, charity draws on two other gifts of Grace, both of which are more difficult to acknowledge: "a supernatural Need-love [in the giver himself] of Himself and a supernatural Need-love of one another." Charity requires us to look not only outward but inward, and to recognize our own fundamental unlovableness, dependence, and neediness, or, as others put it, our own sinfulness. It requires us to recognize that we, just like our beneficiaries, have that within that requires forbearance, tolerance, and forgiveness. Is Lewis right to put such stress on the demands and difficulties inherent in charity? Must we, as he seems to imply, accept the sorrows of suffering if we are truly to be moved or governed by charity? Is there a difference between charitable giving, as Lewis understands it, and generosity? (Compare with Aristotle, on "Generosity.") Or between charitable giving and compassionate giving? (Compare with Genesis 4 and Orwin, on "Princess Diana and Mother Teresa.")

William Morris wrote a poem called "Love Is Enough" and someone is said to have reviewed it briefly in the words "It isn't." Such has been the burden of this book. The natural loves are not self-sufficient. Something else, at first vaguely described as "decency and common sense," but later revealed as goodness, and finally as the whole Christian life in one particular relation, must come to the help of the mere feeling if the feeling is to be kept sweet. . . .

[T]his brings me to the foot of the last steep ascent this book must try to make. We must try to relate the human activities called "loves" to that Love which is God a little more precisely than we have yet done. The precision can, of course, be only that of a model or a symbol, certain to fail us in the long run and, even while we use it, requiring correction from other models. The humblest of us, in a state of Grace, can have some "knowledge-by-acquaintance" (*connaître*), some "tasting," of Love Himself; but man even at his highest sanctity and intelligence has no direct "knowledge about" (*savoir*) the ultimate Being—only analogies. We cannot see light, though by light we can see things. Statements about God are extrapolations from the knowledge of other things which the divine illumination enables us to know. I labour these deprecations because, in what follows, my efforts to be clear (and not intolerably lengthy) may suggest a confidence which I by no means feel. I should be mad if I did. Take it as one man's reverie, almost one man's myth. If anything in it is useful to you, use it; if anything is not, never give it a second thought.

God is love. Again, "Herein is love, not that we loved God but that He loved us" (I *John* IV, 10). We must not begin with mysticism, with the creature's love for God, or with the wonderful foretastes of the fruition of God vouchsafed to some in their earthly life. We begin at the real beginning, with love as the Divine energy. This primal love is Gift-love. In God there is no hunger that needs to be filled, only plenteousness that desires to give. The doctrine that God was under no necessity to create is not a piece of dry scholastic speculation. It is essential. Without it we can hardly avoid the conception of what I can only call a "managerial" God; a Being whose function or nature is to "run" the universe, who stands to it as a head-master to a school or a hotelier to a hotel. But to be sovereign of the universe is no great matter to God. In Himself, at home in "the land of the Trinity," he is Sovereign of a far greater realm. We must keep always before our eyes that vision of Lady Julian's in which God carried in His hand a little object like a nut, and that nut was "all that is made." God, who needs nothing, loves into existence wholly superfluous creatures in order that He may love and perfect them. He creates the universe, already foreseeing—or should we say "seeing"? there are no tenses in God—the buzzing cloud of flies about the cross, the flayed back pressed against the uneven stake, the nails driven through the mesial nerves, the repeated incipient suffocation as the body droops, the repeated torture of back and arms as it is time after time, for breath's sake, hitched up. If I may dare the biological image, God is a "host" who deliberately creates His own parasites; causes us to be that we may exploit and "take advantage of" Him. Herein is love. This is the diagram of Love Himself, the inventor of all loves.

God, as Creator of nature, implants in us both Gift-loves and Need-loves. The Gift-loves are natural images of Himself; proximities to Him by resemblance which are not necessarily and in all men proximities of approach. A devoted mother, a beneficent ruler or teacher, may give and give, continually exhibiting the likeness, without making the approach. The Need-loves, so far as I have been able to see, have no resemblance to the Love which God is. They are rather correlatives, opposites; not as evil is the opposite of good, of course, but as the form of the blancmange is an opposite to the form of the mould.

But in addition to these natural loves God can bestow a far better gift; or rather, since our minds must divide and pigeon-hole, two gifts.

He communicates to men a share of His own Gift-love. This is different from the Gift-loves He has built into their nature. These never quite seek simply the good of the loved object for the object's own sake. They are biased in favour of those goods they can themselves bestow, or those which they would like best themselves, or those which fit in with a pre-conceived picture of the life they want the object to lead. But Divine Gift-love—Love Himself working in a man—is wholly disinterested and desires what is simply best for the beloved. Again, natural Gift-love is always directed to objects which the lover finds in some way intrinsically lovable—objects to which Affection or Eros or a shared point of view attracts him, or, failing that, to the grateful and the deserving, or perhaps to those whose helplessness is of a winning and appealing kind. But Divine Gift-love in the man enables him to love what is not naturally lovable; lepers, criminals, enemies, morons, the sulky, the superior and the sneering. Finally, by a high paradox, God enables men to have a Gift-love towards Himself. There is of course a sense in which no one can give to God anything which is not already His; and if it is already His what have you given? But since it is only too obvious that we can withhold ourselves, our wills and hearts, from God, we can, in that sense, also give them. What is His by right and would not exist for a moment if it ceased to be His (as the song is the singer's), He has nevertheless made ours in such a way that we can freely offer it back to Him. "Our wills are ours to make them Thine." And as all Christians know there is another way of giving to God; every stranger whom we feed or clothe is Christ. And this apparently is Gift-love to God whether we know it or not. Love Himself can work in those who know nothing of Him. The "sheep" in the parable had no idea either of the God hidden in the prisoner whom they visited or of the God hidden in themselves when they made the visit. (I take the whole parable to be about the judgment of the heathen. For it begins by saying, in the Greek, that the Lord will summon all "the nations" before Him—presumably, the Gentiles, the *Goyim*.)

That such a Gift-love comes by Grace and should be called Charity, everyone will agree. But I have to add something which will not perhaps be so easily admitted. God, as it seems to me, bestows two other gifts; a supernatural Need-love of Himself and a supernatural Need-love of one another. By the first I do not mean the Appreciative love of Himself, the gift of adoration. What little I have to say on that higher—that highest—subject will come later. I mean a love which does not dream of disinterestedness, a bottomless indigence. Like a river making its own channel, like a magic wine which in being poured out should simultaneously create the glass that was to hold it, God turns our need of Him into Need-love of Him. What is stranger still is that He creates in us a more than natural receptivity of Charity from our fellow-men. Need is so near greed and we are so greedy already that it seems a strange grace. But I cannot get it out of my head that this is what happens.

Let us consider first this supernatural Need-love of Himself, bestowed by Grace. Of course the Grace does not create the need. That is there already; "given" (as the mathematicians say) in the mere fact of our being creatures, and incalculably increased by our being fallen creatures. What the Grace gives is the full recognition, the sensible awareness, the complete acceptance—even, with certain reservations, the glad acceptance—of this Need. For, without Grace, our wishes and our necessities are in conflict.

All those expressions of unworthiness which Christian practice puts into the believer's mouth seem to the outer world like the degraded and insincere grovelings of a sycophant before a tyrant, or at best a *façon de parler* like the self-depreciation of a Chinese gentleman when he calls himself "this coarse and illiterate person." In reality, however, they express the continually renewed, because continually necessary, attempt to negate that misconception of ourselves and of our relation to God which nature, even while we pray, is always recommending to us. No sooner do we believe that God loves us than there is an impulse to believe that He does so, not because He is Love, but because we are intrinsically lovable. The Pagans obeyed this impulse unabashed; a good man was "dear to the gods" because he was good. We, being better taught, resort to subterfuge. Far be it from us to think that we have virtues for which God could love us. But then, how magnificently we have repented! As Bunyan says, describing his first and illusory conversion, "I thought there was no man in England that pleased God better than I." Beaten out of this, we next offer our own humility to God's admiration. Surely He'll like *that?* Or if not that, our clear-sighted and humble recognition that we still lack humility. Thus, depth beneath depth and subtlety within subtlety, there remains some lingering idea of our own, our very own, attractiveness. It is easy to acknowledge, but almost impossible to realize for long, that we are mirrors whose brightness, if we are bright, is wholly derived from the sun that shines upon us. Surely we must have a little—however little—native luminosity? Surely we can't be *quite* creatures?

For this tangled absurdity of a Need, even a Need-love, which never fully acknowledges its own neediness, Grace substitutes a full, childlike and delighted acceptance of our Need, a joy in total dependence. We become "jolly beggars." The good man is sorry for the sins which have increased his Need. He is not entirely sorry for the fresh Need they have produced. And he is not sorry at all for the innocent Need that is inherent in his creaturely condition. For all the time this illusion to which nature clings as her last treasure, this pretence that we have anything of our own or could for one hour retain by our own strength any goodness that God may pour into us, has kept us from being happy. We have been like bathers who want to keep their feet—or one foot—or one toe—on the bottom, when to lose that foothold would be to surrender themselves to a glorious tumble in the surf. The consequences of parting with our last claim to intrinsic freedom, power, or worth, are real freedom, power and worth, really ours just because God gives them and because we know them to be (in another sense) not "ours." Anodos has got rid of his shadow.

But God also transforms our Need-love for one another, and it requires equal transformation. In reality we all need at times, some of us at most times, that Charity from others which, being Love Himself in them, loves the unlovable. But this, though a sort of love we need, is not the sort we want. We want to be loved for our cleverness, beauty, generosity, fairness, usefulness. The first hint that anyone is offering us the highest love of all is a terrible shock. This is so well recognized that spiteful people will pretend to be loving us with Charity precisely because they know that it will wound us. To say to one who expects a renewal of Affection, Friendship, or Eros, "I forgive you as a Christian" is merely a way of continuing the quarrel. Those who say it are of course lying. But the thing would not be falsely said in order to wound unless, if it were true, it would be wounding.

How difficult it is to receive, and to go on receiving, from others a love that does not depend on our own attraction can be seen from an extreme case. Suppose yourself a man struck down shortly after marriage by an incurable disease which may not kill you for many years; useless, impotent, hideous, disgusting; dependent on your wife's earnings; impoverishing where you hoped to enrich; impaired even in intellect and shaken by gusts of uncontrollable temper, full of unavoidable demands. And suppose your wife's care and pity to be inexhaustible. The man who can take this sweetly, who can receive all and give nothing without resentment, who can abstain even from those tiresome self-depreciations which are really only a demand for petting and reassurance, is doing something which Need-love in its merely natural condition could not attain. (No doubt such a wife will also be doing something beyond the reach of a natural Gift-love, but that is not the point at present). In such a case to receive is harder and perhaps more blessed than to give. But what the extreme example illustrates is universal. We are all receiving Charity. There is something in each of us that cannot be naturally loved. It is no one's fault if they do not so love it. Only the lovable can be naturally loved. You might as well ask people to like the taste of rotten bread or the sound of a mechanical drill. We can be forgiven, and pitied, and loved in spite of it, with Charity; no other way. All who have good parents, wives, husbands, or children, may be sure that at some times— and perhaps at all times in respect of some one particular trait or habit—they are receiving Charity, are loved not because they are lovable but because Love Himself is in those who love them.

Thus God, admitted to the human heart, transforms not only Gift-love but Need-love; not only our Need-love of Him, but our Need-love of one another. This is of course not the only thing that can happen. He may come on what seems to us a more dreadful mission and demand that a natural love be totally renounced. A high and terrible vocation, like Abraham's may constrain a man to turn his back on his own people and his father's house. Eros, directed to a forbidden object, may have to be sacrificed. In such instances, the process, though hard to endure, is easy to understand. What we are more likely to overlook is the necessity for a transformation even when the natural love is allowed to continue.

In such a case the Divine Love does not *substitute* itself for the natural—as if we had to throw away our silver to make room for the gold. The natural loves are summoned to become modes of Charity while also remaining the natural loves they were.

One sees here at once a sort of echo or rhyme or corollary to the Incarnation itself. And this need not surprise us, for the Author of both is the same. As Christ is perfect God and perfect Man, the natural loves are called to become perfect Charity and also perfect natural loves. As God becomes Man "Not by conversion of the Godhead into flesh, but by taking of the Manhood into God," so here; Charity does not dwindle into merely natural love but natural love is taken up into, made the tuned and obedient instrument of, Love Himself.

How this can happen, most Christians know. All the activities (sins only excepted) of the natural loves can in a favoured hour become works of the glad and shameless and grateful Need-love or of the selfless, unofficious Gift-love, which are both Charity. Nothing is either too trivial or too animal to be thus transformed. A game, a joke, a drink together, idle chat, a walk, the act of Venus—all these can be modes in which we forgive or accept forgiveness, in which we console or are reconciled, in which we "seek not our own." Thus in our very instincts, appetites and recreations, Love has prepared for Himself "a body."

But I said "in a favoured hour." Hours soon pass. The total and secure transformation of a natural love into a mode of Charity is a work so difficult that perhaps no fallen man has ever come within sight of doing it perfectly. Yet the law that loves must be so transformed is, I suppose, inexorable.

One difficulty is that here, as usual, we can take a wrong turn. A Christian—a somewhat too vocally Christian—circle or family, having grasped this principle, can make a show, in their overt behaviour and especially in their words, of having achieved the thing itself—an elaborate, fussy, embarrassing and intolerable show. Such people make every trifle a matter of explicitly spiritual importance—out loud and to one another (to God, on their knees, behind a closed door, it would be another matter). They are always unnecessarily asking, or insufferably offering, forgiveness. Who would not rather live with those ordinary people who get over their tantrums (and ours) unemphatically, letting a meal, a night's sleep, or a joke mend all? The real work must be, of all our works, the most secret. Even as far as possible secret from ourselves. Our right hand must not know what our left is doing. We have not got far enough if we play a game of cards with the children "merely" to amuse them or to show that they are forgiven. If this is the best we can do we are right to do it. But it would be better if a deeper, less conscious, Charity threw us into a frame of mind in which a little fun with the children was the thing we should at that moment like best.

We are, however, much helped in this necessary work by that very feature of our experience at which we most repine. The invitation to turn our natural loves into Charity is never lacking. It is provided by those frictions and frustrations that meet us in all of them; unmistakable evidence that (natural) love is not going to be "enough"—unmistakable, unless we are blinded by egotism. When we are, we use them absurdly. "If only I had been more fortunate in my children (that boy gets more like his father every day) I could have loved them perfectly." But every child is sometimes infuriating; most children are not infrequently odious. "If only my husband were more considerate, less lazy, less extravagant" . . . "If only my wife had fewer moods and more sense, and were less extravagant" . . . "If my father wasn't so infernally prosy and close-fisted." But in everyone, and of course in ourselves, there is that which requires forbearance, tolerance, forgiveness. The necessity of practicing these virtues first sets us, forces us, upon the attempt to turn—more strictly, to let God turn—our love into Charity. These frets and rubs are beneficial. It may even be that where there are fewest of them the conversion of natural love is most difficult. When they are plentiful the necessity of rising above it is obvious. To rise above it when it is as fully satisfied and as little impeded as earthly conditions allow—to see that we must rise when all seems so well already—this may require a subtler conversion and a more delicate insight. In this way also it may be hard for "the rich" to enter the Kingdom.

And yet, I believe, the necessity for the conversion is inexorable; at least, if our natural loves are to enter the heavenly life. That they can enter it most of us in fact believe. We may hope that the resurrection of the body means also the resurrection of what may be called our "greater body"; the general fabric of our earthly life with its affections and relationships. But only on a condition; not a condition arbitrarily laid down by God, but one necessarily inherent in the character of Heaven: nothing can enter there which cannot become heavenly. "Flesh and blood," mere nature, cannot inherit that Kingdom. Man can ascend to Heaven only because the Christ, who died and ascended to Heaven, is "formed in him." Must we not suppose that the same is true of a man's loves? Only those into which Love Himself has entered will ascend to Love Himself. And these can be raised with Him only if they have, in some degree and fashion, shared His death; if the natural element in them has submitted—year after year, or in some sudden agony—to transmutation. The fashion of this world passes away. The very name of nature implies the transitory. Natural loves can hope for eternity only in so far as they have allowed themselves to be taken into the eternity of Charity; have at least allowed the process to begin here on earth, before the night comes when no man can work. And the process will always involve a kind of death. There is no escape. In my love for wife or friend the only eternal element is the transforming presence of Love Himself. By that presence, if at all, the other elements may hope, as our physical bodies hope, to be raised from the dead. For this only is holy in them, this only is the Lord.

Theologians have sometimes asked whether we shall "know one another" in Heaven, and whether the particular love-relations worked out on earth would then continue to have any significance. It seems reasonable to reply: "It may depend what kind of love it had become, or was becoming, on earth." For, surely, to meet in the eternal world someone for whom your love in this, however strong, had been merely natural, would not be (on that ground) even interesting. Would it not be like meeting in adult life someone who had seemed to be a great friend at your preparatory school solely because of common interests and occupations? If there was nothing more, if he was not a kindred soul, he will now be a total stranger. Neither of you now plays conkers. You no longer want to swop your help with his French exercise for his help with your arithmetic. In Heaven I suspect, a love that had never embodied Love Himself would be equally irrelevant. For Nature has passed away. All that is not eternal is eternally out of date.

But I must not end on this note, I dare not—and all the less because longings and terrors of my own prompt me to do so—leave any bereaved and desolate reader confirmed in the widespread illusion that reunion with the loved dead is the goal of the Christian life. The denial of this may sound harsh and unreal in the ears of the broken hearted, but it must be denied.

"Thou has made us for thyself," said St. Augustine, "and our heart has no rest till it comes to Thee." This, so easy to believe for a brief moment before the altar or, perhaps, half-praying, half-meditating in an April wood, sounds like mockery beside a deathbed. But we shall be far more truly mocked if, casting this way, we pin our comfort on the hope—perhaps even with the aid of *séance* and necromancy—of some day, this time forever, enjoying the earthly Beloved again, and no more. It is hard not to imagine that such an endless prolongation of earthly happiness would be completely satisfying.

But, if I may trust my own experience, we get at once a sharp warning that there is something wrong. The moment we attempt to use our faith in the other world for this purpose, that faith weakens. The moments in my life when it was really strong have all been moments when God Himself was central in my thoughts. Believing in Him, I could then believe in Heaven as a corollary. But the reverse process—believing first in reunion with the Beloved, and then, for the sake of that reunion, believing in Heaven, and finally, for the sake of Heaven, believing in God—this will not work. One can of course imagine things. But a self-critical person will soon be increasingly aware that the imagination at work is his own; he knows he is only weaving a fantasy. And simpler souls will find the phantoms they try to feed on void of all comfort and nourishment, only to be stimulated into some semblance of reality by pitiful efforts of self-hypnotism, and perhaps by the aid of ignoble pictures and hymns and (what is worse) witches.

We find thus by experience that there is no good applying to Heaven for earthly comfort. Heaven can give heavenly comfort; no other kind. And earth cannot give earthly comfort either. There is no earthly comfort in the long run.

For the dream of finding our end, the thing we were made for, in a Heaven of purely human love could not be true unless our whole Faith were wrong. We were made for God. Only by being in some respect like Him, only by being a manifestation of His beauty, loving kindness, wisdom or goodness, has any earthly Beloved excited our love. It is not that we have loved them too much, but that we did not quite understand what we were loving. It is not that we shall be asked to turn from them, so dearly familiar, to a Stranger. When we see the face of God we shall know that we have always known it. He has been a party to, has made, sustained and moved moment by moment within, all our earthly experiences of innocent love. All that was true love in them was, even on earth, far more His than ours, and ours only because His. In Heaven there will be no anguish and no duty of turning away from our earthly Beloveds. First, because we shall have turned already; from the portraits to the Original, from the rivulets to the Fountain, from the creatures He made lovable to Love Himself. But secondly, because we shall find them all in Him. By loving him more than them we shall love them more than we now do.

But all that is far away in "the land of the Trinity," not here in exile, in the weeping valley. Down here it is all loss and renunciation. The very purpose of the bereavement (so far as it affects ourselves) may have been to force this upon us. We are then compelled to try to believe, what we cannot yet feel, that God is our true Beloved. That is why bereavement is in some ways easier for the unbeliever than for us. He can storm and rage and shake his fist at the universe, and (if he is a genius) write poems like Housman's or Hardy's. But we, at our lowest ebb, when the least effort seems too much for us, must begin to attempt what seem impossibilities.

"Is it easy to love God?" asks an old author. "It is easy," he replies, "to those who do it." I have included two Graces under the word Charity. But God can give a third. He can awake in man, towards Himself, a supernatural Appreciative love. This is of all gifts the most to be desired. Here, not in our natural loves, nor even in ethics, lies the true center of all human and angelic life. With this all things are possible.

And with this, where a better book would begin, mine must end. I dare not proceed. God knows, not I, whether I have ever tasted this love. Perhaps I have only imagined the tasting. Those like myself whose imagination far exceeds their obedience are subject to a just penalty; we easily imagine conditions far higher than any we have really reached. If we describe what we have imagined we may make others, and make ourselves, believe that we have really been there. And if I have only imagined it, is it a further delusion that even the imagining has at some moments made all other objects of desire—yes, even peace, even to have no more fears—look like broken toys and faded flowers? Perhaps. Perhaps, for many of us, all experience merely defines, so to speak, the shape of that gap where our love of God ought to be. It is not enough. It is something. If we cannot "practice the presence of God," it is something to practice the absence of God, to become increasingly aware of our unawareness till we feel like men who should stand beside a great cataract and hear no noise, or like a man in a story who looks in a mirror and finds no face there, or a man in a dream who stretches out his hand to visible objects and gets no sensation of touch. To know that one is dreaming is to be no longer perfectly asleep. But for news of the fully waking world you must go to my betters.

I.7

"Jeeves Takes Charge"

P. G. Wodehouse

The world created by P. G. Wodehouse (1881–1975), prolific English-born novelist, short-story writer, and playwright, has been said to stand "at a slight angle to the universe, unreachable by anything but laughter itself." In the cycle of Wodehouse's writings represented in this selection, Bertram Wilberforce Wooster (a.k.a. Bertie), an upper-class English bachelor, probably in his late twenties or early thirties, takes center stage. Though many Wodehouse enthusiasts find him lovable, all nevertheless agree that Bertie is remarkably foolish, inept, lazy, and abidingly proud, and that his valet, Jeeves, is the real "hero" of the cycle, far more interesting and important than his master. Jeeves takes a proprietary interest in everything that comes before him. He appears as if from nowhere and moves silently about like a "healing zephyr," seemingly without expecting any reward. He is competent, prudent, efficient, courageous, and resourceful.

In this story, we learn how Bertie first came to employ Jeeves. His capacity to command is evident from the start, and even his master unabashedly refers to him as a genius. Given his many talents and character, one can't help but wonder why Jeeves chooses to stay and serve Bertie. Do you admire him for doing so? Some people regard Jeeves (thanks to his name, as well as his comportment) as a Christ-like man, that is, as a paradigmatic servant or keeper. Is there a warrant for doing so?

Now, touching this business of old Jeeves—my man, you know—how do we stand? Lots of people think I'm much too dependent on him. My Aunt Agatha, in fact, has even gone so far as to call him my keeper. Well, what I say is: Why not? The man's a genius. From the collar upward he stands alone. I gave up trying to run my own affairs within a week of his coming to me. That was about half a dozen years ago, directly after the rather rummy business of Florence Craye, my Uncle Willoughby's book, and Edwin, the Boy Scout.

The thing really began when I got back to Easeby, my uncle's place in Shropshire. I was spending a week or so there, as I generally did in the summer; and I had had to break my visit to come back to London to get a new valet. I had found

From *Carry on, Jeeves* by P. G. Wodehouse (New York: A. L. Burt Company, 1927), pp. 11–42. Reprinted with the permission of A. P. Watt Ltd. on behalf of The Trustees of the Wodehouse Estate.

Meadowes, the fellow I had taken to Easeby with me, sneaking my silk socks, a thing no bloke of spirit could stick at any price. It transpiring, moreover, that he had looted a lot of other things here and there about the place, I was reluctantly compelled to hand the misguided blighter the mitten and go to London to ask the registry office to dig up another specimen for my approval. They sent me Jeeves.

I shall always remember the morning he came. It so happened that the night before I had been present at a rather cheery little supper, and I was feeling pretty rocky. On top of this I was trying to read a book Florence Craye had given me. She had been one of the house-party at Easeby, and two or three days before I left we had got engaged. I was due back at the end of the week, and I knew she would expect me to have finished the book by then. You see, she was particularly keen on boosting me up a bit nearer her own plane of intellect. She was a girl with a wonderful profile, but steeped to the gills in serious purpose. I can't give you a better idea of the way things stood than by telling you that the book she'd given me to read was called "Types of Ethical Theory," and that when I opened it at random I struck a page beginning:—

"The postulate or common understanding involved in speech is certainly co-exten-sive, in the obligation it carries, with the social organism of which language is the in-strument, and the ends of which it is an effort to subserve."

All perfectly true, no doubt; but not the sort of thing to spring on a lad with a morning head.

I was doing my best to skim through this bright little volume when the bell rang. I crawled off the sofa and opened the door. A kind of darkish sort of respectful Johnnie stood without.

"I was sent by the agency, sir," he said. "I was given to understand that you required a valet."

I'd have preferred an undertaker; but I told him to stagger in, and he floated noiselessly through the doorway like a healing zephyr. That impressed me from the start. Meadowes had had flat feet and used to clump. This fellow didn't seem to have any feet at all. He just streamed in. He had a grave, sympathetic face, as if he, too, knew what it was to sup with the lads.

"Excuse me, sir," he said gently.

Then he seemed to flicker, and wasn't there any longer. I heard him moving about in the kitchen, and presently he came back with a glass on a tray.

"If you would drink this, sir," he said, with a kind of bedside manner, rather like the royal doctor shooting the bracer into the sick prince. "It is a little preparation of my own invention. It is the Worcester Sauce that gives it its colour. The raw egg makes it nutritious. The red pepper gives it its bite. Gentlemen have told me they have found it extremely invigorating after a late evening."

I would have clutched at anything that looked like a life-line that morning. I swallowed the stuff. For a moment I felt as if somebody had touched off a bomb inside the old bean and was strolling down my throat with a lighted torch, and then everything seemed suddenly to get all right. The sun shone in through the window; birds twittered in the tree-tops; and, generally speaking, hope dawned once more.

"You're engaged!" I said, as soon as I could say anything.

I perceived clearly that this cove was one of the world's workers, the sort no home should be without.

"Thank you, sir. My name is Jeeves."

"You can start in at once?"

"Immediately, sir."

"Because I'm due down at Easeby, in Shropshire, the day after to-morrow."

"Very good, sir." He looked past me at the mantelpiece. "That is an excellent likeness of Lady Florence Craye, sir. It is two years since I saw her ladyship. I was at one time in Lord Worplesdon's employment. I tendered my resignation because I could not see eye to eye with his lordship in his desire to dine in dress trousers, a flannel shirt, and a shooting coat."

He couldn't tell me anything I didn't know about the old boy's eccentricity. This Lord Worplesdon was Florence's father. He was the old buster who, a few years later, came down to breakfast one morning, lifted the first cover he saw, said "Eggs! Eggs! Eggs! Damn all eggs!" in an overwrought sort of voice, and instantly legged it for France, never to return to the bosom of his family. This, mind you, being a bit of luck for the bosom of the family, for old Worplesdon had the worst temper in the county.

I had known the family ever since I was a kid, and from boyhood up this old boy had put the fear of death into me. Time, the great healer, could never remove from my memory the occasion when he found me—then a stripling of fifteen—smoking one of his special cigars in the stables. He got after me with a hunting-crop just at the moment when I was beginning to realize that what I wanted most on earth was solitude and repose, and chased me more than a mile across difficult country. If there was a flaw, so to speak, in the pure joy of being engaged to Florence, it was the fact that she rather took after her father, and one was never certain when she might erupt. She had a wonderful profile, though.

"Lady Florence and I are engaged, Jeeves," I said.

"Indeed, sir?"

You know, there was a kind of rummy something about his manner. Perfectly all right and all that, but not what you'd call chirpy. It somehow gave me the impression that he wasn't keen on Florence. Well, of course, it wasn't my business. I supposed that while he had been valeting old Worplesdon she must have trodden on his toes in some way. Florence was a dear girl, and, seen sideways, most awfully good-looking; but if she had a fault it was a tendency to be a bit imperious with the domestic staff.

At this point in the proceedings there was another ring at the front door. Jeeves shimmered out and came back with a telegram. I opened it. It ran:

Return immediately. Extremely urgent. Catch first train. Florence.

"Rum!" I said.

"Sir?"

"Oh, nothing!"

It shows how little I knew Jeeves in those days that I didn't go a bit deeper into the matter with him. Nowadays I would never dream of reading a rummy communication without asking him what he thought of it. And this one was devilish odd. What I mean is, Florence knew I was going back to Easeby the day after to-morrow, anyway; so why the hurry call? Something must have happened, of course; but I couldn't see what on earth it could be.

"Jeeves," I said, "we shall be going down to Easeby this afternoon. Can you manage it?"

"Certainly, sir."

"You can get your packing done and all that?"

"Without any difficulty, sir. Which suit will you wear for the journey?"

"This one."

I had on a rather sprightly young check that morning, to which I was a good deal attached; I fancied it, in fact, more than a little. It was perhaps rather sudden till you got used to it, but, nevertheless, an extremely sound effort, which many lads at the club and elsewhere had admired unrestrainedly.

"Very good, sir."

Again there was that kind of rummy something in his manner. It was the way he said it, don't you know. He didn't like the suit. I pulled myself together to assert myself. Something seemed to tell me that, unless I was jolly careful and nipped this lad in the bud, he would be starting to boss me. He had the aspect of a distinctly resolute blighter.

Well, I wasn't going to have any of that sort of thing, by Jove! I'd seen so many cases of fellows who had become perfect slaves to their valets. I remember poor old Aubrey Fothergill telling me—with absolute tears in his eyes, poor chap!—one night at the club, that he had been compelled to give up a favourite pair of brown shoes simply because Meekyn, his man, disapproved of them. You have to keep these fellows in their place, don't you know. You have to work the good old iron-hand-in-the-velvet-glove wheeze. If you give them a what's-its-name, they take a thingummy.

"Don't you like this suit, Jeeves?" I said coldly.

"Oh, yes, sir."

"Well, what don't you like about it?"

"It is a very nice suit, sir."

"Well, what's wrong with it? Out with it, dash it!"

"If I might make the suggestion, sir, a simple brown or blue, with a hint of some quiet twill—"

"What absolute rot!"

"Very good, sir."

"Perfectly blithering, my dear man!"

"As you say, sir."

I felt as if I had stepped on the place where the last stair ought to have been, but wasn't. I felt defiant, if you know what I mean, and there didn't seem anything to defy.

"All right, then," I said.

"Yes, sir."

And then he went away to collect his kit, while I started in again on "Types of Ethical Theory" and took a stab at a chapter headed. "Idiopsychological Ethics."

Most of the way down in the train that afternoon, I was wondering what could be up at the other end. I simply couldn't see what could have happened. Easeby wasn't one of those country houses you read about in the society novels, where young girls are lured on to play baccarat and then skinned to the bone of their jewellery, and so on. The house-party I had left had consisted entirely of law-abiding birds like myself.

Besides, my uncle wouldn't have let anything of that kind go on in his house. He was a rather stiff, precise sort of old boy, who liked a quiet life. He was just finishing a history of the family or something, which he had been working on for the last year, and didn't stir much from the library. He was rather a good instance of what they say about its being a good scheme for a fellow to sow his wild oats. I'd been told that in his youth Uncle Willoughby had been a bit of a rounder. You would never have thought it to look at him now.

When I got to the house, Oakshott, the butler, told me that Florence was in her room, watching her maid pack. Apparently there was a dance on at a house about twenty miles away that night, and she was motoring over with some of the Easeby lot and would be away some nights. Oakshott said she had told him to tell her the moment I arrived; so I trickled into the smoking-room and waited, and presently in she came. A glance showed me that she was perturbed, and even peeved. Her eyes had a goggly look, and altogether she appeared considerably pipped.

"Darling!" I said, and attempted the good old embrace; but she side-stepped like a bantam weight.

"Don't!"

"What's the matter?"

"Everything's the matter! Bertie, you remember asking me, when you left, to make myself pleasant to your uncle?"

"Yes."

The idea being, of course, that as at that time I was more or less dependent on Uncle Willoughby I couldn't very well marry without his approval. And though I knew he wouldn't have any objection to Florence, having known her father since they were at Oxford together, I hadn't wanted to take any chances; so I had told her to make an effort to fascinate the old boy.

"You told me it would please him particularly if I asked him to read me some of his history of the family."

"Wasn't he pleased?"

"He was delighted. He finished writing the thing yesterday afternoon, and read me nearly all of it last night. I have never had such a shock in my life. The book is an outrage. It is impossible. It is horrible!"

"But, dash it, the family weren't so bad as all that."

"It is not a history of the family at all. Your uncle has written his reminiscences! He calls them 'Recollections of a Long Life'!"

I began to understand. As I say, Uncle Willoughby had been somewhat on the tabasco side as a young man, and it began to look as if he might have turned out something pretty fruity if he had started recollecting his long life.

"If half of what he has written is true," said Florence, "your uncle's youth must have been perfectly appalling. The moment we began to read he plunged straight into a most scandalous story of how he and my father were thrown out of a music-hall in 1887!"

"Why?"

"I decline to tell you why."

It must have been something pretty bad. It took a lot to make them chuck people out of music-halls in 1887.

"Your uncle specifically states that father had drunk a quart and a half of champagne before beginning the evening," she went on. "The book is full of stories like that. There is a dreadful one about Lord Emsworth."

"Lord Emsworth? Not the one we know? Not the one at Blandings?"

A most respectable old Johnnie, don't you know? Doesn't do a thing nowadays but dig in the garden with a spud.

"The very same. That is what makes the book so unspeakable. It is full of stories about people one knows who are the essence of propriety to-day, but who seem to have behaved, when they were in London in the 'eighties, in a manner that would not have been tolerated in the fo'c'sle of a whaler. Your uncle seems to remember everything disgraceful that happened to anybody when he was in his early twenties. There is a story about Sir Stanley Gervase-Gervase at Rosherville Gardens which is ghastly in its perfection of detail. It seems that Sir Stanley—but I can't tell you!"

"Have a dash!"

"No!"

"Oh, well, I shouldn't worry. No publisher will print the book if it's as bad as all that."

"On the contrary, your uncle told me that all negotiations are settled with Riggs and Ballinger, and he's sending off the manuscript to-morrow for immediate publication. They make special thing of that sort of book. They published Lady Carnaby's 'Memories of Eighty Interesting Years.'"

"I read 'em!"

"Well, then, when I tell you that Lady Carnaby's Memories are simply not to be compared with your uncle's Recollections, you will understand my state of mind. And father appears in nearly every story in the book! I am horrified at the things he did when he was a younger man!"

"What's to be done?"

"The manuscript must be intercepted before it reaches Riggs and Ballinger, and destroyed!"

I sat up.

This sounded rather sporting.

"How are you going to do it?" I enquired.

"How can I do it? Didn't I tell you the parcel goes off to-morrow? I am going to the Murgatroyds' dance to-night and shall not be back till Monday. You must do it. That is why I telegraphed to you."

"What!"

She gave me a look.

"Do you mean to say you refuse to help me, Bertie?"

"No; but—I say!"

"It's quite simple."

"But even if I—— What I mean is—— Of course, anything I can do—but—if you know what I mean——"

"You say you want to marry me, Bertie?"

"Yes, of course; but still——"

For a moment she looked exactly like her old father.

"I will never marry you if those Recollections are published."

"But, Florence, old thing!"

"I mean it. You may look on it as a test, Bertie. If you have the resource and courage to carry this thing through, I will take it as evidence that you are not the vapid and shiftless person most people think you. If you fail, I shall know that your Aunt Agatha was right when she called you a spineless invertebrate and advised me strongly not to marry you. It will be perfectly simple for you to intercept the manuscript, Bertie. It only requires a little resolution."

"But suppose Uncle Willoughby catches me at it? He'd cut me off with a bob."

"If you care more for your uncle's money than for me——"

"No, no! Rather not!"

"Very well, then. The parcel containing the manuscript will, of course, be placed on the hall table to-morrow for Oakshott to take to the village with the letters. All you have to do is to take it away and destroy it. Then your uncle will think it has been lost in the post."

It sounded thin to me.

"Hasn't he got a copy of it?"

"No; it has not been typed. He is sending the manuscript just as he wrote it."

"But he could write it over again."

"As if he would have the energy!"

"But——"

"If you are going to do nothing but make absurd objections, Bertie——"

"I was only pointing things out."

"Well, don't! Once and for all, will you do me this quite simple act of kindness?"

The way she put it gave me an idea.

"Why not get Edwin to do it? Keep it in the family, kind of, don't you know. Besides, it would be a boon to the kid."

A jolly bright idea it seemed to me. Edwin was her young brother, who was spending his holidays at Easeby. He was a ferret-faced kid, whom I had disliked since birth. As a matter of fact, talking of Recollections and Memories, it was young blighted Edwin who, nine years before, had led his father to where I was smoking his cigar and caused all of the unpleasantness. He was fourteen now and had just joined the Boy Scouts. He was one of those thorough kids, and took his responsibilities pretty seriously. He was always in a sort of fever because he was dropping behind schedule with his daily acts of kindness. However hard he tried, he'd fall behind; and then you would find him prowling about the house, setting such a clip to try and catch up with himself that Easeby was rapidly becoming a perfect hell for man and beast.

The idea didn't seem to strike Florence.

"I shall do nothing of the kind, Bertie. I wonder you can't appreciate the compliment I am paying you—trusting you like this."

"Oh, I see that all right, but what I mean is, Edwin would do it so much better than I would. These Boy Scouts are up to all sorts of dodges. They spoor, don't you know, and take cover and creep about, and what not."

"Bertie, will you or will you not do this perfectly trivial thing for me? If not, say so now, and let us end this farce of pretending that you care a snap of the fingers for me."

"Dear old soul, I love you devotedly!"

"Then will you or will you not——"

"Oh, all right," I said. "All right! All right! All right!"

And then I tottered forth to think it over. I met Jeeves in the passage just outside.

"I beg your pardon, sir. I was endeavouring to find you."

"What's the matter?"

"I felt that I should tell you, sir, that somebody has been putting black polish on our brown walking shoes."

"What! Who? Why?"

"I could not say, sir."

"Can anything be done with them?"

"Nothing, sir."

"Damn!"

"Very good, sir."

I've often wondered since then how these murderer fellows manage to keep in shape while they're contemplating their next effort. I had a much simpler sort of job on hand, and the thought of it rattled me to such an extent in the night watches that I was a perfect wreck the next day. Dark circles under the eyes—I give you my word! I had to call on Jeeves to rally round with one of those life-savers of his.

From breakfast on I felt like a bag-snatcher at a railway station. I had to hang about waiting for the parcel to be put on the hall table, and it wasn't put. Uncle Willoughby was a fixture in the library, adding the finishing touches to the great work, I supposed, and the more I thought the thing over the less I liked it. The chances against my pulling it off seemed about three to two, and the thought of what would happen if I didn't gave me cold shivers down the spine. Uncle Willoughby was a pretty mild sort of old boy, as a rule, but I've known him to cut up rough, and, by Jove, he was scheduled to extend himself if he caught me trying to get away with his life work.

It wasn't till nearly four that he toddled out of the library with the parcel under his arm, put it on the table, and toddled off again. I was hiding a bit to the south-east at the moment, behind a suit of armour. I bounded out and legged it for the table. Then I nipped upstairs to hide the swag. I charged in like a mustang and nearly stubbed my toe on young blighted Edwin, the Boy Scout. He was standing at the chest of drawers, confound him, messing about with my ties.

"Hallo!" he said.

"What are you doing here?"

"I'm tidying your room. It's my last Saturday's act of kindness."

"Last Saturday's?"

"I'm five days behind. I was six till last night, but I polished your shoes."

"Was it you——"

"Yes. Did you see them? I just happened to think of it. I was in here, looking round. Mr. Berkeley had this room while you were away. He left this morning. I thought perhaps he might have left something in it that I could have sent on. I've often done acts of kindness that way."

"You must be a comfort to one and all!"

It became more and more apparent to me that this infernal kid must some-how be turned out eftsoons or right speedily. I had hidden the parcel behind my back, and I didn't think he had seen it; but I wanted to get at that chest of draw-ers quick, before anyone else came along."

"I shouldn't bother about tidying the room," I said.

"I like tidying it. It's not a bit of trouble—really."

"But it's quite tidy now."

"Not so tidy as I shall make it."

This was getting perfectly rotten. I didn't want to murder the kid, and yet there didn't seem any other way of shifting him. I pressed down the mental accelerator. The old lemon throbbed fiercely. I got an idea.

"There's something much kinder than that which you could do," I said. "You see that box of cigars? Take it down to the smoking-room and snip off the ends for me. That would save me no end of trouble. Stagger along, laddie."

He seemed a bit doubtful; but he staggered. I shoved the parcel into a drawer, locked it, trousered the key, and felt better. I might be a chump, but, dash it, I could out-general a mere kid with a face like a ferret. I went downstairs again. Just as I was passing the smoking-room door out curveted Edwin. It seemed to me that if he wanted to do a real act of kindness he would commit suicide.

"I'm snipping them," he said.

"Snip on! Snip on!"

"Do you like them snipped much, or only a bit?"

"Medium."

"All right. I'll be getting on, then."

"I should."

And we parted.

Fellows who know all about that sort of thing—detectives, and so on—will tell you that the most difficult thing in the world is to get rid of the body. I remember, as a kid, having to learn by heart a poem about a bird by the name of Eugene Aram, who had the deuce of a job in this respect. All I can recall of the actual poetry is the bit that goes:

"Tum-tum, tum-tum, tum-tumty-tum,
I slew him, tum-tum-tum!"

But I recollect that the poor blighter spent much of his valuable time dumping the corpse into ponds and burying it, and what not, only to have it pop out at him again. It was about an hour after I had shoved the parcel into the drawer when I realised that I had let myself in for just the same sort of thing.

Florence had talked in an airy sort of way about destroying the manuscript; but when one came down to it, how the deuce can a chap destroy a great chunky mass of paper in somebody else's house in the middle of summer? I couldn't ask to have a fire in my bedroom, with the thermometer in the eighties. And if I didn't burn the thing, how else could I get rid of it? Fellows on the battle-field eat dispatches to keep them from falling into the hands of the enemy, but it would have taken me a year to eat Uncle Willoughby's Recollections.

I'm bound to say the problem absolutely baffled me. The only thing seemed to be to leave the parcel in the drawer and hope for the best.

I don't know whether you have ever experienced it, but it's a dashed unpleasant thing having a crime on one's conscience. Towards the end of the day the mere sight of the drawer began to depress me. I found myself getting all on edge; and once when Uncle Willoughby trickled silently into the smoking-room when I was alone there and spoke to me before I knew he was there, I broke the record for the sitting high jump.

I was wondering all the time when Uncle Willoughby would sit up and take notice. I didn't think he would have time to suspect that anything had gone wrong till Saturday morning, when he would be expecting, of course, to get the acknowledgment of the manuscript from the publishers. But early on Friday evening he came out of the library as I was passing and asked me to step in. He was looking considerably rattled.

"Bertie," he said—he always spoke in a precise sort of pompous kind of way—"an exceedingly disturbing thing has happened. As you know, I dispatched the manuscript of my book to Messrs. Riggs and Ballinger, the publishers, yesterday afternoon. It should have reached them by the first post this morning. Why I should have been uneasy I cannot say, but my mind was not altogether at rest respecting the safety of the parcel. I therefore telephoned to Messrs. Riggs and Ballinger a few moments back to make enquiries. To my consternation they informed me that they were not yet in receipt of my manuscript."

"Very rum!"

"I recollect distinctly placing it myself on the hall table in good time to be taken to the village. But here is a sinister thing. I have spoken to Oakshott, who took the rest of the letters to the post office, and he cannot recall seeing it there. He is, indeed, unswerving in his assertions that when he went to the hall to collect the letters there was no parcel among them."

"Sounds funny!"

"Bertie, shall I tell you what I suspect?"

"What's that?"

"The suspicion will no doubt sound to you incredible, but it alone seems to fit the facts as we know them. I incline to the belief that the parcel has been stolen."

"Oh, I say! Surely not!"

"Wait! Hear me out. Though I have said nothing to you before, or to anyone else, concerning the matter, the fact remains that during the past few weeks a number of objects—some valuable, others not—have disappeared in this house. The conclusion to which one is irresistibly impelled is that we have a kleptomaniac in our midst. It is a peculiarity of kleptomania, as you are no doubt aware, that the subject is unable to differentiate between the intrinsic values of objects. He will purloin an old coat as readily as a diamond ring, or a tobacco pipe costing but a few shillings with the same eagerness as a purse of gold. The fact that this manuscript of mine could be of no possible value to any outside person convinces me that——"

"But, uncle, one moment; I know all about those things that were stolen. It was Meadowes, my man, who pinched them. I caught him snaffling my silk socks. Right in the act, by Jove!"

He was tremendously impressed.

"You amaze me, Bertie! Send for the man at once and question him."

"But he isn't here. You see, directly I found that he was a sock-sneaker I gave him the boot. That's why I went to London—to get a new man."

"Then, if the man Meadowes is no longer in the house it could not be he who purloined my manuscript. The whole thing is inexplicable."

After which we brooded for a bit. Uncle Willoughby pottered about the room, registering baffledness, while I sat sucking at a cigarette, feeling rather like a chappie I'd once read about in a book, who murdered another cove and hid the body under the dining-room table, and then had to be the life and soul of a dinner party, with it there all the time. My guilty secret oppressed me to such an extent that after a while I couldn't stick it any longer. I lit another cigarette and started for a stroll in the grounds, by way of cooling off.

It was one of those still evenings you get in the summer, when you can hear a snail clear its throat a mile away. The sun was sinking over the hills and the gnats were fooling about all over the place, and everything smelled rather topping—what with the falling dew and so on—and I was just beginning to feel a little soothed by the peace of it all when suddenly I heard my name spoken.

"It's about Bertie."

It was the loathsome voice of young blighted Edwin! For a moment I couldn't locate it. Then I realised that it came from the library. My stroll had taken me within a few yards of the open window.

I had often wondered how those Johnnies in books did it—I mean the fellows with whom it was the work of a moment to do about a dozen things that ought to have taken them about ten minutes. But, as a matter of fact, it was the work of a moment with me to chuck away my cigarette, swear a bit, leap about ten yards, dive into a bush that stood near the library window, and stand there with my ears flapping. I was as certain as I've ever been of anything that all sorts of rotten things were in the offing.

"About Bertie?" I heard Uncle Willoughby say.

"About Bertie and your parcel. I heard you talking to him just now. I believe he's got it."

When I tell you that just as I heard these frightful words a fairly substantial beetle of sorts dropped from the bush down the back of my neck, and I couldn't even stir to squash the same, you will understand that I felt pretty rotten. Everything seemed against me.

"What do you mean, boy? I was discussing the disappearance of my manuscript with Bertie only a moment back, and he professed himself as perplexed by the mystery as myself."

"Well, I was in his room yesterday afternoon, doing him an act of kindness, and he came in with a parcel. I could see it, though he tried to keep it behind his back. And then he asked me to go to the smoking-room and snip some cigars for him; and about two minutes afterwards he came down—and he wasn't carrying anything. So it must be in his room."

I understand they deliberately teach these dashed Boy Scouts to cultivate their powers of observation and deduction and what not. Devilish thoughtless and inconsiderate of them, I call it. Look at the trouble it causes.

"It sounds incredible," said Uncle Willoughby, thereby bucking me up a trifle.

"Shall I go and look in his room?" asked young blighted Edwin. "I'm sure the parcel's there."

"But what could be his motive for perpetrating this extraordinary theft?"

"Perhaps he's a—what you said just now."

"A kleptomaniac? Impossible!"

"It might have been Bertie who took all those things from the very start," suggested the little brute hopefully. "He may be like Raffles."

"Raffles?"

"He's a chap in a book who went about pinching things."

"I cannot believe that Bertie would—ah—go about pinching things."

"Well, I'm sure he's got the parcel. I'll tell you what you might do. You might say that Mr. Berkeley wired that he had left something here. He had Bertie's room, you know. You might say you wanted to look for it."

"That would be possible. I——"

I didn't wait to hear any more. Things were getting too hot. I sneaked softly out of my bush and raced for the front door. I sprinted up to my room and made for the drawer where I had put the parcel. And then I found I hadn't the key. It wasn't for the deuce of a time that I recollected I had shifted it to my evening trousers the night before and must have forgotten to take it out again.

Where the dickens were my evening things? I had looked all over the place before I remembered that Jeeves must have taken them away to brush. To leap at the bell and ring it was, with me, the work of a moment. I had just rung it when there was a footstep outside, and in came Uncle Willoughby.

"Oh, Bertie," he said, without a blush, "I have—ah—received a telegram from Berkeley, who occupied this room in your absence, asking me to forward him his—er—his cigarette-case, which it would appear, he inadvertently omitted to take with him when he left the house. I cannot find it downstairs; and it has, therefore, occurred to me that he may have left it in this room. I will—er—just take a look around."

It was one of the most disgusting spectacles I've ever seen—this white-haired old man, who should have been thinking of the hereafter, standing there lying like an actor.

"I haven't seen it anywhere," I said.

"Nevertheless, I will search. I must—ah—spare no effort."

"I should have seen it if it had been here—what?"

"It may have escaped your notice. It is—er—possibly in one of the drawers."

He began to nose about. He pulled out drawer after drawer, pottering around like an old bloodhound, and babbling from time to time about Berkeley and his cigarette-case in a way that struck me as perfectly ghastly. I just stood there, losing weight every moment.

Then he came to the drawer where the parcel was.

"This appears to be locked," he said, rattling the handle.

"Yes; I shouldn't bother about that one. It—it's—er—locked, and all that sort of thing."

"You have not the key?"

A soft, respectful voice spoke behind me.

"I fancy sir, that this must be the key you require. It was in the pocket of your evening trousers."

It was Jeeves. He had shimmered in, carrying my evening things, and was standing there holding out the key. I could have massacred the man.

"Thank you," said my uncle.

"Not at all, sir."

The next moment Uncle Willoughby had opened the drawer. I shut my eyes.

"No," said Uncle Willoughby, "there is nothing here. The drawer is empty. Thank you, Bertie. I hope I have not disturbed you. I fancy—er—Berkeley must have taken his case with him after all."

When he had gone I shut the door carefully. Then I turned to Jeeves. The man was putting my evening things out on a chair.

"Er—Jeeves!"

"Sir?"

"Oh, nothing."

It was deuced difficult to know how to begin.

"Er—Jeeves!"

"Sir?"

"Did you—— Was there—— Have you by chance——"

"I removed the parcel this morning, sir."

"Oh—ah—why?"

"I considered it more prudent, sir."

I mused for a while.

"Of course, I suppose all this seems tolerably rummy to you, Jeeves?"

"Not at all, sir. I chanced to overhear you and Lady Florence speaking of the matter the other evening, sir."

"Did you, by Jove?"

"Yes, sir."

"Well—er—Jeeves, I think that, on the whole, if you were to—as it were—freeze on to that parcel until we get back to London——"

"Exactly, sir."

"And then we might—er—so to speak—chuck it away somewhere—what?"

"Precisely, sir."

"I'll leave it in your hands."

"Entirely, sir."

"You know, Jeeves, you're by way of being rather a topper."

"I endeavour to give satisfaction, sir."

"One in a million, by Jove!"

"It is very kind of you to say so, sir."

"Well, that's about all, then, I think."

"Very good, sir."

Florence came back on Monday. I didn't see her till we were all having tea in the hall. It wasn't till the crowd had cleared away a bit that we got a chance of having a word together.

"Well, Bertie?" she said.

"It's all right."

"You have destroyed the manuscript?"

"Not exactly; but——"

"What do you mean?"

"I mean I haven't absolutely——"

"Bertie, your manner is furtive!"

"It's all right. It's this way——"

And I was just going to explain how things stood when out of the library came leaping Uncle Willoughby looking as braced as a two-year-old. The old boy was a changed man.

"A most remarkable thing, Bertie! I have just been speaking with Mr. Riggs on the telephone, and he tells me he received my manuscript by the first post this morning. I cannot imagine what can have caused the delay. Our postal facilities are extremely inadequate in the rural districts. I shall write to headquarters about it. It is insufferable if valuable parcels are to be delayed in this fashion."

I happened to be looking at Florence's profile at the moment, and at this juncture she swung round and gave me a look that went right through me like a knife. Uncle Willoughby meandered back to the library, and there was a silence that you could have dug bits out of with a spoon.

"I can't understand it," I said at last. "I can't understand it, by Jove!"

"I can. I can understand it perfectly, Bertie. Your heart failed you. Rather than risk offending your uncle you——"

"No, no! Absolutely!"

"You preferred to lose me rather than risk losing the money. Perhaps you did not think I meant what I said. I meant every word. Our engagement is ended."

"But—I say!"

"Not another word!"

"But, Florence, old thing!"

"I do not wish to hear any more. I see now that your Aunt Agatha was perfectly right. I consider that I have had a very lucky escape. There was a time when I thought that, with patience, you might be moulded into something worth while. I see now that you are impossible!"

And she popped off, leaving me to pick up the pieces. When I had collected the *debris* to some extent I went to my room and rang for Jeeves. He came in looking as if nothing had happened or was ever going to happen. He was the calmest thing in captivity.

"Jeeves!" I yelled. "Jeeves, that parcel has arrived in London!"

"Yes, sir?"

"Did you send it?"

"Yes, sir. I acted for the best, sir. I think that both you and Lady Florence overestimated the danger of people being offended at being mentioned in Sir Willoughby's Recollections. It has been my experience, sir, that the normal person enjoys seeing his or her name in print, irrespective of what is said about them. I have an aunt, sir, who a few years ago was a martyr to swollen limbs. She tried Walkinshaw's Supreme Ointment and obtained considerable relief—so much so that she sent them an unsolicited testimonial. Her pride at seeing her photograph in the daily papers in connection with descriptions of her lower limbs before taking, which were nothing less than revolting, was so intense that it lead me to believe that publicity, of whatever sort, is what nearly everybody desires. Moreover, if you have ever studied psychology, sir, you will know that respectable old gentlemen are by no means averse to having it advertised that they were extremely wild in their youth. I have an uncle——"

I cursed his aunts and his uncles and him and all the rest of the family.

"Do you know that Lady Florence has broken off her engagement with me?"

"Indeed, sir?"

Not a bit of sympathy! I might have been telling him it was a fine day.

"You're sacked!"

"Very good, sir."

He coughed gently.

"As I am no longer in your employment, sir, I can speak freely without appearing to take a liberty. In my opinion you and Lady Florence were quite unsuitably matched. Her ladyship is of a highly determined and arbitrary temperament, quite opposed to your own. I was in Lord Worplesdon's service for nearly a year, during which time I had ample opportunities of studying her ladyship. The opinion of the servants' hall was far from favourable to her. Her ladyship's temper caused a good deal of adverse comment among us. It was at times quite impossible. You would not have been happy, sir!"

"Get out!"

"I think you would also have found her educational methods a little trying, sir. I have glanced at the book her ladyship gave you—it has been lying on your table since our arrival—and it is, in my opinion, quite unsuitable. You would not have enjoyed it. And I have it from her ladyship's own maid, who happened to overhear a conversation between her ladyship and one of the gentlemen staying here—Mr. Maxwell, who is employed in an editorial capacity by one of the reviews—that it was her intention to start you almost immediately upon Nietzsche. You would not enjoy Nietzsche, sir. He is fundamentally unsound."

"Get out!"

"Very good, sir."

It's rummy how sleeping on a thing often makes you feel quite different about it. It's happened to me over and over again. Somehow or other, when I woke next morning the old heart didn't feel half so broken as it had done. It was a perfectly topping day, and there was something about the way the sun came in at the window and the row of birds were kicking up in the ivy that made me half wonder whether Jeeves wasn't right. After all, though she had wonderful profile, was it such a catch being engaged to Florence Craye as the casual observer might imagine? Wasn't there something in what Jeeves had said about her character? I began to realize that my ideal wife was something quite different, something a lot more clinging and drooping and prattling, and what not.

I had got as far as this in thinking the thing out when that "Types of Ethical Theory" caught my eye. I opened it, and I give you my honest word this was what hit me:

> *Of the two antithetic terms in the Greek philosophy one only was real and self-subsisting; and that one was Ideal Thought as opposed to that which it has to penetrate and mould. The other, corresponding to our Nature, was in itself phenomenal, unreal, without any permanent footing, having no predicates that held true for two moments together; in short, redeemed from negation only by including indwelling realities appearing through.*

Well—I mean to say—what? And Nietzsche, from all accounts, a lot worse than that!

"Jeeves," I said, when he came in with my morning tea, "I've been thinking it over. You're engaged again."

"Thank you, sir."

I sucked down a cheerful mouthful. A great respect for this bloke's judgment began to soak through me.

"Oh, Jeeves," I said; "about that check suit."

"Yes, sir?"

"Is it really a frost?"

"A trifle too bizarre, sir, in my opinion."

"But lots of fellows have asked me who my tailor is."

"Doubtless in order to avoid him, sir."

"He's supposed to be one of the best men in London."

"I am saying nothing against his moral character, sir."

I hesitated a bit. I had a feeling that I was passing into this chappie's clutches, and that if I gave in now I should become just like poor old Aubrey Fothergill, unable to call my soul my own. On the other hand, this was obviously a cove of rare intelligence, and it would be a comfort in a lot of ways to have him doing the thinking for me. I made up my mind.

"All right, Jeeves," I said. "You know! Give the bally thing away to somebody!"

He looked down at me like a father gazing tenderly at the wayward child.

"Thank you, sir. I gave it to the under-gardener last night. A little more tea, sir?"

I.8

"The Prayers of Thanksgiving"

William F. May

In his essay "Images That Shape the Public Obligations of the Minister," from which this selection is excerpted, Protestant theologian and ethicist William F. May (born in 1927) explores, among other things, what the liturgically formed citizen looks like. Taking his bearings from the Christian worship service, May includes this brief discussion of the way in which commonly uttered prayers of thanksgiving shape congregants as givers. Of special interest to us, May compares the motives that lead congregants to give with those of philanthopists. Church giving, he asserts, draws on an ethics of gratitude, which teaches givers to see themselves, primordially, as receivers: one gives because one has received. By contrast, philanthropic giving presupposes a fundamental distinction between givers, who see themselves as "relatively self-sufficient," and receivers, who are needy: one gives, May implies, at best out of something like noblesse oblige. May seems clearly to advocate church giving over philanthropy. Are the two necessarily mutually exclusive? Is the distinction May draws as clear as he would have us believe? Must one be a believer to be moved by an ethics of gratitude?

These prayers [of thanksgiving] impel the church toward giving—toward its service function—but with a different motive than inspires philanthropic giving. The ideal of philanthropy (which informs so much of the giving of voluntary communities, conscientious professionals and corporations with a conscience) commends a love of humankind that issues in concrete deeds of service to others. The ideal of philanthropy tends to divide the human race in two: relatively self-sufficient benefactors and needy beneficiaries. It presupposes a unilateral or one-way transfer from giver to receiver. This assumption of asymmetry dominates not only private charity, professional *pro bono* work, and corporate philanthropy, but also the conventional self-interpretation of America as philanthropist among the nations and the American church as patron to the churches in the Third World.

This idealist's picture of a social world divided into givers and receivers, while morally superior to a callous neglect of the needy, overlooks the fact that

Selection currently appears in *The Beleaguered Rulers: The Public Obligation of the Professional* (Westminster: John Knox Press, 2001). Reprinted by permission of William F. May.

the benefactor receives as well as gives. A two-way street of giving and receiving marks human community, and not merely in the setting of the family. Long before Americans discussed a Marshall Plan, they received much of their heritage from the continent. The would-be philanthropic nation receives richly from other nations; and the American Church, from other churches. Just so, professionals receive nothing less than their vocation from patients, clients, and parishioners who allow them to practice the therewith to be themselves. And corporations receive their identity not only from stockholders who invest their money but workers who invest their lives, and other stakeholders in the enterprise—suppliers, consumers, and neighbors, to say nothing of the state and the society at large that charter its life, grant it protection, and endow its enterprises with a public significance.

The prayers of thanksgiving, as scripture helps shape them, provide the transcendent setting for an ethics of gratitude that differs from the ideal of philanthropy. Scripture provides powerful warrants for giving but always within the setting of a primordial receiving. The Scriptures of Israel urge the Jewish farmer, in harvesting, not to pick his crops too clean. He should leave some for the sojourner, for he was once a sojourner in Egypt. Thus God's own actions, his care for Israel while a stranger in Egypt, prompts and measures Israel's treatment of the stranger in her midst. The imperative to give rests upon the account of a gift already received. Thus the moral/legal element in scripture (the *halacha*) rests upon a narrative base (the *agada*). Similarly, the New Testament reads, "Herein is love: not that we loved God but that God first loved us. So we ought to love one another." The imperative derives from the disclosive event of the divine love.

These passages push the believer toward a different notion of love from the philosopher's principle of beneficence. The rational principle of beneficence presupposes the structural relationship of *benefactor* to *beneficiary,* of a giver to receiver. How shall I act so as to construct a better future for others? But these scriptural passages put human giving in the context of a primordial receiving. Love others as God loved you while you were yet a stranger. The virtue in question is not self-derived benevolence but a responsive love that impels the receiver reflexively beyond the ordinary circle of family and friendship. These sacred narratives about God's actions and deeds do not merely illustrate moral principles derived from elsewhere. They reposition the agent; they open up a disclosive horizon in which the potential benefactor discovers himself to be a beneficiary. His petty benefactions merely signify love already received beyond his deserving. . . .

I.9

"The Social Psychology of the Gift"

Barry Schwartz

In this essay, contemporary American sociologist Barry Schwartz (born in 1938) emphasizes the giving (and receiving) of gifts as an essentially self-regarding activity. Drawing on the research of such noted social anthropologists as Marcel Mauss and Ruth Benedict, as well as from everyday life in our own society, he invites us to think about gift-giving as our way of defining ourselves and others, which we do for the sake of such things as influence, power, control, status, or justice. Indeed, Schwartz seems to take as a self-evident truth the proposition (made famous by Marcel Mauss) that there is no such thing as a free gift: "Gift exchange," he asserts, "is governed by the norm of reciprocity." Given Schwartz's assumptions, does it make any sense to speak of anyone as a philanthropist? Is there any way of squaring Schwartz's views with the more idealistic views of human nature and human impulses implicit in some of the other selections in this part? For example, is Aristotle's claim that the truly generous person gives for the sake of the noble merely a noble lie? Is Lewis's idea of "Gift-love" that desires what is simply best for the beloved just an illusion?

The Gift as a Generator of Identity

. . . Gifts are one of the ways in which the pictures that others have of us in their minds are transmitted. This point is seen in recurrent controversies over the prevalence of "war toys" on American gift lists. And the function of "masculine" and "feminine" gifts relative to sexual identification is clear enough. By the giving of different types of "masculine" gifts, for example, the mother and father express their image of the child as "a little soldier" or "a little chemist or engineer." Doubtlessly, an analysis of the gift-buying habits of parents would be a significant contribution to our knowledge of socialization. One important aspect of such an investigation would surely focus upon the increasing popularity of educational toys, the bisexual distribution of which may contribute to and reflect the lessening differentiation of American sex roles.

"The Social Psychology of the Gift," by Barry Schwartz, *American Journal of Sociology* 73, no. 1 (1967): 1–11. Reprinted by permission of the University of Chicago Press and Barry Schwartz.

The gift as an imposition of identity is well seen in its burlesqued form, the "Office Pollyanna," the ideal type of which obtains when gift recipients are chosen at random and presented with inexpensive items which make comical or witty reference to that part of their personal makeup which, in the eyes of the giver, is most worthy of exaggeration.

If gift giving socializes and serves as a generator of identity, it becomes necessary to acknowledge the existence of gifts which facilitate or impede maturation. One way in which upwardly mobile parents cause anxiety in their children is to provide gifts for which they are not yet ready—or even gifts whose level they have long ago outgrown. In this light, regressive possibilities exist on both sides of every gift-giving relationship. What has been implied here is that gift giving plays a role in status maintenance and locomotion. This is illustrated best in the "rites of passage" which gifts normally accompany. In such instances, they not only serve the recipient (e.g., a newlywed) as tools with which to betray more easily his or her former self but symbolize as well the social support necessary for such betrayal.

The Giver

The gift imposes an identity upon the giver as well as the receiver. On the one hand, gifts, as we noted, are frequently given which are consonant with the character of the recipient; yet, such gifts reveal an important secret: the idea which the recipient evokes in the imagination of the giver. . . . Indeed, gift giving is a way of free associating about the recipient in his presence and sometimes in the presence of others. This principle is recognized by the maker of a last will who is obliged to distribute benefits among two or more persons. The identity he thereby generates for himself is perhaps the most important of a long career of identity pronouncements, for it is his last—and is unalterable.

The act of giving is self-defining in a more direct way. Men tend to confirm their own identity by presenting it to others in objectified form. An extreme instance of this type of self-presentation is the display of masculinity through the giving of gift cigars following the birth of a child. Emerson, in fact, has suggested that this tendency toward self-objectification be made explicit (and in so doing provides insight into that which the new father's gift cigar symbolizes):

> The only gift is a portion of thyself. . . . Therefore the poet brings his poem; the shepherd, his lamb; the farmer, corn; the miner, a gem; the sailor, coral and shells; the painter, his picture; the girl, a handkerchief of her own sewing. This is right and pleasing, for it restores society in so far to its primary basis, when a man's biography is conveyed in a gift.

It is common knowledge that men present themselves publicly by the conspicuous presentation of gifts. Generous contributions to charity have always been a source of prestige in the United States. This is especially true when such gestures are made by individuals rather than corporations, and has been carried to an extreme by the members of movie society, for whom giving is an aspect of public relations. But professional fund raisers recognize this tendency in general society as well and therefore provide "I Gave" stickers which are generally affixed to the front door as certification of the family's willingness and ability to give away wealth. The charity potlatch is an important mode of the public presentation of self.

In middle-and upper-class society, the wife is a ceremonial consumer of goods, for decency "requires the wife to consume some goods conspicuously for the reputability of the household and its head." Thus, the husband elaborates his identity by the bestowal of gifts upon the wife, who becomes the public exponent of his selfhood. Children, furthermore, are more and more assuming the role of family status representatives as the adult female moves from the social to the economic sphere. The gift presentation of automobiles and other expensive items to children and teenagers testifies to this drift. Of course, the negative side of an excessive giving—receiving ratio in favor of the parents consists of a denial to the child of those rewards to self-hood which accompany the giving of gifts, the chief of which is an image of oneself as a source of gratification to others.

This leads into the interesting area of the giving of gifts to oneself. This is normally spoken of in terms of "self-indulgence," opposition to which, stripped to its essentials, represents an unwillingness on the part of the ego to strike a bargain with the id. This inflexibility is dangerous when other people (as sources of satisfaction) are not available, for it makes adjustment to hostile or impersonal environments unlikely. Deprived of material demonstrations of recognition from others, the internalization of such disregard can only be avoided by the utilization of one-self as a source of pleasure. The "self-gratifier" is an interesting product of the non-intimate community who, despite his pervasiveness, has received little attention from the social sciences. This is the person who, without significant affectional bonds, somehow makes it through life in one piece. He creates his own (emotional) "nutrition" and survives.

Gift Rejection

Earlier, in our treatment of the gift as an imposition of identity, it was suggested that the acceptance of a present is in fact an acceptance of the giver's ideas as to what one's desires and needs are. Consequently, to accept a gift is to accept (at least in part) an identity, and to reject a gift is to reject a definition of oneself. It follows that the receipt of gifts from two incompatible persons or groups raises questions as to the real source of one's identification.

At another extreme are found outright rejections of gifts with a conscious view to affirming the selfhood whose status an acceptance would threaten. A radical illustration from Ruth Benedict makes this type of reaction clear in our minds:

> Throw Away invited the clan of his friend to a feast of salmon berries and care-lessly served the grease and berries in canoes that had not been cleaned suffi-ciently to do them honor. Fast Runner chose to take this as a gross insult. He refused the food, lying down with his black bear blanket drawn over his face, and all his relatives, seeing he was displeased, followed his example.

The covering of the face suggests that Fast Runner is defending himself against the disparaging definitions of his selfhood which the dirty canoes imply. And from the standpoint of the giver of the rejected gift, we see an immediate world that has somehow lost its dependability. As Helen M. Lynd notes, the giver trusts himself to "a situation that is not there" and is thereby forced to cope with the dilemma of shame.

Gift Exchange, Control and Subordination

Levi-Strauss has written that "goods are not only economic commodities but vehicles and instruments for realities of another order: influence, power, sym-pathy, status, emotion; and the skillful game of exchange consists of a complex totality of maneuvers, conscious or unconscious, in order to gain security and to fortify one's self against risks incurred through alliances and rivalry." In other words, the regulation of one's bonds to others is very much part of the matter of the exchange of goods. . . . Furthermore, it is generally true that men maintain ascendancy by regulating the indebtedness of others to them. An exaggerated instance of this is described in Korn and McCorkle's essay on prison socializa-tion:

> Once an inmate has accepted any material symbol of service it is understood that the donor of these gifts has thereby established personal rights over the receiver. The extreme degree to which these mutual aid usages have been made dependent to power struggles is illustrated by the custom of forcing other inmates to accept cigarettes. . . . Aggressive inmates will go to extraordinary lengths to place gifts in the cells of inmates they have selected for personal domination. These intended victims, in order to escape the threatened bondage, must find the owner and insist that the gifts be taken back.

The principle of reciprocity, then, may be used as a tool in the aspiration for and protection of status and control. William F. Whyte, for instance, notes that the leader takes care not to fall into debt to his followers but to insure, on the con-trary, that the benefits he renders unto others are never fully repaid. Parents are especially aware of the fact that the child pays the cost of social inferiority when he accepts a gift from them and fails to reciprocate. "What is more," notes Homans, "he may, in becoming an inferior, become also a subordinate: the only way he can pay his debt may be to accept the orders of the giver." This principle is perhaps nowhere better seen than through the character of Santa Claus, the greatest of all gift givers, whose powers of surveillance and ability to grant and withhold benefits are annually exploited by parents as instruments of control over their children.

Santa Claus should not be taken lightly by the sociologist for, as we have seen, he plays an important role with respect to social control. It must also be noticed that he is not only a Christian but a Caucasian—and a blue-eyed Nordic one at that. This has particular significance for the non-Christian and non-Caucasian. That little Jewish boys and girls, for example, must depend upon a blue-eyed Christian for their gifts may lead to many hypotheses concerning the role of the myth in general and of St. Nicholas in particular with respect to ethnic dominance. Most Jewish parents are very aware of Santa's great seductive powers and of his ability to confound the developmental problem of ethnic identification. Therefore, the existence of Santa Claus is sometimes denied straightaway, and in his stead the hero of the Jewish holiday of Hanukkah, Judas Maccabee, is placed. But there is no contest: first of all, Judas is not a gift giver and as such is due neither promises of loyalty nor obedience. Further, there is no connection between the Hanukkah gift and the Maccabees. It is little wonder that Jewish children feel themselves shortchanged in December, for Hanukkah is indeed an imitation Christmas—and the very existence of imitation implies a dominant object and an inferior one. The Hanukkah gift, moreover, lacks the sociological quality of the Christmas present. The former, often given in the form of cash or Hanukkah *gelt*, merely (in Simmelian terms) "expresses the general element contained in all exchangeable objects, that is, their exchange value, it is incapable of expressing the individual element in them." By contrast, the concrete Christmas present, especially chosen in terms of the personality of giver and receiver, is more specifically reflective of and incorporable into their respective life systems. To this extent, the giver of Hanukkah *gelt* inevitably surrenders to the recipient a measure of control because money, unlike a particular commodity, does not presume a certain life system: it may be used in any way and thus becomes a more flexible instrument of the possessor's volition.

Incidentally, the above point, it seems, is relevant to the area of public assistance, where there has been some debate about whether benefits to the needy should be given in the form of cash or goods. Social workers are more prone to argue in favor of the former alternative, often on the basis of its implications for the psychological autonomy of the recipient. Opponents of this policy argue that the presentation of money severely limits the welfare department's band of control, for cash may be spent on disapproved commodities. Its abstractness dissolves the authority of the giver, which is inherent in concrete items.

Gift Giving as an Unfriendly Act

Once a connection is made between gift exchange and social control, it becomes necessary to explore the possibility of unfriendliness as a component of gift giving. One need not look far before ample evidence for such a possibility is found. . . . [T]he popular warning, "Never look a gift horse in the mouth," is [a] . . . direct acknowledgement of gifts as expressions of hostility. And the practical joke is an instance of man's need to give gifts which hurt or embarrass the recipient: "hot" chewing gum, cigars that blow up, gift-wrapped boxes containing a replica of a portion of feces, etc., are all purchased with a view to the direct or indirect satisfaction of this need.

The very nature of the gift exchange provides a condition for unfriendliness. Although gift giving is itself rewarding . . . it is accompanied by obvious deprivation as well, for the giver presents to another that which could have been employed for self-gratification. While he may receive a gift in return, there is certainly some loss of personal control over income and output of goods and money. The recipient in this light becomes a depriver about whom various degrees of ambivalence may emerge. . . .

One expresses unfriendliness through gift giving by breaking the rule of approximate reciprocity (returning a gift in near, but not exact, value of that received). Returning "tit for tat" transforms the relation into an economic one and expresses a refusal to play the role of grateful recipient. This offense represents a desire to end the relationship or at least define it on an impersonal, nonsentimental level. An exact return, then, is essentially a refusal to *accept* a "token of regard," which is to Mauss, [in many cultures,] "the equivalent of a declaration of war; it is a refusal of friendship and intercourse."

Both gift giver and receiver evaluate presents according to some frame of reference. A giver may therefore express contempt for the recipient by purchasing for him an inferior gift (in comparison with his gifts to others). Thus unfriendliness is shown by the mere invocation of a frame of reference. This mechanism, of course, is what enables the last will and testament to become partly an instrument for the expression of hostility.

We might also mention the object-derogation ritual by means of which the gift to be presented is "cursed." This ritual is reserved especially for those occasions where a presentation of a token of regard is mandatory. Thus children, in relaying a Christmas gift from their parents to the teacher, will feign a spit upon the package—or suggest its use as toilet paper, with an indecent gesture. Such rituals have as their purpose the "contamination" of the item with unfriendly sentiment. The ritual yields its fruit when the teacher accepts the contaminated gift with pleasure and thanks. On the other hand, the recipient may be aware of the contempt of the giver and, though obliged to accept the gift, may prevent contamination by destroying it, failing to use it, forgetting about it, etc.

Gifts may reflect unfriendliness in at least two final ways. First, the gold watch presented at retirement is normally more representative of a feeling of good riddance than of recognition for achievement; it is indeed a gilded "pink slip." Lastly, psychoanalytic theories of symbolism suggest that death wishes may be expressed in such gift objects as electric trains, satin blankets, ships, and other vehicles which take "long journeys." Inasmuch as such theories are valid, the popularity of electric trains as Christmas gifts has enormous implications.

Unfriendliness in the Recipient

What has been said about unfriendliness in gift giving should not draw attention away from hostility in the receiver. Ralph Waldo Emerson reminds us of this point in his essay:

> The law of benefits is a difficult channel, which requires careful sailing. . . . We wish to be self sustained. We do not quite forgive a giver. The hand that feeds us is in some danger of being bitten. We can receive anything from love, for that is a way of receiving it from ourselves; but not from *anyone* who assumes to bestow. We sometimes hate the meat which we eat, because there seems something of degrading dependence in living by it.

Emerson here suggests that an understanding or meaningful analysis of gift exchange requires a knowledge of the relationship between giver and receiver.

Status Anxiety

The possibility of unfriendliness in the gift exchange is recognized by most people. This is best supported by reference once again to popular slogans and proverbs which warn against being deceived by the gift. Translated sociologically, there is a general awareness that gift givers and receivers do not always believe in the role they are playing: the thought behind the gift may run anywhere from cynicism to sincerity. Insofar as persons employ one another as "social looking glasses," this variability in role sincerity gives rise to an uncertainty which may be called "status anxiety." Yet, it might also be suggested that the cynical giver (or the cynical role player, in general) is himself plagued by two sources of discomfort: there exists both the fear of "being found out" and a degree of guilt over the insincerity itself. When ambivalence reaches a certain point, the *compulsive* gift giver emerges who protects himself from both guilt and the unmasking anxiety by ritualistic presentations. In general, then, the ritual of gift exchange is not understandable by its anxiety-reducing qualities alone; it is itself a generator of anxiety, for if it is not properly executed, the public front of sincerity is likely to be jeopardized.

Awards

Gifts as ceremonial tokens of regard may be distributed analytically into two overlapping categories: those presented in recognition of status and those presented in recognition of achievement. In the former grouping are found Christmas, birthday, and anniversary gifts, Mother's Day and Father's Day presents, and so forth. We find the purest forms of the achievement gift in prizes, trophies, etc. Mixed forms involve achievement gifts for persons of a certain (usually kinship) status, for example, graduation presents.

It is important, however, to note that status gifts are often presented *publicly* as achievement gifts. Levi-Strauss, for example, writes, "the refinement of selection [of Christmas cards], their outstanding designs, their price, the quantity sent or received, give evidence (ritually exhibited on the mantlepiece during the week of celebration), of the recipient's social bonds and the degree of his prestige." Thus status and achievement gifts share a characteristic which provides insight into one of their more important properties: both are objectifications of past or present social relationships. The ceremonial display of such objectifications is a powerful tendency in social life: persons invariably seek to make known their social bonds in daily encounters. Veblen suggests that in advanced societies this tendency "develops into a system of rank titles, degrees and insignia, typical examples of which are heraldic devices, medals and honorary decorations." The presentation of self, then, is often made with symbols of one's connections to others. And gifts represent the purest forms of such symbols. These may of course be displayed with such elaboration and ostentation as to bring down the displeasure of the audience. Thus, the gift diamond, automobile, or other trophies must be displayed tactfully and with a certain degree of humility.

Gift Exchange, Reciprocity, and Distributive Justice

Gift exchange is governed by the norm of reciprocity. The degree to which this norm has been fulfilled in a given exchange of gifts may be stated in terms of distributive justice, which obtains when social rewards are proportional to costs and to investments. The concept of distributive justice is important in itself for it leads to interesting and non-obvious statements about human behavior. The principle tells us, for example, that a gift giver will experience discomfort if reciprocity fails to occur; but the idea that over-reciprocation will produce disturbance in the original giver is more interesting and leads into the area of undeserved rewards, to which shame, according to Helen M. Lynd, is connected. The use of a reward (often in the form of a gift) *as a punishment* is a device employed by many sets of contemporary "love-oriented" parents and may be subsumed under the general category of "shaming techniques," which consist of three separate operations: (1) the provision for the child of an unfavorable derogation-praise ratio, (2) the presentation of a gift, and (3) a verbal declaration of the lack of commensurability between the child's merit and the gift he has received. ("Daddy and mommy are giving you a present even though you've been a bad boy!") Shame is therefore doubly established by a statement of one's knowledge of another's sins and the giving of a reward despite them.

Distributive justice is particularly interesting in view of the rule which prohibits an equal-return "payment" in gift exchange. This suggests that every gift-exchanging dyad (or larger group) is characterized by a certain "balance of debt" which must never be brought into equilibrium, for a perfect level of distributive justice is typical of the economic rather than the social exchange relationship. It has, in fact, already been suggested that the greater the correspondence in value between gift received and gift returned, the less the sentimental component in the relationship is likely to be. But this proposition needs to be qualified by our noting that an absence or inadequate amount of reciprocity is not at all functional for the intimate relationship. There exists, then, a band—between complete and incomplete or inadequate reciprocity—within which the giver of the return gift must locate its value.

The continuing balance of debt—now in favor of one member, now in favor of the other—insures that the relationship between the two continue, for gratitude will always constitute a part of the bond linking them. Gouldner, in this connection, considered gift exchange as a "starting mechanism" for social relationships. Simmel likened the phenomenon to "inertia" in his essay on "Faithfulness and Gratitude":

> An action between men may be engendered by love or greed of gain, obedience or hatred, sociability or lust for domination alone, but this action usually does not exhaust the creative mood which, on the contrary, somehow lives on in the sociological situation it has produced. Gratitude is definitely such a continuance. . . . If every grateful action, which lingers on from good turns received in the past, were suddenly eliminated, society (at least as we know it) would break apart.

It must be noted that gratitude binds not only the living, but connects the living and the dead as well. The will is an institutionalization of such a connection. Inherited benefits, insofar as they cannot be reciprocated, generate eternal indebtedness and thereby link together present and past. Thus the absence of a sense of family tradition among the poor is due not only to familial instability, for example, "serial monogamy," but to a lack of willable commodities, that is, gratitude imperatives.

Simmel makes another important observation which implies that every gift-exchanging dyad is characterized by a moral dominance of one member over another. This has to do with the initiation of benefit exchange:

Once we have received something good from another person, once he has preceded us with his action, we no longer can make up for it completely, no matter how much our return gift or service may objectively or legally surpass his own. The reason is that his gift, because it was first, has a voluntary character which no return gift can have. For, to return the benefit we are obliged ethically; we operate under a coercion which, though neither social nor legal but moral, is still a coercion. The first gift is given in full spontaneity; it has a freedom without any duty, even without the duty of gratitude.

Following the same line of thought leads us to observe the tendency for initial aggression to be opposed with a disproportional amount of hostility, for the original aggressive act contains the decisive element of freedom. The object of the initial attack justifies his own retaliation, no matter how superior or devastating it may be, by simply noting the voluntary character of the original hostility. It is perhaps for this reason that vengeance is restrained in ancient (*lex talionis*) and modern law—and in moral interdictions as well. ("Vengeance is mine, saith the Lord.")

In order to draw our discussion on obligation balance to its logical completion, we are required to note that, while a gift exchange of items of nearly equal value generates gratitude, which binds the relation long after the exchange has actually taken place, an absence of reciprocity will inject into the bond an element of hostility that will be equally persistent. Simmel, then, failed to recognize the negative consequences of the norm of reciprocity, which prescribe vengeance, or at least grudge, for harm done, just as their counterparts call for reimbursement and gratitude for benefits received. It is, in this regard, worth noting that man could not altogether cease to show vengeance without ceasing to show gratitude as well, for both reflect and depend upon the internalized imperative of reciprocity.

Suspense and Social Exchange

We have just completed a discussion of that quality of gift exchange which provides a social relationship with inertia, in the form of gratitude or grudge. It remains to point out that the gift has a binding effect upon the relation before it is actually given and received. The growing cohesion of two potential exchangers, for example, obviously results from mutual expectation of a gift. Now, mutual expectation is reflective of an important fact about social life; that is, its easy predictability: the institutionalization of social action provides for this. But the substance of social life is as unpredictable as its form is certain—and this property of social exchange saves us from the tedium of perfect knowledge.

Without suspense, the entire tone of the gift exchange is altered—and with it, the relationship, which is correspondingly deprived of its mystery and surprise. Gifts are hidden or kept secret for the sake of the giver as well as the receiver for, as noted, the recipient's reaction to the present is crucial to the giver.

Suspense is most prevalent in childhood, since gifts differ greatly from year to year as a result of maturation. In contrast, the adult's status is more stable, and the types of gifts he receives will normally follow a set pattern. . . .

I.10

"Princess Diana and Mother Teresa: Compassion and Christian Charity"

Clifford Orwin

Among the various motives we may have for giving, compassion ranks
near the top. Most people today regard compassion as a—if not the—
bedrock of morality, and hence, too, as the proper governing principle
for our philanthropic practices. In this probing essay (usefully compared
with the selection by C. S. Lewis), political theorist Clifford Orwin (born
in 1947) helps us to understand what this means and how it has come to
pass. Beginning from a comparison of the charitable ways of Princess
Diana and Mother Teresa—two women vastly different in life, but in
death both canonized as saints of compassion—Orwin expounds the
fundamental difference between compassion and Christian charity,
thereby illuminating the compassionate humanitarianism that so summons our allegiance today. He locates the core of the difference in the
stance each takes with respect to suffering. For adherents of compassionate humanitarianism, he argues, "suffering is the main enemy and its
eradication the final goal." For practitioners of traditional Christian
charity, by contrast, "suffering, while distressing," is nevertheless recognized as "necessary to the salvation of sinful human beings." For the former, charity has become "a merely human virtue with a merely human
point of reference—the relief of earthly suffering." For the latter, suffering is redemptive and charity is a manifestation of our aspiration to godliness. Orwin's analysis invites us to ponder some very basic questions:
What is the meaning of human limitation and human suffering? How
should we stand toward them? Are our reasons for giving ultimately
linked to aspirations for perfection or immortality or holiness?

The women died just a few days apart, the lovely young princess and the homely
old nun. In life their lots had differed vastly. In death, however, both were canonized, if not (or, in Mother Teresa's case, not yet) by the Church of Rome, then
by the still more universal church of journalism. It pronounced them saints of
compassion, the one form of sanctity that commands universal respect today.

Unpublished manuscript. Used by permission of Clifford Orwin.

It was the blend of celebrity, accessibility and vulnerability that rendered Diana morally bewitching. She was the jet setting princess who "reached out" to ordinary people. Her causes, while numerous, were carefully selected. They were fashionable, and under her patronage became still more so. In particular her patronage of the campaign to ban land mines helped it to extraordinary successes.

But Diana did not become the "people's princess" solely through her solicitude for the distress of others. Equally endearing was her willingness to let us share *her* pain. If the nun relieved more suffering than the Princess, the Princess (at least as most people saw it) endured more than the nun. As Germaine Greer has written, "her suffering, as a wife disliked and scorned, as a lover betrayed and humiliated, was [every woman's]." Spurned by her uncaring husband, mistreated by her kin, she was prey to bulimia and other unroyal ailments. Her death was both terrible and poignant, the lover with whom she shared it one from whom sensible fathers locked up their daughters. Such happiness as they enjoyed could not possibly have lasted, and this too was one of the things that made Diana so contemporary.

It's easy to be cynical about Diana's celebrity, as about celebrity generally. From the very beginning of her public life, she was a creature of the media; Charles seems to have chosen her with them in mind. In the end it was she, not he, who excelled at manipulating the media. Inevitably, her good works were somewhat diminished by the public relations wars that dominated her life. Whatever her kindness toward the humble of the earth, she stopped at nothing to humiliate her unfaithful husband and those other stuffy unfeeling royals. That her death forced Queen Elizabeth to unstiffen her upper lip represented an extraordinary triumph for Diana. To have compelled her hated in-laws to abandon their cold gray dignity for her compassion: that was impressively cruel.

Diana was "with it" as only the young can be. While her death was sad, was it as sad as her growing old would have been? Would her repertory have included dignity in decay? That's something few of our celebrities manage. In any case destiny spared her this challenge.

Mother Teresa will be remembered longer, Mother Teresa who followed a much older script. The self-enforced austerities, the reticence, the unwavering fidelity to dogmatic theology and the authority of the Holy See—all seemed to mark her as in our time but not really of it. Her effect on worldly people was extraordinary, as if the odors of Calcutta provided a last whiff of a holiness otherwise long vanished. No wonder Christopher Hitchens seems to have regarded her life as an affront to his own.

Hitchens is a British journalist who lives in America and wages class struggle where it hurts the rich the most, in the pages of *Vanity Fair*. While he is usually nothing if not urbane, the appalling spectacle of Mother Teresa reduced him to juvenility. As if *The Missionary Position* were not a gross enough title for a book about her, he also collaborated on a documentary called *Hell's Angel*.

Despite such occasional lapses Hitchens is an accomplished debunker who dispenses his vitriol with style. Still, Mother Teresa is not the only anachronism of the two. "If the baffled and fearful prehistory of our species ever comes to an end, if we ever get off our knees . . . , there will be no need for smoking altars and forbidding temples with which to honor the freethinking humanists who scorned to use the fear of death to coerce and flatter the poor." No, that's not Tom Paine speaking, but Hitchens himself. And it's hot stuff—for 1789. Lest we miss the point Hitchens also showers us with epigraphs from actual Enlightenment priest-haters. He covets a role vacant in the West since the deaths of Jean-Paul Sartre and Sidney Hook: that of the great public atheist.

Hitchen's case against Mother Teresa (then still very much alive) runs roughly as follows. Far from being a saint unwillingly plucked from obscurity, she earned her halo only through relentless self-promotion, abetted by various sinister interests. She was not a humanitarian but a reactionary, who exploited her reputation to campaign against abortion and contraception. Of those who contributed money to her cause, quite a few were rich, and one or two were tyrants. Nor, despite the wealth so accumulated, did she dispense first-rate medical care. She cared more about how her patients died than whether they lived, and was more concerned to console them in their distress than to ease it by administering morphine. Hitchens even alleges that she sanctioned the practice of deathbed baptisms without the knowledge of the patient. Her Nobel Peace Prize was a travesty, as appears sufficiently from her speech accepting it, which dwelled on the evils of abortion. On close examination everything about her reeks of sectarianism and intolerance.

In the end Hitchens just can't forgive Mother Teresa her Christianity. Yet he grasps something crucial about her that others not bent on character assassination have missed: that she was not in fact a saint of compassion. The fad for her among worldly people—including Princess Diana herself—was due at least partly to misunderstanding.

Maybe Mother Teresa was unprofessional as a medical practitioner. But a professional medical practitioner she never claimed to be. "We are first of all religious. We are not social workers, not teachers, not nurses or doctors. We are religious sisters. We serve Jesus in the poor. We nurse him, feed him, clothe him, visit him, comfort him in the poor, the abandoned, the sick, the orphans, the dying." (Note the surprising absence of any reference to curing.) "Our lives are very much woven with the Eucharist. We have a deep faith in Jesus' Blessed Sacrament. Because of this faith, it is not so difficult to see Christ and touch him in the distressing disguise of the poor."

Mother Teresa's example calls on us to grasp the difference between compassion and Christian charity, between the virtue that now commands the conscience of the West and the one that used to do so. Compassion, like most social phenomena, is as important for what it isn't as for what it is. The crucial thing it isn't—what those great geniuses who launched it into the world in the 18th Century specifically designed it not to be—is Christian charity.

Mother Teresa was deeply sensitive to human suffering; if that is what we mean by compassion she certainly did not lack it. In her zeal to console the afflicted, however, she aspired to heights to which not even compassion could bear her. She strove to love her fellow human beings because and as she loved God, and the lowliest among them because He had so instructed: "Inasmuch as ye do this unto one of these the least of My brethren, so do ye it also unto Me." As she saw it, she imitated God by ministering unto his human form. She followed Jesus by treating every patient as Jesus, with all the love the Christian owes to Jesus. Her approach to her patients was not primarily a clinical one, directed to healing their bodies or, that failing, to minimize their pain. As a practitioner of charity, she addressed the problem of suffering differently than if she were acting from compassion.

"Charity" doesn't trip smoothly off our tongues these days, and it's worth considering why not. It is a tepid word, old-fashioned and even mildly pejorative. Its connotations seem cramped and outworn. A *charity* is an organization that helps people in need, and so we have the plural *charities*. (This institutional sense of the term is a wholly modern one.) *Charity* without the article is the practice of helping those in need or the attitude presumed to accompany such help. The protest "I don't want your lousy charity" suggests the problem here. We often think of charity as something extended *de haut en bas*, which affronts the dignity of the recipient and thereby our own egalitarianism. So most philanthropies find words other than charity to describe themselves and what they practice.

For access to the older, more expansive view of charity we need only turn to Abraham Lincoln. Of all modern statesmen he was the most indebted to the Bible and the most capable of evoking its sublimity. When in his Second Inaugural Address he called upon the citizens of the Union to treat their defeated brethren "with malice toward none and with charity toward all," he mined depths of charity largely forgotten today.

The Almighty has His own purposes. "Woe unto the world because of offenses! For it must needs be that offenses come: but woe to that man by whom the offense cometh!" If we suppose that American Slavery is one of those offenses which, in the providence of God, must needs come, but which, having continued through His appointed time, He now wills to remove, and that He gives to both North and South, this terrible war, as the woe due those by whom the offence came, shall we discern therein any departure from those divine attributes which the believers in a Living God always ascribe to him? Fondly do we hope—fervently do we pray— that this mighty scourge of war may speedily pass away. Yet, if God wills that it continue, until all the wealth piled by the bond-man's two hundred and fifty years of unrequited toil shall be sunk, and until every drop of blood drawn with the lash shall be paid by another drawn with the sword, as was said three thousand years ago, so still it must be said "the judgments of the Lord are righteous altogether."

With malice toward none, with charity for all; with firmness in the right, as God gives us to see the right, let us strive on to finish the work we are in; to bind up the nation's wounds. . . .

We associate compassion with egalitarianism: generally speaking, the party of compassion today is also that of greater social equality. Of such greater social equality Lincoln was unquestionably a prophet. In urging charity, however, he evoked at the same time an older and very different notion of human equality— the equality of all human beings as stained by original sin. In his political re-working of this notion, the awareness of common responsibility for slavery and therefore for the war that it brought is to save Northerners from pride and ha-tred. If all Americans have suffered greatly in war it is because all shared greatly in transgression. Because Northerners and Southerners were companions in sin they must become companions in charity. Because charity implies the most per-fect forgiveness, it lays the basis for the most perfect reconciliation with him.

Lincoln's appeal to charity as the final test of the mettle of a nation on which the ordeal of war had imposed so many others reminds us of how demanding a virtue Christians have traditionally understood it to be. Like the Latin *caritas* of which it is the English rendering, charity in its original Christian sense means something both broader and more specific than it does today. It is not just one virtue among many but the perfection of all the virtues, and, far from being able to achieve it on her own, the Christian owes it to divine grace. It is not an ac-quired but (to adopt the term of St. Thomas Aquinas) an "infused" virtue, for which, as a leading Catholic authority has written "strictly speaking, no human analogue exists . . . ; only the justifying power of the Holy Spirit causes [it] to come about in the believer." Charity is not human but divine, and can only be a gift of the Divine. It attests to God's love for humankind that he permits us to participate in this love and so to reciprocate it.

The practice of charity relates the believer directly to God. Precisely in so doing, however, it also embraces the neighbor—i.e., other human beings with-out exception—for they are created in the image of God. The more the Chris-tian aspires to love God, to take up His Cross and to follow His way, the more she will love her neighbor.

Among the merely human qualities that charity perfects is compassion. The Christ of the Gospels displays it, and his miracles notably include the curing of bodily sufferings. Likewise the Good Samaritan, whom Christ's parable offers as the model for our treatment of our neighbor, delivers a man fallen into worldly misfortunes. Precisely in its emphasis on the imitation of the divine, Christian-ity has been the most "humanitarian" of the world's great religions. This point seems especially worth making in view of the striking contrast in this regard between Christianity and Buddhism. The latter has been plausibly described as "the most compassionate of the world's great faiths." Yet Buddhist humanitarianism dates only to the 19th Century and Buddhism's encounter with Christianity.

Perhaps because this fact about Christianity is so obvious, we tend to take it for granted. Or perhaps because Christians have so often strayed from charity—toward fanaticism, sectarianism, oppression of non-Christians and so on—we may lean to cynicism toward it. It remains of capital importance, and crucial for grasping the deepest roots of the current culture of compassion. For what was true of Christian theology, as known only to the tiny handful of the educated in medieval Europe, was even truer of popular morals. In fact our very word "pity" was once one and the same word as "piety." "For pity's sake" was originally an appeal to piety. This held not only in English but also in French (*pitié*) and Italian (*pietà*). Only in the 16th Century did the words and their meanings diverge. Piety toward God was inseparable from pity toward man: piety was as pity did.

Consider finally yet another sense of this same term. In its Italian version of *pietà*, pity/piety came to name a central image of Christian iconography. The Incarnate God, tormented and crucified, subjected to that death that was in his day both the most disgraceful and the most agonizing, displays the wounds of his Passion. Of all scenes this one evokes in the Christian at the same time the keenest pity and the deepest piety.

The Christian God burst upon the world as everything one could want in a God, including an impenetrable contradiction. One and omnipotent, infinite and incorporeal, creator and king of all, He was also—strange to tell—the greatest of sufferers. Classical paganism had adorned its temples with images of resplendent beings, perfect in their beauty, beyond change and so beyond pity. The suffering on view in these shrines was not that of the gods, but of those insolent enough to offend them. While such images of torment could be heart-rending—think of the Laocoon—their official purpose at least was not to solicit compassion. It was to warn of the high price of *hubris*. The gods of Olympus may not have demanded much from human beings, but they didn't forgive much either.

Admittedly, the pagan gods had not been utter strangers to suffering. They were too much the work of poets—of Homer and Hesiod and all who followed them—to hope to escape all travail: suffering gods make for good stories. Besides, since the Olympians carried anthropomorphism so far as to lust after mortals, they were vulnerable on the side of parenthood. While they were immortal, their children by human consorts were not. Thus Homer's Zeus grieves bitterly that he must acquiesce in the death before Troy of his son Sarpedon.

Even more striking were the mystery cults, open only to initiates, with their deities of death and renewal. Nietzsche was to erect a whole theory of the birth of tragedy on the notion of the suffering Dionysus. While the Olympian gods forbade human beings to imitate them by pretending to the prerogatives of deathlessness—such imitation was the very core of *hubris*—the initiate into the mysteries assumed the persona of his divine patron. He ritually re-enacted the god's suffering so as to share in his rebirth. And such deities, having known affliction themselves, were presumed sensitive to human affliction. Even outside the framework of the mysteries, women revered Demeter and Kore/Persephone, the divine mother and daughter whose annual round of separation and reunion, barrenness and fertility, disposed them to pity mortal females. Thus not only suffering but the redemption of human beings from it had figured in the portfolios even of classical deities.

Other paganisms, such as those of West Asia, also propitiated gods subject to death and renewal. Yet the vulnerability of this throng of multiple and therefore petty gods, deficient in power and justice and fitful even in their mercy, worked no moral revolution in the world. For the very reasons the gods were sometimes fit objects for pity they could never be counted on to supply it. Lacking transcendence and omnipotence, subject themselves to all-too-human passions, they lacked the distance on humankind to embrace it with universal benevolence. They were similarly short of moral authority. Not being holy gods, they did not inspire charity or any other form of holiness in mortals.

In this as in all else, Judaism was profoundly different. It preached a God who was One, Eternal, Omnipotent, Just, and Merciful. According to the Talmud, indeed, it was God as *Adonai* (i.e., in His mercy) rather than as *Elohim* (i.e., in His justice) who created the world. By placing an unprecedented emphasis on divine mercy, Judaism vastly elevated its standing among the human virtues. The Hebrew Bible twice describes instances of human mercy as *chesed Adonai*—the lovingkindness of the Lord. It was equally characteristic of Judaism to blur the distinction between justice and mercy by subsuming what Christianity would present as acts of charity under the requirements of justice or righteousness (*tzedakah*).

Still, it was left to Christianity to confound the world by introducing an omnipotent God who "so loved mankind" that He became flesh and suffered more than flesh could bear that men might be redeemed from eternal suffering. By interpreting the Jewish image of the Suffering Servant of God (Isaiah) as the human incarnation of God, Christianity combined the poignancy of the pagan notion of a suffering god with the sublimity of the Jewish God. By presenting a God who was not merely embodied (like Dionysus or Demeter) but, though incorporeal, had actually willed his incarnation in a human body, it rendered his sufferings more comprehensible in one sense and less so in another. The sufferings of Christ were those of a man like us, yet at the same time those of a God who had spontaneously taken it upon himself to share our fate.

And could spiritual subtlety imagine any *more dangerous* bait than this? Anything to equal the enticing, intoxicating, overwhelming and undermining power of that symbol of the "holy cross," that ghastly paradox of a "God on the cross," that mystery of an unimaginable ultimate cruelty and self-crucifixion of God *for the salvation of man*? (Nietzsche, *On the Genealogy of Morals*)

Christians will disagree with Nietzsche as to the ghastliness of this symbol, but not as to its power. A god—the One True God—who stands pagan iconography on its head by freely subjecting Himself to sufferings more bitter than those previously decreed for the obdurate enemies of the Gods? Through His supreme commiseration for men, the Christian God becomes, in His tormented incarnation, the supreme *object* of man's commiseration. Only in Christian iconography does the very Principle of Being cry out to us in anguish.

The Christian life, accordingly, was that of the imitation of Christ, inspired by contemplation of his Passion. In every Catholic Church to this day that contemplation is evoked by the itinerary of the Stations of the Cross. The good Christian "takes up the Cross"; he takes upon himself the sufferings to which Christ submitted for his sake. Through suffering God has reached out to him and through suffering he must reach out to God.

Christians saints suffered, then, not as a punishment for disobedience to God but from their emulation of Him. Martyred or self-mortifying, they comprised an aristocracy unlike any previously known, pre-eminent not in power but in willing submission to affliction. The images of God crucified or deposed from the cross often portray him in the company of His grieving mother and others of his legion of saints. Sometimes too a donor is depicted in solemn contemplation of the doleful spectacle, reminding us that in bewailing the sufferings of Christ the saints serve as models for the viewer; that to respond to the scene is to participate in it.

So it was not only that the Christian followed Christ primarily by emulating His suffering. It was also, as witness the prominence of such images as the Flagellation, the *ecce homo*, the way to Calvary, the Crucifixion, and the *pietà*, through compassion that the Christian approached Him in the first place. It is only by appreciating how He has suffered for us that we become filled with eagerness to suffer for Him. Pity thus serves as the basis of piety, of love of God and of imitation of him. All suffering of the true Christian is suffering-along-with God; and all human suffering is meaningful if suffused with this light. For then it is the pathway to redemption of the soul. And charity, as love-of-God-in-mankind and love-of-mankind-in-God, must aim at such redemption, the only satisfactory answer to the riddle of human suffering.

There is then at least one further possible paradox in Christianity. The imitation of Christ culminates in the practice of his charity, which aims at the alleviation of suffering—as God assumed human form to suffer to redeem us from sin and suffering, so are we to devote ourselves to relieve the suffering of our fellows. At the same time, the Christian cannot simply will the abolition of [this-worldly] suffering, for it is through such suffering alone that sinful humans can approach Christ. Hitchens, as we have seen, damns Mother Teresa for eschewing the task of ending human suffering. In this she was indeed at odds with the devotees of secular compassion. For them, suffering is the main enemy and its eradication the final goal. In her view, however, suffering, while distressing, was necessary to the salvation of sinful human beings. [In Mother Teresa's words:]

> Suffering in itself is nothing, but suffering shared with Christ's passion is a wonderful gift of human life. It is the most beautiful gift that we can share in the passion of Christ.
> Suffering is a sign of love because this is how God the Father proved that he loved the world—by giving his Son to die for us and expiate our sin.
> Suffering in itself does not bring joy, but Christ as seen in suffering does.
> All of us are called to sanctity because as Jesus himself said, we must be perfect "like the Father," and in order to become saints we must suffer much, for suffering begets life in the soul.

If suffering in itself is nothing, shared it becomes the vehicle of the greatest human good, the joyful holiness available only through sharing in the sufferings of God. The task of the Christian is not to put an end to suffering but to help the sufferer see Christ in it and thereby find joy in it.

The compassionate or "humanitarian" reader will find this endorsement of suffering troubling. She'll balk at the suggestion that suffering be accepted not just as a permanent feature of human life but even as God's greatest gift to us. While she may not follow Hitchens down the path of vituperation, she will view Mother Teresa's project as very different from her own. What then of the presumed kinship between compassion and Christian charity? Is this just a misunderstanding?

Yes and no. And insofar as the answer is yes, the misunderstanding is not wholly accidental. If the pervasiveness of Christianity was a condition of the rise of compassion in the West, so too was the decline of Christianity, especially among the members of that avant-garde that conducted the Enlightenment. This decline was due in part to the overzealous practice of charity itself. Premodern Christian societies, being therefore also preliberal, were not permissive in matters of religion. They recognized no right of the individual to worship God as he saw fit. Charity obliged every Christian to leave no stone unturned in laboring for the salvation of his neighbor. Salvation depended on faith and so on the true faith—there could be no salvation in blasphemy and error. So every Christian state and ruler was conscience bound to propagate that true faith. Orthodoxy was to be not only taught but enforced; heresy not only refuted but suppressed. Where eternal damnation and salvation were at stake, neutrality or permissiveness was itself damnable. As interpreted by all too many Christians, charity not only permitted persecution but demanded it. In vain did the Unitarian Servetus flee Spain for Protestant Geneva; the flames to which Calvin consigned him there could not have been any hotter in Seville.

It's hard for us today even to grasp this position, let alone enter into the souls of those Christians who for so many centuries took it for granted. The notion that love of our fellow man could drive us to afflict and even kill him in order to suppress his theological opinions seems abominable to us. Indeed, there is no clearer test of a modern Christian (of course including Mother Teresa) than that she rejects persecution, and does so precisely in the name of charity. Yet this great revolution required a thoroughgoing reinterpretation of charity, one that culminated in assimilating it to compassion.

There is much plausibility to the claim that compassion or "humanity" represents the rump of Christian charity in our post-Christian world, the world of which Princess Diana was so much more representative than Mother Teresa. The key term is post-Christian. The crucial adaptation to modern moral tastes has been the reworking of charity as a merely human virtue with a merely human point of reference—the relief of earthly suffering. Compassion or "humanity" is charity without God. The offspring not of a marriage but of a divorce, it is our aspiration to benevolence "liberated" from our aspiration to godliness.

This project, a crucial aspect of the broader modern project of human "liberation," has proved ongoing and irresistible. In its early stages, however, compassion hardly dared breathe its name; it stirred only under cover of charity. Writing for Christian readers in a Christian world (in which indeed Christianity was officially enforced by every government in Europe) the trailblazers of the modern sensibility played down their innovation. They marketed their heady new wine in comfortably old bottles. They sought to exploit the Christian predisposition to charity that was the habit of seventeen centuries while purging it of Christian otherworldliness and sectarianism. Any account of this reform of charity must begin with the Enlightenment and its project of religious toleration. It would include a discussion of such towering figures as Spinoza and Locke, Bayle and Voltaire, Lessing and Moses Mendelssohn, Jefferson and Madison.

I am going to focus, however, on Jean-Jacques Rousseau. Rousseau too argued passionately for toleration as a requirement of true charity, and in many ways his critique of the Christianity of his day echoed that of the Enlightenment. But he far surpassed it in conceiving that the modern substitute for charity, and hence the modern reinterpretation of charity, must rest squarely on compassion.

Like any proponent of a purified Christianity, Rousseau purveyed his own version of the teaching of Christ, one allegedly founded in the Gospels and free of priestly incrustations. He begins by rejecting all theology, save for what we might call moral theology: those tenets of faith required to support good works.

God's existence, His goodness, His Providential care for mankind and in particular His solicitude for justice and just men: this is as much as we need to know and anything more would be too much, as it would set us to theological wrangling than which nothing is less conducive to love of neighbor. Rousseau explicitly renounces the dogma of original sin as without scriptural basis and as incompatible with the keystone of his own philosophical system, the doctrine of the natural goodness of man. According to this last doctrine, human beings as we know them are indeed evil, but they are so not because of sin but because of society. Similarly, they suffer not from sin but from society. Most simply, the Christian teaching on charity presumes the insufficiency of nature (and hence the necessity of the theological virtues, available only by grace) while Rousseau's promotion of compassion presumes the natural goodness of man.

As I have already suggested, Rousseau accepts his predecessors' critique of Christianity: if anything, he extends it. In discussing Christianity as it actually was he stresses not its charity but its repressiveness. And the Christian teaching on charity he casts as Exhibit A of Christian repressiveness. In enjoining us to love others as much as we love ourselves, it demands what we cannot possibly supply. Indeed it fosters a deadly collaboration of ambition, fanaticism, and mutual hatred.

For Rousseau, the very designation of charity as a theological virtue underscores the problem with it. It is because of the (re-?) definition of Christian faith in theological terms that salvation comes to depend on adherence to the proper set of abstruse metaphysical doctrines and charity comes to require the zealous enforcement of these doctrines.

Thus must we display our supposed love of our neighbor by striving to impose our dogmas upon him. Those whom we love in this manner are bound to resent our love far more than they would our indifference. We, in turn, are bound to experience their stubborn resistance as a mortal affront as well as a challenge to our own creed which therefore we must repel at all cost. If in theory Christianity teaches universal love, in practice it must stoke fierce hatreds. Rather than unite believers of all nations, it sharply divides them, albeit (due to its universalist pretensions) along sectarian lines rather than political ones. This Rousseau regards as the worst of both worlds: theological Christianity pits citizen against citizen, brother against brother.

The effectual truth of Christian charity as a theological virtue is fanaticism, as expressed in Crusades against unbelievers and heretics. "One must think as I do in order to be saved. This is the frightful dogma that lays waste the world" (Rousseau, *Geneva Manuscript*). Rousseau quotes with ironic approval a Dominican writer's praise of St. Dominic, "who, while preaching against the Albigensians, had the charity to join . . . [in taking] the trouble to exterminate corporeally, with the material sword, those heretics whom [it had not proved possible] to vanquish with the sword of the word of God" (*Letter to Beaumont*).

(Whether or not the saint had actually so acted, it was enough for Rousseau that a Dominican writer had thought so and had praised him for it.)

In keeping with this general polemical position, Rousseau tends not to reject charity but to seek to reinterpret it as compassion. That this task is not wholly implausible confirms the genuineness of his debt to Christianity. After all, he can point out that in placing even faith itself below charity he is only following St. Paul (*Letter to Beaumont*). And from this it would seem to follow that differences of faith (i.e., of interpretation of the true faith) should cede to that charity incumbent upon all. In the first of his *Letters written from the Mountain,* he imagines a people living according to the Christianity earlier expounded in the "Profession of Faith of the Savoyard Vicar" (expounded in his *Emile*). When confronted by a Christian dogmatist, such a people would invoke charity against dogmatism. It would grasp the essence of Christianity as the practice of charity in its new non-dogmatic garb of humanity and beneficence. " . . . That which is necessary in religion consists in practice; . . . not only must one be beneficent, merciful, humane, charitable; but . . . whoever is truly such believes enough to be saved." Not going so far as to argue for justification by works alone, Rousseau instead contends that works and works alone offer sufficient evidence of the faith that justifies. From this it follows that to concern oneself with the salvation of one's fellow becomes identical with setting him an example of those works (and therefore that faith) on which his salvation depends. Because all dogma beyond what is necessary to ground good works is to be deemed indifferent to our prospects for salvation, any focus on it detracts from those prospects by distracting us from what is needful to them.

It should go without saying, then, that a people of true Christians would reject persecution as a means of imposing dogma. For once doctrines are disjoined from faith, their imposition stands exposed not as a requirement of charity but as incompatible with it. "Charity is not murderous. Love of neighbor does not motivate to massacre. Thus it is not zeal for the salvation of men that is the cause of persecution: it is pride and amour-propre" ["vanity"]. Rousseau reinterprets faith (as in "the true faith") in terms of sincerity or "good faith." Not surprisingly, he does this in bad faith. For him as for his orthodox adversaries only the true faith qualifies as in good faith. The difference is that the criterion of good faith that he preaches is not dogmatic but moral. The sincerity of the tolerant and compassionate is accepted without question, while that of the intolerant and dogmatizing is rejected out of hand.

Viewed globally, Rousseau's religion of humanity splits the difference between true Christianity on the one hand and classical paganism, on the other. It seeks to combine the universality of the former with the this-worldliness of the latter. It thereby fosters a morality that is, as we would say today, not so much political as "social." It is not primarily as a fellow American (or even a fellow Christian) that our neighbor may lay claim to our concern but as a fellow human being. For Rousseau, we might say, Christianity begins and ends with the parable of the Good Samaritan. Inasmuch as the chief natural or earthly prop of our decency toward our fellows is compassion, the stirrings of compassion are the voice of God.

There is a final aspect of Rousseau's critique of charity that deserves notice for its relevance to our current situation. As I have mentioned, he breaks with Christianity by attributing human suffering not to sin but to society. Much of the suffering of society, moreover, he lays at the door of Christianity itself. The good Christian feels sinful and therefore guilty while a bad one may thrive on manipulating these feelings in others. Guilt appears to compassion, however, as just one more form of suffering to be relieved and if possible eradicated. Confronted with a human being so afflicted, compassion tends to address not the sin (for sin is not a category it acknowledges) but the sense of sinfulness. Confronted with a preacher of sinfulness, it tends to become indignant: there is enough suffering in life without man tormenting himself and others with bugbears.

To be sure, we are encouraged to feel guilty if we commit the one sin that is cardinal under the new dispensation: that of showing insufficient compassion. Of this sort of rhetoric Rousseau himself was an incomparable master. One of the many things that Rousseau invented was liberal guilt; prior to him liberals (i.e., partisans of Enlightenment) had lived quite free of guilt. If, however, we pronounce our compassion sufficient (and in gauging it we are of course acting as judges in our own cause), we are free to feel good about ourselves.

It follows that an important task of the morality of compassion is to cure us of being too "judgmental" (that is, too cruel) whether toward others or toward ourselves. This has gone very far in our own day, further than Rousseau could have imagined, and further than he would have approved. The whole "self-esteem" movement can be understood as an implication of the morality of compassion. "Non-judgmentalness" grows from compassion because to pronounce an adverse judgment on someone is not to dispel whatever other distress may afflict him but rather to compound it. It would be insensitive, and the last thing that the morality of compassion can sanction is insensitivity. To this Princess Diana, as a woman of our time, was perfectly attuned. Hence her devotion to the campaign against AIDS and on behalf of its sufferers, the non-judgmental—and anti-judgmental—cause *par excellence*.

Not that the necessity that a Christian make moral judgments is supposed to limit his charity. As God's love for human beings excludes no one, so the commandment to love our neighbor is absolute. Mother Teresa too strove on behalf of AIDS sufferers. To "be there" for someone, however, means something different to the Christian than it does on our soap operas and talk shows. It doesn't mean to refrain from all judgment. True, forgiveness must always be extended and final judgment left to God. Still, as charity commands love of neighbor, so it commands hatred of sin (as bad for the neighbor and everybody else) and exertion to free him from it. Indeed there is no evil comparable to sin and so no love comparable to that which seeks to dispel it. Whether or not Mother Teresa's homilies against contraception and abortion are (as Hitchens thinks) blots on her humanitarianism, they do not tarnish her charity.

If Rousseau were to return to earth today he would have to admit that Christianity has proved far more amenable to being cured of the tendency toward persecution than he anywhere admitted. The pontificates of John XXIII and John Paul II would have left him gaping, as would the transformation of the harsh Calvinism and Lutheranism of his day. In the world today, as in that of the early martyrs, Christians are far more likely to be the victims of persecution than its practitioners; virtually all Christianity everywhere is in the decisive respects tolerant.

True, certain issues, such as abortion, try this tolerance, but even quite conservative Christians accept the rights of conscience and the separation of church and state. We can go much further, and state that many if not most Christians today largely accept the reinterpretation of charity as compassion. From the Social Gospel of early 20th Century North American Protestantism to the left liberal social agenda of the mainstream churches today, the increasing this-worldliness of the Christian concern with the neighbor is only too obvious.

Rousseau would have recognized Princess Diana as an offspring of his rhetoric of compassion. He would also have recognized Christopher Hitchens, so angrily and blithely unaware of the shortcomings of Enlightenment. Yet he would have joined Hitchens in being wary of Mother Teresa.

Let me finish with a favorite anecdote of hers.

> I never forget one day when I met a lady who was dying of cancer and I could see the way she was struggling with that terrible pain. And I said to her, I said, you know this is but the kiss of Jesus, a sign that you have come so close to Him on the cross that He can kiss you. And she joined her hands together and said, "Mother Teresa, please tell Jesus to stop kissing me."

Undaunted by this response, Mother Teresa continues.

> This is the joy of suffering, the kiss of Jesus. Do not be afraid to share in that joy of suffering with Him because He will never give us more suffering than we are able to bear.

Mother Teresa retold this anecdote in the course of a commencement address at a Catholic women's college in California. We can only wonder what the Valley Girls in the audience made of it. Charity, as she understood it, makes extraordinary demands of sufferers—even as it invests extraordinary hopes in suffering. Compassion does neither. From the standpoint of charity, compassion is lax and superficial; from that of compassion, charity is exacting and cruel.

I.11

"Toward a Fourth Philanthropic Response: American Philanthropy and Its Public"

Elizabeth M. Lynn and D. Susan Wisely

Looked at from the point of view of individuals, motives or purposes for giving and serving can appear as individuated as we are. But from the point of view of organized philanthropy, there appear to be primarily three traditional reasons for giving: relief of personal suffering, improvement of individuals, and reform of society. In this selection, Elizabeth M. Lynn (born in 1958), Director of the Project on Civic Reflection and Consultant on Evaluation for the Lilly Foundation, and D. Susan Wisely (born in 1945), Director of Program Evaluation for the Lilly Endowment, provide a brief overview of these three traditions. Their assessment of the strengths and weaknesses of these traditions leads them to advance a newly burgeoning "tradition" on the philanthropic landscape, the promotion of "civic engagement": the effort to build up local community by engaging its citizens with one another and enabling them to work together on their shared concerns. To what extent do the various traditions discussed here mutually imply or depend upon each other? If you were made chairman of a philanthropic board, which one would you emphasize? Why?

As has often been observed, the private foundation is a curious creature on the landscape of American society. It is an institution poised somewhere between public and private—private in its operations, yet public in its regard. The ambiguity of this position has haunted foundations since their inception, and it presents special problems in the early twenty-first century, when the American public itself seems ready to dissolve into an array of diverse communities, defined less by commonalities than by differences. In such a time, when all Americans are pressed to think about the nature of their relationship to a larger public, foundation personnel must be especially reflective. How are we, in our institutional capacities, related to the changing arena of public life? And how can we best participate in the urgent task of reweaving the bonds of community

Adapted from "A Foundation's Relationship to Its Public" (Indiana University Center on Philanthropy, No. 17).

in this country, in a way that is respectful of diversity yet hopeful for a common future?

Answers to these questions are not easily forthcoming, perhaps for good reason. We live in a time between times, no longer confidently progressive in our social programs, but not sure of our ambitions for the future. The word "change" may be on the tip of every politician's tongue and at the center of every organizational logo. But no one seems certain about the true or desired direction of change.

Even as we strive to move forward, we might do well to acknowledge our uncertainty and allow this "time between times" to become something of an opportunity—an opportunity to reflect, to converse together, and to learn from the past. As always, we should try to learn from the mistakes and delusions of the past, especially insofar as those mistakes and delusions determine our present situation. But we can also learn from the hopes and dreams of the past, and from the visions of previous generations that impelled them to think and act in new ways, and to create new institutions that would carry their work forward. To chart a course for the future, we would do well to understand the several traditions of hope that have shaped the work of American philanthropy.

Making Connections

Central to the history of philanthropy in the United States is a vision of human connectedness. As historian Ellen Condliffe Lagemann has written, American philanthropy represents "a long tradition of . . . efforts to establish the values, shape the beliefs, and define the behaviors that would join people to one another."

Yet though they have all sought to cultivate connection among the members of this society, American philanthropists have not always understood that task in the same way. In the brief history of this nation, we have seen three distinctive philanthropic traditions: Relief, Improvement, and Social Reform. Within each of these traditions, the principles and purposes of philanthropic practice have been defined differently. Philanthropy understood as *relief* operates on the principle of compassion and seeks to alleviate human suffering. Philanthropy understood as *improvement* operates on the principle of progress and seeks to maximize individual human potential. Philanthropy understood as *reform* operates on the principle of justice and seeks to solve social problems. Let us briefly explore each of these traditions.

Philanthropy as Relief

The poor you will always have with you. . . .
John 12:8

The tradition of philanthropy as relief represents the most ancient form of philanthropy—what is sometimes called "charity." Animated by the principle of compassion, this kind of philanthropy is mainly concerned with *alleviating human suffering.*

Of all of the traditions contributing to the contemporary practice of philanthropy, the tradition of benevolence is most obviously rooted in a religious worldview. Charity, from the Latin term *caritas,* means other-regarding love, prompted without regard for status or merit, as in God's love for humanity. The benevolent impulse proceeds from the recognition that we are all connected to one another as part of God's creation. Even our accumulated wealth is God's gift, not our own achievement, and therefore is to be shared freely with God's other creatures.

In "On Christian Charity," a now famous sermon delivered to his fellow Puritans while sailing to America in 1630, John Winthrop gave these principles exemplary expression. Because we are "knit . . . together in the bond of brotherly affection," he said, "it appears plainly that no man is made more honorable than another or more wealthy, etc., out of any particular and singular respect to himself, but for the glory of his creator and the common good of the creature, man." We are therefore commanded to love our neighbors as ourselves.

> [T]his law requires two things: first, that every man afford his help to another in every want and distress; secondly, that he perform this out of the same affection which makes him careful of his own good according to that of our savior: "Whatsoever ye would that men should do to you" (Matthew:12).

As "members of the same body," he concluded, "we must delight in each other, make others' conditions as our own, rejoice together, mourn together, labor and suffer together."

The tradition of charity has been an important part of American philanthropy from Winthrop's day forward, and it continues today to animate philanthropies large and small, organized and individual, modest and lavish. When a foundation commits funds for the needy, it participates in the tradition of relief. Likewise, when we as individuals make a donation to the Red Cross, provide goods to a food pantry, shovel out an elderly neighbor or carry food to a fire victim, we too are participating in the tradition of relief.

The tradition of relief has many strengths (imagine a world without it!). It allows us to express love or empathy for others, without regard for status or merit. It highlights our personal obligation to respond to others. It meets clear and pressing needs. And, precisely because it is an act of compassion, a matter of "feeling with" others, charitable philanthropy is responsive to those it serves, rather than actively trying to shape or lead them.

At its worst, however, this tradition of benevolence can waste precious resources by failing to address the causes of suffering. It can also cultivate passivity toward "the way things are" by inviting us to respond to pressing needs rather than change the conditions that created them. Winthrop expressed this attitude of acquiescence to "the order of things" in the opening words of his sermon, when he declared that "God Almighty . . . hath so disposed of the condition of mankind as in all times some must be rich, some poor; some high and eminent in power and dignity, others mean in subjection." For better or worse, charity is a tradition resigned to the inevitability of social inequality. "The poor you will always have with you" might well be its motto.

Philanthropy as Improvement

Give a man a fish, feed him for a day.
Teach him to fish, feed him for a lifetime.
Anon.

The second great tradition of American philanthropy developed at least partly in response to the perceived futility of relief. Questioning the wisdom and effectiveness of "almsgiving," philanthropists like Benjamin Franklin and Andrew Carnegie sought instead to *maximize human potential.* Their distinctive style of giving established a great American tradition of providing opportunities for individual and civic improvement. To this day, many of us choose to give by underwriting fellowships for talented individuals, sponsoring cultural and artistic activities, or supporting educational and other "improving" organizations.

Andrew Carnegie provides an especially interesting example of philanthropy as improvement. In establishing one of the first modern foundations, he consciously rejected the old tradition of charity. Like those who practice benevolence, Carnegie hoped his philanthropy would foster human connectedness. His essay "The Gospel of Wealth" begins: "The problem of our age is the proper administration of wealth, so that the ties of brotherhood may still bind together the rich and poor in harmonious relationship." But he believed that the revolutionary changes wrought by industrialization and urbanization in the last third of the nineteenth century called for a fundamentally new approach to philanthropy.

For Carnegie, as for a number of Victorian philanthropists, the traditional forms of charity and almsgiving perpetuated the very ills they sought to alleviate. Far better, he believed, were charitable efforts that aim at improvement:

> In bestowing charity, the main consideration should be to help those who will help themselves; to provide part of the means by which those who desire to improve may do so; to give those who desire to rise the aids by which they may rise; to assist, but rarely or never to do all. Neither the individual nor the race is improved by almsgiving. . . . [T]he best means of benefiting the community is to place within its reach the ladders upon which the aspiring can rise—parks, and

means of recreation, by which men are helped in body and mind; works of art, certain to give pleasure and improve the public taste, and public institutions of various kinds, which will improve the general condition of the people.

According to Carnegie, proper philanthropy sets out ladders for those who have initiative and climbing skill. Individuals are then responsible for taking advantage of the ladders set before them. The libraries funded by Carnegie are an excellent example of this kind of giving. As is often the case in improvement philanthropy, they were inspired by Carnegie's own boyhood experiences of using a library.

More than a hundred years after Carnegie published "The Gospel of Wealth," the improvement tradition remains a vital part of American philanthropy, practiced especially by individual givers who want to make opportunities of the sort they experienced available to others. This kind of philanthropy has many inviting qualities that insure its continued vitality. It allows us to express gratitude for special opportunities we have received by extending the same opportunities to others. It emphasizes individual responsibility and encourages individual initiative.

Yet the tradition of improvement, like the tradition of relief, has weaknesses. In the latter half of the twentieth century, American philanthropy increasingly confronted a society in which its improving efforts seemed chiefly to benefit the well-situated and highly motivated members of the community. (Ladders, after all, are useful only to those with climbing skills, and fishing lessons only help those with access to the pond!) The concept of "individual opportunities" is of diminished value if entire groups are effectively blocked—for social, legal, and economic reasons—from taking advantage of such opportunities.

Philanthropy as Social Reform

A Catalyst for Change.
(MacArthur Foundation slogan)

Just as Carnegie reacted to the flaws in the relief tradition, so too foundation leaders felt it necessary to respond to the flaws in the improvement tradition. In a retrospective published in 1981, a spokesperson for Carnegie's own foundation noted that, in the early 1960s, the staff and board of the Carnegie Corporation had become "painfully aware of the urgent problems of race, poverty, and equality that were besetting the nation." Looking back on a tradition of encouraging educational opportunities, they concluded that "it was not reasonable to expect that schooling alone could create equality of opportunity when equality did not exist in the world of jobs, of social relations, or of politics." Like the Rockefeller and Ford Foundations, the Carnegie Corporation shifted its grant-making strategies in a new direction: it began to attack perceived underlying circumstances of inequality. Many of America's largest foundations now dedicated themselves not to charity or improvement but to social reform.

This third great tradition in American philanthropy—the tradition of reform—has roots in America's past: recall the abolitionists of the 1800s, for instance, or the muckrakers of the progressive era. Yet the goal of social reform has achieved special prominence in recent years, to the point where it now characterizes the self-understanding of most large foundations and of many smaller and more traditional charitable organizations as well.

Philanthropy as social reform is, above all, dedicated to encouraging social change. Its practitioners believe that societal circumstances are often more powerful in shaping human destiny than the actions of individuals themselves; hence, they argue, philanthropy must strive to change the circumstances. Indeed, its motto might well be the MacArthur Foundation's own: "A Catalyst for Change."

As this motto suggests, the philanthropic tradition of social reform takes a proactive, even directive role in public life. Rather than responding to the requests of others, it actively attempts to define and solve public problems, often through experimentation and the innovative use of venture capital. According to proponents of this approach, a foundation has the resources, freedom and expertise necessary to experiment on social problems. It should therefore seek innovative solutions that can in time be adopted by others.

One classic statement of social reform is the Carnegie Corporation report quoted above. Other exemplary expressions of this tradition can be found in the writings of national commissions established in the early 1970s to articulate the public role of foundations. Consider, for instance, the following statement from the Peterson Commission in 1970: "Our society . . . is in obvious need of philanthropic institutions standing outside the frame of government but in support of the public interest," it declared . "[J]ust as scouts move in advance of a body of troops to probe what lies ahead," so too philanthropic institutions "can spot emergent problems, diagnose them, and test alternative ways to deal with them."

The tradition of social reform has obvious strengths. It acknowledges the power of societal circumstances and seeks to change them. It intentionally experiments with alternative solutions to social problems and seeks to learn from those solutions. But social experimentation has brought with it some difficulties. Often, when foundations look to others to adopt the experiments they have fostered, they count on public revenue or hope to influence governmental policy. Modern foundations have naturally been tempted to see themselves as a kind of "shadow government," not just as supporters of experiments that might inspire further thinking but as the very makers of future social policy. Paul Ylvisaker indicates this tendency in *The Handbook on Private Foundations,* when he writes that modern philanthropy has been dedicated "to finding systemic so-lutions to underlying causes of poverty and other social ills, and over time has become a recognized social process, in effect *a set of private legislatures* defining public problems, setting goals and priorities, and allocating resources toward general solutions" (emphasis added). The result can be a kind of arrogance in advocating for social change "on behalf of" the public, and a failure to listen carefully to that public.

A Fourth Philanthropic Response?

. . . Only Connect.
E. M. Forster

The three types of philanthropy outlined above are not mutually exclusive. In-deed, most modern foundations participate to some degree in all three tradi-tions. Yet, on the whole, organized American philanthropy has in recent decades moved increasingly in the direction of social reform, relying on individual givers to fund opportunities for self-improvement and relegating the tradition-ally charitable work of relief to governmental and religious bodies.

The future direction of American philanthropy is less clear. Events of recent years have put new pressure upon foundations to rethink their fundamental strategies for serving the American public. Effective solutions to social problems have proven more elusive than had been hoped. Despite the social reform ef-forts of both government and philanthropy, ours is more than ever a society di-vided into rich and poor, a society still very much challenged to alleviate human suffering and to maximize human potential by providing significant opportu-nities for all its members.

Nor is it clear, in the new century, just *who* should be proposing solutions. We hear calls for different voices in public life—not just the voice of the suc-cessful, not just the voice of the expert, but the voice of the citizen. And yet, with the increased complexity and ambitions of the philanthropic enterprise, philan-thropy's relation to its public—its capacity to hear and learn from the public—has, if anything, diminished. The philanthropist who funds libraries or experi-ments with social policy stands at a far greater remove from those served than the relief worker who ladles soup in a soup kitchen.

In response, foundations and other philanthropic organizations have begun to turn toward a fourth philanthropic way, which some people refer to as *civic engagement.* They are investing resources in strengthening relationships and nurturing conversations among citizens, in order to build, as the President of the Public Education Network, Wendy Puriefoy, put it, "more reflective and re-sourceful local communities." Study circles, neighborhood associations, and the forums sponsored by the Kettering Foundation are examples of this fourth philanthropic response, as is the more ambitious recent initiative of the Annie E. Casey Foundation to "partner" with communities in cultivating local resources for addressing poverty. Ultimately, the goal of these investments may be to relieve, improve, or reform the communities they serve. Yet the focus of the work, and the standard of its success, is building up connections among ordinary citizens.

American interest in civic engagement is not new. In 1889, the same year Andrew Carnegie published his reflections on wealth, Jane Addams started Hull House in Chicago. Taking inspiration from London's Toynbee Hall, Addams established this settlement house with the conviction that we must connect with one another in order to help one another. In *Democracy and Social Ethics,* published in 1902, she cautions against the indiscriminate giving of relief and the stern policy of justice, and points the reader toward another way:

> 'To love mercy' and at the same time 'to do justly' is the difficult task; to fulfill the first requirement alone is to fall into the error of indiscriminate giving with all its disastrous results; to fulfill the second solely is to obtain the stern policy of withholding, and it results in such a dreary lack of sympathy and understanding that the establishment of justice is impossible. It may be that the combination of the two can never be attained save as we fulfill the third requirement—'to walk humbly with God,' which may mean to walk for many dreary miles beside the lowliest of His creatures.

The help Hull House offered its neighbors took many forms—sometimes relief from pain, sometimes improved individual opportunity, sometimes advocacy for social change. But its first and final value, for Addams, lay in building relationships among citizens so that they could better understand and assist one another. Addams did not call this work philanthropy, much less civic engagement. Yet in her writings and practices one can find many echoes of our contemporary need to build up meaningful connections among citizens.

As Addams would have been the first to acknowledge, civic engagement suffers from the perennial frustrations of democracy. It can be slow, contentious, prone to more talk than action, and difficult to render into measurable outcomes. But it can also empower those who might not otherwise participate in public life. It encourages attention to local needs and, in the language of our own time, recognizes local assets. And it builds community by engaging its citizens with one another and enabling them to work together on their shared concerns.

Each of the first three philanthropic traditions outlined earlier has made significant contributions to the well-being of the American public. But each, if taken alone, also displays weaknesses. The tradition of relief can encourage a philanthropy that is passive, reacting to pressing needs rather than trying to change the conditions that create those needs. The tradition of improvement can encourage philanthropy that benefits only selected members of the community. The tradition of social reform can lead foundation workers or other donors into unilateral decision-making "on behalf of" the public, without much openness to the wisdom or will of that public.

In this time between times, when new wisdom is needed, civic engagement may be an especially important philanthropic response. Citizens have untapped wisdom and resources for public service in their own practical experience which, for a variety of reasons, they have not been able to discover or recover. To put it simply, people need opportunities to learn from themselves and about themselves, from others and about others. A foundation can help those whom it would serve to tap these deep veins of wisdom, thereby discerning more clearly appropriate directions for public service in their own particular places and in their own particular ways.

One timely contribution foundations as well as individual donors can make, then, is to promote civic engagement and encourage public moral discourse, by cultivating hospitable spaces for reflection and by bringing diverse people and perspectives into conversation. Rather than trying to force a specific vision of the future (which could turn out to be an unexamined extension of the past), we can create the conditions for conversation, in the hope that new vision and fresh action will eventually emerge. In doing so, we are not forcing our own experimental answers or simply repeating the predictable answers a little louder for all to hear. Instead, we will be furthering public deliberation and promoting discovery of new ways of seeing.

PART TWO

How Should I Give?

Part II: Table of Contents

Matthew 25:1–46, Three Parables

Homer, *The Odyssey:* The Meeting of Nausikaa and Odysseus

Moses Maimonides, *Laws Concerning Gifts to the Poor:* "The Book of Seeds"

Sarah Orne Jewett, "The Spur of the Moment"

Isaac Peretz, "Motl Prince"

Jane Addams, "Charitable Effort"

O. Henry, "The Chair of Philanthromathematics"

Edith Wharton, "The Rembrandt"

Rudyard Kipling, "The Record of Badalia Herodsfoot"

Sylvia Warner, "A Work of Art"

John Reed, "Another Case of Ingratitude"

Gwendolyn Brooks, "The Lovers of the Poor"

II.1

Three Parables

Matthew 25:1–46

This chapter of Matthew's Gospel consists of three of Jesus' parables. As in many other parables, judgments are rendered, on the basis of which we are invited to infer what are better and worse ways of comporting ourselves with respect to our neighbors. But perhaps even more than other parables, these invite close scrutiny. Not only is each of them perplexing in its own right, but taken together, their teachings seem, at least on first impression, to be contradictory. For example, the "ten virgins" of the first parable seem to be praised for doing what appears to be condemned in the second—that is, for prudently guarding their gifts—and for not doing what appears to be praised in the third—that is, for not acting compassionately or hospitably to needy others. Can the sort of prudence that appears to be praised in the first parable be reconciled with the creativity rewarded in the second or with the compassion praised in the third? Is it possible for the same person simultaneously to act prudently, creatively, and compassionately toward his/her neighbors? Is it desirable to aspire to do so? If one acts prudently, how does one avoid being calculating? If one takes risks and tries to be creative, how does one avoid the temptation to be overly proud of one's accomplishments? If one is simply compassionate, how does one avoid the temptation to become condescending?

The Parable of the Ten Virgins

25 Then shall the kingdom of heaven be likened unto ten virgins, which took their lamps, and went forth to meet the bridegroom.

2 And five of them were wise, and five *were* foolish.

3 They that *were* foolish took their lamps, and took no oil with them:

4 but the wise took oil in their vessels with their lamps.

5 While the bridegroom tarried, they all slumbered and slept.

6 And at midnight there was a cry made, Behold, the bridegroom cometh; go ye out to meet him.

From *The Holy Bible,* King James version (New York: American Bible Company).

7 Then all those virgins arose, and trimmed their lamps.

8 And the foolish said unto the wise, Give us of your oil; for our lamps are gone out.

9 But the wise answered, saying, *Not so;* lest there be not enough for us and you: but go ye rather to them that sell, and buy for yourselves.

10 And while they went to buy, the bridegroom came; and they that were ready went in with him to the marriage: and the door was shut.

11 Afterward came also the other virgins, saying, Lord, Lord, open to us.

12 But he answered and said, Verily I say unto you, I know you not.

13 Watch therefore; for ye know neither the day nor the hour wherein the Son of man cometh.

The Parable of the Talents

14 ¶ For *the kingdom of heaven is* as a man traveling into a far country, *who* called his own servants, and delivered unto them his goods.

15 And unto one he gave five talents, to another two, and to another one; to every man according to his several ability; and straightway took his journey.

16 Then he that had received the five talents went and traded with the same, and made *them* other five talents.

17 And likewise he that *had received* two, he also gained other two.

18 But he that had received one went and digged in the earth, and hid his lord's money.

19 After a long time the lord of those servants cometh, and reckoneth with them.

20 And so he that had received five talents came and brought other five talents, saying, Lord, thou deliveredst unto me five talents: behold, I have gained beside them five talents more.

21 His lord said unto him, Well done, *thou* good and faithful servant: thou has been faithful over a few things, I will make thee ruler over many things: enter thou into the joy of thy lord.

22 He also that had received two talents came and said, Lord, thou deliveredst unto me two talents: behold, I have gained two other talents beside them.

23 His lord said unto him, Well done, good and faithful servant; thou has been faithful over a few things, I will make thee ruler over many things: enter thou into the joy of thy Lord.

24 Then he which had received the one talent came and said, Lord, I knew thee that thou art a hard man, reaping where thou has not sown, and gathering where thou has not strewed:

25 and I was afraid, and went and hid thy talent in the earth: lo, *there* thou hast *that* is thine.

26   His lord answered and said unto him, *Thou* wicked and slothful servant, thou knewest that I reap where I sowed not, and gather where I have not strewed:

27   thou oughtest therefore to have put my money to the exchangers, and *then* at my coming I should have received mine own with usury.

28   Take therefore the talent from him, and give *it* unto him which hath ten talents.

29   For unto every one that hath shall be given, and he shall have abundance: but from him that hath not shall be taken away even that which he hath.

30   And cast ye the unprofitable servant into outer darkness: there shall be weeping and gnashing of teeth.

The Judgment of the Nations

31   ¶ When the Son of man shall come in his glory, and all the holy angels with him, then shall he sit upon the throne of his glory:

32   and before him shall be gathered all nations: and he shall separate them one from another, as a shepherd divideth his sheep from the goats:

33   and he shall set the sheep on his right hand, but the goats on the left.

34   Then shall the King say unto them on his right hand, Come, ye blessed of my Father, inherit the kingdom prepared for you from the foundation of the world:

35   for I was ahungered, and ye gave me meat: I was thirsty, and ye gave me drink: I was a stranger, and ye took me in:

36   naked, and ye clothed me: I was sick, and ye visited me: I was in prison, and ye came unto me.

37   Then shall the righteous answer him, saying, Lord, when saw we thee ahungered, and fed thee? or thirsty, and gave thee drink?

38   When saw we thee a stranger, and took thee in? or naked, and clothed thee?

39   Or when saw we thee sick, or in prison, and came unto thee?

40   And the King shall answer and say unto them, Verily I say unto you, Inasmuch as ye have done it unto one of the least of these my brethren, ye have done it unto me.

41   Then shall he say also unto them on the left hand, Depart from me, ye cursed, into everlasting fire, prepared for the devil and his angels:

42   for I was ahungered, and ye gave me no meat: I was thirsty, and ye gave me no drink:

43   I was a stranger, and ye took me not in: naked, and ye clothed me not: sick, and in prison, and ye visited me not.

44   Then shall they also answer him, saying, Lord, when saw we thee ahungered, or athirst, or a stranger, or naked, or sick, or in prison, and did not minister unto thee?

45   Then shall he answer them, saying, Verily I say unto you, Inasmuch as ye did it not to one of the least of these, ye did *it* not to me.

46   And these shall go away into everlasting punishment: but the righteous into life eternal.

II.2

The Odyssey:
The Meeting of Nausikaa and Odysseus

Homer

Homer (circa ninth century B.C.), the earliest Greek poet of whom we are aware, is often regarded as the maker of the Greeks. Through his two epic poems, *The Iliad* and *The Odyssey,* he taught the ancient Greeks how to think about themselves, as well as about the gods. The deeds of his oversized heroes stand out, but often his lesser-known characters play equally important roles. For example, Nausikaa, the young Phaiakian princess in this selection from *The Odyssey,* is a case in point. As Odysseus awakens on the shore of Phaiakia, he hears the joyful sounds of young women at play. Though he looks like a "hill-kept lion," and feels even worse, "his belly is urgent upon him." Very cautiously, he readies himself to face the young maidens, the first human beings he has seen in more than seven years. As he approaches, everyone but Nausikaa flees in fright. In this selection, we observe and listen in on Odysseus's winning supplication and Nausikaa's response.

Several days and much hospitality later (in a part of the epic not reproduced below), Odysseus and Nausikaa meet for a second and last time, during which we learn what Nausikaa's brave deed here has meant to Odysseus. Nausikaa makes one short speech: "Goodbye, stranger," she says. "Think of me sometimes when you are back at home, how I was the first you owed your life [in Greek, *zoë*] to." In effect, she asks Odysseus to remember her for giving him the stuff of life—*zoë*—food, clothing, and shelter. But Odysseus, answering her, says, "Nausikaa, daughter of great-hearted Alkinoos, even so may Zeus, high-thundering husband of Hera, grant me to reach my house and see my day of homecoming. So even when I am there I will pray to you, as to a goddess, all the days of my life. For, maiden, my life [in Greek, *bios*] was your gift" (IX.457–468). Odysseus, in effect, says that he will remember her for giving him back his human life—his *bios*. He will remember her for "en-humaning" him. If we take Odysseus at his word, and under the circumstances there seems little reason not to, Nausikaa may well be regarded as "philanthropist par excellence." How does Nausikaa bring about the change with which Odysseus credits her? Can ancient Homer's Nausikaa provide a philanthropic model relevant for people of the twenty-first century?

Excerpt from "Book VI" from *The Odyssey of Homer* by Richmond Lattimore. Copyright © 1965, 1967 by Richmond Lattimore. Reprinted by permission of HarperCollins Publishers, Inc.

So long-suffering great Odysseus slept in that place
in an exhaustion of sleep and weariness, and now Athene
went her way to the district and city of the Phaiakian
men, who formerly lived in the spacious land, Hypereia,
next to the Cyclopes, who were men too overbearing,
and who had kept harrying them, being greater in strength. From here
godlike Nausithoös had removed and led a migration,
and settled in Scheria, far away from men who eat bread,
and driven a wall about the city, and built the houses,
and made the temples of the gods, and allotted the holdings.
But now he had submitted to his fate, and gone to Hades',
and Alkinoös, learned in designs from the gods, now ruled there.
It was to his house that the gray-eyed goddess Athene
went, devising the homecoming of great-hearted Odysseus,
and she went into the ornate chamber, in which a girl
was sleeping, like the immortal goddesses for stature and beauty,
Nausikaa, the daughter of great-hearted Alkinoös,
and beside her two handmaidens with beauty given from the Graces
slept on either side of the post with the shining doors closed.
She drifted in like a breath of wind to where the girl slept,
and came and stood above her head and spoke a word to her,
likening herself to the daughter of Dymas, famed for seafaring,
a girl of the same age, in whom her fancy delighted.
In this likeness the gray-eyed Athene spoke to her:
'Nausikaa, how could your mother have a child so careless?
The shining clothes are lying away uncared for, while your
marriage is not far off, when you should be in your glory
for clothes to wear, and provide too for those who attend you.
It is from such things that a good reputation among people
springs up, giving pleasure to your father and the lady your mother.
So let us go on a washing tomorrow when dawn shows. I too
will go along with you and help you, so you can have all
done most quickly, since you will not long stay unmarried.
For already you are being courted by all the best men
of the Phaiakians hereabouts, and you too are a Phaiakian.
So come, urge your famous father early in the morning
to harness the mules and wagon for you, and it shall carry
the sashes and dresses and shining coverlets for you. In this way
it will be so much more becoming than for you to go there
on foot, for the washing places are a long way from the city.'
      So the gray-eyed Athene spoke and went away from her
to Olympos, where the abode of the gods stands firm and unmoving
forever, they say, and is not shaken with winds nor spattered
with rains, nor does snow pile ever there, but the shining bright air

stretches cloudless away, and the white light glances upon it.
And there, and all their days, the blessed gods take their pleasure.
There the Gray-eyed One went, when she had talked with the young girl.

And the next the Dawn came, throned in splendor, and wakened the well-robed
girl Nausikaa, and she wondered much at her dreaming,
and went through the house, so as to give the word to her parents,
to her dear father and her mother. She found them within there;
the queen was sitting by the fireside with her attendant
women, turning sea-purple yarn on a distaff; her father
she met as he was going out the door to the council
of famed barons, where the proud Phaiakians used to summon him.
She stood very close up to her dear father and spoke to him:
'Daddy dear, will you not have them harness me the wagon,
the high one with the good wheels, so that I can take the clothing
to the river and wash it? Now it is lying about, all dirty,
and you yourself, when you sit among the first men in council
and share their counsels, ought to have clean clothing about you;
and also, you have five dear sons who are grown in the palace,
two of them married, and the other three are sprightly bachelors,
and they are forever wanting clean fresh clothing, to wear it
when they go to dance, and it is my duty to think about all this.'

So she spoke, but she was ashamed to speak of her joyful
marriage to her dear father, but he understood all and answered:
'I do not begrudge you the mules, child, nor anything
else. So go, and the serving men will harness the wagon,
the high one with the good wheels that has the carrying basket.'

He spoke, and gave the order to the serving men. These obeyed,
and brought the mule wagon with good wheels outside and put it
together, and led the mules under the yoke and harnessed them,
and the girl brought the bright clothing out from the inner chamber
and laid it in the well-polished wagon. Meanwhile her mother
put in a box all manner of food, which would preserve strength,
and put many good things to eat with it, and poured out
wine in a goatskin bottle, and her daughter put that in the wagon.
She gave her limpid olive oil in a golden oil flask
for her and her attendant women to use for anointing.
Nausikaa took up the whip and the shining reins, then
whipped them into a start and the mules went noisily forward
and pulled without stint, carrying the girl and the clothing.
She was not alone. The rest, her handmaidens, walked on beside her.

Now when they had come to the delightful stream of the river,
where there was always a washing place, and plenty of glorious
water that ran through to wash what was ever so dirty,
there they unyoked the mules and set them free from the wagon,

and chased them out along the bank of the swirling river
to graze on the sweet river grass, while they from the wagon
lifted the wash in their hands and carried it to the black water,
and stamped on it in the basins, making a race and game of it
until they had washed and rinsed all dirt away, then spread it
out in line along the beach of the sea, where the water
of the sea had washed the most big pebbles up on the dry shore.
Then they themselves, after bathing and anointing themselves with olive oil,
ate their dinner all along by the banks of the river
and waited for the laundry to dry out in the sunshine.
But when she and her maids had taken their pleasure in eating,
they all threw off their veils for a game of ball, and among them
it was Nausikaa of the white arms who led in the dancing;
and as Artemis, who showers arrows, moves on the mountains
either along Taÿgetos or on high-towering
Erymanthos, delighting in boars and deer in their running,
and along with her the nymphs, daughters of Zeus of the aegis,
range in the wilds and play, and the heart of Leto is gladdened,
for the head and the brows of Artemis are above all the others,
and she is easily marked among them, though all are lovely,
so this one shone among her handmaidens, a virgin unwedded.

But now, when she was about ready once more to harness
the mules, and fold the splendid clothing, and start on the way home,
then the gray-eyed goddess Athene thought what to do next;
how Odysseus should awake, and see the well-favored young girl,
and she should be his guide to the city of the Phaiakians.
Now the princess threw the ball toward one handmaiden,
and missed the girl, and the ball went into the swirling water,
and they all cried out aloud, and noble Odysseus wakened
and sat up and began pondering in his heart and his spirit:
'Ah me, what are the people whose land I have come to this time,
and are they violent and savage, and without justice,
or hospitable to strangers, with a godly mind? See now
how an outcry of young women echoes about me,
of nymphs, who keep the sudden and sheer high mountain places
and springs of the rivers and grass of the meadows, or am I truly
in the neighborhood of human people I can converse with?
But come now, I myself shall see what I can discover.'

So speaking, great Odysseus came from under his thicket,
and from the dense foliage with his heavy hand he broke off
a leafy branch to cover his body and hide the male parts,
and went in the confidence of his strength, like some hill-kept lion,
who advances, though he is rained on and blown by the wind, and both eyes
kindle; he goes out after cattle or sheep, or it may be

deer in the wilderness, and his belly is urgent upon him
to get inside of a close steading and go for the sheepflocks.
So Odysseus was ready to face young girls with well-ordered
hair, naked though he was, for the need was on him; and yet
he appeared terrifying to them, all crusted with dry spray,
and they scattered one way and another down the jutting beaches.
Only the daughter of Alkinoös stood fast, for Athene
put courage into her heart, and took the fear from her body,
and she stood her ground and faced him, and now Odysseus debated
whether to supplicate the well-favored girl by clasping
her knees, or stand off where he was and in words of blandishment
ask if she would show him the city, and lend him clothing.
Then in the division of his heart this way seemed best to him,
to stand well off and supplicate in words of blandishment,
for fear that, if he clasped her knees, the girl might be angry.
So blandishingly and full of craft he began to address her:
'I am at your knees, O queen. But are you mortal or goddess?
If indeed you are one of the gods who hold wide heaven,
then I must find in you the nearest likeness to Artemis
the daughter of great Zeus, for beauty, figure, and stature.
But if you are one among those mortals who live in this country,
three times blessed are your father and the lady your mother,
and three times blessed your brothers too, and I know their spirits
are warmed forever with happiness at the thought of you, seeing
such a slip of beauty taking her place in the chorus of dancers;
but blessed at the heart, even beyond these others, is that one
who, after loading you down with gifts, leads you as his bride
home. I have never with these eyes seen anything like you,
neither man nor woman. Wonder takes me as I look on you.
Yet in Delos once I saw such a thing, by Apollo's altar.
I saw the stalk of a young palm shooting up. I had gone there
once, and with a following of a great many people,
on that journey which was to mean hard suffering for me.
And as, when I looked upon that tree, my heart admired it
long, since such a tree had never yet sprung from the earth, so
now, lady, I admire you and wonder, and am terribly
afraid to clasp you by the knees. The hard sorrow is on me.
Yesterday on the twentieth day I escaped the wine-blue
sea; until then the current and the tearing winds had swept me
along from the island Ogygia, and my fate has landed me
here; here too I must have evil to suffer; I do not
think it will stop; before then the gods have much to give me.
Then have pity, O queen. You are the first I have come to
after much suffering, there is no one else that I know of

here among the people who hold this land and this city.
Show me the way to the town and give me some rag to wrap me
in, if you had any kind of piece of cloth when you came here,
and then may the gods give you everything that your heart longs for;
may they grant you a husband and a house and sweet agreement
in all things, for nothing is better than this, more steadfast
than when two people, a man and his wife, keep a harmonious
household; a thing that brings much distress to the people who hate them
and pleasure to their well-wishers, and for them the best reputation.'

Then in turn Nausikaa of the white arms answered him:
'My friend, since you seem not like a thoughtless man, nor a mean one,
it is Zeus himself, the Olympian, who gives people good fortune,
to each single man, to the good and the bad, just as he wishes;
and since he must have given you yours, you must even endure it.
But now, since it is our land and our city that you have come to,
you shall not lack for clothing nor anything else, of those gifts
which should befall the unhappy suppliant on his arrival;
and I will show you our town, and tell you the name of our people.
It is the Phaiakians who hold this territory and city,
and I myself am the daughter of great-hearted Alkinoös,
whose power and dominion are held by right, given from the Phaiakians.'

She spoke, and to her attendants with well-ordered hair gave instruction:
'Stand fast, girls. Where are you flying, just because you have looked on
a man? Do you think this is some enemy coming against us?
There is no such man living nor can there ever be one
who can come into the land of the Phaiakians bringing
warlike attack; we are so very dear to the immortals,
and we live far apart by ourselves in the wash of the great sea
at the utter end, nor do any other people mix with us.
But, since this is some poor wanderer who has come to us,
we must now take care of him, since all strangers and wanderers
are sacred in the sight of Zeus, and the gift is a light and a dear one.
So, my attendants, give some food and drink to the stranger,
and bathe him, where there is shelter from the wind, in the river.'

II.3

Laws Concerning Gifts to the Poor: "The Book of Seeds"

Moses Maimonides

Spanish-born philosopher Moses Maimonides (1135–1204), also known as Moses Ben Maimon, or more commonly "RaMBaM," is one of Judaism's most revered rabbis (teachers). The famous selection below, excerpted from the final chapter of *Hilchot Matanot Ani'im* [*Laws Concerning Gifts to the Poor*], appears in a tractate called *Sefer Zera'im* [*Book of Seeds*], which is part of the *Mishneh Torah* [*Retelling of the Torah*, i.e., of the first five books of the Hebrew Bible]. For Maimonides, giving to the poor is but one instance of distributing growing things, which is why it appears in this tractate.

In this selection, Maimonides speaks of eight levels of *tzedakah*, a term often translated as "charity" but perhaps better translated as "righteousness" or "equity."* His term "levels"—as opposed, say, to degrees—suggests differences of kind. Is each level really different in kind from the next? Can you discern the (a?) reason for Maimonides' order? Should you, as benefactor, feel obliged to regard yourself as a partner of your beneficiary (the best way to proceed, according to Maimonides)? If so, how is such a partnership to be construed? Who should determine when it ought to be terminated? Why might anonymity of giver and recipient (Maimonides' second level) be important and/or desirable? If total anonymity is impossible, is it more important (better?) that the receiver remain anonymous (Maimonides' third level) than that the giver be so (Maimonides' fourth level)? Should one give before (fifth level) or after (sixth level) being asked? Does it ultimately make any difference whether one gives pleasantly (seventh level) or sorrowfully (eight level)? How can

Translated from the Hebrew by Judah Mandelbaum

"Sefer Zera'im (The Book of Seeds)," in *Laws Concerning Gifts to the Poor*, unpublished translation by Judah Mandelbaum, from chapter 10. Permission to reprint granted by Judah Mandelbaum.

*The Hebrew term *tzedakah* has the same root as *tzedek*, which means justice. In Jewish thought, acts of *tzedakah* are looked upon primarily as a rectification of social imbalance. They are thought to be fueled more by a sense of fairness or justice than by mercy, pangs of conscience, or compassion. Such deeds constitute the fulfillment, it is taught, of the obligations one incurs by virtue of having wealth or owning property. Hence, it is best to translate *tzedakah* as "righteousness" or "equity." In Jewish thought, it should be noted, ownership is tantamount to custodianship. In biblical times, for example, farmers were required to leave crops standing in the corners of their fields for the poor, as well as any crop that fell in the course of harvesting. This arrangement provided for the needy, but it also necessitated the able-bodied poor to engage in the harvesting of the corners and the gathering of the fallen crops. This is no doubt, at least in part, why the topic of this selection appears in the tractate *The Book of Seeds*.

one who gives rightly—that is, in one of the ways suggested by Maimonides—avoid the temptation to become calculating, manipulative, or hypocritical?

There are eight levels of *tzedakah,* one better than the next. A high level, of which none is higher, is where one takes the hand of an Israelite and gives him a gift or loan, or makes a partnership with him, or finds him employment, in order to strengthen him until he needs to ask help of no one. *Concerning this it says, "And you will give strength to the resident alien, so he may live among you," as if to say, strengthen him until he will not falter or need.*

Below this is one who gives *tzedakah* to the poor, not knowing to whom he gives, while the poor person does not know from whom he takes. *For this is [fulfillment of a] commandment for its own sake. . . .*

Below this, the giver knows to whom he gives, and the poor person does not know from whom he takes. *For example: the rabbinic sages who went in secret, tossing coins in the door openings of the poor. In this case, it is proper and good if the alms officers do not behave precisely.*

Below this, the poor person knows from whom he takes, and the giver does not know: *as per example of the greatest of the sages who would bundle small change in their sheets, and throw them over their shoulders, in sight of the poor, who took, so they would have no shame.*

Below this, one puts into another's hand before [the latter] asks.

Below this, one gives another after [the latter] asks.

Below this, one gives another less than is appropriate, in a pleasant manner.

Below this, one gives sorrowfully.

II.4

"The Spur of the Moment"

Sarah Orne Jewett

In this story, American novelist and short-story writer Sarah Orne Jewett (1849–1909) invites reflection not only on the philanthropic value of im-pulse-giving, but also on how to (indeed, whether we can ever) evaluate our philanthropic deeds. As Mrs. Dartmouth stares out her window, her attention alights on the cabman in the street, who is continually jerking at his horse's reins in order to keep the poor specimen of a creature from nodding off. Spurred, so it seems, as much by her own boredom, restless-ness, and self-disgust as by the actions of the "horrid" cabman, Mrs. Dart-mouth impulsively summons the cabman to drive to Miss Peet's, to "see if she has any errands for an hour or two." Unbeknownst to Mrs. Dart-mouth, this small, spur-of-the-moment gesture becomes a great benefac-tion, for both the cabman and Miss Peet. In concluding her story, Jewett generalizes the point the drama appears to enact: "There is always the hope that 'our unconscious benefactions may outweigh our unconscious cruelties,' but the world moves on, and we seldom really know how much we have to do with other people's lives." Should Mrs. Dartmouth be re-garded as a philanthropist? In general, should we regard as philanthropic impulsive deeds that spring, as hers seem to, more from negative than from positive motives? Is it true that we "seldom really know" how we af-fect other people's lives? If so, does it—should it—matter how or in what spirit we give, or, for that matter, whether we give at all?

＊＊＊

Mrs. Dartmouth sat at a front window looking out upon very bad weather and a most uninteresting street. She had turned her back to the large room, as if all the books and pictures, which were badly enough lighted that day, only filled her with impatience. At the end of the room there was a cheerful fire. It looked as if the lady had just been sitting in a low chair beside it; there was a book dropped face downward on the rug.

"I never was so tired of myself in all my life!" grumbled the watcher at the window, and then smiled, as if she must recognize those who would be sure to protest at such a speech if they were only present.

From *The Uncollected Short Stories of Sarah Orne Jewett,* edited by Richard Cary (Waterville, Maine: Colby College Press, 1971). Reprinted by permission of Colby College.

The public square outside looked country-like that winter day, with fresh snow outlining the trees, and the broad walks quite empty of those figures which usually came and went and gave an air of hurry which belongs to the center of a great city. The sloping ground, snow-covered and deserted, might have been a part of some large rural estate; there were no foot-tracks, and you could not see, for the misty weather, the buildings that stood beyond. The lady at the window was not fond of the country for its own sake, and liked to see plenty of figures in all her landscapes; it was very seldom that she was left to pass a dull winter afternoon alone.

Now and then a carriage plodded by; the snow-storm was fast turning to rain, and the clogged wheels left black tracks in the thin snow and spattered mud into the white gutters. Across the street stood a poor-looking cab with a dreary white horse that kept nodding his heavy head down to comfortless sleep and being detected by his driver, who sat miserably on the box and jerked the reins as if he had nothing to do but to keep the poor creature broad awake. There was a roof of snow on the cab and on the driver's hat; once, happily, he fell into a doze himself and swayed about dangerously, until he waked with a start and pulled at the reins again and looked anxiously at the opposite houses.

The lady flushed with displeasure as she watched, and then suddenly availed herself with satisfaction of even so poor and unrewarding an occasion of interest.

"Horrid, hard-hearted man!" she said aloud. "Why can't he let that poor horse sleep?" Then she rose and went a step or two closer to the window to see if there were any prospect of a customer for the waiting cab; she wished that the poor appealing establishment would take itself off. Sometimes people came hurrying across the square and chartered this cab to carry them the rest of the way to a railway station back of the hill; but it now occurred to Mrs. Dartmouth that such patronage was never frequent in either the best or worst of weather; the cab seemed to be on its stand much oftener than it was absent on its brief errands.

"Nobody would want such a poor-looking thing for visits," she thought; she had never really given two thoughts to the matter before. "That has been a good horse once." Her vague grievances and sense of dullness were fast giving way to this new interest.

"Why doesn't the foolish fellow get a better turnout? Why doesn't he try what a little varnish might do? A trig little brougham would tempt dozens of persons that pass him by. I'm sure that I never should get into such a thing unless I were in some strait or other—caught in a shower perhaps. I dare say he's poor enough, but he must be a slack cabby, too. A little varnish certainly wouldn't ruin him—(Oh, don't jerk that poor horse so; you hurt his mouth!)" She fairly stamped her foot with impatience, but she could not stop looking. "I wonder where he lives. Why doesn't he go home out of the rain? They'll both be stiff with cold; there's not a creature in sight. Oh, dear, this is worse than thinking about nothing!"

The white horse drooped his patient head again. The cabman was either asleep himself or in a despondent brown study; at any moment he might twitch the reins.

"I cannot bear this another moment," exclaimed the watcher, who rapped such impatient, determined blows with her paper-cutter on the window that the driver heard them only too easily, looked up, touched his dripping snow-topped hat with a smart air, seized his whip and turned across the street toward the high, handsome house to take a most welcome order.

"Oh, what shall I do with him? Dear me!" cried the lady now, and at that very moment a man-servant came in to mend the fire.

"No. Don't move my chair, Jenks," she said. "Please light the gas; it was really growing too dark to read there." She crossed the room to the writing-table and opened a drawer. "Will you take this money; there is a cabman at the door, ask him to go—to go to Miss Peet's, 18 Blight Street, and see if she has any errands for an hour or two."

"Miss Peet's, 18 Blight Street," repeated Jenks who promptly disappeared. The mistress of the house gave a sigh of relief and seated herself by the fire. "Dear me!" she exclaimed again with a sigh of relief, "if that wasn't the spur of the moment! But what an afternoon!"

Miss Peet was sitting by the window all this time in quite another part of the city. Everybody had called her old Miss Peet for at least twenty years, and she was hardly seventy yet. Some persons always look out of place in spring and summer; they seem to belong only to winter, as if they were the dried stalks of what had once been growing, but one might feel a reasonable doubt as to whether poor Miss Peet had ever really been in bloom. She had an unhappy way of telling you more things to other people's disadvantage than to their credit, and when she had told you, and you saw fit to join in with blame, she looked satisfied at first and then grew severe and prim and reminded you that one must endeavor to be charitable. But somehow she never liked to hear others praised; she would say, "Oh, but she has so *much* money!" or, "Oh, it's *very* easy to make use of such opportunities as hers," or, "I have heard it said that he is very close about little things and does something large now and then because he likes to have it known!" Nearly all the really generous and kind actions of her old friend Mrs. Dartmouth had been at one time or another arranged under one of these three heads. In short, Miss Peet was one of those sad, unhappy souls who cannot help looking upon the prosperity of others except as some injustice to themselves.

She was now grumbling at the weather, and with some reason, for it was certainly bad weather, and was also preventing her from going to a funeral. It might be expected that such occasions possessed great attraction for so gloomy a disposition, though Miss Peet was by no means one of those who can only look on at the distress of their fellows as if it were a scene in a play. The poor lady's lack of sympathy so often prevented her being asked by younger people to join in any friendly occasions that she made the most of those public or semi-public social functions that fell in her way. This was the funeral of a friend who through all his lifetime had been indulgent to Miss Peet, and often affectionate; he had once been the younger business partner of her father. After going down with the rest of the company in the sad crash of 1857, he alone had regained his footing and been able to climb again to the top of the hill of fortune. He had been most kind in his remembrance of this poor, sharp-tempered lady's sorrows and needs, and his Christmas cheque had long been her main dependence. Perhaps she mourned the loss of this as much as the loss of the giver. She could not bear to think that the weather was going to make her miss going to such a funeral, but she sighed to think that none of his children would remember to send a carriage for her, as he had touchingly remembered to do years before when his wife died. This had seemed to Miss Peet only a proper tribute to the daughter of his former friend and associate.

Miss Peet had put on her best clothes and was ready and waiting. There was something most appealing in her appearance; you felt anew that she was one of those unhappy persons from whom every year has taken something away; whether it was her own fault or other people's, the fact remained that nearly everything pleasant had gone. She sat by the window watching the rain and sleet come down into the empty street. There were some bright little children bobbing and smiling and beckoning from a window opposite, but she did not see them.

"It's too late now; I shouldn't see the people come in, anyway," Miss Peet said, ruefully. "I believe I'll take off my things. I should think somebody might have remembered to call for me; I can't walk and run the risk of getting cold again, but nobody thinks of me now," and she leaned forward to give a last look up the street.

There was an old white horse just turning the corner, and her heart really beat a little faster with sudden hope; then she drew back. "It may be somebody coming to see me," she thought, "but I'm sure they'd take poor me to the funeral if I told the circumstances."

Hardly five minutes afterward Miss Peet was safe in the cab and only disturbed because the man did not drive faster. The pavements were growing icy now and the horse slipped, while the driver did not seem to know how to help him to keep his feet. Luckily, they had not far to go. "What made Mary Dartmouth send such a miserable old horse and cab as this!" grumbled our friend as she settled the limp bows of her bonnet. "Providence does sometimes provide for us," she handsomely acknowledged a moment later, when she was well on her way and had time to remember how great her disappointment would have been but for this accident of a friend's thought.

The line of waiting carriages seemed to darken all the gloomy street. Miss Peet was helped out of the cab and well sheltered under a large umbrella on her way up the steps, and the cabman drove away to take his humble place behind the more comfortable turnouts. Everything was cold and forlorn, dripping and icy and cheerless. The coachmen were well wrapped; their backs looked round enough under their mackintoshes, but nobody liked the weather, and the poor horses were badly off. Two or three men at a time left the line and drove discreetly to the corner and back. They spoke to one another from box to box, and appeared to be on friendly and even intimate terms. The cabman who came last was a stranger among them, and belonged, at any rate, to a far lower grade of the business than the private coachmen who were his neighbors.

Half an hour went by, and the conversation became more and more frank, and so distinctly audible that the undertaker's man on the hearse waved a rebuking hand.

"Nobody can't hear us in the house with this storm a-pelting down," said one of the most comfortable-looking and loudest-complaining men. "They'll not be out for another hour, I dessay, and keep us freezing. I don't want to be up all night over my team." (The delays of those who ride in carriages often seem foolishly unnecessary and thoughtless to those who drive them.)

"He was an awful kind-hearted, nice old gentleman, anyway," said the next coachman, a very large old man. "I knew him 'most forty years ago, when I first went to be helper to Mr. Duncan next door—long before I was ever on a carriage box. I used to bring round his ridin' horse an' Mr. Duncan's together; our stable was next door to each other on Chestnut Street. Many's the quarter he's give me, and quarters was quarters then. I come near going to him for helper when Mr. Duncan died, but one o' the sons kept me on, and give me the place as coachman after a year or two. I was there twenty-two years, and I'm with Wallis's goin' on twelve."

"Must be stupid," said the next man. "For me, I like a change. Hosses an' you gettin' old and fat together an' doin' the same bloomin' things over an' over— oh, *land!* I go off in summer, anyway, and I make a winter shift to New York every two-three year."

"Have to take a trick o' livery work in between; up all night with them big parties worst season o' the year," observed a neighbor, scornfully. He had been so indiscreet as to wear a bearskin cap, and it looked like a thatched roof fringed with icicles, which now and then broke off and slipped inside his collar.

"Know that missionary on the cab, back there?" inquired a coachman who was stirring his horses again.

"He ain't no edicated cabman; he come a few days ago to that stand o' old Dumphy's—Dumphy's laid up with a lung fever," said the big man, who seemed to be in receipt of every particular. "He looks natural to me; he used to live somewheres out in Broadwood, I think, but I can't place him."

"Looks as if he were down on his luck; handles his reins as if he was fast to a fish," said the other. "That's been a plaguy good horse he's tryin' to drive; die game he will, too; drop down dead in's harness. Messenger colt, old Mr. Haines on Hill Street gave an awful price for when he was young; no style, but passed everything on the road and kep' it up all day. Lord! if I was rich I'd build a nice 'ospit'l for them game old horses, right out in the country in a snug place where they'd have good feed all summer and be out o' the wind come winter. I'd pay a lot o' old chaps like us, that's gettin' old for regular work and knowed how to use 'em well; top wages they should have to tend 'em up like cossets!"

There was a sound of approval from all the carriages within hearing.

"I know that fellow!" exclaimed the big coachman a moment afterward. "He's a man I want to see, too. I've got to start my team; I'll go up and speak to him," and he drove slowly to the end of the procession and halted next to the poor white horse.

"Your name Fallon?"

"Yes, it is," said the cabby, half rising on his box. He was soaked through, and his face was all lilac and yellow with cold. The rain-water dripped from his clothes; he had put both the poor blankets over the horse.

"Keep your sitting!" said the pompous private coachman, with a mock insolence that betokened warm good fellowship. "You used to live out at old Mrs. Douglas's place at Broadwood; you used to be a gardener out there, didn't you? an' went out West after a solid-gold job?"

"All so," acknowledged the cabby; "worst thing ever I done, too."

"Sportin' any?" asked the elder man, frankly.

"No, *sir!*" was the sorrowful answer. "Hard luck done it. I broke my arm all to pieces, an' then got burnt out just as we started in to keep house, folks got sick, an' everything. I guess I been one o' them that draws misfortune; 'twa'n't no gardenin' neighborhood, anyway, and I was too poor to leave."

"Don't say!" exclaimed the listener.

"Got back this fall; wife's stopping with some o' her folks—been sick all winter. I ain't used to drivin', but Dumphy's their neighbor and he's down sick and I'm spelling him two-three weeks or so. I went right out to Douglas's an' asked if they'd take me on. 'Not till spring'—that's what everybody says. So I'm driving this chari't o' victory. To-day's last day."

"You go right out to Douglas's again!" exclaimed the harbinger of good fortune. "The old lady heard you'd been there, and she remembered you and said you was lucky with some of her old-fashioned things in the greenhouse. She's been passin' the word to have us all look out for you. I didn't know you when I first see you, either. I guess you'll find you've got it all safe in your hand this time."

"I was goin' to start to-morrow an' tramp it back to New York," said the poor fellow, and then he could not speak. The warm color rushed into his cold, despairing face. "I know them things she means, sir," he added almost gayly to his benefactor; "them old daphnes and lemon-trees; she used to say they belonged to her mother before her. I kind o' favored 'em along, and nussed 'em into bloomin' well. Well, I've thought all day long I see my finish."

The door of the house opened, the big coachman made a lordly gesture as he went on duty again, and moved away to his place. The funeral pomps went on in solemn orderliness and the street was empty after the procession passed.

Poor little Miss Peet had been the last of the funeral guests to slip into the house, and she felt an odd sinking of the heart in the warm, rich-colored, familiar old rooms whence her best friend had departed. She even began to accuse herself for once, instead of other people, and wished that she had done more for Mr. Walton; he had been an invalid for some time, and she was one of the few persons who could talk with him about old times and early interests. She now felt a curious nearness to him and his affectionate kindness, and remembered with an unaccustomed pang how anxiously she had thought of what she might get for herself, instead of thinking of what could be done for him. But the old sense of his affectionate kindness, all lost forever, came over her as she stood in the doorway.

"He knew my lot was hard," she lamented, "but his lot was hard, too. I believe I've been sort of ungrateful and *selfish!*" said Miss Peet. Some persons learn a great many lessons in their lives, and others are all their lifetime learning only one.

Miss Peet was standing in the light just at the doorway of the room where the mourners sat, and before any one had time to bring her a chair and she sat down and was lost in the indistinguishable group, some one had time to notice her pale face and look of sincere feeling. It was the old friend's daughter, who lived at a great distance and who had not seen Miss Peet for many years; who might never have thought of her again. This was something that brought the tears afresh into one's eyes. Mrs. Ashton remembered all her father's patience and loyal interest and kindness; she also felt a curious thrill of nearness to his heart, and a new sense of loss; she said to herself that she would find out what he had done for his old acquaintance, and continue it for his dear and generous sake. Miss Peet had provoked her many a time in earlier years, but how old she looked now, and how lonely! She must try to see her, and do all that could be done. And Miss Peet little knew that, while she let go one friendly hand, another was being held out to her that would never let her fall unbefriended in her stony and narrow little path of life.

Oddly enough, Mrs. Dartmouth could never understand why her old friend Mrs. Douglas sent her such exquisite offerings of flowers from time to time after this. She had often sent some fine roses or a bunch of violets, but she no longer chose them herself, and one can hardly expect one's gardeners to put much sentiment into the choice of flowers for unknown persons. Yet now, when Mrs. Douglas's flowers were announced, they were always a wonder and delight, and Fallon always brought them himself so that they would not get shaken, and left them with Mrs. Douglas's compliments at the door. We all have our little superstitions; and poor Fallon could never forget the handsome lady who sat at the window and watched him that hopeless afternoon, and gave him the order for an hour's work that turned his luck.

Oddly enough, too, Miss Peet happened to be calling upon Mrs. Dartmouth one day when the flowers came. Her face lightened at the sight of them, and she went away with a lovely bunch in her hand. Mrs. Dartmouth could not help noticing that she seemed better pleased with life, and more cheerful than she used to be, and said much less about her own troubles.

There is always the hope that "our unconscious benefactions may outweigh our unconscious cruelties," but the world moves on, and we seldom really know how much we have to do with other people's lives.

II.5

"Motl Prince"

Isaac Peretz

Few of us need instruction to beware the philanthropist who draws attention to his own magnanimity, even fewer to beware the one whose philanthropy comes with mockery of his beneficiaries. In "Motl Prince," Polish-born Yiddish poet, playwright, and short-story writer Isaac Peretz (1851?–1915) gives us an example with which to test these intuitions. Motl is, like many of Peretz's characters, at once very parochial—he is very much a part of Peretz's own, now lost, eastern European Jewish community and culture—and very familiar. Far more prosperous than his neighbors, Motl gives abundant and frequent gifts, but in doing so he consciously draws attention to his own self-importance and, by contrast, to everyone else's neediness. He turns each gift into an occasion to exercise his theatrical powers and to perpetrate what is essentially a practical joke. His recipients are inevitably diminished either by being shamed and humiliated or by being made to experience excessive fear and even terror. Thus, he is known as Motl Prince, not because of his princely or noble origins, but because of his affected lordliness. Not until he is visited by a powerful dream in which he dies and is transported to a "paradise" of torment—that is, not until he is himself diminished—is Motl made aware of the offensiveness of his ways. As his rabbi explains, "When one gives charity as a joke, paradise becomes a mockery." In response, Motl immediately changes his ways. Henceforth, we are told, he practices his charity in secret (anonymously?), and he is known simply as Motl. Does Motl overreact? Is there no room at all for humor when it comes to charity? Is Peretz implicitly suggesting that anonymous giving is simply best, or that it is best for Motl, that is, as a corrective for Motl's particular excesses? Either way, is he right? Is Motl's spirit rightly redirected, or is it broken?

There was once a Jew whose name was Motl. But he was called Motl Prince.

He dealt in timber and grain. He had free entry to the homes of the nobility, so he acted a bit like an aristocrat himself. He wore silk stockings. He painted

Translated from the Yiddish by Shlomo Katz
From *Selected Stories* by I. L. Peretz, edited by Irving Howe and Eliezer Greenberg, copyright © 1974 by Schocken Books. Used by permission of Schocken Books, a division of Random House, Inc.

the chairs in his house red—no other paint was available in town—and a dainty red handkerchief peeked out of his pocket. Even his charity he dispensed in a lordly manner.

Now, it is known that Jews love goose. First, because it is good to eat, and second, because it is economical—there is the meat, and goose fat for Passover, and cracklings to eat with an onion. Feathers for a pillow are also useful. To this day, when a Jew goes to a restaurant he asks for a listing of the entire menu and in the end orders a piece of goose.

It happened, however, that the rabbi of this town loved ducks. A God-fearing scholar but with a weakness for duck meat. People talked about it, and it reached Motl Prince.

It was before Purim and Motl Prince ordered a duck to be bought and fattened as a Purim gift for the rabbi. And he further ordered that, when it came to stuffing the duck after it had been made properly kosher, he should be informed.

On the eve of Purim he was informed: the time has come to stuff the duck.

Motl Prince took eighteen golden Polish zlotys out of his dresser, ordered that they be made kosher by washing them in seven waters, and that the duck be stuffed with them.

Why?

Motl Prince wanted to know which the rabbi liked more, duck or Polish zlotys.

Once Motl went strolling down the synagogue alley. It was the eve of the Sabbath, on a summer day, and from time to time he took out his dainty red handkerchief, ostensibly to wipe the perspiration from his brow. Each time he pulled out the handkerchief he let slip a roulon to the ground.

What is a *roulon?*

At that time there was no paper money in circulation, no credit bills. What was used in trade were gold coins. Merchants would pack the gold coins into paper tubes, seal them with their seals, and write the sum on the tubes. It was these tubes, called roulons, that circulated from hand to hand without the contents being counted. There was a bit more trust and confidence then.

Motl strolled along and let slip such *roulons.*

How come?

He took old Polish pennies and packed them into the tubes as if they were gold coins.

Poor people walking in the street would find them. If the finder was honest, he would run after him and return the find, and Motl Prince would reward him with gracious thanks and a gold coin for returning the loss. If the finder was not an honest man, he would grab his find, conceal it, and happily run home with it—but all he would end up with would be a few pennies.

Once on the eve of Passover he played this trick. Since he was *parnas,* the communal provider, he sat in the community house and distributed *ma'ot hittin,* wheat money. Poor Jews came in rags and in tatters, and he would remark to one and then another, "You stingy fellow, will you at least indulge yourself and order some new clothes for the holiday?"

The paupers laughed.

On the eve of *Shabbat Hagadol,* the great Sabbath before Passover, poor people left the bathhouse late—they had to wait till the *ba'ale batim,* the solid citizens, had their turn first. When they came to the cooling room where they had left their clothes—not a trace. Outcries, shouting. Who stole the clothes? How would they get home? They blamed the bathhouse attendant. Motl Prince came in, pretending to have been delayed. He ruled: the paupers were right. The bathhouse attendant was paid for his work and so he must pay.

Well, since Motl Prince so ruled, the attendant went into the adjoining house and returned with a heap of clothes, fresh from the needle, nothing missing, and proceeded to dress and shod the naked ones.

In mid-winter, after a snow had freshly fallen, he plays a trick like this.

In the same synagogue alley, poor people wake early in their little houses; they barely scramble out from amid the rags in which they had wrapped themselves, they pour water on their finger tips, dress, and want to go to early prayer and then to market to earn whatever the good God would provide. But the doors don't open. They must be blocked from outside, sealed, for the frost is sharp. They try the doors again but they do not yield. Terror seizes them. They yell; the men shout, the women shout, the children wail. All of those in the synagogue alley shout. The cry is heard in other streets; people jump out of their beds, they run out of their houses, they come to the synagogue alley, and . . .

Before every door is piled a load of wood.

Motl Prince had ordered the wood brought from the forest during the night. The snowfall had been heavy and nobody heard a sound.

Once Motl Prince came home weary from the forest, lay down to rest before his meal, and dozed off thinking what new charity joke he could play. The door opens and two attendants of the Burial and Pallbearers Society enter and declare: "Motl Prince, be informed that you have passed away."

He answers calmly, "Blessed be the True Judge."

Should anyone speculate who is best prepared for paradise, he would be told by all: Motl Prince.

What has a man like him to fear?

They approach him, take some straw from their pockets and spread it; they raise him up, light a candle at his head, and walk out.

One says he is going to buy cerements. The other, that he is going at once to order a tombstone. On it would be engraved "Motl Prince," nothing more.

Motl Prince thinks to himself: it's quite enough.

He wants to consider why he doesn't see anyone from his household, he wants to recall whether he had said farewell to them, whether or not he had recited the confession—but two strange figures come in; they are not angels, they are not people, they are not beasts. They have thin wings, like bats, and they ask him whether he wants to go to paradise at once.

He forgets about everything else and smiles, "Why not?"

They lift him and hoist him through the chimney to the roof.

He knows that the chimney had not been cleaned in a long time, and he comes out black, asking, "What have I done to deserve this?"

They answer, "One doesn't get to paradise without first being blackened."

Well, if that is the rule!

"Now," they say, "we will fly up, we on our wings, but what will you fly on?"

There appears before him on the roof the broom which stands on his porch and which poor people coming to visit him use for brushing their boots. They say to him, "Get on it."

The broom is not clean. Well, one has to go through with it.

"Such is the custom," they tell him. "As long as the soul still doesn't have its own wings, it rides on a broom."

They hold him between them and fly off.

"Will we be flying long?"

"It's a long way to heaven yet," they tell him.

He understands. It takes time. So they fly on.

He asks, "What time of the year is it?"

They say, "The eve of Sukkoth." And they ask if he wants to sit in a *sukkah*.

It's true that the dead are relieved of all commandments; still, why not sit in a *sukkah*? "Very well," he says. And as he speaks there floats toward them a *sukkah* with walls and a roof of branches.

"This is King David's *sukkah*," they say.

He goes in gaily and sits down. "Will the divine visitors come?" he asks.

But before they answer, the *sukkah* collapses over him and he is barely dragged out, beat up and battered, covered with white dust on top of the black soot from the chimney.

"What have I done to deserve this?" he asks.

"There is no other way to get to paradise than beat up and battered," they tell him.

He submits humbly and they fly on. Then they stop.

"Are we there?" But he sees nothing.

They tell him that though he sees nothing they are already near paradise and it is therefore necessary to blindfold him.

"What for?"

Every saint is entitled to see his own chamber only, they explain to him. Only later, when other saints come to visit and invite him to their chambers is it possible to see paradise. Since it will be necessary to pass through the chambers of other saints, they must blindfold him.

He submits. They take his dainty, red handkerchief, blindfold him, and fly on. Then they stop again.

"You are already in your chamber."

"Please," he begs, "remove the blindfold."

"Right away." First they must get everything in readiness. First he must change his clothes.

They rip off his old clothes and dress him in others and say, "These are royal garments." They even rip the new clothes, but that is probably the way it has to be.

They set him down and say, "This is your golden throne."

They shove something under his feet. "This is your footstool."

They put something on his head. "This is your golden crown."

They shove something in front of him. "This is your table set with the Leviathan and the preserved wine."

And suddenly there is laughter from all sides, and what laughter! Apparently they are in stitches from laughter.

He rips off the blindfold and sees before him a wooden kitchen table, and on it tin plates, like those in a poor house, with black vermin dipped in tar.

His clothes are of pig bristles and they itch. On his head an old sleeping cap, under his feet a cold fire pot, and he sits on a stool with a hole in the center.

Motl awakes from his dream and sees the rabbi sitting at the head of his bed. He had come to ask for a donation and waited for Motl to wake up.

He relates to him the dream just as it was. "Rabbi," he sighs, "why?"

The rabbi lowers his long brows, thinks a while, and answers with a smile: "What did you expect, Motl? When one gives charity as a joke, paradise becomes a mockery."

From that time on Motl gave charity only in secret. In time people began to call him simply Motl. The name "Prince" was forgotten.

II.6

"Charitable Effort"

Jane Addams

Social reformer, prolific social critic, and Nobel Peace Laureate (1931) Jane Addams (1860–1935) began her long and flourishing career as founder and head of Hull House in Chicago, one of the first social settlements in North America. Founded in 1889, Hull House eventually included among its facilities a day nursery, a gymnasium, a community kitchen, and a boarding club for working girls. In addition to offering social services and a full range of cultural and educational activities, it provided opportunities for young social workers to acquire training.

In the first of her many books, *Democracy and Social Ethics* (1902), from which this selection is taken, Addams drew on her already vast personal experience to address the theme that became her hallmark: the right way to give charity. Addams vividly contrasts the values and beliefs that inform many middle-class social workers with those of the clients they seek to serve, in order to show (arguably for the first time) that the working-class poor represent not merely a class but a markedly different culture. Like many a cultural anthropologist before and since, she encourages all would-be social workers to assume a culturally relative stance and to recognize that the failure of many poor people to be, for example, frugal and industrious does not necessarily mean that they are wasteful or lazy or unworthy. But unlike most cultural anthropologists, Addams is not simply content to describe cultural differences; nor does she simply eschew so-called middle-class values. She criticizes social workers for "*too sternly* forcing their standards on others" (emphasis added), not because their standards as such are wrong, but because their clients are ill-prepared to heed them. She rebukes them for thinking "much more of what a man ought to be than of what he is," yet encourages them to think of what "he may become." In concluding, Addams advises us to guide our charitable efforts in the spirit of the prophet: to "love mercy, do justice, and walk humbly with God." She would have us exercise compassion and judgment, and at the same time put ourselves in the shoes of those whom we seek to help—literally to walk with them, to live with them, to see things as they do, in their language, in their way. Addams is well aware of how difficult it is to be compassionate and humble, and at the same time to judge. Is it ever really possible?

From *Democracy and Social Ethics* by Jane Addams (New York: The Macmillan Company, 1902), pp. 13–25, 30–41, 44–51, 58–70.

All those hints and glimpses of a larger and more satisfying democracy, which literature and our own hopes supply, have a tendency to slip away from us and to leave us sadly unguided and perplexed when we attempt to act upon them.

Our conceptions of morality, as all our other ideas, pass through a course of development; the difficulty comes in adjusting our conduct, which has become hardened into customs and habits, to these changing moral conceptions. When this adjustment is not made, we suffer from the strain and indecision of believing one hypothesis and acting upon another.

Probably there is no relation in life which our democracy is changing more rapidly than the charitable relation—that relation which obtains between benefactor and beneficiary; at the same time there is no point of contact in our modern experience which reveals so clearly the lack of that equality which democracy implies. We have reached the moment when democracy has made such inroads upon this relationship, that the complacency of the old-fashioned charitable man is gone forever; while, at the same time, the very need and existence of charity, denies us the consolation and freedom which democracy will at last give.

It is quite obvious that the ethics of none of us are clearly defined, and we are continually obliged to act in circles of habit, based upon convictions which we no longer hold. Thus our estimate of the effect of environment and social conditions has doubtless shifted faster than our methods of administering charity have changed. Formerly when it was believed that poverty was synonymous with vice and laziness, and that the prosperous man was the righteous man, charity was administered harshly with a good conscience; for the charitable agent really blamed the individual for his poverty, and the very fact of his own superior prosperity gave him a certain consciousness of superior morality. We have learned since that time to measure by other standards, and have ceased to accord to the money-earning capacity exclusive respect; while it is still rewarded out of all proportion to any other, its possession is by no means assumed to imply the possession of the highest moral qualities. We have learned to judge men by their social virtues as well as by their business capacity, by their devotion to intellectual and disinterested aims, and by their public spirit, and we naturally resent being obliged to judge poor people so solely upon the industrial side. Our democratic instinct instantly takes alarm. It is largely in this modern tendency to judge all men by one democratic standard, while the old charitable attitude commonly allowed the use of two standards, that much of the difficulty adheres. We know that unceasing bodily toil becomes wearing and brutalizing, and our position is totally untenable if we judge large numbers of our fellows solely upon their success in maintaining it.

The daintily clad charitable visitor who steps into their little house made untidy by the vigorous efforts of her hostess, the washerwoman, is no longer sure of her superiority to the latter; she recognizes that her hostess after all represents social value and industrial use, as over against her own parasitic cleanliness and a social standing attained only through status.

The only families who apply for aid to the charitable agencies are those who have come to grief on the industrial side; it may be through sickness, through loss of work, or for other guiltless and inevitable reasons; but the fact remains that they are industrially ailing, and must be bolstered and helped into industrial health. The charity visitor, let us assume, is a young college woman, well-bred and open-minded; when she visits the family assigned to her, she is often embarrassed to find herself obliged to lay all the stress of her teaching and advice upon the industrial virtues, and to treat the members of the family almost exclusively as factors in the industrial system. She insists that they must work and be self-supporting, that the most dangerous of all situations is idleness, that seeking one's own pleasure, while ignoring claims and responsibilities, is the most ignoble of actions. The members of her assigned family may have other charms and virtues—they may possibly be kind and considerate of each other, generous to their friends, but it is her business to stick to the industrial side. As she daily holds up these standards, it often occurs to the mind of the sensitive visitor, whose conscience has been made tender by much talk of brotherhood and equality, that she has no right to say these things; that her untrained hands are no more fitted to cope with actual conditions than those of her brokendown family.

The grandmother of the charity visitor could have done the industrial preaching very well, because she did have the industrial virtues and housewifely training. In a generation our experiences have changed, and our views with them; but we still keep on in the old methods, which could be applied when our consciences were in line with them, but which are daily becoming more difficult as we divide up into people who work with their hands and those who do not. The charity visitor belonging to the latter class is perplexed by recognitions and suggestions which the situation forces upon her. Our democracy has taught us to apply our moral teaching all around, and the moralist is rapidly becoming so sensitive that when his life does not exemplify his ethical convictions, he finds it difficult to preach.

Added to this is a consciousness, in the mind of the visitor, of a genuine misunderstanding of her motives by the recipients of her charity, and by their neighbors. Let us take a neighborhood of poor people, and test their ethical standards by those of the charity visitor, who comes with the best desire in the world to help them out of their distress. A most striking incongruity, at once apparent, is the difference between the emotional kindness with which relief is given by one poor neighbor to another poor neighbor, and the guarded care with which relief is given by a charity visitor to a charity recipient. The neighborhood mind is at once confronted not only by the difference of method, but by an absolute clashing of two ethical standards.

A very little familiarity with the poor districts of any city is sufficient to show how primitive and genuine are the neighborly relations. There is the greatest willingness to lend or borrow anything, and all the residents of the given tenement know the most intimate family affairs of all the others. The fact that the economic condition of all alike is on a most precarious level makes the ready outflow of sympathy and material assistance the most natural thing in the world. There are numberless instances of self-sacrifice quite unknown in the circles where greater economic advantages make that kind of intimate knowledge of one's neighbors impossible. An Irish family in which the man has lost his place, and the woman is struggling to eke out the scanty savings by day's work, will take in the widow and her five children who have been turned into the street, without a moment's reflection upon the physical discomforts involved. The most maligned landlady who lives in the house with her tenants is usually ready to lend a scuttle full of coal to one of them who may be out of work, or to share her supper. A woman for whom the writer had long tried in vain to find work failed to appear at the appointed time when employment was secured at last. Upon investigation it transpired that a neighbor further down the street was taken ill, that the children ran for the family friend, who went of course, saying simply when reasons for her non-appearance were demanded, "It broke my heart to leave the place, but what could I do?" A woman whose husband was sent up to the city prison for the maximum term, just three months, before the birth of her child found herself penniless at the end of that time, having gradually sold her supply of household furniture. She took refuge with a friend whom she supposed to be living in three rooms in another part of town. When she arrived, however, she discovered that her friend's husband had been out of work so long that they had been reduced to living in one room. The friend, however, took her in, and the friend's husband was obliged to sleep upon a bench in the park every night for a week, which he did uncomplainingly if not cheerfully. Fortunately it was summer, "and it only rained one night." The writer could not discover from the young mother that she had any special claim upon the "friend" beyond the fact that they had formerly worked together in the same factory. The husband she had never seen until the night of her arrival, when he at once went forth in search of a midwife who would consent to come upon his promise of future payment.

The evolutionists tell us that the instinct to pity, the impulse to aid his fellows, served man at a very early period, as a rude rule of right and wrong. There is no doubt that this rude rule still holds among many people with whom charitable agencies are brought into contact, and that their ideas of right and wrong are quite honestly outraged by the methods of these agencies. When they see the delay and caution with which relief is given, it does not appear to them a conscientious scruple, but as the cold and calculating action of a selfish man. It is not the aid that they are accustomed to receive from their neighbors, and they do not understand why the impulse which drives people to "be good to the poor" should be so severely supervised. They feel, remotely, that the charity visitor is moved by motives that are alien and unreal. They may be superior motives, but they are different, and they are "agin nature." They cannot comprehend why a person whose intellectual perceptions are stronger than his natural impulses, should go into charity work at all. The only man they are accustomed to see whose intellectual perceptions are stronger than his tenderness of heart, is the selfish and avaricious man who is frankly "on the make." If the charity visitor is such a person, why does she pretend to like the poor? Why does she not go into business at once?

We may say, of course, that it is a primitive view of life, which thus confuses intellectuality and business ability; but it is a view quite honestly held by many poor people who are obliged to receive charity from time to time. In moments of indignation the poor have been known to say: "What do you want, anyway? If you have nothing to give us, why not let us alone and stop your questionings and investigations?" "They investigated me for three weeks, and in the end gave me nothing but a black character," a little woman has been heard to assert. This indignation, which is for the most part taciturn, and a certain kindly contempt for her abilities, often puzzles the charity visitor. The latter may be explained by the standard of worldly success which the visited families hold. Success does not ordinarily go, in the minds of the poor, with charity and kind-heartedness, but rather with the opposite qualities. The rich landlord is he who collects with sternness, who accepts no excuse, and will have his own. There are moments of irritation and of real bitterness against him, but there is still admiration, because he is rich and successful. The good-natured landlord, he who pities and spares his poverty-pressed tenants, is seldom rich. He often lives in the back of his house, which he has owned for a long time, perhaps has inherited; but he has been able to accumulate little. He commands the genuine love and devotion of many a poor soul, but he is treated with a certain lack of respect. In one sense he is a failure. The charity visitor, just because she is a person who concerns herself with the poor, receives a certain amount of this good-natured and kindly contempt, sometimes real affection, but little genuine respect. The poor are accustomed to help each other and to respond according to their kindliness; but when it comes to worldly judgment, they use industrial success as the sole standard. In the case of the charity visitor who has neither natural kindness nor dazzling riches, they are deprived of both standards, and they find it of course utterly impossible to judge of the motive of organized charity. . . .

The neighborhood understands the selfish rich people who stay in their own part of town, where all their associates have shoes and other things. Such people don't bother themselves about the poor; they are like the rich landlords of the neighborhood experience. But this lady visitor, who pretends to be good to the poor, and certainly does talk as though she were kind-hearted, what does she come for, if she does not intend to give them things which are so plainly needed?

The visitor says, sometimes, that in holding her poor family so hard to a standard of thrift she is really breaking down a rule of higher living which they formerly possessed; that saving, which seems quite commendable in a comfortable part of town, appears almost criminal in a poorer quarter where the next-door neighbor needs food, even if the children of the family do not.

She feels the sordidness of constantly being obliged to urge the industrial view of life. The benevolent individual of fifty years ago honestly believed that industry and self-denial in youth would result in comfortable possessions for old age. It was, indeed, the method he had practised in his own youth, and by which he had probably obtained whatever fortune he possessed. He therefore reproved the poor family for indulging their children, urged them to work long hours, and was utterly untouched by many scruples which afflict the contemporary charity visitor. She says sometimes, "Why must I talk always of getting work and saving money, the things I know nothing about? If it were anything else I had to urge, I could do it; anything like Latin prose, which I had worried through myself, it would not be so hard." But she finds it difficult to connect the experiences of her youth with the experiences of the visited family.

Because of this diversity in experience, the visitor is continually surprised to find that the safest platitude may be challenged. She refers quite naturally to the "horrors of the saloon," and discovers that the head of her visited family does not connect them with "horrors" at all. He remembers all the kindnesses he has received there, the free lunch and treating which goes on, even when a man is out of work and not able to pay up; the loan of five dollars he got there when the charity visitor was miles away and he was threatened with eviction. He may listen politely to her reference to "horrors," but considers it only "temperance talk."

The charity visitor may blame the women for lack of gentleness toward their children, for being hasty and rude to them, until she learns that the standard of breeding is not that of gentleness toward the children so much as the observance of certain conventions, such as the punctilious wearing of mourning garments after the death of a child. The standard of gentleness each mother has to work out largely by herself, assisted only by the occasional shame-faced remark of a neighbor. "That they do better when you are not too hard on them"; but the wearing of mourning garments is sustained by the definitely expressed sentiment of every woman in the street. The mother would have to bear social blame, a certain social ostracism, if she failed to comply with that requirement. It is not comfortable to outrage the conventions of those among whom we live, and, if our social life be a narrow one, it is still more difficult. The visitor may choke a little when she sees the lessened supply of food and the scanty clothing provided for the remaining children in order that one may be conventionally mourned, but she doesn't talk so strongly against it as she would have done during her first month of experience with the family since bereaved.

The subject of clothes indeed perplexes the visitor constantly, and the result of her reflections may be summed up somewhat in this wise: The girl who has a definite social standing, who has been to a fashionable school or to a college, whose family live in a house seen and known by all her friends and associates, may afford to be very simple, or even shabby as to her clothes, if she likes. But the working girl, whose family lives in a tenement, or moves from one small apartment to another, who has little social standing and has to make her own place, knows full well how much habit and style of dress has to do with her position. Her income goes into her clothing, out of all proportion to the amount which she spends upon other things. But, if social advancement is her aim, it is the most sensible thing she can do. She is judged largely by her clothes. Her house furnishing, with its pitiful little decorations, her scanty supply of books, are never seen by the people whose social opinions she most values. Her clothes are her background, and from them she is largely judged. It is due to this fact that girls' clubs succeed best in the business part of town, where "working girls" and "young ladies" meet upon an equal footing, and where the clothes superficially look very much alike. Bright and ambitious girls will come to these downtown clubs to eat lunch and rest at noon, to study all sorts of subjects and listen to lecturers, when they might hesitate a long time before joining a club identified with their own neighborhood, where they would be judged not solely on their own merits and the unconscious social standing afforded by good clothes, but by other surroundings which are not nearly up to these. For the same reason, girls' clubs are infinitely more difficult to organize in little towns and villages, where every one knows every one else, just how the front parlor is furnished, and the amount of mortgage there is upon the house. These facts get in the way of a clear and unbiased judgment; they impede the democratic relationship and add to the self-consciousness of all concerned. Every one who has had to do with downtown girls' clubs has had the experience of going into the home of some bright, well-dressed girl, to discover it uncomfortable and perhaps wretched, and to find the girl afterward carefully avoiding her, although the working girl may not have been at home when the call was made, and the visitor may have carried herself with the utmost courtesy throughout. In some very successful down-town clubs the home address is not given at all, and only the "business address" is required. Have we worked out our democracy further in regard to clothes than anything else?

The charity visitor has been rightly brought up to consider it vulgar to spend much money upon clothes, to care so much for "appearances." She realizes dimly that the care for personal decoration over that for one's home or habitat is in some way primitive and undeveloped; but she is silenced by its obvious need. She also catches a glimpse of the fact that the disproportionate expenditure of the poor in the matter of clothes is largely due to the exclusiveness of the rich who hide from them the interior of their houses, and their more subtle pleasures, while of necessity exhibiting their street clothes and their street manners. Every one who goes shopping at the same time may see the clothes of the richest women in town, but only those invited to her receptions see the Corot on her walls or the bindings in her library. The poor naturally try to bridge the difference by reproducing the street clothes which they have seen. They are striving to conform to a common standard which their democratic training presupposes belongs to all of us. The charity visitor may regret that the Italian peasant woman has laid aside her picturesque kerchief and substituted a cheap street hat. But it is easy to recognize the first attempt toward democratic expression.

The charity visitor finds herself still more perplexed when she comes to consider such problems as those of early marriage and child labor; for she cannot deal with them according to economic theories, or according to the conventions which have regulated her own life. She finds both of these fairly upset by her intimate knowledge of the situation, and her sympathy for those into whose lives she has gained a curious insight. She discovers how incorrigibly bourgeois her standards have been, and it takes but a little time to reach the conclusion that she cannot insist so strenuously upon the conventions of her own class, which fail to fit the bigger, more emotional, and freer lives of working people. The charity visitor holds well-grounded views upon the imprudence of early marriages, quite naturally because she comes from a family and circle of professional and business people. A professional man is scarcely equipped and started in his profession before he is thirty. A business man, if he is on the road to success, is much nearer prosperity at thirty-five than twenty-five, and it is therefore wise for these men not to marry in the twenties; but this does not apply to the workingman. In many trades he is laid upon the shelf at thirty-five, and in nearly all trades he receives the largest wages in his life between twenty and thirty. If the young workingman has all his wages to himself, he will probably establish habits of personal comfort, which he cannot keep up when he has to divide with a family—habits which he can, perhaps, never overcome.

The sense of prudence, the necessity for saving, can never come to a primitive, emotional man with the force of a conviction; but the necessity of providing for his children is a powerful incentive. He naturally regards his children as his savings-bank; he expects them to care for him when he gets old, and in some trades old age comes very early. A Jewish tailor was quite lately sent to the Cook County poorhouse, paralyzed beyond recovery at the age of thirty-five. Had his little boy of nine been but a few years older, he might have been spared this sorrow of public charity. He was, in fact, better able to well support a family when he was twenty than when he was thirty-five, for his wages had steadily grown less as the years went on. Another tailor whom I know, who is also a Socialist, always speaks of saving as a bourgeois virtue, one quite impossible to the genuine workingman. He supports a family consisting of himself, a wife and three children, and his two parents on eight dollars a week. He insists it would be criminal not to expend every penny of this amount upon food and shelter, and he expects his children later to care for him.

This economic pressure also accounts for the tendency to put children to work overyoung and thus cripple their chances for individual development and usefulness, and with the avaricious parent also leads to exploitation. "I have fed her for fourteen years, now she can help me pay my mortgage" is not an unusual reply when a hard-working father is expostulated with because he would take his bright daughter out of school and put her into a factory. . . .

. . . The struggle for existence, which is so much harsher among people near the edge of pauperism, sometimes leaves ugly marks on character, and the charity visitor finds these indirect results most mystifying. Parents who work hard and anticipate an old age when they can no longer earn, take care that their children shall expect to divide their wages with them from the very first. Such a parent, when successful, impresses the immature nervous system of the child thus tyrannically establishing habits of obedience, so that the nerves and will may not depart from this control when the child is older. The charity visitor, whose family relation is lifted quite out of this, does not in the least understand the industrial foundation for this family tyranny.

The head of a kindergarten training-class once addressed a club of working women, and spoke of the despotism which is often established over little children. She said that the so-called determination to break a child's will many times arose from a lust of dominion, and she urged the ideal relationship founded upon love and confidence. But many of the women were puzzled. One of them remarked to the writer as she came out of the club room, "If you did not keep control over them from the time they were little, you would never get their wages when the are grown up." Another one said, "Ah, of course she (meaning the speaker) doesn't have to depend upon her children's wages. She can afford to be lax with them, because even if they don't give money to her, she can get along without it."

There are an impressive number of children who uncomplainingly and constantly hand over their weekly wages to their parents, sometimes receiving back ten cents or a quarter for spending-money, but quite as often nothing at all; and the writer knows one girl of twenty-five who for six years has received two cents a week from the constantly falling wages which she earns in a large factory. Is it habit or virtue which holds her steady in this course? If love and tenderness had been substituted for parental despotism, would the mother have had enough affection, enough power of expression to hold her daughter's sense of money obligation through all these years? This girl who spends her paltry two cents on chewing-gum and goes plainly clad in clothes of her mother's choosing, while many of her friends spend their entire wages on those clothes which factory girls love so well, must be held by some powerful force.

The charity visitor finds these subtle and elusive problems most harrowing. The head of a family she is visiting is a man who has become black-listed in a strike. He is not a very good workman, and this, added to his agitator's reputation, keeps him out of work for a long time. The fatal result of being long out of work follows: he becomes less and less eager for it, and gets a "job" less and less frequently. In order to keep up his self-respect, and still more to keep his wife's respect for him, he yields to the little self-deception that this prolonged idleness follows because he was once black-listed, and he gradually becomes a martyr. Deep down in his heart perhaps—but who knows what may be deep down in his heart? Whatever may be in his wife's, she does not show for an instant that she thinks he has grown lazy, and accustomed to see her earn, by sewing and cleaning, most of the scanty income for the family. The charity visitor, however, does see this, and she also sees that the other men who were in the strike have gone back to work. She further knows by inquiry and a little experience that the man is not skillful. She cannot, however, call him lazy and good-for-nothing, and denounce him as worthless as her grandmother might have done, because of certain intellectual conceptions at which she has arrived. She sees other workmen come to him for shrewd advice; she knows that he spends many more hours in the public library reading good books than the average workman has time to do. He has formed no bad habits and has yielded only to those subtle temptations toward a life of leisure which come to the intellectual man. He lacks the qualifications which would induce his union to engage him as a secretary or organizer, but he is a constant speaker at workingmen's meetings, and takes a high moral attitude on the questions discussed there. He contributes a certain intellectuality to his friends, and he has undoubted social value. The neighboring women confide to the charity visitor their sympathy with his wife, because she has to work so hard, and because her husband does not "provide." Their remarks are sharpened by a certain resentment toward the superiority of the husband's education and gentle manners. The charity visitor is ashamed to take this point of view, for she knows that it is not altogether fair. She is reminded of a college friend of hers, who told her that she was not going to allow her literary husband to write unworthy potboilers for the sake of earning a living. "I insist that we shall live within my own income; that he shall not publish until he is ready, and can give his genuine message." The charity visitor recalls what she has heard of another acquaintance, who urged her husband to decline a lucrative position as a railroad attorney, because she wished him to be free to take municipal positions, and handle public questions without the inevitable suspicion which unaccountably attaches itself in a corrupt city to a corporation attorney. The action of these two women seemed noble to her, but in their cases they merely lived on a lesser income. In the case of the workingman's wife, she faced living on no income at all, or on the precarious one which she might be able to get together.

She sees that this third woman has made the greatest sacrifice, and she is utterly unwilling to condemn her while praising the friends of her own social position. She realizes, of course, that the situation is changed by the fact that the third family needs charity, while the other two do not; but, after all, they have not asked for it, and their plight was only discovered through an accident to one of the children. The charity visitor has been taught that her mission is to preserve the finest traits to be found in her visited family, and she shrinks from the thought of convincing the wife that her husband is worthless and she suspects that she might turn all this beautiful devotion into complaining drudgery. To be sure, she could give up visiting the family altogether, but she has become much interested in the progress of the crippled child who eagerly anticipates her visits, and she also suspects that she will never know many finer women than the mother. She is unwilling, therefore, to give up the friendship, and goes on bearing her perplexities as best she may. . . .

. . . The greatest difficulty is experienced when the two standards come sharply together, and when both sides make an attempt at understanding and explanation. The difficulty of making clear one's own ethical standpoint is at times insurmountable. A woman who had bought and sold school books stolen from the school fund,—books which are all plainly marked with a red stamp,—came to Hull House one morning in great distress because she had been arrested, and begged a resident "to speak to the judge." She gave as a reason the fact that the House had known her for six years, and had once been very good to her when her little girl was buried. The resident more than suspected that her visitor knew the school books were stolen when buying them, and any attempt to talk upon that subject was evidently considered very rude. The visitor wished to get out of her trial, and evidently saw no reason why the House should not help her. The alderman was out of town, so she could not go to him. After a long conversation the visitor entirely failed to get another point of view and went away grieved and disappointed at a refusal, thinking the resident simply disobliging; wondering, no doubt, why such a mean woman had once been good to her; leaving the resident, on the other hand, utterly baffled and in the state of mind she would have been in, had she brutally insisted that a little child should lift weights too heavy for its undeveloped muscles.

Such a situation brings out the impossibility of substituting a higher ethical standard for a lower one without similarity of experience, but it is not as painful as that illustrated by the following example, in which the highest ethical standard yet attained by the charity recipient is broken down, and the substituted one not in the least understood:—

A certain charity visitor is peculiarly appealed to by the weakness and pathos of forlorn old age. She is responsible for the well-being of perhaps a dozen old women to whom she sustains a sincerely affectionate and almost filial relation. Some of them learn to take her benefactions quite as if they came from their own relatives, grumbling at all she does, and scolding her with a family freedom. One of these poor old women was injured in a fire years ago. She has but the fragment of a hand left, and is grievously crippled in her feet. Through years of pain she had become addicted to opium, and when she first came under the visitor's care, was only held from the poorhouse by the awful thought that she would there perish without her drug. Five years of tender care have done wonders for her. She lives in two neat little rooms, where with her thumb and two fingers she makes innumerable quilts, which she sells and gives away with the greatest delight. Her opium is regulated to a set amount taken each day, and she has drawn away from much drinking. She is a voracious reader, and has her head full of strange tales made up from books and her own imagination. At one time it seemed impossible to do anything for her in Chicago, and she was kept for two years in a suburb, where the family of the charity visitor lived, and where she was nursed through several hazardous illnesses. She now lives a better life than she did, but she is still far from being a model old woman. The neighbors are constantly shocked by the fact that she is supported and comforted by a "charity lady," while at the same time she occasionally "rushes the growler,"*scolding at the boys lest they jar her in her tottering walk. The care of her has broken through even that second standard, which the neighborhood had learned to recognize as the standard of charitable societies, that only the "worthy poor" are to be helped; that temperance and thrift are the virtues which receive the plums of benevolence. The old lady herself is conscious of this criticism. Indeed, irate neighbors tell her to her face that she doesn't in the least deserve what she gets. In order to disarm them, and at the same time to explain what would otherwise seem loving-kindness so colossal as to be abnormal, she tells them that during her sojourn in the suburb she discovered an awful family secret,—a horrible scandal connected with the long-suffering charity visitor; that it is in order to prevent the divulgence of this that she constantly receives her ministrations. Some of her perplexed neighbors accept this explanation as simple and offering a solution of this vexed problem. Doubtless many of them have a glimpse of the real state of affairs, of the love and patience which ministers to need irrespective of worth. But the standard is too high for most of them, and it sometimes seems unfortunate to break down the second standard, which holds that people who "rush the growler" are not worthy of charity, and that there is a certain justice attained when they go to the poorhouse. It is certainly dangerous to break down the lower, unless the higher is made clear.

Just when our affection becomes large enough to care for the unworthy among the poor as we would care for the unworthy among our own kin, is

---

*A "growler" is a beer container.

certainly a perplexing question. To say that it should never be so, is a comment upon our democratic relations to them which few of us would be willing to make.

Of what use is all this striving and perplexity? Has the experience any value? It is certainly genuine, for it induces an occasional charity visitor to live in a tenement house as simply as the other tenants do. It drives others to give up visiting the poor altogether, because, they claim, it is quite impossible unless the individual becomes a member of a sisterhood, which requires, as some of the Roman Catholic sisterhoods do, that the member first take the vows of obedience and poverty, so that she can have nothing to give save as it is first given to her, and thus she is not harassed by a constant attempt at adjustment.

Both the tenement-house resident and the sister assume to have put themselves upon the industrial level of their neighbors, although they have left out the most awful element of poverty, that of imminent fear of starvation and a neglected old age.

The young charity visitor who goes from a family living upon the most precarious industrial level to her own home in a prosperous part of the city, if she is sensitive at all, is never free from perplexities which our growing democracy forces upon her.

We sometimes say that our charity is too scientific, but we would doubtless be much more correct in our estimate if we said that it is not scientific enough. We dislike the entire arrangement of cards alphabetically classified according to streets and names of families, with the unrelated and meaningless details attached to them. Our feeling of revolt is probably not unlike that which afflicted the students of botany and geology in the middle of the last century, when flowers were tabulated in alphabetical order, when geology was taught by colored charts and thin books. No doubt the students, wearied to death, many times said that it was all too scientific, and were much perplexed and worried when they found traces of structure and physiology which their so-called scientific principles were totally unable to account for. But all this happened before science had become evolutionary and scientific at all, before it had a principle of life from within. The very indications and discoveries which formerly perplexed, later illumined and made the study absorbing and vital.

We are singularly slow to apply this evolutionary principle to human affairs in general, although it is fast being applied to the education of children. We are at last learning to follow the development of the child; to expect certain traits under certain conditions; to adapt methods and matter to his growing mind. No "advanced educator" can allow himself to be so absorbed in the question of what a child ought to be as to exclude the discovery of what he is. But in our charitable efforts we think much more of what a man ought to be than of what he is or of what he may become; and we ruthlessly force our conventions and standards upon him, with a sternness which we would consider stupid indeed did an educator use it in forcing his mature intellectual convictions upon an underdeveloped mind.

Let us take the example of a timid child, who cries when he is put to bed because he is afraid of the dark. The "soft-hearted" parent stays with him, simply because he is sorry for him and wants to comfort him. The scientifically trained parent stays with him, because he realizes that the child is in a stage of development in which his imagination has the best of him, and in which it is impossible to reason him out of a belief in ghosts. These two parents, wide apart in point of view, after all act much alike, and both very differently from the psuedo-scientific parent, who acts from dogmatic conviction and is sure he is right. He talks of developing his child's self-respect and good sense, and leaves him to cry himself to sleep, demanding powers and self-control and development which the child does not possess. There is no doubt that our development of charity methods has reached this pseudo-scientific and stilted stage. We have learned to condemn unthinking, ill-regulated kind-heartedness, and we take pride in mere repression much as the stern parent tells the visitor below how admirably he is rearing the child, who is hysterically crying upstairs and laying the foundation for future nervous disorders. The pseudo-scientific spirit, or rather, the undeveloped stage of our philanthropy, is perhaps most clearly revealed in our tendency to lay constant stress on negative action. "Don't give!" "don't break down self-respect," we are constantly told. We distrust the human impulse as well as the teachings of our own experience, and in their stead substitute dogmatic rules for conduct. We forget that the accumulation of knowledge and the holding of convictions must finally result in the application of that knowledge and those convictions to life itself; that the necessity for activity and a pull upon the sympathies is so severe, that all the knowledge in the possession of the visitor is constantly applied, and she has a reasonable chance for an ultimate intellectual comprehension. Indeed, part of the perplexity in the administration of charity comes from the fact that the type of person drawn to it is the one who insists that her convictions shall not be unrelated to action. Her moral concepts constantly tend to float away from her, unless they have a basis in the concrete relation of life. She is confronted with the task of reducing her scruples to action, and of converging many wills, so as to unite the strength of all of them into one accomplishment, the value of which no one can foresee.

On the other hand, the young woman who has succeeded in expressing her social compunction through charitable effort finds that the wider social activity, and the contact with the larger experience, not only increases her sense of social obligation but at the same time recasts her social ideals. She is chagrined to discover that in the actual task of reducing her social scruples to action, her humble beneficiaries are far in advance of her, not in charity or singleness of purpose, but in self-sacrificing action. She reaches the old-time virtue of humility by a social process, not in the old way, as the man who sits by the side of the road and puts dust upon his head, calling himself a contrite sinner, but she gets the dust upon her head because she has stumbled and fallen in the road through her efforts to push forward the mass, to march with her fellows. She has socialized her virtues not only through a social aim but by a social process.

The Hebrew prophet made three requirements from those who would join the great forward-moving procession led by Jehovah. "To love mercy" and at the same time "to do justly" is the difficult task; to fulfil the first requirement alone is to fall into the error of indiscriminate giving with all its disastrous results; to fulfil the second solely is to obtain the stern policy of withholding, and it results in such a dreary lack of sympathy and understanding that the establishment of justice is impossible. It may be that the combination of the two can never be attained save as we fulfil still the third requirement—"to walk humbly with God," which may mean to walk for many dreary miles beside the lowliest of His creatures, not even in that peace of mind which the company of the humble is popularly supposed to afford, but rather with the pangs and throes to which the poor human understanding is subjected whenever it attempts to comprehend the meaning of life.

II.7

"The Chair of Philanthromathematics"

O. Henry

O. Henry is often remembered for his sardonic and insightful wit, which
is well illustrated in this short story. There is little doubt that Jeff and
Andy, the story's main protagonists, are two fast-talking swindlers. But
there is also little doubt that they have genuinely philanthropic impulses,
and that the cure they administer for the disease that besets them—
"philanthropitis"—is admirable. Finding themselves in possession of too
much money to be "implicated in plain charity" and too little to "make
restitution," they take a middle course and found "one of the finest free
educational institutions in the world." All seems fine until their money
well begins to run dry and the new source of funds is as corrupt as the
original. Does Jeff's and Andy's tainted money, or their subsequently
shady fundraising practices, call into question either the value or the usefulness of their benefaction? Is it necessarily wrong to make—or even try
to make—a profit from philanthropy? Does business strategy have any
place in the world of philanthropy?

"I see that the cause of Education has received the princely gift of more than
fifty millions of dollars," said I.

I was gleaning the stray items from the evening papers while Jeff Peters
packed his briar pipe with plug cut.

"Which same," said Jeff, "calls for a new deck, and a recitation by the entire
class in philanthromathematics."

"Is that an allusion?" I asked.

"It is," said Jeff. "I never told you about the time when me and Andy Tucker
was philanthropists, did I? It was eight years ago in Arizona. Andy and me was
out in the Gila Mountains with a two-horse wagon prospecting for silver. We
struck it, and sold out to parties in Tucson for $25,000. They paid our check at
the bank in silver—a thousand dollars in a sack. We loaded it in our wagon and
drove east a hundred miles before we recovered our presence of intellect.
Twenty-five thousand dollars don't sound like so much when you're reading the
annual report of the Pennsylvania Railroad or listening to an actor talking about

From *The Complete Works of O. Henry* (Garden City, N.Y.: Doubleday & Co., 1953).

his salary; but when you can raise up a wagon sheet and kick around your bootheel and hear every one of 'em ring against another it makes you feel like you was a night-and-day bank with the clock striking twelve.

"The third day we drove into one of the most specious and tidy little towns that Nature or Rand and McNally ever turned out. It was in the foothills, and mitigated with trees and flowers and about 2,000 head of cordial and dilatory inhabitants. The town seemed to be called Floresville, and Nature had not contaminated it with many railroads, fleas or Eastern tourists.

"Me and Andy deposited our money to the credit of Peters and Tucker in the Esperanza Savings Bank, and got rooms at the Skyview Hotel. After supper we lit up, and sat out on the gallery and smoked. Then was when the philanthropy idea struck me. I suppose every grafter gets it sometime.

"When a man swindles the public out of a certain amount he begins to get scared and wants to return part of it. And if you'll watch close and notice the way his charity runs you'll see that he tries to restore it to the same people he got it from. As a hydrostatical case, take, let's say, A. A made his millions selling oil to poor students who sit up nights studying political economy and methods for regulating the trusts. So, back to the universities and colleges goes his conscience dollars.

"There's B got his from the common laboring man that works with his hands and tools. How's he to get some of the remorse fund back into their overalls?

"'Aha!' says B, 'I'll do it in the name of Education. I've skinned the laboring man,' says he to himself, 'but, according to the old proverb, "Charity covers a multitude of skins."'

"So he puts up eighty million dollars' worth of libraries; and the boys with the dinner pail that builds 'em gets the benefit.

"'Where's the books?' asks the reading public.

"'I dinna ken,' says B. 'I offered ye libraries; and there they are. I suppose if I'd given ye preferred steel trust stock instead ye'd have wanted the water in it set out in cut glass decanters. Hoot, for ye!'

"But, as I said, the owning of so much money was beginning to give me philanthropitis. It was the first time me and Andy had ever made a pile big enough to make us stop and think how we got it.

"'Andy,' says I, 'we're wealthy—not beyond the dreams of average; but in our humble way we are comparatively as rich as Greasers. I feel as if I'd like to do something for as well as to humanity.'

"'I was thinking the same thing, Jeff,' says he. 'We've been gouging the public for a long time with all kinds of little schemes for selling self-igniting celluloid collars to flooding Georgia with Hoke Smith presidential campaign buttons. I'd like, myself, to hedge a bet or two in the graft game if I could do it without actually banging the cymbalines in the Salvation Army or teaching a bible class by the Bertillon system.'

"'What'll we do?' says Andy. 'Give free grub to the poor or send a couple of thousand to George Cortelyou?'

"'Neither,' says I. 'We've got too much money to be implicated in plain charity; and we haven't got enough to make restitution. So, we'll look about for something that's about half way between the two.'

"The next day in walking around Floresville we see on a hill a big red brick building that appears to be disinhabited. The citizens speak up and tell us that it was begun for a residence several years before by a mine owner. After running up the house he finds he only had $2.80 left to furnish it with, so he invests that in whiskey and jumps off the roof on a spot where he now requiescats in pieces.

"As soon as me and Andy saw that building the same idea struck both of us. We would fix it up with lights and pen wipers and professors, and put an iron dog and statues of Hercules and Father John on the lawn, and start one of the finest free educational institutions in the world right there.

"So we talks it over to the prominent citizens of Floresville, who falls in fine with the idea. They give a banquet in the engine house to us, and we make our bow for the first time as benefactors to the cause of progress and enlightenment. Andy makes an hour-and-a-half speech on the subject of irrigation in Lower Egypt, and we have a moral tune on the phonograph and pineapple sherbet.

"Andy and me didn't lose any time in philanthropping. We put every man in town that could tell a hammer from a step ladder to work on the building, dividing it up into class rooms and lecture halls. We wire to Frisco for a carload of desks, footballs, arithmetics, penholders, dictionaries, chairs for the professors, slates, skeletons, sponges, twenty-seven cravenetted gowns and caps for the senior class, and an open order for all the truck that goes with a first-class university. I took it on myself to put a campus and a curriculum on the list; but the telegraph operator must have got the words wrong, being an ignorant man, for when the goods come we found a can of peas and a curry-comb among 'em.

"While the weekly papers was having chalkplate cuts of me and Andy we wired an employment agency in Chicago to express us f.o.b., six professors immediately—one English literature, one up-to-date dead languages, one chemistry, one political economy—democrat preferred—one logic, and one wise to painting, Italian and music, with union card. The Esperanza bank guaranteed salaries, which was to run between $800 and $800.50.

"Well, sir, we finally got in shape. Over the front door was carved the words: 'The World's University; Peters & Tucker, Patrons and Proprietors.' And when September the first got a cross-mark on the calendar, the comeons begun to roll in. First the faculty got off the tri-weekly express from Tucson. They was mostly young, spectacled and red-headed, with sentiments divided between ambition and food. Andy and me got 'em billeted on the Floresvillians and then laid for the students.

"They came in bunches. We had advertised the University in all the state papers, and it did us good to see how quick the country responded. Two hundred and nineteen husky lads aging along from 18 up to chin whiskers answered the clarion call of free education. They ripped open that town, sponged the seams, turned it, lined it with new mohair; and you couldn't have told it from Harvard or Goldfields at the March term of court.

"They marched up and down the streets waving flags with the World's University colors—ultra-marine and blue—and they certainly made a lively place of Floresville. Andy made them a speech from the balcony of the Skyview Hotel, and the whole town was out celebrating.

"In about two weeks the professors got the students disarmed and herded into classes. I don't believe there's any pleasure equal to being a philanthropist. Me and Andy bought high silk hats and pretended to dodge the two reporters of the Floresville *Gazette*. The paper had a man to kodak us whenever we appeared on the street, and ran our pictures every week over the column headed 'Educational Notes.' Andy lectured twice a week at the University; and afterward I would rise and tell a humorous story. Once the Gazette printed my pictures with Abe Lincoln on one side and Marshall P. Wilder on the other.

"Andy was as interested in philanthropy as I was. We used to wake up of nights and tell each other new ideas for booming the University.

"'Andy,' says I to him one day, 'there's something we overlooked. The boys ought to have dromedaries.'

"'What's that?' Andy asks.

"'Why, something to sleep in, of course,' says I. 'All colleges have 'em.'

"'Oh, you mean pajamas,' says Andy.

"'I do not,' says I. 'I mean dromedaries.' But I never could make Andy understand; so we never ordered 'em. Of course, I meant them long bedrooms in colleges where the scholars sleep in a row.

"Well, sir, the World's University was a success. We had scholars from five States and territories, and Floresville had a boom. A new shooting gallery and a pawn shop and two more saloons started; and the boys got up a college yell that went this way:

"*Raw, raw, raw,*
Done, done, done,
Peters, Tucker,
Lots of fun.
Bow-wow-wow,
Haw-hee-haw,
World University,
Hip hurrah!'

"The scholars was a fine lot of young men, and me and Andy was as proud of 'em as if they belonged to our own family.

"But one day about the last of October Andy come to me and asks if I have any idea how much money we had left in the bank. I guesses about sixteen thousand. 'Our balance,' says Andy, 'is $821.62.'

"'What!' says I, with a kind of a yell. 'Do you mean to tell me that them infernal clod-hopping, dough-headed, pup-faced, goose-brained, gate-stealing, rabbit-eared sons of horse thieves have soaked us for that much?'

"'No less,' says Andy.

"'Then, to Helvetia with philanthropy,' says I.

"'Not necessarily,' says Andy. 'Philanthropy,' says he, 'when run on a good business basis is one of the best grafts going. I'll look into the matter and see if it can't be straightened out.'

"The next week I am looking over the payroll of our faculty when I run across a new name—Professor James Darnley McCorkle, chair of mathematics; salary $100 per week. I yells so loud that Andy runs in quick.

"'What's this,' says I. 'A Professor of mathematics at more than $5,000 a year? How did this happen? Did he get in through the window and appoint himself?'

"'I wired to Frisco for him a week ago,' says Andy. 'In ordering the faculty we seemed to have overlooked the chair of mathematics.'

"'A good thing we did,' says I. 'We can pay his salary two weeks, and then our philanthropy will look like the ninth hole on the Skibo golf links.'

"'Wait a while,' says Andy, 'and see how things turn out. We have taken up too noble a cause to draw out now. Besides, the further I gaze into the retail philanthropy business the better it looks to me. I never thought about investigating it before. Come to think of it now,' goes on Andy, 'all the philanthropists I ever knew had plenty of money. I ought to have looked into the matter long ago, and located which was the cause and which was the effect.'

"I had confidence in Andy's chicanery in financial affairs, so I left the whole thing in his hands. The University was flourishing fine, and me and Andy kept our silk hats shined up, and Floresville kept on heaping honors on us like we was millionaires instead of almost busted philanthropists.

"The students kept the town lively and prosperous. Some stranger came to town and started a faro bank over the Red Front livery stable, and began to amass money in quantities. Me and Andy strolled up one night and piked a dollar or two for sociability. There were about fifty of our students there drinking rum punches and shoving high stacks of blues and reds about the table as the dealer turned the cards up.

"'Why, dang it, Andy,' says I, 'these free-school-hunting, gander-headed, silk-socked little sons of sapsuckers have got more money than you and me ever had. Look at the rolls they're pulling out of their pistol pockets!'

"'Yes,' says Andy, 'a good many of them are sons of wealthy miners and stockmen. It's very sad to see 'em wasting their opportunities this way.'

"At Christmas all the students went home to spend the holidays. We had a farewell blowout at the University and Andy lectured on 'Modern Music and

Prehistoric Literature of the Archipelagos.' Each one of the faculty answered to toasts, and compared me and Andy to Rockefeller and the Emperor Marcus Autolycus. I pounded on the table and yelled for Professor McCorkle; but it seems he wasn't present on the occasion. I wanted a look at the man that Andy thought could earn $100 a week in philanthropy that was on the point of making an assignment.

"The students all left on the night train; and the town sounded as quiet as the campus of a correspondence school at midnight. When I went to the hotel I saw a light in Andy's room and I opened the door and walked in.

"There sat Andy and the faro dealer at a table dividing a two-foot high stack of currency in thousand-dollar packages.

"'Correct,' says Andy. 'Thirty-one thousand apiece. Come in, Jeff,' says he. 'This is our share of the profits of the first half of the scholastic term of the World's University, incorporated and philanthropated. Are you convinced now,' says Andy, 'that philanthropy when practiced in a business way is an art that blesses him who gives as well as him who receives?'

"'Great!' says I, feeling fine. 'I'll admit you are the doctor this time.'

"'We'll be leaving on the morning train,' says Andy. 'You'd better get your collars and cuffs and press clippings together.'

"'Great!' says I. 'I'll be ready. But, Andy,' says I, 'I wish I could have met that Professor James Darnley McCorkle before he went. I had a curiosity to know that man.'

"'That'll be easy,' says Andy, turning around to the faro dealer.

"'Jim,' says Andy, 'shake hands with Mr. Peters.'"

II.8

"The Rembrandt"

Edith Wharton

American writer Edith Wharton, née Edith Newbold Jones (1862–1937), is best known for her observant and oftentimes satiric portrayals of the complexities of social life. In this short story, it is not entirely clear when or whether she is being satiric. Or is it? When the museum curator in the story sees the "Rembrandt," he knows instantly that it is worthless. But at the same time, he sees what is at stake in saying so: its owner, a destitute old woman, would be utterly bereft, because her pride and happiness seem to depend on her faith in the authenticity of the picture. Caught in this dilemma, he chooses deception over honesty, in fact, twice over. He misleads the old woman and cheats the museum for which he works. In the end, no one appears to be harmed; indeed, everybody concerned seems to gain positively. But is this true? Should we be sanguine about the results of the curator's deed or his tactics? Should he have acted differently? If so, when and how? Of the various characters in the story, which one, if any, acts philanthropically?

"You're *so* artistic," my cousin Eleanor Copt began.

Of all Eleanor's exordiums it is the one I most dread. When she tells me I'm so clever I know this is merely the preamble to inviting me to meet the last literary obscurity of the moment: a trial to be evaded or endured, as circumstances dictate; whereas her calling me artistic fatally connotes the request to visit, in her company, some distressed gentlewoman whose future hangs on my valuation of her old Saxe or of her grandfather's Marc Antonios. Time was when I attempted to resist these compulsions of Eleanor's; but I soon learned that, short of actual flight, there was no refuge from her beneficent despotism. It is not always easy for the curator of a museum to abandon his post on the plea of escaping a pretty cousin's importunities; and Eleanor, aware of my predicament, is none too magnanimous to take advantage of it. Magnanimity is, in fact, not in Eleanor's line. The virtues, she once explained to me, are like bonnets: the very ones that look best on other people may not happen to suit one's own particular style; and she

From *Crucial Instances* by Edith Wharton (New York: Charles Scribner's Sons), 1901, pp. 123–149.

added, with a slight deflection of metaphor, that none of the ready-made virtues ever *had* fitted her: they all pinched somewhere, and she'd given up trying to wear them.

Therefore when she said to me, "You're *so* artistic," emphasizing the conjunction with a tap of her dripping umbrella (Eleanor is out in all weathers: the elements are as powerless against her as man), I merely stipulated, "It's not old Saxe again?"

She shook her head reassuringly. "A picture—a Rembrandt!"

"Good Lord! Why not a Leonardo?"

"Well"—she smiled—"that, of course, depends on *you*."

"On me?"

"On your attribution. I dare say Mrs. Fontage would consent to the change—though she's very conservative."

A gleam of hope came to me and I pronounced: "One can't judge of a picture in this weather."

"Of course not. I'm coming for you to-morrow."

"I've an engagement to-morrow."

"I'll come before or after your engagement."

The afternoon paper lay at my elbow and I contrived a furtive consultation of the weather-report. It said "Rain to-morrow," and I answered briskly: "All right, then; come at ten"—rapidly calculating that the clouds on which I counted might lift by noon.

My ingenuity failed of its due reward; for the heavens, as if in league with my cousin, emptied themselves before morning, and punctually at ten Eleanor and the sun appeared together in my office.

I hardly listened, as we descended the Museum steps and got into Eleanor's hansom, to her vivid summing-up of the case. I guessed beforehand that the lady we were about to visit had lapsed by the most distressful degrees from opulence to a "hall-bedroom"; that her grandfather, if he had not been Minister to France, had signed the Declaration of Independence; that the Rembrandt was an heirloom, sole remnant of disbanded treasures; that for years its possessor had been unwilling to part with it, and that even now the question of its disposal must be approached with the most diplomatic obliquity.

Previous experience had taught me that all Eleanor's "cases" presented a harrowing similarity of detail. No circumstance tending to excite the spectator's sympathy and involve his action was omitted from the history of her beneficiaries; the lights and shades were indeed so skillfully adjusted that any impartial expression of opinion took on the hue of cruelty. I could have produced closetfuls of "heirlooms" in attestation of this fact; for it is one more mark of Eleanor's competence that her friends usually pay the interest on her philanthropy. My one hope was that in this case the object, being a picture, might reasonably be rated beyond my means; and as our cab drew up before a blistered brown-stone door-step I formed the self-defensive resolve to place an extreme valuation on Mrs. Fontage's Rembrandt. It is Eleanor's fault if she is sometimes fought with her own weapons.

The house stood in one of those shabby provisional-looking New York streets that seem resignedly awaiting demolition. It was the kind of house that, in its high days, must have had a bow-window with a bronze in it. The bow-window had been replaced by a plumber's *devanture,* and one might conceive the bronze to have gravitated to the limbo where Mexican onyx tables and bric-à-brac in buffalo-horn await the first signs of our next aesthetic reaction.

Eleanor swept me through a hall that smelled of poverty, up unlit stairs to a bare slit of a room. "And she must leave this in a month!" she whispered across her knock.

I had prepared myself for the limp widow's weed of a woman that one figures in such a setting; and confronted abruptly with Mrs. Fontage's white-haired erectness I had the disconcerting sense that I was somehow in her presence at my own solicitation. I instinctively charged Eleanor with this reversal of the situation; but a moment later I saw it must be ascribed to a something about Mrs. Fontage that precluded the possibility of her asking any one a favor. It was not that she was of forbidding, or even majestic, demeanor; but that one guessed, under her aquiline prettiness, a dignity nervously on guard against the petty betrayal of her surroundings. The room was unconcealably poor: the little faded "relics," the high-stocked ancestral silhouettes, the steel-engravings after Raphael and Correggio, grouped in a vain attempt to hide the most obvious stains on the wall-paper, served only to accentuate the contrast of a past evidently diversified by foreign travel and the enjoyment of the arts. Even Mrs. Fontage's dress had the air of being a last expedient, the ultimate outcome of a much-taxed ingenuity in darning and turning. One felt that all the poor lady's barriers were falling save that of her impregnable manner.

To this manner I found myself conveying my appreciation of being admitted to a view of the Rembrandt.

Mrs. Fontage's smile took my homage for granted. "It is always," she conceded, "a privilege to be in the presence of the great masters." Her slim wrinkled hand waved me to a dusky canvas near the window.

"It's *so* interesting, dear Mrs. Fontage," I heard Eleanor exclaiming, "and my cousin will be able to tell you exactly—" Eleanor, in my presence, always admits that she knows nothing about art; but she gives the impression that this is merely because she hasn't had time to look into the matter—and has had me to do it for her.

Mrs. Fontage seated herself without speaking, as though fearful that a breath might disturb my communion with the masterpiece. I felt that she thought

Eleanor's reassuring ejaculations ill-timed; and in this I was of one mind with her; for the impossibility of telling her exactly what I thought of her Rembrandt had become clear to me at a glance.

My cousin's vivacities began to languish and the silence seemed to shape itself into a receptacle for my verdict. I stepped back, affecting a more distant scrutiny; and as I did so my eye caught Mrs. Fontage's profile. Her lids trembled slightly. I took refuge in the familiar expedient of asking the history of the picture, and she waved me brightly to a seat.

This was indeed a topic on which she could dilate. The Rembrandt, it appeared, had come into Mr. Fontage's possession many years ago, while the young couple were on their wedding-tour, and under circumstances so romantic that she made no excuse for relating them in all their parenthetic fullness. The picture belonged to an old Belgian Countess of redundant quarterings, whom the extravagances of an ungovernable nephew had compelled to part with her possessions (in the most private manner) about the time of the Fontages' arrival. By a really remarkable coincidence, it happened that their courier (an exceptionally intelligent and superior man) was an old servant of the Countess's, and had thus been able to put them in the way of securing the Rembrandt under the very nose of an English Duke, whose agent had been sent to Brussels to negotiate for its purchase. Mrs. Fontage could not recall the Duke's name, but he was a great collector and had a famous Highland castle, where somebody had been murdered, and which she herself had visited (by moonlight) when she had traveled in Scotland as a girl. The episode had in short been one of the most interesting "experiences" of a tour almost chromo-lithographic in vivacity of impression; and they had always meant to go back to Brussels for the sake of reliving so picturesque a moment. Circumstances (of which the narrator's surroundings declared the nature) had persistently interfered with the projected return to Europe, and the picture had grown doubly valuable as representing the high-water mark of their artistic emotions. Mrs. Fontage's moist eye caressed the canvas. "There is only," she added with a perceptible effort, "one slight drawback: the picture is not signed. But for that the Countess, of course, would have sold it to a museum. All the connoisseurs who have seen it pronounce it an undoubted Rembrandt, in the artist's best manner; but the museums"—she arched her brows in smiling recognition of a well-known weakness—"give the preference to signed examples—"

Mrs. Fontage's words evoked so touching a vision of the young tourists of fifty years ago, entrusting to an accomplished and versatile courier the direction of their helpless zeal for art, that I lost sight for a moment of the point at issue. The old Belgian Countess, the wealthy Duke with a feudal castle in Scotland, Mrs. Fontage's own maiden pilgrimage to Arthur's Seat and Holyrood, all the accessories of the naïf transaction, seemed a part of that vanished Europe to which our young race carried its indiscriminate ardors, its tender romantic credulity: the legendary castellated Europe of keepsakes, brigands and old masters, that compensated, by one such "experience" as Mrs. Fontage's, for an after-life of aesthetic privation.

I was restored to the present by Eleanor's looking at her watch. The action mutely conveyed that something was expected of me. I risked the temporizing statement that the picture was very interesting; but Mrs. Fontage's polite assent revealed the poverty of the expedient. Eleanor's impatience overflowed.

"You would like my cousin to give you an idea of its value?" she suggested.

Mrs. Fontage grew more erect. "No one," she corrected with great gentleness, "can know its value quite as well as I, who live with it—"

We murmured our hasty concurrence.

"But it might be interesting to hear"—she addressed herself to me—"as a mere matter of curiosity—what estimate would be put on it from the purely commercial point of view—if such a term may be used in speaking of a work of art."

I sounded a note of deprecation.

"Oh, I understand, of course," she delicately anticipated me, "that that could never be *your* view, your personal view; but since occasions *may* arise—do arise—when it becomes necessary to—to put a price on the priceless, as it were—I have thought—Miss Copt has suggested—"

"Some day," Eleanor encouraged her, "you might feel that the picture ought to belong to some one who has more—more opportunity of showing it—letting it be seen by the public—for educational reasons—"

"I have tried," Mrs. Fontage admitted, "to see it in that light."

The crucial moment was upon me. To escape the challenge of Mrs. Fontage's brilliant composure I turned once more to the picture. If my courage needed re-inforcement, the picture amply furnished it. Looking at the lamentable canvas seemed the surest way of gathering strength to denounce it; but behind me, all the while, I felt Mrs. Fontage's shuddering pride drawn up in a final effort of self-defense. I hated myself for my sentimental perversion of the situation. Reason argued that it was more cruel to deceive Mrs. Fontage than to tell her the truth; but that merely proved the inferiority of reason to instinct in situations involving any concession to the emotions. Along with her faith in the Rembrandt I must destroy not only the whole fabric of Mrs. Fontage's past, but even that lifelong habit of acquiescence in untested formulas that makes the best part of the average feminine strength. I guessed the episode of the picture to be inextricably interwoven with the traditions and convictions which served to veil Mrs. Fontage's destitution not only from others but from herself. Viewed in that light the Rembrandt had perhaps been worth its purchase-money; and I regretted that works of art do not commonly sell on the merit of the moral support they may have rendered.

From this unavailing flight I was recalled by the sense that something must be done. To place a fictitious value on the picture was at best a provisional measure; while the brutal alternative of advising Mrs. Fontage to sell it for a hundred dollars at least afforded an opening to the charitably disposed purchaser. I intended, if other resources failed, to put myself forward in that light; but delicacy of course forbade my coupling my unflattering estimate of the Rembrandt with an immediate offer to buy it. All I could do was to inflict the wound: the healing unguent must be withheld for later application.

I turned to Mrs. Fontage, who sat motionless, her finely-lined cheeks touched with an expectant color, her eyes averted from the picture which was so evidently the one object they beheld.

"My dear madam—" I began. Her vivid smile was like a light held up to dazzle me. It shrouded every alternative in darkness and I had the flurried sense of having lost my way among the intricacies of my contention. Of a sudden I felt the hopelessness of finding a crack in her impenetrable conviction. My words slipped from me like broken weapons. "The picture," I faltered, "would of course be worth more if it were signed. As it is, I—I hardly think—on a conservative estimate—it can be valued at—at more—than—a thousand dollars, say—"

My deflected argument ran on somewhat aimlessly till it found itself plunging full tilt against the barrier of Mrs. Fontage's silence. She sat as impassive as though I had not spoken. Eleanor loosed a few fluttering words of congratulation and encouragement, but their flight was suddenly cut short. Mrs. Fontage had risen with a certain solemnity.

"I could never," she said gently—her gentleness was adamantine—"under any circumstances whatever, consider, for a moment even, the possibility of parting with the picture at such a price."

II

WITHIN three weeks a tremulous note from Mrs. Fontage requested the favor of another visit. If the writing was tremulous, however, the writer's tone was firm. She named her own day and hour, without the conventional reference to her visitor's convenience.

My first impulse was to turn the note over to Eleanor. I had acquitted myself of my share in the ungrateful business of coming to Mrs. Fontage's aid, and if, as her letter denoted, she had now yielded to the closer pressure of need, the business of finding a purchaser for the Rembrandt might well be left to my cousin's ingenuity. But here conscience put in the uncomfortable reminder that it was I who, in putting a price on the picture, had raised the real obstacle in the way of Mrs. Fontage's rescue. No one would give a thousand dollars for the Rembrandt; but to tell Mrs. Fontage so had become as unthinkable as murder. I had, in fact, on returning from my first inspection of the picture, refrained from imparting to Eleanor my opinion of its value. Eleanor is porous, and I knew that sooner or later the unnecessary truth would exude through the loose texture of her dissimulation. Not infrequently she thus creates the misery she alleviates; and I have sometimes suspected her of paining people in order that she might be sorry for them. I had, at all events, cut off retreat in Eleanor's direction; and the remaining alternative carried me straight to Mrs. Fontage.

She received me with the same commanding sweetness. The room was even barer than before—I believe the carpet was gone—but her manner built up about her a palace to which I was welcomed with high state; and it was as a mere incident of the ceremony that I was presently made aware of her decision to sell the Rembrandt. My previous unsuccess in planning how to deal with Mrs. Fontage had warned me to leave my farther course to chance; and I listened to her explanation with complete detachment. She had resolved to travel for her health; her doctor advised it, and as her absence might be indefinitely prolonged she had reluctantly decided to part with the picture in order to avoid the expense of storage and insurance. Her voice drooped at the admission, and she hurried on, detailing the vague itinerary of a journey that was to combine long-promised visits to impatient friends with various "interesting opportunities" less definitely specified. The poor lady's skill in rearing a screen of verbiage about her enforced avowal had distracted me from my own share in the situation, and it was with dismay that I suddenly caught the drift of her assumptions. She expected me to buy the Rembrandt for the Museum; she had taken my previous valuation as a tentative bid, and when I came to my senses she was in the act of accepting my offer.

Had I had a thousand dollars of my own to dispose of, the bargain would have been concluded on the spot; but I was in the impossible position of being materially unable to buy the picture and morally unable to tell her that it was not worth acquiring for the Museum.

I dashed into the first evasion in sight. I had no authority, I explained, to purchase pictures for the Museum without the consent of the committee.

Mrs. Fontage coped for a moment in silence with the incredible fact that I had rejected her offer; then she ventured, with a kind of pale precipitation: "But I understood—Miss Copt tells me that you practically decide such matters for the committee." I could guess what the effort had cost her.

"My cousin is given to generalizations. My opinion may have some weight with the committee—"

"Well, then—" she timidly prompted.

"For that very reason I can't buy the picture."

She said, with a drooping note, "I don't understand."

"Yet you told me," I reminded her, "that you knew museums didn't buy unsigned pictures."

"Not for what they are worth! Every one knows that. But I—I understood—the price you named—" Her pride shuddered back from the abasement. "It's a misunderstanding then," she faltered.

To avoid looking at her, I glanced desperately at the Rembrandt. Could I—? But reason rejected the possibility. Even if the committee had been blind—and they all *were* but Crozier—I simply shouldn't have dared to do it. I stood up, feeling that to cut the matter short was the only alleviation within reach.

Mrs. Fontage had summoned her indomitable smile; but its brilliancy dropped, as I opened the door, like a candle blown out by a draught.

"If there's any one else—if you knew any one who would care to see the picture, I should be most happy—" She kept her eyes on me, and I saw that, in her case, it hurt less than to look at the Rembrandt. "I shall have to leave here, you know," she panted, "if nobody cares to have it—"

III

THAT evening at my club I had just succeeded in losing sight of Mrs. Fontage in the fumes of an excellent cigar, when a voice at my elbow evoked her harassing image.

"I want to talk to you," the speaker said, "about Mrs. Fontage's Rembrandt."

"There isn't any," I was about to growl; but looking up I recognized the confiding countenance of Mr. Jefferson Rose.

Mr. Rose was known to me chiefly as a young man suffused with a vague enthusiasm for Virtue and my cousin Eleanor.

One glance at his glossy exterior conveyed the assurance that his morals were as immaculate as his complexion and his linen. Goodness exuded from his moist eye, his liquid voice, the warm damp pressure of his trustful hand. He had always struck me as one of the most uncomplicated organisms I had ever met. His ideas were as simple and inconsecutive as the propositions in a primer, and he spoke slowly, with a kind of uniformity of emphasis that made his words stand out like the raised type for the blind. An obvious incapacity for abstract conceptions made him peculiarly susceptible to the magic of generalization, and one felt he would have been at the mercy of any Cause that spelled itself with a capital letter. It was hard to explain how, with such a superabundance of merit, he managed to be a good fellow: I can only say that he performed the astonishing feat as naturally as he supported an invalid mother and two sisters on the slender salary of a banker's clerk. He sat down beside me with an air of bright expectancy.

"It's a remarkable picture, isn't it?" he said.

"You've seen it?"

"I've been so fortunate. Miss Copt was kind enough to get Mrs. Fontage's permission; we went this afternoon."

I inwardly wished that Eleanor had selected another victim; unless indeed the visit were part of a plan whereby some third person, better equipped for the cultivation of delusions, was to be made to think the Rembrandt remarkable. Knowing the limitations of Mr. Rose's resources I began to wonder if he had any rich aunts.

"And her buying it in that way, too," he went on with his limpid smile, "from that old Countess in Brussels, makes it all the more interesting, doesn't it? Miss Copt tells me it's very seldom old pictures can be traced back for more than a generation. I suppose the fact of Mrs. Fontage's knowing its history must add a good deal to its value?"

Uncertain as to his drift, I said: "In her eyes it certainly appears to."

Implications are lost on Mr. Rose, who glowingly continued: "That's the reason why I wanted to talk to you about it—to consult you. Miss Copt tells me you value it at a thousand dollars."

There was no denying this, and I grunted a reluctant assent.

"Of course," he went on earnestly, "your valuation is based on the fact that the picture isn't signed—Mrs. Fontage explained that; and it *does* make a difference, certainly. But the thing is—if the picture's really good—ought one to take advantage—? I mean—one can see that Mrs. Fontage is in a tight place, and I wouldn't for the world—"

My astonished stare arrested him.

"*You* wouldn't—?"

"I mean—you see, it's just this way"; he coughed and blushed: "I can't give more than a thousand dollars myself—it's as big a sum as I can manage to scrape together—but before I make the offer I want to be sure I'm not standing in the way of her getting more money."

My astonishment lapsed to dismay. "You're going to buy the picture for a thousand dollars?"

His blush deepened. "Why, yes. It sounds rather absurd, I suppose. It isn't much in my line, of course. I can see the picture's very beautiful, but I'm no judge—it isn't the kind of thing, naturally, that I could afford to go in for; but in this case I'm very glad to do what I can; the circumstances are so distressing; and knowing what you think of the picture I feel it's a pretty safe investment—"

"I don't think!" I blurted out.

"You—?"

"I don't think the picture's worth a thousand dollars; I don't think it's worth ten cents; I simply lied about it, that's all."

Mr. Rose looked as frightened as though I had charged him with the offense.

"Hang it, man, can't you see how it happened? I saw the poor woman's pride and happiness hung on her faith in that picture. I tried to make her understand that it was worthless—but she wouldn't; I tried to tell her so—but I couldn't. I behaved like a maudlin ass, but you shan't pay for my infernal bungling—you mustn't buy the picture!"

Mr. Rose sat silent, tapping one glossy boot-tip with another. Suddenly he turned on me a glance of stored intelligence. "But you know," he said good-humoredly, "I rather think I must."

"You haven't—already?"

"Oh, no; the offer's not made."

"Well, then—"

His look gathered a brighter significance.

"But if the picture's worth nothing, nobody will buy it—"

I groaned.

"Except," he continued, "some fellow like me, who doesn't know anything. *I* think it's lovely, you know; I mean to hang it in my mother's sitting-room." He rose and clasped my hand in his adhesive pressure. "I'm awfully obliged to you for telling me this; but perhaps you won't mind my asking you not to mention our talk to Miss Copt? It might bother her, you know, to think the picture isn't exactly up to the mark; and it won't make a rap of difference to me."

IV

MR. ROSE left me to a sleepless night. The next morning my resolve was formed, and it carried me straight to Mrs. Fontage's. She answered my knock by stepping out on the landing, and as she shut the door behind her I caught a glimpse of her devastated interior. She mentioned, with a careful avoidance of the note of pathos on which our last conversation had closed, that she was preparing to leave that afternoon; and the trunks obstructing the threshold showed that her preparations were nearly complete. They were, I felt certain, the same trunks that, strapped behind a rattling vettura, had accompanied the bride and groom on that memorable voyage of discovery of which the booty had till recently adorned her walls; and there was a dim consolation in the thought that those early "finds" in coral and Swiss wood-carving, in lava and alabaster, still lay behind the worn locks, in the security of worthlessness.

Mrs. Fontage, on the landing, among her strapped and corded treasures, maintained the same air of stability that made it impossible, even under such conditions, to regard her flight as anything less dignified than a departure. It was the moral support of what she tacitly assumed that enabled me to set forth with proper deliberation the object of my visit; and she received my announcement with an absence of surprise that struck me as the very flower of tact. Under cover of these mutual assumptions the transaction was rapidly concluded; and it was not till the canvas passed into my hands that, as though the physical contact had unnerved her, Mrs. Fontage suddenly faltered. "It's the giving it up—" she stammered, disguising herself to the last; and I hastened away from the collapse of her splendid effrontery.

I need hardly point out that I had acted impulsively, and that reaction from the most honorable impulses is sometimes attended by moral perturbation. My motives had indeed been mixed enough to justify some uneasiness, but this was allayed by the instinctive feeling that it is more venial to defraud an institution than a man. Since Mrs. Fontage had to be kept from starving by means not wholly defensible, it was better that the obligation should be borne by a rich institution than an impecunious youth. I doubt, in fact, if my scruples would have survived a night's sleep, had they not been complicated by some uncertainty as to my own future. It was true that, subject to the purely formal assent of the committee, I had full power to buy for the Museum, and that the one member of the committee likely to dispute my decision was opportunely traveling in Europe; but the picture once in place I must face the risk of any expert criticism to which chance might expose it. I dismissed this contingency for future study, stored the Rembrandt in the cellar of the Museum, and thanked heaven that Crozier was abroad.

Six months later he strolled into my office. I had just concluded, under conditions of exceptional difficulty, and on terms unexpectedly benign, the purchase of the great Bartley Reynolds; and this circumstance, by relegating the matter of the Rembrandt to a lower stratum of consciousness, enabled me to welcome Crozier with unmixed pleasure. My security was enhanced by his appearance. His smile was charged with amiable reminiscences, and I inferred that his trip had put him in the humor to approve of everything, or at least to ignore what fell short of his approval. I had therefore no uneasiness in accepting his invitation to dine that evening. It is always pleasant to dine with Crozier and never more so than when he is just back from Europe. His conversation gives even the food a flavor of the Café Anglais.

The repast was delightful, and it was not till we had finished a Camembert which he must have brought over with him, that my host said, in a tone of after-dinner perfunctoriness: "I see you've picked up a picture or two since I left."

I assented. "The Bartley Reynolds seemed too good an opportunity to miss, especially as the French government was after it. I think we got it cheap—"

"*Connu, connu,*" said Crozier pleasantly. "I know all about the Reynolds. It was the biggest kind of a haul and I congratulate you. Best stroke of business we've done yet. But tell me about the other picture—the Rembrandt."

"I never said it was a Rembrandt." I could hardly have said why, but I felt distinctly annoyed with Crozier.

"Of course not. There's 'Rembrandt' on the frame, but I saw you'd modified it to 'Dutch School'; I apologize." He paused, but I offered no explanation. "What about it?" he went on. "Where did you pick it up?" As he leaned to the flame of the cigar-lighter his face seemed ruddy with enjoyment.

"I got it for a song," I said.

"A thousand, I think?"

"Have you seen it?" I asked abruptly.

"Went over the place this afternoon and found it in the cellar. Why hasn't it been hung, by the way?"

I paused a moment. "I'm waiting—"

"To—?"

"To have it varnished."

"Ah!" He leaned back and poured himself a second glass of Chartreuse. The smile he confided to its golden depths provoked me to challenge him with—

"What do you think of it?"

"The Rembrandt?" He lifted his eyes from the glass. "Just what you do."

"It isn't a Rembrandt."

"I apologize again. You call it, I believe, a picture of the same period?"

"I'm uncertain of the period."

"H'm." He glanced appreciatively along his cigar. "What are you certain of?"

"That it's a damned bad picture," I said savagely.

He nodded. "Just so. That's all we wanted to know."

"*We?*"

"We—I—the committee, in short. You see, my dear fellow, if you hadn't been certain it was a damned bad picture our position would have been a little awkward. As it is, my remaining duty—I ought to explain that in this matter I'm acting for the committee—is as simple as it's agreeable."

"I'll be hanged," I burst out, "if I understand one word you're saying!"

He fixed me with a kind of cruel joyousness. "You will—you will," he assured me; "at least you'll begin to, when you hear that I've seen Miss Copt."

"Miss Copt?"

"And that she has told me under what conditions the picture was bought."

"She doesn't know anything about the conditions! That is," I added, hastening to restrict the assertion, "she doesn't know my opinion of the picture." I thirsted for five minutes with Eleanor.

"Are you quite sure?" Crozier took me up. "Mr. Jefferson Rose does."

"Ah—I see."

"I thought you would," he reminded me. "As soon as I'd laid eyes on the Rembrandt—I beg your pardon!—I saw that it—well, required some explanation."

"You might have come to me."

"I meant to; but I happened to meet Miss Copt, whose encyclopædic information has often before been of service to me. I always go to Miss Copt when I want to look up anything; and I found she knew all about the Rembrandt."

"*All?*"

"Precisely. The knowledge was in fact causing her sleepless nights. Mr. Rose, who was suffering from the same form of insomnia, had taken her into his confidence, and she—ultimately—took me into hers."

"Of course!"

"I must ask you to do your cousin justice. She didn't speak till it became evident to her uncommonly quick perceptions that your buying the picture on its

merits would have been infinitely worse for—for everybody—than your divert-
ing a small portion of the Museum's funds to philanthropic uses. Then she told
me the moving incident of Mr. Rose. Good fellow, Rose. And the old lady's case
was desperate. Somebody had to buy that picture." I moved uneasily in my seat.

"Wait a moment, will you? I haven't finished my cigar. There's a little head of
Il Fiammingo's that you haven't seen, by the way; I picked it up the other day in
Parma. We'll go in and have a look at it presently. But meanwhile what I want to
say is that I've been charged—in the most informal way—to express to you the
committee's appreciation of your admirable promptness and energy in captur-
ing the Bartley Reynolds. We shouldn't have got it at all if you hadn't been uncommonly wide-awake, and to get it at such a price is a double triumph. We'd
have thought nothing of a few more thousands—"

"I don't see," I impatiently interposed, "that, as far as I'm concerned, that al-
ters the case."

"The case—?"

"Of Mrs. Fontage's Rembrandt. I bought the picture because, as you say, the
situation was desperate, and I couldn't raise a thousand myself. What I did was
of course indefensible; but the money shall be refunded to-morrow—"

Crozier raised a protesting hand. "Don't interrupt me when I'm talking ex
cathedrâ. The money's been refunded already. The fact is, the Museum has sold
the Rembrandt."

I stared at him wildly. "Sold it? To whom?"

"Why—to the committee.—Hold on a bit, please.—Won't you take another
cigar? Then perhaps I can finish what I've got to say.—Why, my dear fellow, the
committee's under an obligation to you—that's the way we look at it. I've investigated Mrs. Fontage's case, and—well, the picture had to be bought. She's eating meat now, I believe, for the first time in a year. And they'd have turned her
out into the street that very day, your cousin tells me. Something had to be done
at once, and you've simply given a number of well-to-do and self-indulgent
gentlemen the opportunity of performing, at very small individual expense, a
meritorious action in the nick of time. That's the first thing I've got to thank you
for. And then—you'll remember, please, that I have the floor—that I'm still
speaking for the committee—and secondly, as a slight recognition of your services in securing the Bartley Reynolds at a very much lower figure than we were
prepared to pay, we beg you—the committee begs you—to accept the gift of
Mrs. Fontage's Rembrandt. Now we'll go in and look at that little head. . . ."

II.9

"The Record of Badalia Herodsfoot"

Rudyard Kipling

We have no way of knowing whether Rudyard Kipling (1865–1936), England's poet laureate, was familiar with the teachings of Jane Addams (see Addams's "Charitable Effort" earlier in this part). But his heroine in this short story certainly seems to have been. By Addams's standards, Badalia Herodsfoot is a model relief worker: she exercises compassion but also judgment, she fully understands the people with whom she works, and she speaks their language. In part, this is because, like Addams, she lives where she works, on Gunnison Street, alongside its poor, despairing people; in part, it is because, as Kipling tells us, "in the beginning of things she [too] had been unregenerate." Others try to offer relief from the violence and corruption of Gunnison Street, but only Badalia seems to have the toughness and resilience to succeed. All the others come, naturally and increasingly, to rely on her. Yet in the end, Badalia shows herself to be as vulnerable and impotent as the rest. Why does Badalia succumb where so many others, far weaker than she, would not? How does it happen? Does Badalia's own sad end cause you to question the ways and means of her otherwise seemingly successful charitable efforts?

> The year's at the spring
> And day's at the morn;
> Morning's at seven;
> The hill-side's dew-pearled;
> The lark's on the wing;
> The snail's on the thorn;
> God's in his heaven—
> All's right with the world!
>
> *Pippa passes.*

This is not that Badalia whose spare names were Joanna, Pugnacious, and Mc-Canna, as the song says, but another and much nicer lady.

From *The Day's Work, Part Two* by Rudyard Kipling (New York: Charles Scribner's Sons, 1916), pp. 185–221.

In the beginning of things she had been unregenerate; had worn the heavy, fluffy fringe which is the ornament of the costermonger's girl, and there is a legend in Gunnison-street that on her wedding-day she, a flare-lamp in either hand, danced dances on a discarded lover's winkle-barrow, till a policeman interfered, and then Badalia danced with the Law amid shoutings. Those were her days of fatness, and they did not last long, for her husband after two years took to himself another woman, and passed out of Badalia's life, over Badalia's senseless body; for he stifled protest with blows. While she was enjoying her widowhood the baby that the husband had not taken away died of croup, and Badalia was altogether alone. With rare fidelity she listened to no proposals for a second marriage according to the customs of Gunnison-street, which do not differ from those of the Barralong. "My man," she explained to her suitors, "'e'll come back one o' these days, an' then, like as not, 'e'll take an' kill me if I was livin' 'long o' you. You don't know Tom; I do. Now you go. I can do for myself—not 'avin' a kid." She did for herself with a mangle, some tending of babies, and an occasional sale of flowers. This latter trade is one that needs capital, and takes the vendor very far westward, in so much that the return journey from, let us say, the Burlington Arcade to Gunnison-street, E., is an excuse for drink, and then, as Badalia pointed out, "You come 'ome with your shawl arf off of your back an' your bonnick under your arm, and the price of nothing-at-all in your pocket, let alone a slop takin' care o' you." Badalia did not drink, but she knew her sisterhood, and gave them rude counsel. Otherwise she kept herself to herself, and meditated a great deal upon Tom Herodsfoot, her husband, who would come back some day, and the baby that would never return. In what manner these thoughts wrought upon her mind will not be known.

Her entry into society dates from the night when she rose literally under the feet of the Reverend Eustace Hanna, on the landing of No. 17, Gunnison-street, and told him that he was a fool, without discernment in the dispensation of his district charities.

"You give Lascar Loo custids," said she, without the formality of introduction; "give her pork-wine. Garn! Give 'er blankits. Garn 'ome! 'Er mother, she eats 'em all, and drinks the blankits. Gits 'em back from the shop, she does, before you come visiting again, so as to 'ave 'em all handy an' proper; an' Lascar Loo she sez to you, 'Oh, my mother's that good to me!' she do. Lascar Loo 'ad better talk so, bein' sick abed, 'r else 'er mother would kill 'er. Garn! you're a bloomin' gardener—you an' yer custids! Lascar Loo don't never smell of 'em even."

Thereon the curate, instead of being offended, recognized in the heavy eyes under the fringe the soul of a fellow worker, and so bade Badalia mount guard over Lascar Loo, when the next jelly or custard should arrive, to see that the invalid actually ate it. This Badalia did, to the disgust of Lascar Loo's mother, and the sharing of a black eye between the three; but Lascar Loo got her custard, and coughing heartily, rather enjoyed the fray.

Later on, partly through the Reverend Eustace Hanna's swift recognition of her uses, and partly through certain tales poured out with moist eyes and flushed cheeks by Sister Eva, youngest and most impressionable of the Little Sisters of the Red Diamond, it came to pass that Badalia, arrogant, fluffy-fringed and perfectly unlicensed in speech, won a recognized place among such as labour in Gunnison-street.

These were a mixed corps, zealous or hysterical, faint-hearted or only very wearied of battle against misery, according to their lights. The most part were consumed with small rivalries and personal jealousies, to be retailed confidentially to their own tiny cliques in the pauses between wrestling with death for the body of a moribund laundress, or scheming for further mission-grants to resole a consumptive compositor's very consumptive boots. There was a rector that lived in dread of pauperising the poor, would fain have held bazaars for fresh altar cloths, and prayed in secret for a new large brass bird, with eyes of red glass, fondly believed to be carbuncles. There was Brother Victor, of the Order of Little Ease, who knew a great deal about altar cloths but kept his knowledge in the background while he strove to propitiate Mrs. Jessel, the Secretary of the Tea Cup Board, who had money to dispense but hated Rome—even though Rome would, on its honour, do no more than fill the stomach, leaving the dazed soul to the mercies of Mrs. Jessel. There were all the Little Sisters of the Red Diamond, daughters of the horseleech, crying "Give" when their own charity was exhausted, and pitifully explaining to such as demanded an account of their disbursements in return for one half-sovereign, that relief work in a bad district can hardly be systematised on the accounts side without expensive duplication of staff. There was the Reverend Eustace Hanna who worked impartially with Ladies' Committees, Androgynous Leagues and Guilds, Brother Victor, and anybody else who could give him money, boots, or blankets, or that more precious help that allows itself to be directed by those who know. And all these people learned, one by one, to consult Badalia on matters of personal character, right to relief, and hope of eventual reformation in Gunnison-street. Her answers were seldom cheering, but she possessed special knowledge and complete confidence in herself.

"I'm Gunnison street," she said to the austere Mrs. Jessel. "I know what's what, *I* do, an' they don't want your religion, Mum, not a single——. Excuse me. It's all right when they comes to die, Mum, but till they die what they wants is things to eat. The men they'll shif' for themselves. That's why Nick Lapworth sez to you that 'e wants to be confirmed an' all that. 'E won't never lead no new life, nor 'is wife won't get no good out o' all the money you gives 'im. No more you can't pauperise them as 'asn't things to begin with. They're bloomin' well pauped. The women they can't shif' for themselves—'specially bein' always confined. 'Ow should they? They wants things if they can get 'em anyways. If not they dies, and a good job too, for women is cruel put upon in Gunnison-street."

"Do you believe that—that Mrs. Herodsfoot is altogether a proper person to trust funds to?" said Mrs. Jessel to the curate after this conversation. "She seems to be utterly godless in her speech at least."

The curate agreed. She was godless according to Mrs. Jessel's views, but did not Mrs. Jessel think that since Badalia knew Gunnison-street and its needs, as none other knew it, she might in a humble way be, as it were, the scullion of charity from purer sources, and that if, say, the Tea Cup Board could give a few shillings a week, and the Little Sisters of the Red Diamond a few more, and yes, he himself could raise yet a few more, the total, not at all likely to be excessive, might be handed over to Badalia to dispense among her associates. Thus Mrs. Jessel herself would be set free to attend more directly to the spiritual wants of certain large-limbed, hulking men who sat picturesquely on the lower benches of her gatherings and sought for truth—which is quite as precious as silver, when you know the market for it.

"She'll favour her own friends," said Mrs. Jessel. The curate refrained from mirth, and, after wise flattery, carried his point. To her unbounded pride Badalia was appointed the dispenser of a grant—a weekly trust, to be held for the benefit of Gunnison-street.

"I don't know what we can get together each week," said the curate to her. "But here are seventeen shillings to start with. You do what you like with them among your people, only let me know how it goes so that we shan't get muddled in the accounts. D'you see?"

"Ho yuss! 'Taint much though, is it?" said Badalia, regarding the white coins in her palm. The sacred fever of the administrator, only known to those who have tasted power, burned in her veins. "Boots is boots, unless they're give you, an' then they ain't fit to wear unless they're mended top an' bottom; an' jellies is jellies; an' I don't think anything o' that cheap pork-wine, but it all comes to something. It'll go quicker 'n a quartern of gin—seventeen bob. An' I'll keep a book—same as I used do before Tom went an' took up 'long o' that pan-faced slut in Henessy's Rents. We was the only barrer that kep' regular books, me an'—'im."

She bought a large copy-book—her unschooled handwriting demanded room—and in it she wrote the story of her war; boldly, as befits a general, and for no other eyes than her own and those of the Reverend Eustace Hanna. Long ere the pages were full the mottled cover had been soaked in kerosine—Lascar Loo's mother, defrauded of her percentage on her daughter's custards, invaded Badalia's room in 17, Gunnison-street, and fought with her to the damage of the lamp and her own hair. It was hard, too, to carry the precious "pork-wine" in one hand and the book in the other through an eternally thirsty land; so red stains were added to those of the oil. But the Reverend Eustace Hanna, looking at the matter of the book, never objected. The generous scrawls told their own tale, Badalia every Saturday night supplying the chorus between the written statements thus:—

Mrs. Hikkey, very ill brandy 3d. Cab for hospital, she had to go, 1s. Mrs. Poone confined. In money for tea (she took it I know, sir) 6d. Met her husband out looking for work.

"I slapped 'is face for a bone-idle beggar! 'E won't get no work this side o'—excuse me, sir. Won't you go on?" The curate continued—

Mrs. Vincent. Confid. No linning for baby. Most untidy. In money 2s. 6d. Some cloths from Miss Evva.

"Did Sister Eva do that?" said the curate very softly. Now charity was Sister Eva's bounden duty, yet to one man's eyes each act of her daily toil was a manifestation of angelic grace and goodness—a thing to perpetually admire.

"Yes, sir. She went back to the Sisters' 'Ome an' took 'em off 'er own bed. Most beautiful marked too. Go on, sir, That makes up four and thruppence."

Mrs. Junnett to keep good fire coals is up. 7d.

Mrs. Lockhart took a baby to nurse to earn a triffle but mother can'd pay husband summons over and over. He won't help. Cash 2s. 2d. Worked in a ketchin but had to leave. Fire, tea, and shin o beef, 1s. 7 1/2 d.

"There was a fight there, sir," said Badalia. "Not me, sir. 'Er 'usband, o' course 'e come in at the wrong time, was wishful to 'ave the beef, so I calls up the next floor an' down comes that mulatter man wot sells the sword-stick canes, top o' Ludgate-'ill. 'Muley,' sez I, 'you big black beast, you, take an' kill this big white beast 'ere.' I knew I couldn't stop Tom Lockart 'alf drunk, with the beef in 'is 'ands. 'I'll beef'm,' sez Muley, an' 'e did it, with that pore woman a-cryin' in the next room, an' the top banisters on that landin' is broke out, but she got 'er beef-tea, an' Tom 'e's got 'is gruel. Will you go on, sir?"

"No, I think it will be all right. I'll sign for the week," said the curate. One gets so used to these things profanely called human documents.

"Mrs. Churner's baby's got diptheery," said Badalia, turning to go.

"Where's that? The Churners of Painter's-alley, or the other Churners on Houghton-street?"

"Houghton-street. The Painter's-alley people, they're sold out an' left."

"Sister Eva's sitting one night a week with old Mrs. Probyn in Houghton-street—isn't she?" said the curate, uneasily.

"Yes; but she won't sit no longer. *I've* took up Mrs. Probyn. I can't talk'er no religion, but she don't want it; an' Miss Eva she don't want no diptheery tho' she sez she does. Don't *you* be afraid for Miss Eva."

"But—but you'll get it, perhaps."

"Like as not." She looked the curate between the eyes, and her own eyes flamed under the fringe. "Maybe I'd like to get it, for aught you know."

The curate thought upon these words for a little time till he began to think of Sister Eva in the grey cloak with the white bonnet ribbons under the chin. Then he thought no more of Badalia.

What Badalia thought was never expressed in words, but it is known in Gunnison-street that Lascar Loo's mother, sitting blind drunk on her own doorstep, was that night captured and wrapped up in the war-cloud of Badalia's wrath, so that she did not know whether she stood on her head or her heels, and after being soundly bumped on every particular stair up to her room, was set down on Badalia's bed, there to whimper and quiver till the dawn, protesting that all the world was against her, and calling on the names of children long since slain by dirt and neglect. Badalia, snorting, went out to war, and since the hosts of the enemy were many, found enough work to keep her busy till the dawn.

As she had promised, she took Mrs. Probyn into her own care, and began by nearly startling the old lady into a fit with the announcement that "there ain't no God like as not, an' if there *is* it don't matter to you or me, an' any'ow you take this jelly." Sister Eva objected to being shut off from her pious work in Houghton-street, but Badalia insisted, and by fair words and the promise of favours to come so prevailed on three or four of the more sober men of the neighbourhood that they blockaded the door whenever Sister Eva attempted to force an entry, and pleaded the diphtheria as their excuse. "I've got to keep 'er out o' arm's way," said Badalia, "an' out she keeps. The curick won't care a—for me, but—he wouldn't any'ow."

The effect of that quarantine was to shift the sphere of Sister Eva's activity to other streets, and notably those most haunted by the Reverend Eustace Hanna and Brother Victor, of the Order of Little Ease. There exists, for all their human bickerings, a very close brotherhood in the ranks of those whose work lies in Gunnison-street. To begin with, they have seen pain—pain that no word or deed of theirs can alleviate—life born into Death, and Death crowded down by unhappy life. Also they understand the full significance of drink, which is a knowledge hidden from very many well-meaning people, and some of them have fought with the beasts at Ephesus. They meet at unseemly hours in unseemly places, exchange a word or two of hasty counsel, advice, or suggestion, and pass on to their appointed toil, since time is precious and lives hang in the balance of five minutes. For many, the gas-lamps are their sun, and the Covent Garden wains the chariots of the twilight. They have all in their station begged for money, so that the freemasonry of the mendicant binds them together.

To all these influences there was added in the case of two workers that thing which men have agreed to call Love. The possible chance of Sister Eva's catching diphtheria did not enter into the curate's head till Badalia had spoken. Then it seemed a thing intolerable and monstrous that she should be exposed not only to this risk, but any accident whatever of the streets. A wain coming round a corner might kill her; the rotten staircases on which she trod daily and nightly might collapse and maim her; there was danger in the tottering coping-stones of certain crazy houses that he knew well; danger more deadly within those houses. What if one of a thousand drunken men crushed out that precious life? A woman had once flung a chair at the curate's head. Sister Eva's arm would not be strong enough to ward off a chair. There were also knives that were apt to fly. These and other considerations cast the soul of the Reverend Eustace Hanna into torment, that no leaning upon Providence could relieve. God was indubitably great and terrible—one had only to walk through Gunnison-street to see that much—but it would be better, vastly better, that Eva should have the protection of his own arm. And the world that was not too busy to watch might have seen a woman, not too young, light-haired and light-eyed, slightly assertive in her speech, and very limited in such ideas as lay beyond the immediate sphere of her duty, where the eyes of the Reverend Eustace Hanna turned to follow the footsteps of a Queen crowned in a little grey bonnet with white ribbons under the chin.

If that bonnet appeared for a moment at the bottom of a courtyard, or nodded at him on a dark staircase, then there was hope yet for Lascar Loo, living on one lung and the memory of past excesses, hope even for whining, sodden Nick Lapworth, blaspheming in the hope of money over the pangs of a "true conversion this time, s'elp me Gawd, sir." If that bonnet did not appear for a day, the mind of the curate was filled with lively pictures of horror, visions of stretchers, a crowd at some villainous crossing, and a policeman—he could see that policeman—jerking out over his shoulder the details of the accident, and ordering the man who would have set his body against the wheels—heavy dray wheels, he could see them—to "move on." Then there was less hope for the salvation of Gunnison-street and all in it.

Which agony Brother Victor beheld one day when he was coming from a death-bed. He saw the light in the eye, the relaxing muscles of the mouth, and heard a new ring in the voice that had told flat all the forenoon. Sister Eva had turned into Gunnison-street after a forty-eight hours' eternity of absence. She had not been run over. Brother Victor's heart must have suffered in some human fashion, or he would never have seen what he saw. But the law of his Church made suffering easy. His duty was to go on with his work until he died, even as Badalia went on. She, magnifying her office, faced the drunken husband; coaxed the doubly shiftless, thriftless girl wife into a little forethought, and begged clothes when and where she could for the scrofulous babes that multiplied like the green scum on the water cisterns.

The story of her deeds was written in the book that the curate signed weekly, but she never told him any more of fights and tumults in the street. "Mis' Eva does 'er work 'er way. I does mine mine. But I do more than Mis' Eva ten times over, an' 'Thank yer, Badalia,' sez 'e—'that'll do for this week.' I wonder what Tom's doin' now long o' that—other woman. 'Seems like as if I'd go an' look at 'im one o' these days. But I'd cut 'er liver out—couldn't 'elp myself. Better not go, p'raps."

Hennessy's Rents lay more than two miles from Gunnison-street, and were inhabited by much the same class of people. Tom had established himself there with Jenny Wabstow, his new woman, and for weeks lived in great fear of Badalia's suddenly descending upon him. The prospect of actual fighting did not scare him: but he objected to the police-court that would follow, and the orders for maintenance and other devices of a law that cannot understand the simple rule that "when a man's tired of a woman 'e ain't such a bloomin' fool as to live with 'er no more, an' that's the long an' short of it." For some months his new wife wore very well, and kept Tom in a state of decent fear and consequent orderliness. Also work was plentiful. Then a baby was born, and, following the law of his kind, Tom, little interested in the children he helped to produce, sought distraction in drink. He had confined himself, as a rule, to beer, which is stupefying and comparatively innocuous: at least, it clogs the legs, and though the heart may ardently desire to kill, sleep comes swiftly, and the crime often remains undone. Spirits, being more volatile, allow both the flesh and the soul to work together—generally to the inconvenience of others. Tom discovered that there was merit in whiskey—if you only took enough of it—cold. He took as much as he could purchase or get given him, and by the time that his woman was fit to go abroad again, the two rooms of their household were stripped of many valuable articles. Then the woman spoke her mind, not once, but several times, with point, fluency, and metaphor; and Tom was indignant at being deprived of peace at the end of his day's work, which included much whiskey. He therefore withdrew himself from the solace and companionship of Jenny Wabstow, and she therefore pursued him with more metaphors. At the last, Tom would turn round and hit her—sometimes across the head, and sometimes across the breast, and the bruises furnished material for discussion on doorsteps among such women as had been treated in like matter by their husbands. They were not few.

But no very public scandal had occurred till Tom one day saw fit to open negotiations with a young woman on the subject of matrimony according to the laws of free selection. He was getting very tired of Jenny and the young woman was earning enough from flower-selling to keep him in comfort, whereas Jenny was expecting another baby and most unreasonably expected consideration on this account. The shapelessness of her figure revolted him, and he said as much in the language of his breed. Jenny cried till Mrs. Hart, lineal descendant, and Irish of the "mother to Mike of the donkey-cart," stopped her on her own staircase and whispered: "God be good to you, Jenny, my woman, for I see how 'tis with you." Jenny wept more than ever, and half dazed with the sickness that makes the banisters swim in the morning, gave Mrs. Hart a penny and some kisses, while Tom was conducting his own wooing at the corner of the street.

The young woman, prompted by pride, not by virtue, told Jenny of his offers, and she spoke to Tom that night. The altercation began in their own rooms, but

Tom tried to escape; and in the end all Hennessy's Rents gathered themselves upon the pavement and formed a court to which Jenny appealed from time to time, her hair loose on her neck, her raiment in extreme disorder, and her steps astray from drink. "When your man drinks, you'd better drink too! It don't 'urt so much when 'e 'its you then," says the Wisdom of the Women. And surely they ought to know.

"Look at 'im!" shrieked Jenny. "Look at 'im, standin' there without any word to say for himself, that 'ud smitch off and leave me an' never so much as a shilllin' lef be'ind! You call yourself a man—you call yourself the bleedin' shadow of a man? I've seen better men than you made outer chewed paper and sput out arterwards. Look at 'im! 'E's been drunk since Thursday last, an' e'll be drunk s' long's 'e can get drink. 'Es took all I've got, an' me—an' me—as you see——"

A murmur of sympathy from the women.

"Took it all, he did, an' atop of his blasted pickin' an' stealin'—yes, you, you thief—'e goes off an' tries to take up long o' that"—here followed a complete and minute description of the young woman aforementioned. Luckily, she was not on the spot to hear. "'E'll serve 'er as 'e served me! 'E'll drink every bloomin' copper she makes an' then leave 'er alone, same as 'e done me! O women, look you, I've bore 'im one an' there's another on the way, an' e'd up an' leave me as I am now—the stinkin' dorg. An' you may leave me. I don't want none o' your leavin's. Go away. Get away!" The hoarseness of passion overpowered the voice. The crowd attracted a policeman as Tom began to slink away.

"Look at 'im," said Jenny, grateful for the new listener. "Ain't there no law for such as 'im? 'E's took all my money, 'e's beat me once twice an' over, 'E's swine drunk when 'e aint mad drunk, an' now, an' now 'e's trying to pick up along o' another woman. 'Im I give up a four times better man for. Ain't there no law?"

"What's the matter now? You go on into your 'ouse. I'll see to the man. 'As 'e been 'itting you?" said the policeman.

"'Ittin' me? 'E's cut my 'eart in two, an' 'e stands there grinnin' a tho' 'twas all a play to 'im."

"You go on into your 'ouse an' lie down a bit."

"I'm a married woman, I tell you, an' I'll 'ave my 'usband!"

"I ain't done her no bloomin' 'arm," said Tom from the edge of the crowd. He felt that public opinion was running against him.

"You ain't done me any bloomin' good, you dorg. I'm a married woman, I am, an' I won't 'ave my 'usband took from me."

"Well, if you are a married woman, go into the 'ouse," said the policeman soothingly. He was used to domestic brawls.

"Shan't—thank you for your impidence. Look 'ere!" She tore open her dishevelled bodice and showed such crescent-shaped bruises as are made by a well applied chair-back. "That's what 'e done to me acause my heart wouldn't break quick enough! 'E's tried to get in an' break it. Look at that, Tom, that you gave me last night; an' I made it up with you. But that was before I knew what you were tryin' to do long o' that woman——"

"D'you charge 'im?" said the policeman. "'E'll get a month for it, pre'aps."

"No," said Jenny firmly. It was one thing to expose her man to the scorn of the street, and another to lead him to jail.

"Then you go in an' lie down, and you"—this to the crowd— "pass along the pavement, there. Pass along. 'Taint nothing to laugh at." To Tom, who was being sympathised with by his friends, "It's good for you she didn't charge you, but mind this now, the next time," &c.

Tom did not at all appreciate Jenny's forbearance, nor did his friends help to compose his mind. He had whacked the woman because she was a nagging nuisance. For precisely the same reason he had cast about for a new mate. And all his kind acts had ended in a truly painful scene in the street, a most unjustifiable exposure by and of his woman, and a certain loss of caste—this he realized dimly—among his associates. Consequently, all women were nuisances, and consequently whiskey was a good thing. His friends condoled with him. Perhaps he had been more hard on his woman than she deserved, but her disgraceful conduct under provocation excused all offence.

"I wouldn't 'ave no more to do with 'er—a woman like that there," said one comforter.

"Let 'er go an' dig for her bloomin' self. A man wears 'isself out to a skeleton shovin' meat down their mouths, while they sit at 'ome easy all day; an' the very fust time, mark you, you 'as a bit of difference, an' very proper too for a man as *is* a man, she ups an' 'as you out into the street, callin' you Gawd knows what all. What's the good o' that, I arx you?" So spoke the second comforter.

The whiskey was the third, and his suggestion struck Tom as the best of all. He would return to Badalia his wife. Probably she would have been doing something wrong while he had been away, and he could then vindicate his authority as a husband. Certainly she would have money. Single women always seemed to possess the pence that God and the Government denied to hard-working men. He refreshed himself with more whiskey. It was beyond any doubt that Badalia would have done something wrong. She might even have married another man. He would wait till the new husband was out of the way, and after kicking Badalia, would get money and a long absent sense of satisfaction. There is much virtue in a creed or law, but when all is prayed and suffered, drink is the only thing that will make clean all a man's deeds in his own eyes. Pity it is that the effects are not permanent.

Tom parted with his friends, bidding them tell Jenny that he was going to Gunnison-street, and would return to her arms no more. Because this was the devil's message, they remembered and severally delivered it, with drunken distinctness, in Jenny's ears. Then Tom took more drink till his drunkenness rolled back and stood off from him as a wave rolls back and stands off the wreck it will swamp. He reached the traffic-polished black asphalte of a side street and trod warily among the reflections of the shop-lamps that burned in gulfs of pitchy darkness, fathoms beneath his bootheels. He was very sober indeed. Looking down his past, he beheld that he was justified of all his actions so entirely and perfectly that if Badalia had in his absence dared to lead a blameless life he would smash her for not having gone wrong.

Badalia at that moment was in her own room after the regular nightly skirmish with Lascar Loo's mother. To a reproof as stinging as a Gunnison-street tongue could make it, the old woman, detected for the hundredth time in the theft of the poor delicacies meant for the invalid, could only cackle and answer—

"D'you think Loo's never bilked a man in 'er life? She's dyin' now—on'y she's so cunning long about it. Me! I'll live for twenty years yet."

Badalia shook her, more on principle than in any hope of curing her, and thrust her into the night, where she collapsed on the pavement and called upon the devil to slay Badalia.

He came upon the word in the shape of a man with a very pale face who asked for her by name. Lascar Loo's mother remembered. It was Badalia's husband—and the return of a husband to Gunnison-street was generally followed by beatings.

"Where's my wife?" said Tom. "Where's my slut of a wife?"

"Upstairs an' be —— to her," said the old woman, falling over on her side. "'Ave you come back for 'er, Tom?"

"Yes. 'Oo's she took up while I've bin gone?"

"All the bloomin' curicks in the parish. She's that set up you wouldn't know 'er."

"'Strewth she is!"

"Oh, yuss. Mor'n that, she's always round an' about with them sniffin' Sisters of Charity an' the curick. Mor'n that, 'e gives 'er money—pounds an' pounds a week. Been keepin' her that way for months, 'e 'as. No wonder you wouldn't 'ave nothin' to do with 'er when you left. An' she keeps me outer the food-stuff they gets for me lyin' dyin' out 'ere like a dorg. She's been a blazin' bad 'un has Badalia since you lef."

"Got the same room still, 'as she?" said Tom, striding over Lascar Loo's mother, who was picking at the chinks between the pave-stones.

"Yes, but so fine you wouldn't know it."

Tom went up the stairs and the old lady chuckled. Tom was angry. Badalia would not be able to bump people for some time to come, or to interfere with the heaven-appointed distribution of custards.

Badalia, undressing to go to bed, heard feet on the stair that she knew well. Ere they stopped to kick at her door she had, in her own fashion, thought through several volumes of the book of human life.

"Tom's back," she said to herself. "An' I'm glad . . . spite o' the curick an' everythink."

She opened the door, crying his name.

The man pushed her aside.

"I don't want none o' your kissin's an' slaverin's. I'm sick of 'em," said he.

"You ain't 'ad so many neither to make you sick these two years past."

"I've 'ad better. Got any money?"

"On'y a little—orful little."

"That's a —— lie, an' you know it."

"'Taint—and, oh, Tom, what's the use o' talkin' money the minute you come back? Didn't you like Jenny? I knowed you wouldn't."

"Shut your 'ead. Ain't you got enough to make a man drunk fair?"

"You don't want bein' made more drunk any. You're drunk a'ready. You come to bed, Tom."

"To you?"

"Ay, to me. Ain't I nothin'—spite o' Jenny?"

She put out her arms as she spoke. But the drink held Tom fast.

"Not for me," said he, steadying himself against the wall. "Don't I know 'ow you've been goin' on while I was away, yah!"

"Arsk about!" said Badalia, indignantly, drawing herself together, "'Oo sez anythink agin me 'ere?"

"'Oo sez? W'y, everybody. I ain't come back more 'n a minute fore I finds you've been with the curick Gawd knows where. Wot curick was 'e?"

"The curick that's 'ere always," said Badalia, hastily. She was thinking of anything rather than the Rev. Eustace Hanna at that moment. Tom sat down gravely in the only chair in the room. Badalia continued her arrangements for going to bed.

"Pretty thing that," said Tom, "to tell your own lawful married 'usband—an' I guv five bob for the weddin' ring. Curick that's 'ere always! Cool as brass you are. Ain't you got no shame? Ain't 'e under the bed now?"

"Tom, you're bleedin' drunk. I ain't done nothin' to be shamed of."

"You! You don't know wot shame is. But I ain't come 'ere o mess with you. Give me wot you've got, an' then I'll dress you down an' go to Jenny."

"I ain't got nothin' 'cept some coppers an' a shillin' or so."

"Wot's that about the curick keepin' you on five poun' a week?"

"'Oo told you that?"

"Lascar Loo's mother, lyin' on the pavemint outside, an' more honest than you'll ever be. Give me wot you've got!!"

Badalia passed over to a little shell pincushion on the mantelpiece, drew thence four shillings and threepence—the lawful earnings of her mangle—and held them out to the man who was rocking in his chair and surveying the room with wide-opened rolling eyes.

"That ain't five poun'," said he, drowsily.

"I ain't got no more. Take it an' go—if you won't stay."

Tom rose slowly, gripping the arms of the chair. "Wot about the curick's money that 'e guv you?" said he. "Lascar Loo's mother told me. You give it over to me now, or I'll make you."

"Lascar Loo's mother don't know anything about it."

"She do, an' more than you want her to know."

"She don't. I've bumped the eart out of 'er, and I can't give you the money. Anythin' else but that, Tom, an' everythin else but that, Tom, I'll give willin' and true. 'Tain't my money. Won't the dollar be enough? That money's my trust. There's a book along of it too."

"Your trust? Wot are you doin with any trust that your 'usband don't know of? You an' your trust! Take you that !"

Tom stepped towards her and delivered a blow of the clenched fist across the mouth. "Give me wot you've got," said he, in the thick, abstracted voice of one talking in dreams.

"I won't," said Badalia, staggering to the washstand. With any other man than her husband she would have fought savagely as a wild cat; but Tom had been absent two years, and, perhaps, a little timely submission would win him back to her. None the less, the weekly trust was sacred.

The wave that had so long held back descended on Tom's brain. He caught Badalia by the throat and forced her to her knees. It seemed just to him in that hour to punish an erring wife for two years of wilful desertion; and the more, in that she had confessed her guilt by refusing to give up the wage of sin.

Lascar Loo's mother waited on the pavement without for the sounds of lamentation, but none came. Even if Tom had released her gullet, Badalia would not have screamed.

"Give it up, you slut!" said Tom. "Is that 'ow you pay me back for all I've done?"

"I can't. 'Tain't my money. Gawd forgive you, Tom, for wot you're—" the voice ceased as the grip tightened, and Tom heaved Badalia against the bed. Her forehead struck the bed-post, and she sank, half kneeling, on the floor. It was impossible for a self-respecting man to refrain from kicking her: so Tom kicked with the deadly intelligence born of whiskey. The head drooped to the floor, and Tom kicked at that till the crisp tingle of hair striking through his nailed boot with the chill of cold water, warned him that it might be as well to desist.

"Where's the curick's money, you kep' woman?" he whispered in the blood-stained ear. But there was no answer—only a rattling at the door, and the voice of Jenny Wabstow crying ferociously, "Come out o' that, Tom, an' come 'ome with me! An' you, Badalia, I'll tear your face off its bones!"

Tom's friends had delivered their message, and Jenny, after the first flood of passionate tears, rose up to follow Tom, and, if possible, to win him back. She was prepared even to endure an exemplary whacking for her performances in Hennessy's Rents. Lascar Loo's mother guided her to the chamber of horrors, and chuckled as she retired down the staircase. If Tom had not banged the soul out of Badalia, there would at least be a royal fight between that Badalia and Jenny. And Lascar Loo's mother knew well that Hell has no fury like a woman fighting above the life that is quick in her.

Still there was no sound audible in the street. Jenny swung back the unbolted door, to discover her man stupidly regarding a heap by the bed. An eminent murderer has remarked that if people did not die so untidily most men, and all women, would commit at least one murder in their lives. Tom was reflecting on the present untidiness, and the whiskey was fighting with the clear current of his thoughts.

"Don't make that noise" he said. "Come in quick."

"My Gawd!" said Jenny, checking like a startled wild beast. "Wot's all this 'ere? You ain't——"

"Dunno. 'Spose I did it."

"Did it! You done it a sight too well this time."

"She was aggravatin'," said Tom, thickly, dropping back into the chair. "That aggravatin' you'd never believe. Livin' on the fat o' the land among these aristocratic parsons an' all. Look at them white curtings on the bed. *We* ain't got no white curtings. What I want to know is——" The voice died as Badalia's had died, but from a different cause. The whiskey was tightening its grip after the accomplished deed, and Tom's eyes were beginning to close. Badalia on the floor breathed heavily.

"No, nor like to 'ave," said Jenny. "You've done for 'er this time. You go!"

"Not me. She won't hurt. Do 'er good. I'm goin' to sleep. Look at those there clean sheets! Are you comin' too?"

Jenny bent over Badalia, and there was intelligence in the battered woman's eyes—intelligence and much hate.

"I never told 'im to do such," Jenny whispered. "'Twas Tom's own doin'— none o' mine. Shall I get 'im took, dear?"

The eyes told their own story. Tom, who was beginning to snore, must not be taken by the law.

"Go," said Jenny. "Get out! Get out of 'ere."

"You—told—me—that—this afternoon," said the man very sleepily. "Lemme go asleep."

"That wasn't nothing. You'd only 'it me. This time it's murder—murder— murder! Tom, you've killed 'er now." She shook the man from his rest, and understanding with cold terror filled his fuddled brain.

"I done it for your sake, Jenny," he whimpered feebly, trying to take her hand.

"You killed 'er for the money, same as you would ha' killed me. Get out o' this. Lay 'er on the bed first, you brute!"

They lifted Badalia on to the bed, and crept forth silently.

"I can't be took along o' you—and if you was took you'd say I made you do it, an' try to get me 'anged. Go away—anywhere outer 'ere," said Jenny, and she dragged him down the stairs.

"Goin' to look for the curick?" said a voice from the pavement. Lascar Loo's mother was still waiting patiently to hear Badalia squeal.

"Wot curick?" said Jenny, swiftly. There was a chance of salving her conscience yet in regard to the bundle upstairs.

"'Anna—63, Roomer-terrace—close 'ere," said the old woman. She had never been favourably regarded by the curate. Perhaps, since Badalia had not squealed, Tom preferred smashing the man to the woman. There was no accounting for tastes.

Jenny thrust her man before her till they reached the nearest main road. "Go away, now," she gasped. "Go off anywheres, but don't come back to me. I'll never go with you again; an', Tom—Tom, d' you 'ear me?—clean your boots."

Vain counsel. The desperate thrust of disgust which she bestowed upon him sent him staggering face down into the kennel, where a policeman showed interest in his welfare.

"Took for a common drunk. Gawd send they don't look at 'is boots! 'Anna, 63, Roomer-terrace!" Jenny settled her hat and ran.

The excellent housekeeper of the Roomer Chambers still remembers how there arrived a young person, blue-lipped and gasping, who cried only: "Badalia, 17, Gunnison-street. Tell the curick to come at once—at once—at once!" and vanished into the night. This message was borne to the Rev. Eustace Hanna, then enjoying his beauty sleep. He saw there was urgency in the demand, and unhesitatingly knocked up Brother Victor across the landing. As a matter of etiquette, Rome and England divided their cases in the district according to the creeds of the sufferers; but Badalia was an institution, and not a case, and there was no district-relief etiquette to be considered. "Something has happened to Badalia," the curate said, "and it's your affair as well as mine. Dress, and come along."

"I am ready," was the answer.

"Is there any hint of what's wrong?"

"Nothing beyond a runaway knock and a call."

"Then it's a confinement or a murderous assault. Badalia wouldn't wake us up for anything less. I'm qualified for both, thank God."

"I'd give much if our Church insisted on decent medical training. I've subscribed to the Thirty-nine Articles, but it would be better if I had subscribed to the *Lancet* intelligently from the beginning. Come along."

The two men raced to Gunnison-street, for there were no cabs abroad, and under any circumstances a cab fare means two days' good firing for such as are perishing with cold. Lascar Loo's mother had gone to bed, and the door was naturally on the latch. They found considerably more than they had expected in Badalia's room, and the Church of Rome acquitted itself nobly with bandages, while the Church of England could only pray to be delivered from the sin of envy. The Order of Little Ease, recognising that the soul is in most cases accessible through the body, take their measures and train their men accordingly.

"She'll do now," said Brother Victor, in a whisper. "It's internal bleeding, I fear, and a certain amount of injury to the brain. She has a husband, of course?"

"They all have, more's the pity."

"Yes, there's a domesticity about these injuries that shows their origin." He lowered his voice. "It's a perfectly hopeless business, you understand. Twelve hours at the longest."

Badalia's right hand began to beat on the counterpane, palm down.

"I think you are wrong," said the Church of England. "She is going."

"No, that's not picking at the counterpane," said the Church of Rome. "She wants to say something; you know her better than I."

The curate bent very low.

"Send for Miss Eva," said Badalia, with a cough.

"In the morning. She will come in the morning," said the curate, and Badalia was content. Only the Church of Rome, who knew something of the human heart, knitted his brows and said nothing. After all, the law of his order was plain. His duty was to watch till the dawn while the grey worn moon went down.

It was a little before her sinking that the Rev. Eustace Hanna said, "Hadn't we better send for Sister Eva? She seems to be going fast."

Brother Victor made no answer, but as early as decency admitted there came one to the door of the house of the Little Sisters of the Red Diamond and demanded Sister Eva, that she might soothe the pain of Badalia Herodsfoot. That man, saying very little, led her to Gunnison-street, No. 17, and into the room where Badalia lay. Then he stood on the landing, and bit the flesh of his fingers in agony, because he was a priest and a man and knew how the hearts of men and women beat back at the rebound, so that Love is born out of horror, and passion declares itself when the soul is quivering with pain.

Badalia, wise to the last, husbanded her strength till the coming of Sister Eva. It is generally maintained by the Little Sisters of the Red Diamond that she died in delirium, but since one Sister at least took a half of her dying advice, this seems uncharitable.

She tried to turn feebly on the bed, and the poor broken human machinery protested according to its nature.

Sister Eva started forward, thinking that she heard the dread forerunner of the death-rattle. Badalia lay still conscious, and spoke with startling distinctness, the irrepressible irreverence of the street-hawker, the girl who had danced on the winkle-barrow, twinkling in her one available eye.

"Sounds jest like Mrs. Jessel, don't it? Before she's 'ad 'er lunch an' 'as been talkin' all the mornin' to her classes."

Neither Sister Eva nor the curate said anything. Brother Victor stood without the door, and the breath came harshly between his clenched teeth. He was in pain.

"Put a cloth over my 'ead," said Badalia. "I've got it good, an' I don't want Miss Eva to see. I ain't pretty this time."

"Who was it?" said the curate.

"Man from outside. Never seed 'im no more'n Adam. Drunk I s'pose. S'elp me Gawd that's truth! Is Miss Eva 'ere?" I can't see under the towel. I've got it good, Miss Eva. Excuse my not shakin' 'ands with you, but I'm not strong, an' it's fourpence for Mrs. Imeny's beef-tea, an' wot you can give 'er for babylinnin. Allus' 'avin' kids, these people. I 'adn't oughter talk, for *my* 'usband 'e never come nigh me these two years, or I'd a-bin as bad as the rest; but 'e never come nigh me. . . . A man come and 'it me over the 'ead, an' 'e kicked me, Miss Eva; so it was just the same 's if I had ha' had a 'usband, ain't it? The book's in the drawer, Mister 'Anna, an' it's all right, an' I never guv' up a copper o' the trust money—not a copper. You look under the chist o' drawers—all wot isn't spent this week is there. . . . An', Miss Eva, don't you wear that grey bonnick no more. I kep' you from the diptheery, an'—an' I didn't want to keep you so, but the curick said it 'ad to be done. I'd a sooner ha' took up with 'im than anyone, only Tom he come, an' then—you see, Miss Eva, Tom 'e never come nigh me for two years, nor I 'aven't seen him yet. S'elp me——, I haven't. Do you 'ear? But you two go along, and make a match of it. I've wished otherways often, but o' course it was not for the likes o' me. If Tom 'ad come back, which 'e never did, I'd ha' been like the rest—sixpence for beef-tea for the baby, a shilling for layin' out the baby. You've seen it in the books, Mister 'Anna. That's what it is; an' o' course, you couldn't never 'ave nothing to do with me. But a woman she wishes as she looks, an' never you 'ave no doubt about 'im, Miss Eva. I've seen it in 'is face time an' agin—time an' agin. . . . Make it a four pound ten funeral—with the pall."

It was a seven pound fifteen shilling funeral, and all Gunnison-street turned out to do it honour. All but two; for Lascar Loo's mother saw that a Power had departed, and that her road lay clear to the custards. Therefore, when the carriages rattled off, the cat on the doorstep heard the wail of the dying unfortunate, who could not die—

"Oh, mother, mother, won't you even let me lick the spoon!"

II.10

"A Work of Art"

Sylvia Warner

"Doing doesn't do" is the credo of Mrs. Bernstein, the philanthropist in this short story by British author and poet Sylvia Townsend Warner (1893–1978). Above all, Mrs. Bernstein strove to avoid "betterment"— spiritual and bodily—or, as she called it, "professional do-goodery." She gave only money. No questions asked. No strings attached. But being wheelchair-bound and of "immense weight," she was forced to employ an administrator, one Fiona MacTavish, to deliver her largesse. Though Miss MacTavish cheerfully abided by her employer's rule for a good long time, when she found Mr. Herzen living in a "frightful place," with an "appalling landlady," she insisted on making some changes, and Mrs. Bernstein gave in, albeit reluctantly. Mr. Herzen dutifully moved to the new apartment that Miss MacTavish arranged for him, but he promptly reconstructed it in his own sickly image, all the time continuing to take Mrs. Bernstein's money. Has Mrs. Bernstein been vindicated or duped? Should we praise or condemn Miss MacTavish's doings? Should one be concerned about the use or misuse of one's gifts?

Private charity still persists in England though mostly it is practised in the disorderly, hole-and-corner style recommended by Jesus. Mrs. Bernstein was so far in step with the welfare state that she used a paid administrator, but she did so for reasons of her own. If you have to go about in a wheel-chair, she said, you can't see things for yourself. Moreover, a benefactress of immense weight carried by grunting porters up to attics or down to basements (and misery is seldom domiciled on ground-floor level) is bound to create remark, and bring every cheat, thief, cadger, and social worker, not to mention hosts of other unfortunates, to settle like blowflies on the benefited one. So she availed herself of Miss MacTavish, whose muscular legs and unobtrusive bearing could get her in anywhere. Miss MacTavish had already got herself into a perfectly satisfactory life of her own. She was an artist, and illustrated children's books for a living. It

From *A Spirit Rises* by Sylvia Townsend Warner, published by Chatto & Windus, 1962, pp. 203–210. Reprinted by permission of The Random House Group Ltd.

was in the intervals of drawing little girls with turned-up noses offering apples to horses with classical profiles that she went about Mrs. Bernstein's business.

Every three months or so, Mrs. Bernstein would engage Miss MacTavish in strategic conversation to see if any professional do-goodery had lodged itself in her administrator's outlook. The results were reassuringly negative. The outlook remained that of the artist; no tendency to confuse making people a trifle better off with making people better clouded Miss MacTavish's appraising eye. It was above all betterment that Mrs. Bernstein wished to avoid. She had been bettered in her youth and was of the opinion that it would be quite as nauseous to be bettered in maturity or in old age. She was even suspicious of bodily betterment, since the body is the envelope of the soul and not always reliably impermeable. Instead of carrying bundles of blankets and parcels of nourishing food, Miss MacTavish carried pound notes, which are easier both to convey and to conceal. But as one must not muzzle the ox that treadeth out the corn, she was free to give advice—provided that the advice was drawn from her own experience and that the money was given first.

'My Uncle Heinrich,' said Mrs. Bernstein, 'did it the other way round. And so I was always being trapped into performing a pound's worth of behaviour and then getting two and sixpence. That's not fair dealing. And one must not do things for them. Even the rich don't trust even the experts who do things for them. For the poor it is impossible. It would crush all the spontaneity of their taking.'

'I wonder that you are prepared to trust me,' said Miss MacTavish.

'Well, yes. Perhaps you'll run off with it. So you wanted it. So that's all right.'

Discovering Mrs. Bernstein was an enlarging experience, just as beginning to paint in oils had been, and Fiona MacTavish blessed the day when she had run up to steady the chair which was about to topple sideways into the Serpentine— an act that had led to a conversation about the Loch Ness monster, the best way of cooking carp, and the first of many invitations to lunch.

For several years she acted as Mrs. Bernstein's emissary without ever questioning the method laid down for her. This was not mere docility. It seemed to her that the method worked uncommonly well. She saw people looking pleased, and could quit them without any sense of having smudged their pleasure. She saw—which is perhaps rarer—people who regularly received money from her and who met her again without the least trace of fear or calculation. Naturally, she did not always see these wonders, but they occurred oftener than she could have expected. Now and then she gave advice, which was warmly reciprocated in valuable recommendations about health, canaries, geranium cuttings, cockroaches, and so on. And in the course of time she became increasingly attached to Mrs. Bernstein, who became increasingly fatter, uglier, richer, and more versed in the *affaire Port Royal*—this last on the ground that it brought her closer to Mme. de Sévigné. It was Mr. Herzen who drove Miss Mac-Tavish to question the absolute inadmissibility of doing things for those you give money to.

Mr. Herzen was solitary, sickly, hypochrondriacal, sometimes charming, always shiftless, and never continuing in one stay. When traced to a new lodging, he would explain that he had not been able to pay the rent, or that he had merely forgotten to do so, with the result that he had been cruelly evicted. Quite often, this was not so at all. He had paid, he had gone—the landlady just couldn't account for it. Disappearing thus for months on end and when traced being sicklier, sadder, shabbier, and distinctly reproachful—since he insisted on thinking he had somehow displeased his kind friends and been cast off by them—Mr. Herzen drove Miss MacTavish to take a stand.

'I really cannot go on looking for Mr. Herzen any longer, Mrs. Bernstein.'

'Still lost, poor man?'

'No, no. I've hunted him down again. This time he's in Finsbury.'

'*Mais qu'avez-vous de mourir si souvent?*' murmured Mrs. Bernstein.

'In the most frightful hole, with the most appalling landlady. And it seems to me that we—that you—will be compelled into doing something for him.'

'I don't approve of doing.'

'I know you don't. I don't like the idea of it myself. But there are times when there's nothing for it but desperate measures. Now, listen. This is what I suggest. . . .'

*   *   *

In the end, she got her way. A small furnished flat was found, with a pleasant landlady. It was redecorated, and to the landlady it was explained that Miss MacTavish was Mr. Herzen's person of business, and that he would pay his rent through her. By thus representing him as someone rich and strange, she hoped to pass off his obvious poverty, settled incompetence, and vagaries of temper. She thought she had done pretty well, but Mrs. Bernstein continued to assert that doing didn't do. So convinced was she of this that, though she still paid his rent and his allowance, she ceased to inquire about him—as though she knew by some private information that he was dead, but respected the privacy.

Presently it appeared that Mr. Herzen shared Mrs. Bernstein's rejection of the Deed. The pleasant landlady, now looking slightly hangdog, said one day, 'You know, dear, you mustn't think I'm taking money under false colours. But that ten bob a week Mr. Herzen pays me over and above for cleaning his rooms and so on—well, I'm only too ready to do for him, but he won't hear of it. And how he manages about the dust and the smuts and the carpet sweepings I'm sure I do not know, for he hasn't brought down as much as a teacupful to the dustbin in the yard. And sometimes it really worries me, quite apart from the furniture, for it's as plain as a pikestaff that he's the kind of gentleman who needs doing for.'

Miss MacTavish said that Mr. Herzen might be afraid of his papers being disarranged.

'Yes, ducks. I recollect you told me he was consecrated in his work and not to be disturbed. Though I don't know when he does it, really. He's always out. He's gone out now.'

The next time she called, Mr. Herzen was out. And the next. Or perhaps it was she who was out—locked out. She had a most distinct impression that on the other side of the door someone was listening. Two could play at that game. Thrusting away all consideration of what Mrs. Bernstein would think of such behaviour—besides, Mr. Herzen was already an exception—she dropped the envelope with the money in it through the letter slot, walked partway downstairs, continued to pat with her feet, and listened. She heard the envelope being torn open. She heard his cough, exasperated by suppression and now let out to do its worst. Knocking on the door, banging on it and shouting, she at last overthrew the silence that lay behind it like a great mattress propped up to intercept bullets.

'Oh, dear! It's Miss MacTavish. I was asleep. Ah, it would be so. The first sleep I have had for days and days. Unlucky, eh?'

The envelope on the floor, the notes sticking out of his pocket, were the only clean things in the room. Dust lay thick on the furniture, cobwebs trailed from the ceiling and latticed the grimy window. Dirty and unshaven, he stood at bay in his den.

'Isn't it terrible? Isn't it terrible? And I have been so ill, I am still so ill, I cannot sleep because of my cough, and whatever I eat, it comes up again, I am poisoned through and through. And the woman downstairs, she does nothing for me, nothing! She puts milk for her cat and forgets me. Not that I have anything against the poor cat, you understand. If I were not so ill I would move, for it is killing me here. All this dust is so bad for my cough.'

'It must be. Poor Mr. Herzen, no wonder you feel ill. Mrs. Bernstein will be sorry to hear all this.'

'No, no! Don't tell her. I do not like to be a trouble to my friends. I shall struggle through somehow. Or I shall not. Every herring must hang by his own tail, eh? I do not like to complain.'

'Do you know what I would advise you to do?'

He started, and glared at her.

'What you need is to have this place given a thorough cleaning. You'll never get well breathing up all this dust. And you're certainly not strong enough to tackle it yourself. What you must do is to go to one of those shops where they sell Hoovers and ask them to send a man to demonstrate it.'

His laugh, still a merry charming laugh under its grime of malevolence, rang out. 'That is what I call a genial idea. Then I tell him I'll think it over, eh? Perhaps it would be surer if I paid a first deposit?'

'I didn't.'

'What? You did this yourself? Splendid!'

For he was so abjectly undeserving, so unsuccourably an alien and a misfit, that she had to re-establish some sort of contact, grease the slide for Mrs. Bernstein's money to flow into that cold quicksand of a pocket. Loyalty to Mrs. Bernstein dictated that. If Mrs. Bernstein did not help him, no one else would, since no one could possibly better him. But as she went homeward to her tidy studio, her tidy modest industry, the illustrations for *Jennifer Sees It Through* on her desk and the blue abstract on her easel, she was so filled with discouragement that she seemed to herself be going nowhere at all.

* * *

Locking the door and waiting to make sure that this time the cheating hag's ugly feet had carried her downstairs and away, Mr. Herzen savoured the moment when he would turn back to his dirt, his solitude, his paradise and great work of art. He turned. There it was, his own, and grimier and grander than ever before, having been acknowledged by her submission and astonishment. How she had stared, pretending not to stare! And she had not seen the whole. She had not seen his bedroom, the skylight opened to the sooty rain, the spatterings from medicine bottles soiling the walls, the morass of dirty socks left steeping in the wash-basin—a splendid passage, one of his best. She had not seen the kitchenette. But she had seen enough to know what he thought of the bright little reformatory they had designed for him—insulting his misery with light paint and flowery walls—and to know that he was not a man to swallow insults. From the first moment of waking in this bourgeois kennel he had realized what to do with it, he had foreseen the masterpiece that he and time would create between them, stroke by patient stroke. 'How do you like it?' the woman had asked, bringing him his money. And he had replied that every day he liked it better. For even then, though she was blind to it, the masterpiece was taking form and the first cobwebs were mustering in the corners. Slow to get under way, tantalizingly slow and fitful, the process of deterioration had gathered impetus, sweeping him along with it, inspiring him to spill and scorch and knock over, so that whatever he did prompted a new invention of filth and squalor. And then, impalpable as a vapour, the quality of perfection had emerged, grave and austere, wrapping his inventions and contrivances and laboured-at dinginess in a solemn veil of inhumanity. Now when he went out, it was not to escape from the discommodities of creation, the dust that choked him, the fœtor that sickened him, but in order to return like a priest returning to the shrine, like a ghoul entering the rich charnel house and musingly rubbing its palms together as it looks round. Absorbed in his task, he had forgotten the motive that dictated it, the piece of grit round which this black pearl had accumulated.

Though the woman's intrusion had brought him that confirming satisfaction, she was superfluous; he did not require the assent of her dismay. Perfection and the Whole had come before her. He would not open the door again.

But the envelope must be attended to. It lay on the floor, pert, crisp and alien. He set his heel on it, grinding it to and fro on the dirty carpet. A cloud of dust flew up. When he lifted his heel and looked at the envelope, it had learned its place. It subserved a work of art.

II.11

"Another Case of Ingratitude"

John Reed

American journalist and author John Reed (1887–1920) was widely known for his eyewitness account of the 1917 October Revolution in Russia, *Ten Days That Shook the World,* as well as for his radical political activities. Shortly after the Russian Revolution, he returned to the United States to organize the Communist Labor Party. Later, when charged with sedition, he fled to Moscow, where he remained until his premature death from typhus. Though this early short story by Reed, "Another Case of Ingratitude" (1913), seems not to carry any overt political teaching, one wonders, by its end, whether one is meant to sympathize with the down-and-out worker or with his would-be benefactor. Reed's seemingly well-intentioned philanthropist takes a poor fellow who is, literally, on his last (and frozen) leg out of the bitter cold, buys him a warm, hearty meal, and gives him money for a night's lodging. As the poor fellow revives, his benefactor tries to engage him in conversation, but the questions he asks are unwelcome, and his motives for doing good are impugned. Should the benefactor have behaved differently? If so, at what point and how? Should the worker have behaved differently? Again, if so, at what point and how?

Walking late down Fifth Avenue, I saw him ahead of me, on the dim stretch of sidewalk between two arc-lights. It was biting cold. Head sunk between hunched-up shoulders, hands in his pockets, he shuffled along, never lifting his feet from the ground. Even as I watched him, he turned, as if in a daze, and leaned against the wall of a building, where it made an angle out of the wind. At first I thought it was shelter he sought, but as I drew nearer I discerned the unnatural stiffness of his legs, the way his cheek pressed against the cold stone, and the glimmer of light that played on his sunken, closed eyes. The man was asleep!

Asleep—the bitter wind searching his flimsy clothes and the holes in his shapeless shoes; upright against the hard wall, with his legs rigid as an epileptic's. There was something bestial in such gluttony of sleep.

From *Adventures of a Young Man: Short Stories from Life* (San Francisco: City Lights, 1975), pp. 47–50.

I shook him by the shoulder. He slowly opened an eye, cringing as though he were often disturbed by rougher hands than mine, and gazed at me with hardly a trace of intelligence.

"What's the matter—sick?" I asked.

Faintly and dully he mumbled something, and at the same time stepped out as if to move away. I asked him what he said, bending close to hear.

"No sleep for two nights," came the thick voice. "Nothing to eat for three days." He stood there obediently under the touch of my hand, swaying a little, staring vacantly at me with eyes that hung listlessly between opening and shutting.

"Well, come on," I said, "we'll go get something to eat and I'll fix you up with a bed." Docilely he followed me, stumbling along like a man in a dream, falling forward and then balancing himself with a step. From time to time his thick lips gave utterance to husky, irrelevant words and phrases. "Got to sleep walking around," he said again and again. "They keep moving me on."

I took his arm and guided him into the white door of an all-night lunch-room. I sat him at a table, where he dropped into a dead sleep. I set before him roast beef, and mashed potatoes, and two ham sandwiches, and a cup of coffee, and bread and butter, and a big piece of pie. And then I woke him up. He looked up at me with a dawning meaning in his expression. The look of humble gratitude, love, devotion was almost canine in its intensity. I felt a warm thrill of Christian brotherhood all through my veins. I sat back and watched him eat.

At first he went at it awkwardly, as if he had lost the habit. Mechanically he employed little tricks of table manners—perhaps his mother had taught them to him. He fumblingly changed knife and fork from right hand to left, and then put down his knife and took a dainty piece of bread in his left hand; removed the spoon from his coffee cup before he drank, and spread butter thinly and painstakingly on his bread. His motions were so somnambulistic that I had a strange feeling of looking on a previous incarnation of the man.

As the dinner progressed, a marvelous change took place. The warmth and nourishment, heating and feeding his thin blood, flooded the nerve centers of that starving body; a quick flush mounted to his cheeks, every part of him started widely awake, his eyes glowed. The little niceties of manner dropped away as if they had never been. He slopped his bread roughly in the gravy, and thrust huge knife-loads of food into his mouth. The coffee vanished in great gulps. He became an individual instead of a descendant; where there had been a beast, a spirit lived; he was a man!

The metamorphosis was so exciting that I could hardly wait to learn more about him. I held in, however, until he had finished his dinner.

As the last of the pie disappeared, I drew forth a box of cigarettes and placed them before him. He took one and accepted one of my matches. "T'anks!" he said.

"How much will it cost you for a bed—a quarter?" I asked.

"Yeh," he answered. "T'anks!"

He sat looking rather nervously at the table—inhaling great clouds of smoke. It was my opportunity.

"What's the matter—no work?"

He looked me in the eye, for the first time since dinner had begun, in a surprised manner. "Sure," he said briefly. I noticed, with somewhat of a shock, that his eyes were gray, whereas I had thought them brown.

"What's your job?"

He didn't answer for a moment. "Bricklayer," he grunted. What was the matter with the man?

"Where do you come from?"

Même jeu. "Albany."

"Been here long?"

"Say," said my guest, leaning over. "Wot do you t'ink I am, a phonygraft?"

For a moment I was speechless with surprise. "Why, I was only asking to make conversation," I said feebly.

"Naw, you wasn't. You t'ought just because you give me a hand-out, I'd do a sob-story all over you. Wot right have you got to ask me all them questions? I know you fellers. Just because you got money you t'ink you can buy me with a meal. . . ."

"Nonsense!" I cried. "I do this perfectly unselfishly. What do you think I get out of feeding you?"

He lit another one of my cigarettes.

"You get all you want," he smiled. "Come on now, don't it make you feel good all over to save a poor starvin' bum's life? God! You're pure and holy for a week!"

"Well, you're a strange specimen," I said angrily. "I don't believe you've got a bit of gratitude in you."

"Gratitude Hell!" said he easily. "Wot for? I'm t'anking my luck, not you— see? It might as well 'a' been me as any other bum. But if you hadn't struck me, you'd 'a' hunted up another down-and-outer. You see," he leaned across the table, explaining, "you just had to save somebody tonight. I understand. I got an appetite like that, too. Only mine's women."

Whereupon I left that ungrateful bricklayer and went to wake up Drusilla, who alone understands me.

II.12

"The Lovers of the Poor"

Gwendolyn Brooks

In this poem, African American poet laureate and novelist Gwendolyn Brooks (1917–2000) provides a rather cynical and devastating portrait of the philanthropic ladies from the "Ladies' Betterment League." The "Ladies" have traveled all the way from their well-appointed, comfortable suburban homes to the homes of their squalid urban neighbors, in order to give them money. "Largesse to the Lost," Brooks calls it. Thanks to her deft and poignant images, as well as to her own omnipresent view, Brooks manages to make every aspect of this charitable effort seem utterly offensive, not only to the ladies but to those they intend to help, as well. Are the "Ladies" as useless as Brooks would have us believe? Might Brooks's own attitude be "another case of ingratitude" (see story by John Reed)? Given what we are told about where the "Ladies" come from and what drives them to want to do good, and assuming that relief for the poor is a worthy end, what advice would you give them about how to proceed in the future?

                          arrive. The Ladies from the Ladies' Betterment League
Arrive in the afternoon, the late light slanting
In diluted gold bars across the boulevard brag
Of proud, seamed faces with mercy and murder hinting
Here, there, interrupting, all deep and debonair,
The pink paint on the innocence of fear;
Walk in a gingerly manner up the hall.
Cutting with knives served by their softest care,
Served by their love, so barbarously fair.
Whose mothers taught: You'd better not be cruel!

You had better not throw stones upon the wrens!
Herein they kiss and coddle and assault
Anew and dearly in the innocence
With which they baffle nature. Who are full,

From *Selected Poems* (New York: Harper & Row Publishers, Inc., 1963), pp. 90–93. Reprinted by permission of the Estate of Gwendolyn Brooks.

Sleek, tender-clad, fit, fiftyish, a-glow, all
Sweetly abortive, hinting at fat fruit,
Judge it high time that fiftyish fingers felt
Beneath the lovelier planes of enterprise.
To resurrect. To moisten with milky chill.
To be a random hitching-post or plush.
To be, for wet eyes, random and handy hem.
              Their guild is giving money to the poor.
The worthy poor. The very very worthy
And beautiful poor. Perhaps just not too swarthy?
Perhaps just not too dirty nor too dim
Nor—passionate. In truth, what they could wish
Is—something less than derelict or dull.
Not staunch enough to stab, though, gaze for gaze!
God shield them sharply from the beggar-bold!
The noxious needy ones whose battle's bald
Nonetheless for being voiceless, hits one down.
              But it's all so bad! and entirely too much for them.
The stench; the urine, cabbage, and dead beans,
Dead porridges of assorted dusty grains,
The old smoke, *heavy* diapers, and, they're told,
Something called chitterlings. The darkness: Drawn
Darkness, or dirty light. The soil that stirs.
The soil that looks the soil of centuries.
And for that matter the general oldness. Old
Wood. Old marble. Old tile. Old old old.
Not homekind Oldness! Not Lake Forest, Glencoe.
Nothing is sturdy, nothing is majestic,
There is no quiet drama, no rubbed glaze, no
Unkillable infirmity of such
A tasteful turn as lately they have left,
Glencoe, Lake Forest, and to which their cars
Must presently restore them. When they're done
With dullards and distortions of this fistic
Patience of the poor and put-upon.
              They've never seen such a make-do-ness as
Newspaper rugs before! In this, this "flat,"
Their hostess is gathering up the oozed, the rich
Rugs of the morning (tattered! the bespattered. . . .)

Readies to spread clean rugs for afternoon.
Here is a scene for you. The Ladies look,
In horror, behind a substantial citizeness
Whose trains clank out across her swollen heart.

Who, arms akimbo, almost fills a door.
All tumbling children, quilts dragged to the floor
And tortured thereover, potato peelings, soft-
Eyed kitten, hunched-up, haggard, to-be-hurt.
                Their League is allotting largesse to the Lost.
But to put their clean, their pretty money, to put
Their money collected from delicate rose-fingers
Tipped with their hundred flawless rose-nails seems . . .
                They own Spode, Lowestoft, candelabra,
Mantels, and hostess gowns, and sunburst clocks,
Turtle soup, Chippendale, red satin "hangings,"
Aubussons and Hattie Carnegie. They Winter
In Palm Beach; cross the Water in June; attend,
When suitable, the nice Art Institute;
Buy the right books in the best bindings; saunter
On Michigan, Easter mornings, in sun or wind.
Oh Squalor! This sick four-story hulk, this fibre
With fissures everywhere! Why, what are bringings
Of loathe-love largesse? What shall peril hungers
So old old, what shall flatter the desolate?
Tin can, blocked fire escape and chitterling
And swaggering seeking youth and the puzzled wreckage
Of the middle passage, and urine and stale shames
And, again, the porridges of the underslung
And children children children. Heavens! That
Was a rat, surely, off there, in the shadows? Long
And long-tailed? Gray? The Ladies from the Ladies'
Betterment League agree it will be better
To achieve the outer air that rights and steadies,
To hie to a house that does not holler, to ring
Bells elsetime, better presently to cater
To no more Possibilities, to get
Away. Perhaps the money can be posted.
Perhaps they two may choose another Slum!
Some serious sooty half-unhappy home!—
Where loathe-love likelier may be invested.
                Keeping their scented bodies in the center
Of the hall as they walk down the hysterical hall,
They allow their lovely skirts to graze no wall,
Are off at what they manage of a canter,
And, resuming all the clues of what they were,
Try to avoid inhaling the laden air.

PART THREE

To Whom or for What Should I Give?

Part III: Table of Contents

Genesis 25:19–34; 27–28:9, Parents and Children: The Case of Jacob and Esau

Matthew 25:14–30, The Parable of the Talents

William Shakespeare, *Timon of Athens,* Act I, Scene 1

William H. McGuffey, "True and False Philanthropy"

Andrew Carnegie, "The Gospel of Wealth"

Henri Barbusse, "The Eleventh"

Stephen Leacock, "Mr. Plumter, B.A., Revisits the Old Shop"

Stephen Crane, "The Men in the Storm"

Leon R. Kass, "Charity and the Confines of Compassion"

III.1

Parents and Children:
The Case of Jacob and Esau

Genesis 25:19–34; 27–28:9

The biblical story of the twin brothers Jacob and Esau turns our attention to matters of inheritance and their effect on families. True, the stakes are higher than they are for most of us: in this case, deciding who gets the inheritance—here referred to as the birthright—is tantamount to deciding not only who will be preeminent in responsibility for the household, but also who will be the leader of the holy nation founded by Abraham. But the questions raised by the story persist. Even when they are still in her womb, Rebekah realizes that there are great differences between her sons, which are borne out as they grow up. Esau (literally the "hairy" or "shaggy" one), the "older" twin, becomes a hunter, a man of the field. Jacob (literally "heel-catcher," "supplanter," or "deceiver"), the "younger," is from the start far more of a homebody. Mother Rebekah favors Jacob, but father Isaac prefers Esau, who, thanks to the practice of primogeniture, is automatically in line to receive the birthright. In time, however, Jacob contrives to get Esau to part with the birthright. Subsequently, Jacob, directed and abetted by Rebekah, tricks Isaac into giving him the blessing intended for Esau, thus sealing his right to the inheritance. Despite the trickery, when Isaac realizes his mistake (27:33), he does not try to rectify it. Indeed, before Jacob leaves home, which he must do in order to escape the ire of his brother, Isaac blesses him again (28:3–4), this time on his own initiative and with the Abrahamic blessing. In the end, so it seems, Isaac endorses Jacob's ambition and Rebekah's preference. Why? Has Jacob shown himself to be the best man for the "job"? Has Esau shown himself to be unfit? Imagine yourself nearing the end of your life and with a similarly, if not equally, precious and important inheritance to give to your children. How would you decide to whom to give it? To what extent would—should—the differences among your children matter? Which differences, if any, ought to matter most?

From *The Holy Bible,* King James version (New York: American Bible Company).

The Birth of Esau and Jacob

25 19 ¶ And these *are* the generations of Isaac, Abraham's son: Abraham begat Isaac:

20 and Isaac was forty years old when he took Rebekah to wife, the daughter of Bethu'el the Syrian of Pa'dan-a'ram, the sister to Laban the Syrian.

21 And Isaac entreated the LORD for his wife, because she *was* barren: and the LORD was entreated of him, and Rebekah his wife conceived.

22 And the children struggled together within her; and she said, If *it be so,* why *am* I thus? And she went to inquire of the LORD.

23 And the LORD said unto her,

> Two nations *are* in thy womb,
> and two manner of people shall be separated from thy bowels:
> and *the one* people shall be stronger than *the other* people;
> and the elder shall serve the younger.

24 And when her days to be delivered were fulfilled, behold, *there were* twins in her womb.

25 And the first came out red, all over like a hairy garment; and they called his name Esau.

26 And after that came his brother out, and his hand took hold on Esau's heel; and his name was called Jacob; and Isaac *was* threescore years old when she bare them.

Esau Sells His Birthright

27 ¶ And the boys grew: and Esau was a cunning hunter, a man of the field; and Jacob *was* a plain man, dwelling in tents.

28 And Isaac loved Esau, because he did eat of *his* venison: But Rebekah loved Jacob.

29 ¶ And Jacob sod pottage: and Esau came from the field, and he *was* faint:

30 and Esau said to Jacob, Feed me, I pray thee, with that same red *pottage;* for I *am* faint: therefore was his name called Edom [literally, red].

31 And Jacob said, Sell me this day thy birthright.

32 And Esau said, Behold, I *am* at the point to die: and what profit shall this birthright do to me?

33 And Jacob said, Swear to me this day; and he sware unto him: and he sold his birthright unto Jacob.

34 Then Jacob gave Esau bread and pottage of lentils; and he did eat and drink, and rose up, and went his way. Thus Esau despised *his* birthright.

Jacob Obtains Isaac's Blessing

27 And it came to pass, that when Isaac was old, and his eyes were dim, so that he could not see, he called Esau his eldest son, and said unto him, My son: and he said unto him, Behold, *here am* I.

2 And he said, Behold now, I am old, I know not the day of my death:

3 now therefore take, I pray thee, thy weapons, thy quiver and thy bow, and go out to the field, and take me *some* venison;

4 and make me savory meat, such as I love, and bring *it* to me, that I may eat; that my soul may bless thee before I die.

5 ¶ And Rebekah heard when Isaac spake to Esau his son. And Esau went to the field to hunt *for* venison, *and* to bring *it.*

6 And Rebekah spake unto Jacob her son, saying, Behold, I heard thy father speak unto Esau thy brother, saying,

7 Bring me venison, and make me savory meat, that I may eat, and bless thee before the LORD before my death.

8 Now therefore, my son, obey my voice according to that which I command thee.

9 Go now to the flock, and fetch me from thence two good kids of the goats; and I will make them savory meat for thy father, such as he loveth:

10 and thou shalt bring *it* to thy father, that he may eat, and that he may bless thee before his death.

11 And Jacob said to Rebekah his mother, Behold, Esau my brother *is* a hairy man, and I *am* a smooth man:

12 my father peradventure will feel me, and I shall seem to him as a deceiver; and I shall bring a curse upon me, and not a blessing.

13 And his mother said unto him, Upon me *be* thy curse, my son: only obey my voice, and go fetch me *them.*

14 And he went, and fetched, and brought *them* to his mother: and his mother made savory meat, such as his father loved.

15 And Rebekah took goodly raiment of her eldest son Esau, which *were* with her in the house, and put them upon Jacob her younger son:

16 and she put the skins of the kids of the goats upon his hands, and upon the smooth of his neck:

17 and she gave the savory meat and the bread, which she had prepared, into the hand of her son Jacob.

18 ¶ And he came unto his father, and said, My father: and he said, Here *am* I; who *art* thou, my son?

19 And Jacob said unto his father, I *am* Esau thy firstborn; I have done according as thou badest me: arise, I pray thee, sit and eat of my venison, that thy soul may bless me.

20 And Isaac said unto his son, How *is it* that thou hast found *it* so quickly, my son? And he said, Because the LORD thy God brought *it* to me.

21 And Isaac said unto Jacob, Come near, I pray thee, that I may feel thee, my son, whether thou *be* my very son Esau or not.

22 And Jacob went near unto Isaac his father; and he felt him, and said, The voice *is* Jacob's voice, but the hands *are* the hands of Esau.

23 And he discerned him not, because his hands were hairy, as his brother Esau's hands: so he blessed him.

24 And he said, *Art* thou my very son Esau? And he said, I *am.*

25 And he said, Bring *it* near to me, and I will eat of my son's venison, that my soul may bless thee. And he brought *it* near to him, and he did eat: and he brought him wine, and he drank.

26 And his father Isaac said unto him, Come near now, and kiss me, my son.

27 And he came near, and kissed him: and he smelled the smell of his raiment, and blessed him, and said,

> See, the smell of my son
> *is* as the smell of a field which the LORD hath blessed:
> 28   therefore God give thee of the dew of heaven,
> and the fatness of the earth,
> and plenty of corn and wine:
> 29   let people serve thee,
>   and nations bow down to thee:
>   be lord over thy brethren,
>   and let thy mother's sons bow down to thee:
>   cursed *be* every one that curseth thee,
>   and blessed *be* he that blesseth thee.

30 ¶ And it came to pass, as soon as Isaac had made an end of blessing Jacob, and Jacob was yet scarce gone out from the presence of Isaac his father, that Esau his brother came in from his hunting.

31 And he also had made savory meat, and brought it unto his father, and said unto his father, Let my father arise, and eat of his son's venison, that thy soul may bless me.

32 And Isaac his father said unto him, Who *art* thou? And he said, I *am* thy son, thy firstborn, Esau.

33 And Isaac trembled very exceedingly, and said, Who? where *is* he that hath taken venison, and brought *it* me, and I have eaten of all before thou camest, and have blessed him? yea, *and* he shall be blessed.

34 And when Esau heard the words of his father, he cried with a great and exceeding bitter cry, and said unto his father, Bless me, *even* me also, O my father.

35   And he said, Thy brother came with subtlety, and hath taken away thy blessing.

36   And he said, Is not he rightly named Jacob? for he hath supplanted me these two times: he took away my birthright; and, behold, now he hath taken away my blessing. And he said, Hast thou not reserved a blessing for me?

37   And Isaac answered and said unto Esau, Behold, I have made him thy lord, and all his brethren have I given to him for servants; and with corn and wine have I sustained him: and what shall I do now unto thee, my son?

38   And Esau said unto his father, Hast thou but one blessing, my father? bless me, *even* me also, O my father. And Esau lifted up his voice, and wept.

39   ¶ And Isaac his father answered and said unto him,

> Behold, thy dwelling shall be the fatness of the earth,
> and of the dew of heaven from above;
> 40   and by thy sword shalt thou live,
> and shalt serve thy brother:
> and it shall come to pass when thou shalt have the dominion, ·
> that thou shalt break his yoke from off thy neck.

Jacob Flees from Esau

41   ¶ And Esau hated Jacob because of the blessing wherewith his father blessed him: and Esau said in his heart, The days of mourning for my father are at hand; then will I slay my brother Jacob.

42   And these words of Esau her elder son were told to Rebekah: and she sent and called Jacob her younger son, and said unto him, Behold, thy brother Esau, as touching thee, doth comfort himself, *purposing* to kill thee.

43   Now therefore, my son, obey my voice; and arise, flee thou to Laban my brother to Haran;

44   and tarry with him a few days, until thy brother's fury turn away;

45   until thy brother's anger turn away from thee, and he forget *that* which thou hast done to him: then I will send, and fetch thee from thence: why should I be deprived also of you both in one day?

46   ¶ And Rebekah said to Isaac, I am weary of my life because of the daughters of Heth [Esau's wives]: if Jacob take a wife of the daughters of Heth, such as these *which are* of the daughters of the land, what good shall my life do me?

28 And Isaac called Jacob, and blessed him, and charged him, and said unto him, Thou shalt not take a wife of the daughters of Canaan.

2   Arise, go to Pa'dan-a'ram, to the house of Bethu'el thy mother's father; and take thee a wife from thence of the daughters of Laban thy mother's brother.

3   And God Almighty bless thee, and make thee fruitful, and multiply thee, that thou mayest be a multitude of people;

4 and give thee the blessing of Abraham, to thee, and to thy seed with thee; that thou mayest inherit the land wherein thou art a stranger, which God gave unto Abraham.

5 And Isaac sent away Jacob: and he went to Pa'dan-a'ram unto Laban, son of Bethu'el the Syrian, the brother of Rebekah, Jacob's and Esau's mother.

6 ❡ When Esau saw that Isaac had blessed Jacob, and sent him away to Pa'-dan-a'ram, to take him a wife from thence; and that as he blessed him he gave him a charge, saying, Thou shalt not take a wife of the daughters of Canaan;

7 and that Jacob obeyed his father and his mother, and was gone to Pa'-dan-a'ram;

8 and Esau seeing that the daughters of Canaan pleased not Isaac his father;

9 then went Esau unto Ish'ma-el, and took unto the wives which he had Ma'-halath the daughter of Ish'ma-el Abraham's son, the sister of Neba'joth, to be his wife.

III.2

The Parable of the Talents

Matthew 25:14–30

Jesus' parables not only speak, at once, to multiple audiences, they often-times carry multiple messages. This is conspicuously true of this parable of the talents. In its immediate context in Matthew's Gospel, as indicated above (see Part II), it seems primarily to invite reflection about how we ought to comport ourselves with respect to our native gifts. Considered by itself, outside of its context, it seems especially to invite reflection about who are fitting beneficiaries. So considered, it seems to shine a bright light on the choices so many of us make, albeit often only subconsciously. Its teaching on this matter seems, at least at first glance, counterintuitive: "Unto every one that hath shall be given, and he shall have abundance: but from him that hath not shall be taken away even that which he hath." Yet consider it. You are a person with a fortune (modest or otherwise) to dispense and a strong interest in supporting struggling artists. Whom do you support? Those who have already demonstrated some talent or those whose talent has yet to be seen? Or imagine yourself the principal of a struggling inner-city elementary school. Whom will you hire to teach first grade? The young idealist, fresh out of college, with a bag full of good intentions and even better ideas, or the person with years of teaching experience and an already proven track record? Evidence of talent and accomplishment—or, at the very least, consideration of such evidence—frequently plays a part in the decisions most of us make, especially when it is a matter of dispensing largesse to people outside the family. But how large a part should it play? What really justifies giving more to those who already have?

⸻

25 14 ⁋ For the *kingdom of heaven is* as a man traveling into a far country, *who* called his own servants, and delivered unto them his goods.

15   And unto one he gave five talents, to another two, and to another one; to every man according to his several ability; and straightway took his journey.

16   Then he that had received the five talents went and traded with the same, and made *them* other five talents.

From *The Holy Bible,* King James version (New York: American Bible Company).

17 And likewise he that *had received* two, he also gained other two.

18 But he that had received one went and digged in the earth, and hid his lord's money.

19 After a long time the lord of those servants cometh, and reckoneth with them.

20 And so he that had received five talents came and brought other five talents, saying, Lord, thou deliveredst unto me five talents: behold, I have gained beside them five talents more.

21 His lord said unto him, Well done, *thou* good and faithful servant: thou hast been faithful over a few things, I will make thee ruler over many things: enter thou into the joy of thy lord.

22 He also that had received two talents came and said, Lord, thou deliveredst unto me two talents: behold, I have gained two other talents beside them.

23 His lord said unto him, Well done, good and faithful servant; thou hast been faithful over a few things, I will make thee ruler over may things: enter thou into the joy of thy lord.

24 Then he which had received the one talent came and said, Lord, I knew thee that thou art a hard man, reaping where thou hast not sown, and gathering where thou hast not strewed:

25 and I was afraid, and went and hid thy talent in the earth: lo, *there* thou hast *that is* thine.

26 His lord answered and said unto him, *Thou* wicked and slothful servant, thou knewest that I reap where I sowed not, and gather where I have not strewed:

27 thou oughtest therefore to have put my money to the exchangers, and *then* at my coming I should have received mine own with usury.

28 Take therefore the talent from him and give *it* unto him which hath ten talents.

29 For unto every one that hath shall be given, and he shall have abundance: but from him that hath not shall be taken away even that which he hath.

30 And cast ye the unprofitable servant into outer darkness: there shall be weeping and gnashing of teeth.

III.3

Timon of Athens, Act I, Scene 1

William Shakespeare

Timon of Athens, one of the lesser-known plays by William Shakespeare (1564–1616) (according to some, in collaboration with Thomas Middleton [1580–1627]), traces the career of a rich and noble Athenian, Timon, from open-handed philanthropy to close-fisted misanthropy. Timon has given freely and often to all who requested assistance—friends, flatterers, and parasites alike—and thus when he, in turn, finds himself in need of help, he naturally turns to his own beneficiaries, some of whom have become well-to-do. Each, in turn, denies his request. Embittered and, in the end, utterly alone, he leaves Athens and becomes as prodigal in his misanthropy as he once was in his philanthropy. Act 1, Scene 1, reprinted in full below, presents a preview of the play's main action in the Poet's description of the allegory he has written. It also provides a vivid picture of the society in which Timon lives and amply makes manifest Timon's philanthropic ways. Even without the help of the allegory, one can probably anticipate what will happen to Timon. But where—with whom? with what?—does the problem lie? Of the various people or causes that Timon gives to in I,i, are there any he should not have responded to as he did? If so, what should he have said or done? How should he have decided whom or what to help? Is it true that most beneficiaries harbor hate for their "Timons"? If so, is there any way for "Timons" to avoid such a fate?

SCENE: *Athens. Timon's house.*

Enter Poet and Painter, Jeweller and Merchant, at several doors.

POET.
    Good day, sir.

PAINTER.   I am glad y'are well.

POET.
    I have not seen you long. How goes the world?

Shakespeare, *Timon of Athens,* Act I, Scene I, edited by G. R. Hibbard (London: Penguin Books, 1970), pp. 55–67.

PAINTER.
     It wears, sir, as it grows.
POET.   Ay, that's well known.
     But what particular rarity? What strange,
     Which manifold record not matches? See,
     Magic of bounty, all these spirits thy power
     Hath conjured to attend! I know the merchant.
PAINTER.
      I know them both; th' other's a jeweller.
MERCHANT.
      O, 'tis a worthy lord!
JEWELLER.   Nay, that's most fixed.
MERCHANT.
     A most incomparable man, breathed, as it were,
     To an untirable and continuate goodness.
     He <u>passes.</u>   excels
JEWELLER.
     I have a jewel here—
MERCHANT.
     O pray, let's see't. For the Lord Timon, sir?
JEWELLER.
     If he will touch the estimate. But for that—
POET *(reciting to himself)*
     'When we for recompense have praised the vile,
     It stains the glory in that happy verse
     Which aptly sings the good.'
MERCHANT *(looking at the jewel)*   'Tis a good form.
JEWELLER.
     And rich. Here is a water, look ye.
PAINTER.
     You are rapt, sir, in some work, some dedication
     To the great lord.
POET.   A thing slipped idly from me.
     Our poesy is as a gum which oozes
     From whence 'tis nourished. The fire i' th' flint
     Shows not till it be struck. Our gentle flame
     Provokes itself, and like the current flies
     Each bound it chafes. What have you there?
PAINTER.
     A picture, sir. When comes your book forth?

POET.

    Upon the heels of my presentment, sir.

    Let's see your piece.

PAINTER.

    'Tis a good piece.

POET.

    So 'tis. This comes off well and excellent.

PAINTER.

    Indifferent.

POET.   Admirable. How this grace

    Speaks his own standing! What a mental power

    This eye shoots forth! How big imagination

    Moves in this lip! To th' dumbness of the gesture

    One might interpret.

PAINTER.

    It is a pretty mocking of the life.

    Here is a touch. Is't good?

POET.   I will say of it,

    It tutors nature. Artificial strife

    Lives in these touches livelier than life.

    Enter certain senators, and pass over the stage.

PAINTER.

    How this lord is followed!

POET.

    The senators of Athens—happy man!

PAINTER.

    Look, more!

POET.

    You see this confluence, this great flood of visitors.

    I have in this rough work shaped out a man

    Whom this beneath world doth embrace and hug

    With amplest entertainment. My free <u>drift</u>   aim

    Halts not particularly, but moves itself

    In a wide sea of tax. No levelled malice

    Infects one comma in the course I hold,

    But flies an eagle flight, bold and forth on,

    Leaving no tract behind.

PAINTER.

    How shall I understand you?

POET.

    I will <u>unbolt</u> to you   *explain*

    You see how all conditions, how all minds,

    As well of glib and slipp'ry creatures as

    Of grave and austere quality, tender down

    Their services to Lord Timon. His large fortune,

    Upon his good and gracious nature hanging,

    Subdues and properties to his love and tendance

    All sorts of hearts; yea, from the glass-faced flatterer

    To Apemantus, that few things loves better

    Than to abhor himself—even he drops down

    The knee before him, and returns in peace

    Most rich in Timon's nod.

PAINTER.

    I saw them speak together.

POET.   Sir,

    I have upon a high and pleasant hill

    Feigned Fortune to be throned. The base o' th' mount

    Is ranked with all deserts, all kind of natures

    That labour on the bosom of this sphere

    To propagate their states. Amongst them all

    Whose eyes are on this sovereign lady fixed

    One do I personate of Lord Timon's frame,

    Whom Fortune with her ivory hand wafts to her,

    Whose present grace <u>to present</u> slaves and servants   *immediately to*

    <u>Translates</u> his rivals.   *transforms*

PAINTER.   'Tis conceived <u>to scope.</u>   *aptly*

    This throne, this Fortune, and this hill, methinks,

    With one man beckoned from the rest below,

    Bowing his head against the steepy mount

    To climb his happiness, would be well expressed

    In our condition.

POET.   Nay sir, but hear me on.

    All those which were his fellows but of late—

    Some better than his value—on the moment

    Follow his strides, his lobbies fill with tendance,

    Rain sacrificial whisperings in his ear,

    Make sacred even his stirrup, and through him

    Drink the free air.

PAINTER.   Ay, marry, what of these?

POET.

> When Fortune in her shift and change of mood
> Spurns down her late beloved, all his dependants,
> Which laboured after him to the mountain's top
> Even on their knees and hands, let him fall down,
> Not one accompanying his declining foot.

PAINTER.

> 'Tis common.
> A thousand moral paintings I can show
> That shall demonstrate these quick blows of Fortune's,
> More pregnantly than words. Yet you do well,
> To show Lord Timon that mean eyes have seen
> The foot above the head.

> *Trumpets sound. Enter Lord Timon, addressing himself courteously to*
> *every suitor; a Messenger from Ventidius (friend of Timon's) talking*
> *with him; Lucilius (Timon's servant) and other servants following.*

TIMON.

> Imprisoned is he, say you?

VENTIDIUS' SERVANT.

> Ay, my good lord. Five talents is his debt,
> His means most short, his creditors most strait.
> Your honourable letter he desires
> To those have shut him up, which failing
> <u>Periods</u> his comfort.   ends

TIMON.   Noble Ventidius! Well,

> I am not of that feather to shake off
> My friend when he must need me. I do know him
> A gentleman that well deserves a help,
> Which he shall have. I'll pay the debt, and free him.

VENTIDIUS' SERVANT.

> Your lordship ever <u>binds him</u>.   attaches by gratitude

TIMON.

> Commend me to him. I will send his ransom;
> And, being enfranchised, bid him come to me.
> 'Tis not enough to help the feeble up,
> But to support him after. Fare you well.

VENTIDIUS' SERVANT.

> All happiness to your honour!   *Exit*

Enter an Old Athenian.

OLD ATHENIAN.
 Lord Timon, hear me speak.
TIMON.   Freely, good father.
OLD ATHENIAN.
 Thou hast a servant named Lucilius.
TIMON.
 I have so. What of him?
OLD ATHENIAN.
 Most noble Timon, call the man before thee.
TIMON.
 Attends he here, or no? Lucilius!
LUCILIUS.
 Here, at your lordship's service.
OLD ATHENIAN.
 This fellow here, Lord Timon, this thy creature,
 By night frequents my house. I am a man
 That from my first have been inclined to thrift,
 And my estate deserves an heir more raised
 Than one which <u>holds a trencher</u>.   waits tables
TIMON.   Well, what further?
OLD ATHENIAN.
 One only daughter have I, no kin else,
 On whom I may confer what I have got.
 The maid is fair, o'th' youngest for a bride,
 And I have bred her at my dearest cost
 In qualities of the best. This man of thine
 Attempts her love. I prithee, noble lord,
 Join with me to forbid him her resort;
 Myself have spoke in vain.
TIMON.   The man is honest.
OLD ATHENIAN.
 Therefore he will be, Timon.
 His honesty rewards him in itself;
 It must not bear my daughter.
TIMON.   Does she love him?
OLD ATHENIAN.
 She is young and apt.
 Our own precedent passions do instruct us
 What levity's in youth.
TIMON *(to Lucilius)*   Love you the maid?

LUCILIUS.

    Ay, my good lord, and she accepts of it.

OLD ATHENIAN.

    If in her marriage my consent be missing,

    I call the gods to witness, I will choose

    Mine heir from forth the beggars of the world,

    And dispossess her all.

TIMON.   How shall she be endowed

    If she be mated with an equal husband?

OLD ATHENIAN.

    Three talents on the present; in future, all.

TIMON.

    This gentleman of mine hath served me long.

    To build his fortune I will strain a little,

    For 'tis a bond in men. Give him thy daughter.

    What you bestow, in him I'll counterpoise,

    And make him weigh with her.

OLD ATHENIAN.   Most noble lord,

    Pawn me to this your honour, she is his.

TIMON.

    My hand to thee; mine honour on my promise.

LUCILIUS.

    Humbly I thank your lordship. Never may

    That state or fortune fall into my keeping

    Which is not owed to you.

    Exit Lucilius and Old Athenian.

POET *(presenting a poem)*

    Vouchsafe my labour, and long live your lordship!

TIMON.

    I thank you; you shall hear from me anon.

    Go not away. *(To Painter)* What have you there, my friend?

PAINTER.

    A piece of painting, which I do beseech

    Your lordship to accept.

TIMON.   Painting is welcome.

    The painting is almost the natural man;

    For since dishonour traffics with man's nature,

    He is but outside; these pencilled figures are

    Even such as they give out. I like your work,

    And you shall find I like it. Wait attendance

    Till you hear further from me.

PAINTER.   The gods preserve ye!

TIMON.

    Well fare you, gentleman. Give me your hand.

    We must needs dine together. *(To Jeweller)* Sir, your jewel

    Hath suffered under praise.

JEWELLER.   What, my lord, dispraise?

TIMON.

    A mere satiety of commendations.

    If I should pay you for't as 'tis extolled,

    It would <u>unclew</u> me quite.   ruin

JEWELLER.   My lord, 'tis rated

    As those which sell would give. But you well know,

    Things of like value, differing in the owners,

    Are prized <u>by</u> their masters. Believe't, dear lord,   according to

    You mend the jewel by the wearing it.

TIMON.

    Well mocked.

    Enter Apemantus. (A Cynic philosopher.)

MERCHANT.

    No, my good lord; he speaks the common tongue

    Which all men speak with him.

TIMON.

    Look who comes here. Will you be chid?

JEWELLER.

    We'll bear, with your lordship.

MERCHANT.   He'll spare none.

TIMON.

    Good morrow to thee, gentle Apemantus.

APEMANTUS.

    Till I be gentle, stay thou for thy good morrow,

    When thou art Timon's dog, and these knaves honest.

TIMON.

    Why dost thou call them knaves? Thou knowest them not.

APEMANTUS.

    Are they not Athenians?

TIMON.

    Yes.

APEMANTUS.

    Then I repent not.

JEWELLER.
> You know me, Apemantus?

APEMANTUS.
> Thou knowest I do. I called thee by thy name.

TIMON.
> Thou art proud, Apemantus.

APEMANTUS.
> Of nothing so much as that I am not like Timon.

TIMON.
> Whither art going?

APEMANTUS.
> To knock out an honest Athenian's brains.

TIMON.
> That's a deed thou'lt die for.

APEMANTUS.
> Right, if doing nothing be death by th' law.

TIMON.
> How likest thou this picture, Apemantus?

APEMANTUS.
> The best, for the innocence.

TIMON.
> Wrought he not well that painted it?

APEMANTUS.   He wrought better that made the painter,
and yet he's but a filthy piece of work.

PAINTER.   Y'are a dog.

APEMANTUS.   Thy mother's of my generation. What's
she, if I be a dog?

TIMON.   Wilt dine with me, Apemantus?

APEMANTUS.   No. I eat not lords.

TIMON.   <u>An</u> thou shouldst, thou'dst anger ladies.   if

APEMANTUS.   O, they eat lords. So they come by great bellies.

TIMON.   That's a lascivious apprehension.

APEMANTUS.   So thou apprehendest it. Take it for thy labour.

TIMON.
> How dost thou like this jewel, Apemantus?

APEMANTUS.   Not so well as plain-dealing, which will
not cost a man a <u>doit.</u>   eighth of a penny

TIMON.   What dost thou think 'tis worth?

APEMANTUS.   Not worth my thinking. How now, poet!

POET.   How now, philosopher!

APEMANTUS.   Thou liest.

POET.   Art not one?

APEMANTUS.   Yes.

POET.   Then I lie not.

APEMANTUS.   Art not a poet?

POET.   Yes.

APEMANTUS.   Then thou liest. Look in thy last work,
    where thou hast feigned him a worthy fellow.

POET.   That's not feigned—he is so.

APEMANTUS.   Yes, he is worthy of thee, and to pay thee
    for thy labour. He that loves to be flattered is worthy
    o'th' flatterer. Heavens, that I were a lord!

TIMON.   What wouldst do then, Apemantus?

APEMANTUS.   E'en as Apemantus does now: hate a lord with my heart.

TIMON.   What, thyself?

APEMANTUS.   Ay.

TIMON.   Wherefore?

APEMANTUS.   That I had no angry wit to be a lord. —Art not thou
    a merchant?

MERCHANT.   Ay, Apemantus.

APEMANTUS.   <u>Traffic</u> confound thee, if the gods will not.   trade

MERCHANT.   If traffic do it, the gods do it.

APEMANTUS.   Traffic's thy god, and thy god confound thee!

    Trumpet sounds. Enter a Messenger.

TIMON.
    What trumpet's that?

MESSENGER.
    'Tis Alcibiades, and some twenty horse,
    All of companionship.

TIMON.
    Pray entertain them, give them guide to us.

                                   Exit some attendants.

    You must needs dine with me. Go not you hence
    Till I have thanked you. When dinner's done,
    Show me this piece. I am joyful of your sights.

    Enter Alcibiades, with the rest.

    Most welcome sir!

APEMANTUS.   So, so, there!
   Aches contract and <u>starve</u> your supple joints!   cause to wither
   That there should be small love amongst these sweet knaves,
   And all this courtesy! The strain of man's <u>bred out</u>   degenerated
   Into baboon and monkey.
ALCIBIADES.
   Sir, you have <u>saved my</u> longing, and I feed   kept me from further
   Most hungerly on your sight.
TIMON.   Right welcome, sir!
   Ere we depart, we'll share a bounteous time
   In different pleasures. Pray you, let us in.

                                Exit all but Apemantus.

   Enter two Lords.

FIRST LORD.   What time o' day is't, Apemantus?
APEMANTUS.   Time to be honest.
FIRST LORD.   That time serves <u>still.</u>   always
APEMANTUS.
   The most accursèd thou that still omittest it.
SECOND LORD.
   Thou art going to Lord Timon's feast?
APEMANTUS.
   Ay, to see meat fill knaves and wine heat fools.
SECOND LORD.
   Fare thee well, fare thee well.
APEMANTUS.
   Thou art a fool to bid me farewell twice.
SECOND LORD.   Why, Apemantus?
APEMANTUS.   Shouldst have kept one to thyself, for I
   mean to give thee none.
FIRST LORD.   Hang thyself.
APEMANTUS.   No, I will do nothing at thy bidding. Make
   thy requests to thy friend.
SECOND LORD.   Away, unpeaceable dog, or I'll spurn thee hence.
APEMANTUS.   I will fly, like a dog, the heels o'th' ass. *Exit.*
FIRST LORD.
   He's <u>opposite</u> to humanity.   hostile
   Come, shall we in
   And taste Lord Timon's bounty? He outgoes
   The very heart of kindness.

SECOND LORD.

    He pours it out. Plutus, the god of gold,

    Is but his steward. No <u>meed</u> but he repays   gift

    Sevenfold above itself; no gift to him

    But breeds the giver a return exceeding

    All <u>use of quittance</u>.   customary repayment

FIRST LORD.   The noblest mind he carries

    That ever governed man.

SECOND LORD.

    Long may he live in fortunes. Shall we in?

FIRST LORD.

    I'll keep you company.   *Exit.*

III.4

"True and False Philanthropy"

William H. McGuffey

Through his *Eclectic Readers*, American educator and preacher William Holmes McGuffey (1800–1873) had a profound effect on education in the United States, particularly in the areas of teacher training and curriculum materials. In the selection below, excerpted from McGuffey's *Newly Revised Eclectic Reader* (published in 1844), Mr. Fantom and Mr. Goodman have a rather heated conversation about how and where philanthropic effort ought to be applied. Both men seem to be moved primarily by the desire to offer relief. But Mr. Fantom thinks globally, whereas Mr. Goodman thinks locally: one wants to address the miseries of the "whole world," the other those of his own "town or neighborhood first." The names that McGuffey assigns to his interlocutors suggest his own preference for local giving over more diffuse and ambitious efforts. Is Goodman persuasive? Are the Fantoms of the world of philanthropy necessarily doomed to chase after illusions? Is the philanthropic way of one "true" and the other "false," as McGuffey's title implies?

Mr. Fantom: I despise a narrow field. O for the reign of universal benevolence! I want to make all mankind good and happy.

Mr. Goodman: Dear me! Sure that must be a wholesale sort of a job: had you not better try your hand at a *town* or *neighborhood* first?

Mr. Fantom: Sir, I have a plan in my head for relieving the miseries of the *whole world*. Every thing is bad as it now stands. I would alter all the laws, and put an end to all the wars in the world. I would put an end to all punishments; I would not leave a single prisoner on the face of the globe. *This* is what I call doing things on a grand scale.

Mr. Goodman: A scale with a vengeance! As to releasing the prisoners, however, I do not much like that, as it would be liberating a few rogues at the expense of all honest men; but as to the rest of your plan, if all countries would be so good as to turn *Christians,* it might be helped on a good deal. There would be still misery enough left indeed; because God intended

From *McGuffey's Newly Revised Eclectic Reader* (1844), reprinted in *America's Voluntary Spirit: A Book of Readings,* edited by Brian O'Connell (New York: Ford Foundation Center, 1983), pp. 59–61.

this world should be earth and not heaven. But, sir, among all your changes, you must destroy human corruption, before you can make the world quite as perfect as you pretend.

Mr. Fantom: *Your* project would rivet the chains which *mine* is designed to *break.*

Mr. Goodman: Sir, I have no projects. Projects are, in general, the offspring of restlessness, vanity, and idleness. I am too busy for projects, too contented for theories, and I hope, have too much honesty and humility for a philosopher. The utmost extent of my ambition at present is, to redress the wrongs of a poor apprentice, who has been cruelly used by his master: indeed, I have another little scheme, which is to prosecute a fellow, who has suffered a poor wretch in the poorhouse, of which he has the care, to perish through neglect, and you must assist me.

Mr. Fantom: Let the town do that. You must not apply to me for the redress of such petty grievances. I own that the wrongs of the Poles and South Americans so fill my mind, as to leave me no time to attend to the petty sorrows of poorhouses, and apprentices. It is provinces, empires, continents, that the benevolence of the philosopher embraces; every one can do a little paltry good to his next neighbor.

Mr. Goodman: Every one *can,* but I do not see that every one *does.* If they would indeed, your business would be ready done to your hands, and your grand ocean of benevolence would be filled with the drops, which private charity would throw into it. I am glad, however, you are such a friend to the prisoners, because I am just now getting a little subscription, to set free your poor old friend Tom Saunders, a very honest brother mechanic, who first got into debt, and then into jail, through no fault of his own, but merely through the pressure of the times. A number of us have given a trifle every week towards maintaining his young family since he has been in prison; but we think we shall do much more service to Saunders, and indeed in the end, lighten our own expense, by paying down, at once, a little sum, to release him, and put him in the way of maintaining his family again. We have made up all the money except five dollars. I am already promised four, and you have nothing to do but to give me the fifth. And so, for a single dollar, without any of the trouble we have had in arranging the matter, you will, at once, have the pleasure of helping to save a worthy family from starving, of redeeming an old friend from jail, and of putting a little of your boasted benevolence into action. Realize! Mr. Fantom: There is nothing like realizing.

Mr. Fantom: Why, hark ye, Mr. Goodman, do not think I value a dollar; no sir, I despise money; it is trash, it is dirt, and beneath the regard of a wise man. It is one of the unfeeling inventions of artificial society. Sir, I could talk to you half a day on the abuse of riches, and my own contempt of money.

Mr. Goodman: O pray do not give yourself that trouble. It will be a much easier way of proving your sincerity, just to put your hand in your pocket, and give me a dollar without saying a word about it: and then to you, who value time so much, and money so little, it will cut the matter short. But come now, (for I see you will give nothing), I should be mighty glad to know what is the sort of good you do yourselves, since you always object to what is done by others.

Mr. Fantom: Sir, the object of a true philosopher is, to diffuse light and knowledge. I wish to see the whole world enlightened.

Mr. Goodman: Well, Mr. Fantom, you are a wonderful man, to keep up such a stock of benevolence, at so small an expense; to love mankind so dearly, and yet *avoid* all opportunities of doing them *good;* to have such a noble zeal for the *millions,* and to feel so little compassion for the units; to long to free *empires* and enlighten *kingdoms,* and deny instruction to your own *village* and comfort to your own *family.* Surely, none but a *philosopher* could indulge so much *philanthropy* and so much *frugality* at the same time. But come, do assist me in a partition I am making in our poorhouse, between the *old,* whom I want to have better *fed,* and the *young,* whom I want to have more *worked.*

Mr. Fantom: Sir, my mind is so engrossed with the partition of Poland, that I cannot bring it down to an object of such insignificance. I despise the man, whose benevolence is swallowed up in the narrow concerns of his own family, or village, or country.

Mr. Goodman: Well, now I have a notion, that it is as well to do one's own duty, as the duty of *another* man; and that to do good at *home,* is as well as to do good abroad. For *my* part, I had as lief help *Tom Saunders* to freedom, as a *Pole* or a *South American,* though I should be very glad to help *them too.* But one must begin to love somewhere; and I think it is as natural to love one's own family, and to do good in one's own neighborhood, as to any body else. And if every man in every family, village, and county did the same, why then all the schemes would be met, and the end of one village or town where I was doing good, would be the beginning of another village where somebody else was doing good; so my schemes would jut into my neighbor's; his projects would unite with those of some other local reformer; and all would fit with a sort of dovetail exactness.

Mr. Fantom: Sir, a man of large views will be on the watch for great occasions to prove his benevolence.

Mr. Goodman: Yes, sir; but if they are so distant that he cannot reach them, or so vast that he cannot grasp them, he may let a thousand little, snug, kind, good actions slip through his fingers in the meanwhile: and so, between the great thing that he *cannot* do, and the little ones that he *will not* do, life passes, and *nothing* will be done.

III.5

"The Gospel of Wealth"

Andrew Carnegie

Andrew Carnegie (1835–1919), Scottish-born American industrialist, led the expansion of the American steel industry in the late nineteenth century and was one of the foremost philanthropists of his era. In the first of the two parts of his "Gospel," Carnegie explains his main principle—that the surplus earned by men of great wealth should be allocated and administered by them, acting as trustees, while they are still alive—and draws out its implications for choosing fitting beneficiaries. In the second part, written in reply to the many responses to the first, Carnegie specifies the most fruitful fields in which men of great wealth should sow.

That Carnegie sees his gospel, at least in its intent, to be in harmony with the spirit of the Christian Gospels is evidenced by his lofty claim that it will solve the problem of the rich and the poor and bring "peace on earth, among men good will." But however Christian the intent of his gospel, both its grounding and its specific recommendations are quintessentially American. Carnegie has unqualified enthusiasm for American individualism and the entrepreneurial outlook it fosters; he stands in firm opposition to giving simply for the sake of relief and insists that help be offered only to those who would help themselves. Indeed, to avoid giving to individuals of questionable merit, Carnegie recommends giving only to institutions. Is it better to give away one's surplus wealth during one's lifetime, rather than as an inheritance? What does it mean to see oneself as a trustee? Can Carnegie avoid the charge of paternalism? Were Carnegie alive today, to what do you think he would urge millionaires to devote their surplus wealth? Though Carnegie is primarily addressing people like himself—those with vast fortunes—he argues that those of us with surplus wealth, however meager, should likewise regard ourselves as trustees and direct our surplus to the sorts of places he specifies. Should we? Should Carnegie's standards for his beneficiaries be applied to our own children?

From *The Gospel of Wealth*, edited by Edward C. Kirkland (Cambridge, Mass.: Harvard University Press, 1962), pp. 14–24. Reprinted with permission from Harvard University Press. Portions of this material may have previously appeared in: *Century Magazine, The North American Review, Forum, Contemporary Review, The Fortnightly Review, Nineteenth Century*, and *The Scottish Leader*.

I. "THE PROBLEM OF THE ADMINISTRATION OF WEALTH"

... The price which society pays for the law of competition, like the price it pays for cheap comforts and luxuries, is also great; but the advantages of this law are also greater still than its cost—for it is to this law that we owe our wonderful material development, which brings improved conditions in its train. But, whether the law be benign or not, ... we cannot evade it; no substitutes for it have been found; and while the law may be sometimes hard for the individual, it is best for the race, because it insures the survival of the fittest in every department. We accept and welcome, therefore, as conditions to which we must accommodate ourselves, great inequality of environment; the concentration of business, industrial and commercial, in the hands of a few; and the law of competition between these, as being not only beneficial, but essential to the future progress of the race. Having accepted these, it follows that there must be great scope for the exercise of special ability in the merchant and in the manufacturer who has to conduct affairs upon a great scale. That this talent for organization and management is rare among men is proved by the fact that it invariably secures enormous rewards for its possessor, no matter where or under what laws or conditions. The experienced in affairs always rate the MAN whose services can be obtained as a partner as not only the first consideration, but such as render the question of his capital scarcely worth considering: for able men soon create capital; in the hands of those without the special talent required, capital soon takes wings. Such men become interested in firms or corporations using millions; and, estimating only simple interest to be made upon the capital invested, it is inevitable that their income must exceed their expenditure and that they must, therefore, accumulate wealth. Nor is there any middle ground which such men can occupy, because the great manufacturing or commercial concern which does not earn at least interest upon its capital soon becomes bankrupt. It must either go forward or fall behind; to stand still is impossible. It is a condition essential to its successful operation that it should be thus far profitable, and even that, in addition to interest on capital, it should make profit. It is a law, as certain as any of the others named, that men possessed of this peculiar talent for affairs, under the free play of economic forces must, of necessity, soon be in receipt of more revenue than can be judiciously expended upon themselves; and this law is as beneficial for the race as the others.

Objections to the foundations upon which society is based are not in order, because the condition of the race is better with these than it has been with any other which has been tried. Of the effect of any new substitutes proposed we cannot be sure. The Socialist or Anarchist who seeks to overturn present conditions is to be regarded as attacking the foundation upon which civilization itself rests, for civilization took its start from the day when the capable, industrious workman said to his incompetent and lazy fellow, "If thou dost not sow, thou shalt not reap," and thus ended primitive Communism by separating the drones from the bees. One who studies this subject will soon be brought face to face with the conclusion that upon the sacredness of property civilization itself depends—the right of the laborer to his hundred dollars in the savings-bank, and equally the legal right of the millionaire to his millions. Every man must be allowed "to sit under his own vine and fig-tree, with none to make afraid," if human society is to advance, or even to remain so far advanced as it is. To those who propose to substitute Communism for this intense Individualism, the answer therefore is: The race has tried that. All progress from that barbarous day to the present time has resulted from its displacement. Not evil, but good, has come to the race from the accumulation of wealth by those who have had the ability and energy to produce it. But even if we admit for a moment that it might be better for the race to discard its present foundation, Individualism,— that it is a nobler ideal that man should labor, not for himself alone, but in and for a brotherhood of his fellows, and share with them all in common, . . . even admit all this, and a sufficient answer is, This is not evolution, but revolution. It necessitates the changing of human nature itself—a work of eons, even if it were good to change it, which we cannot know.

It is not practicable in our day or in our age. Even if desirable theoretically, it belongs to another and long-succeeding sociological stratum. Our duty is with what is practicable now—with the next step possible in our day and generation. . . .

We start, then, with a condition of affairs under which the best interests of the race are promoted, but which inevitably gives wealth to the few. Thus far, accepting conditions as they exist, the situation can be surveyed and pronounced good. The question then arises, . . . What is the proper mode of administering wealth after the laws upon which civilization is founded have thrown it into the hands of the few? And it is of this great question that I believe I offer the true solution. It will be understood that fortunes are here spoken of, not moderate sums saved by many years of effort, the returns from which are required for the comfortable maintenance and education of families. This is not wealth, but only competence, which it should be the aim of all to acquire, and which it is for the best interests of society should be acquired.

There are but three modes in which surplus wealth can be disposed of. It can be left to the families of the decedents; or it can be bequeathed for public purposes; or, finally, it can be administered by its possessors during their lives. Under the first and second modes most of the wealth of the world that has reached the few has hitherto been applied. Let us in turn consider each of these modes. The first is the most injudicious. In monarchical countries, the estates and the greatest portion of the wealth are left to the first son, that the vanity of the parent may be gratified by the thought that his name and title are to descend unimpaired to succeeding generations. The condition of this class in Europe to-day teaches the failure of such hopes or ambitions. The successors have become impoverished through their follies, or from the fall in the value of land. Even in Great Britain the strict law of entail has been found inadequate to maintain an hereditary class. Its soil is rapidly passing into the hands of the stranger. Under republican institutions the division of property among the children is much fairer; but the question which forces itself upon thoughtful men in all lands is, Why should men leave great fortunes to their children? If this is done from affection, is it not misguided affection? Observation teaches that, generally speaking, it is not well for the children that they should be so burdened. Neither is it well for the State. Beyond providing for the wife and daughters moderate sources of income, and very moderate allowances indeed, if any, for the sons, men may well hesitate; for it is no longer questionable that great sums bequeathed often work more for the injury than for the good of the recipients. Wise men will soon conclude that, for the best interests of the members of their families, and of the State, such bequests are an improper use of their means.

It is not suggested that men who have failed to educate their sons to earn a livelihood shall cast them adrift in poverty. If any man has seen fit to rear his sons with a view to their living idle lives, or, what is highly commendable, has instilled in them the sentiment that they are in a position to labor for public ends without reference to pecuniary considerations, then, of course, the duty of the parent is to see that such are provided for in moderation. There are instances of millionaires' sons unspoiled by wealth, who, being rich, still perform great services to the community. Such are the very salt of the earth, as valuable as, unfortunately, they are rare. It is not the exception, however, but the rule, that men must regard; and, looking at the usual result of enormous sums conferred upon legatees, the thoughtful man must shortly say, "I would as soon leave to my son a curse as the almighty dollar," and admit to himself that it is not the welfare of the children, but family pride, which inspires these legacies.

As to the second mode, that of leaving wealth at death for public uses, it may be said that this is only a means for the disposal of wealth, provided a man is content to wait until he is dead before he becomes of much good in the world. Knowledge of the results of legacies bequeathed is not calculated to inspire the brightest hopes of much posthumous good being accomplished by them. The cases are not few in which the real object sought by the testator is not attained, nor are they few in which his real wishes are thwarted. In many cases the bequests are so used as to become only monuments of his folly. It is well to remember that it requires the exercise of not less ability than that which acquires it, to use wealth so as to be really beneficial to the community. Besides this, it may fairly be said that no man is to be extolled for doing what he cannot help doing, nor is he to be thanked by the community to which he only leaves wealth at death. Men who leave vast sums in this way may fairly be thought men who would not have left it at all had they been able to take it with them. The memories of such cannot be held in grateful remembrance, for there is no grace in their gifts. It is not to be wondered at that such bequests seem so generally to lack the blessing.

The growing disposition to tax more and more heavily large estates left at death is a cheering indication of the growth of a salutary change in public opinion. . . . Of all forms of taxation this seems the wisest. Men who continue hoarding great sums all their lives, the proper use of which for public ends would work good to the community from which it chiefly came, should be made to feel that the community, in the form of the State, cannot thus be deprived of its proper share. By taxing estates heavily at death the State marks its condemnation of the selfish millionaire's unworthy life.

It is desirable that nations should go much further in this direction. Indeed, it is difficult to set bounds to the share of a rich man's estate which should go at his death to the public through the agency of the State, and by all means such taxes should be graduated, beginning at nothing upon moderate sums to dependents, and increasing rapidly as the amounts swell, until of the millionaire's hoard, as of Shylock's, at least

> The other half
> Comes to the privy coffer of the State.

This policy would work powerfully to induce the rich man to attend to the administration of wealth during his life, which is the end that society should always have in view, as being by far the most fruitful for the people. Nor need it be feared that this policy would sap the root of enterprise and render men less anxious to accumulate, for, to the class whose ambition it is to leave great fortunes and to be talked about after their death, it will attract even more attention, and, indeed, be a somewhat nobler ambition, to have enormous sums paid over to the State from their fortunes.

There remains, then, only one mode of using great fortunes; but in this we have the true antidote for the temporary unequal distribution of wealth, the reconciliation of the rich and the poor—a reign of harmony, another ideal, differing, indeed, from that of the Communist in requiring only the further evolution of existing conditions, not the total overthrow of our civilization. It is founded upon the present most intense Individualism, and the race is prepared to put it in practice by degrees whenever it pleases. Under its sway we shall have an ideal State, in which the surplus wealth of the few will become, in the best sense, the property of the many, because administered for the common good; and this wealth, passing through the hand of the few, can be made a much more potent force for the elevation of our race than if distributed in small sums to the people themselves. Even the poorest can be made to see this, and to agree that great sums gathered by some of their fellow-citizens and spent for public purposes, from which the masses reap the principal benefit, are more valuable to them than if scattered among themselves in trifling amounts through the course of many years.

If we consider the results which flow from the Cooper Institute, for instance, to the best portion of the race in New York not possessed of means, and compare these with those which would have ensued for the good of the masses from an equal sum distributed by Mr. Cooper in his lifetime in the form of wages, which is the highest form of distribution, being for work done and not for charity, we can form some estimate of the possibilities for the improvement of the race which lie embedded in the present law of the accumulation of wealth. Much of this sum, if distributed in small quantities among the people, would have been wasted in the indulgence of appetite, some of it in excess, and it may be doubted whether even the part put to the best use, that of adding to the comforts of the home, would have yielded results for the race, as a race, at all comparable to those which are flowing and are to flow from the Cooper Institute from generation to generation. Let the advocate of violent or radical change ponder well this thought.

We might even go so far as to take another instance—that of Mr. Tilden's bequest of five millions of dollars for a free library in the city of New York; but in referring to this one cannot help saying involuntarily: How much better if Mr. Tilden had devoted the last years of his own life to the proper administration of this immense sum; in which case neither legal contest nor any other cause of delay could have interfered with his aims. But let us assume that Mr. Tilden's millions finally become the means of giving to this city a noble public library, where the treasures of the world contained in books will be open to all forever, without money and without price. Considering the good of that part of the race which congregates in and around Manhattan Island, would its permanent benefit have been better promoted had these millions been allowed to circulate in small sums through the hands of the masses? Even the most strenuous advocate of Communism must entertain a doubt upon this subject. Most of those who think will probably entertain no doubt whatever.

Poor and restricted are our opportunities in this life, narrow our horizon, our best work most imperfect; but rich men should be thankful for one inestimable boon. They have it in their power during their lives to busy themselves in organizing benefactions from which the masses of their fellows will derive lasting advantage, and thus dignify their own lives. The highest life is probably to be reached, not by such imitation of the life of Christ . . . but, while animated by Christ's spirit, by recognizing the changed conditions of this age, and adopting modes of expressing this spirit suitable to the changed conditions under which we live, still laboring for the good of our fellows, which was the essence of his life and teaching, but laboring in a different manner.

This, then, is held to be the duty of the man of wealth: To set an example of modest, unostentatious living, shunning display or extravagance; to provide moderately for the legitimate wants of those dependent upon him; and, after doing so, to consider all surplus revenues which come to him simply as trust funds, which he is called upon to administer, and strictly bound as a matter of duty to administer in the manner which, in his judgment, is best calculated to produce the most beneficial results for the community—the man of wealth thus becoming the mere trustee and agent for his poorer brethren, bringing to their service his superior wisdom, experience, and ability to administer, doing for them better than they would or could do for themselves.

We are met here with the difficulty of determining what are moderate sums to leave to members of the family; what is modest, unostentatious living; what is the test of extravagance. There must be different standards for different conditions. The answer is that it is as impossible to name exact amounts or actions as it is to define good manners, good taste, or the rules of propriety; but, nevertheless, these are verities, well known, although indefinable. Public sentiment is quick to know and to feel what offends these. So in the case of wealth. The rule in regard to good taste in dress of men or women applies here. Whatever makes one conspicuous offends the canon. If any family be chiefly known for display, for extravagance in home, table, or equipage, for enormous sums ostentatiously spent in any form upon itself—if these be its chief distinctions, we have no difficulty in estimating its nature or culture. So likewise in regard to the use or abuse of its surplus wealth, or to generous, free-handed coöperation in good public uses, or to unabated efforts to accumulate and hoard to the last, or whether they administer or bequeath. The verdict rests with the best and most enlightened public sentiment. The community will surely judge, and its judgments will not often be wrong.

The best uses to which surplus wealth can be put have already been indicated. Those who would administer wisely must, indeed, be wise; for one of the serious obstacles to the improvement of our race is indiscriminate charity. It were better for mankind that the millions of the rich were thrown into the sea than so spent as to encourage the slothful, the drunken, the unworthy. Of every thousand dollars spent in so-called charity to-day, it is probable that nine hundred and fifty dollars is unwisely spent—so spent, indeed, as to produce the very evils which it hopes to mitigate or cure. A well-known writer of philosophic books admitted the other day that he had given a quarter of a dollar to a man who approached him as he was coming to visit the house of his friend. He knew nothing of the habits of this beggar, knew not the use that would be made of this money, although he had every reason to suspect that it would be spent improperly. This man professed to be a disciple of Herbert Spencer; yet the quarter-dollar given that night will probably work more injury than all the money will do good which its thoughtless donor will ever be able to give in true charity. He only gratified his own feelings, saved himself from annoyance—and this was probably one of the most selfish and very worst actions of his life, for in all respects he is most worthy.

In bestowing charity, the main consideration should be to help those who will help themselves; to provide part of the means by which those who desire to improve may do so; to give those who desire to rise the aids by which they may rise; to assist, but rarely or never to do all. Neither the individual nor the race is improved by almsgiving. Those worthy of assistance, except in rare cases, seldom require assistance. The really valuable men of the race never do, except in the case of accident or sudden change. Every one has, of course, cases of individuals brought to his own knowledge where temporary assistance can do genuine good, and these he will not overlook. But the amount which can be wisely given by the individual for individuals is necessarily limited by his lack of knowledge of the circumstances connected with each. He is the only true reformer who is as careful and as anxious not to aid the unworthy as he is to aid the worthy, and, perhaps, even more so, for in almsgiving more injury is probably done by rewarding vice than by relieving virtue.

The rich man is thus almost restricted to following the examples of [those] . . . who know that the best means of benefiting the community is to place within its reach the ladders upon which the aspiring can rise—free libraries, parks, and means of recreation, by which men are helped in body and mind; works of art, certain to give pleasure and improve the public taste; and public institutions of various kinds, which will improve the general condition of the people; in this manner returning their surplus wealth to the mass of their fellows in the forms best calculated to do them lasting good.

Thus is the problem of rich and poor to be solved. The laws of accumulation will be left free, the laws of distribution free. Individualism will continue, but the millionaire will be but a trustee for the poor, intrusted for a season with a great part of the increased wealth of the community, but administering it for the community far better than it could or would have done for itself. The best minds will thus have reached a stage in the development of the race in which it is clearly seen that there is no mode of disposing of surplus wealth creditable to thoughtful and earnest men into whose hands it flows, save by using it year by year for the general good. This day already dawns. Men may die without incurring the pity of their fellows, still sharers in great business enterprises from which their capital cannot be or has not been withdrawn, and which is left chiefly at death for public uses; yet the day is not far distant when the man who dies leaving behind him millions of available wealth, which was free to him to administer during life, will pass away "unwept, unhonored, and unsung," no matter to what uses he leaves the dross which he cannot take with him. Of such as these the public verdict will then be: "The man who dies thus rich dies disgraced."

Such, in my opinion is the true gospel concerning wealth, obedience to which is destined some day to solve the problem of the rich and the poor, and to bring "Peace on earth, among men good will."

II. "THE BEST FIELDS FOR PHILANTHROPY"

... Bearing in mind these considerations, let us endeavor to present some of the best uses to which a millionaire can devote the surplus of which he should regard himself as only the trustee.

First. Standing apart by itself there is the founding of a university by men enormously rich, such men as must necessarily be few in any country. Perhaps the greatest sum ever given by an individual for any purpose is the gift of Senator Stanford, who undertakes to establish a complete university upon the Pacific coast, where he amassed his enormous fortune, which is said to involve the expenditure of ten millions of dollars, and upon which he may be expected to bestow twenty millions of his surplus. He is to be envied. A thousand years hence some orator, speaking his praise upon the then crowded shores of the Pacific, may thus adapt Griffith's eulogy of Wolsey:

> In bestowing, madam,
> He was most princely. Ever witness for him
> This seat of learning, . . .
>   though unfinished, yet so famous.
> So excellent in art, and still so rising,
> That Christendom shall ever speak his virtue.

Here is a noble use of wealth. We have many such institutions,—Johns Hopkins, Cornell, Packer, and others,—but most of these have only been bequeathed, and it is impossible to extol any man greatly for simply leaving what he cannot take with him. Cooper and Pratt and Stanford, and others of this class, deserve credit and admiration as much for the time and attention given during their lives as for their expenditure upon their respective monuments. . . .

Second. The result of my own study of the question, What is the best gift which can be given to a community? is that a free library occupies the first place, provided the community will accept and maintain it as a public institution, as much a part of the city property as its public schools, and, indeed, an adjunct to these. It is, no doubt, possible that my own personal experience may have led me to value a free library beyond all other forms of beneficence. When I was a working-boy in Pittsburgh, Colonel Anderson of Allegheny—a name I can never speak without feelings of devotional gratitude—opened his little library of four hundred books to boys. Every Saturday afternoon he was in attendance at his house to exchange books. No one but he who has felt it can ever know the intense longing with which the arrival of Saturday was awaited, that a new book might be had. My brother and Mr. Phipps, who have been my principal business partners through life, shared with me Colonel Anderson's precious generosity, and it was when reveling in the treasures which he opened to us that I resolved, if ever wealth came to me, that it should be used to establish free libraries, that other poor boys might receive opportunities similar to those for which we were indebted to that noble man. . . .

Third. We have another most important department in which great sums can be worthily used—the founding or extension of hospitals, medical colleges, laboratories, and other institutions connected with the alleviation of human suffering, and especially with the prevention rather than with the cure of human ills. There is no danger of pauperizing a community in giving for such purposes, because such institutions relieve temporary ailments or shelter only those who are hopeless invalids. What better gift than a hospital can be given to a community that is without one?—the gift being conditioned upon its proper maintenance by the community in its corporate capacity. If hospital accommodation already exists, no better method for using surplus wealth can be found than in making additions to it. The late Mr. Vanderbilt's gift of half a million dollars to the Medical Department of Columbia College for a chemical laboratory was one of the wisest possible uses of wealth. It strikes at the prevention of disease by penetrating into its causes. Several others have established such laboratories, but the need for them is still great.

If there be a millionaire in the land who is at a loss what to do with the surplus that has been committed to him as trustee, let him investigate the good that is flowing from these chemical laboratories. No medical college is complete without its laboratory. As with universities, so with medical colleges: it is not new institutions that are required, but additional means for the more thorough equipment of those that exist. The forms that benefactions to these may wisely take are numerous, but probably none is more useful than that adopted by Mr. Osborne when he built a school for training female nurses at Bellevue College. If from all gifts there flows one half of the good that comes from this wise use of a millionaire's surplus, the most exacting may well be satisfied. Only those who have passed through a lingering and dangerous illness can rate at their true value the care, skill, and attendance of trained female nurses. Their employment as nurses has enlarged the sphere and influence of woman. It is not to be wondered at that a senator of the United States, and a physician distinguished in this country for having received the highest distinctions abroad, should recently have found their wives in this class.

Fourth. In the very front rank of benefactions public parks should be placed, always provided that the community undertakes to maintain, beautify, and preserve them inviolate. No more useful or more beautiful monument can be left by any man than a park for the city in which he was born or in which he has long lived, nor can the community pay a more graceful tribute to the citizen who presents it than to give his name to the gift. Mrs. Schenley's gift last month of a large park to the city of Pittsburgh deserves to be noted. This lady, although born in Pittsburgh, married an English gentleman while yet in her teens. It is forty years and more since she took up her residence in London among the titled and the wealthy of the world's metropolis, but still she turns to the home of her childhood and by means of Schenley Park links her name with it forever. A noble use of this great wealth by one who thus becomes her own administrator. If a park be already provided, there is still room for many judicious gifts in connection with it. Mr. Phipps of Allegheny has given conservatories to the park there, which are visited by many every day of the week, and crowded by thousands of working-people every Sunday; for, with rare wisdom, he has stipulated as a condition of the gift that the conservatories shall be open on Sundays. The result of his experiment has been so gratifying that he finds himself justified in adding to them from his surplus, as he is doing largely this year. To lovers of flowers among the wealthy I commend a study of what is possible for them to do in the line of Mr. Phipp's example; and may they please note that Mr. Phipps is a wise as well as a liberal giver, for he requires the city to maintain these conservatories, and thus secures for them forever the public ownership, the public interest, and the public criticism of their management. Had he undertaken to manage and maintain them, it is probable that popular interest in the gift would never have been awakened. . . .

While the bestowal of a park upon a community will be universally approved as one of the best uses for surplus wealth, in embracing such additions to it as conservatories, or in advocating the building of memorial arches and works of adornment, it is probable that many will think I go too far, and consider these somewhat fanciful. The material good to flow from them may not be so directly visible; but let not any practical mind, intent only upon material good, depreciate the value of wealth given for these or for kindred esthetic purposes as being useless as far as the mass of the people and their needs are concerned. As with libraries and museums, so with these more distinctively artistic works: they perform their great use when they reach the best of the masses of the people. It is better to reach and touch the sentiment for beauty in the naturally bright minds of this class than to pander to those incapable of being so touched. For what the improver of the race must endeavor is to reach those who have the divine spark ever so feebly developed, that it may be strengthened and grow. For my part, I think Mr. Phipps put his money to better use in giving the working-men of Allegheny conservatories filled with beautiful flowers, orchids, and aquatic plants, which they, with their wives and children, can enjoy in their spare hours, and upon which they can feed their love for the beautiful, than if he had given his surplus money to furnish them with bread; for those in health who cannot earn their bread are scarcely worth considering by the individual giver, the care of such being the duty of the State. The man who erects in a city a conservatory or a truly artistic arch, statue, or fountain, makes a wise use of his surplus. "Man does not live by bread alone."

Fifth. We have another good use for surplus wealth in providing our cities with halls suitable for meetings of all kinds, and for concerts of elevating music. Our cities are rarely possessed of halls for these purposes, being in this respect also very far behind European cities. Springer Hall, in Cincinnati, a valuable addition to the city, was largely the gift of Mr. Springer, who was not content to bequeath funds from his estate at death, but gave during his life, and, in addition, gave—what was equally important—his time and business ability to insure the successful results which have been achieved. The gift of a hall to any city lacking one is an excellent use for surplus wealth for the good of a community. The reason why the people have only one instructive and elevating, or even amusing, entertainment when a dozen would be highly beneficial, is that the rent of a hall, even when a suitable hall exists, which is rare, is so great as to prevent managers from running the risk of financial failure. If every city in our land owned a hall which could be given or rented for a small sum for such gatherings as a committee or the mayor of the city judged advantageous, the people could be furnished with proper lectures, amusements, and concerts at an exceedingly small cost. The town halls of European cities, many of which have organs, are of inestimable value to the people, utilized as they are in the manner suggested. Let no one underrate the influence of entertainments of an elevating or even of an amusing character, for these do much to make the lives of the people happier and their natures better. If any millionaire born in a small village which has now become a great city is prompted in the day of his success to do something for his birthplace with part of his surplus, his grateful remembrance cannot take a form more useful than that of a public hall with an organ, provided the city agrees to maintain and use it.

Sixth. In another respect we are still much behind Europe. A form of benevolence which is not uncommon there is providing swimming-baths for the people. The donors of these have been wise enough to require the city benefited to maintain them at its own expense, and as proof of the contention that everything should never be done for any one or for any community, but that the recipients should invariably be called upon to do a part, it is significant that it is found essential for the popular success of these healthful establishments to exact a nominal charge for their use. In many cities, however, the school-children are admitted free at fixed hours upon certain days; different hours being fixed for the boys and the girls to use the great swimming-baths, hours or days being also fixed for the use of these baths by women. In addition to the highly beneficial effect of these institutions upon the public health in inland cities, the young of both sexes are thus taught to swim. Swimming clubs are organized, and matches are frequent, at which medals and prizes are given. The reports published by the various swimming-bath establishments throughout Great Britain are filled with instances of lives saved because those who fortunately escaped shipwreck had been taught to swim in the baths; and not a few instances are given in which the pupils of certain bathing establishments have saved the lives of others. If any disciple of the gospel of wealth gives his favorite city large swimming and private baths, provided the municipality undertakes their management as a city affair, he will never be called to account for an improper use of the funds intrusted to him.

Seventh. Churches as fields for the use of surplus wealth have purposely been reserved for the last, because, these being sectarian, every man will be governed in his action in regard to them by his own attachments; therefore gifts to churches, it may be said, are not, in one sense, gifts to the community at large, but to special classes. Nevertheless, every millionaire may know of a district where the little cheap, uncomfortable, and altogether unworthy wooden structure stands at the cross-roads, in which the whole neighborhood gathers on Sunday, and which, independently of the form of the doctrines taught, is the center of social life and source of neighborly feeling. The administrator of wealth makes a good use of a part of his surplus if he replaces that building with a permanent structure of brick, stone, or granite, up whose sides the honeysuckle and columbine may climb, and from whose tower the sweet-tolling bell may sound. The millionaire should not figure how cheaply this structure can be built, but how perfect it can be made. If he has the money, it should be made a gem, for the educating influence of a pure and noble specimen of architecture, built, as the pyramids were built, to stand for ages, is not to be measured by dollars. Every farmer's home, heart, and mind in the district will be influenced by the beauty and grandeur of the church; and many a bright boy, gazing enraptured upon its richly colored windows and entranced by the celestial voice of the organ, will there receive his first message from and in spirit be carried away to the beautiful and enchanting realm which lies far from the material and prosaic conditions which surround him in this workaday world—a real world, this new realm, vague and undefined though its boundaries be. Once within its magic circle, its denizens live there an inner life more precious than the external, and all their days and all their ways, their triumphs and their trials, and all they see, and all they hear, and all they think, and all they do, are hallowed by the radiance which shines from afar upon this inner life, glorifying everything, and keeping all right within. But having given the building, the donor should stop there; the support of the church should be upon its own people. There is not much genuine religion in the congregation or much good to come from the church which is not supported at home.

Many other avenues for the wise expenditure of surplus wealth might be indicated. I enumerate but a few—a very few—of the many fields which are open, and only those in which great or considerable sums can be judiciously used. It is not the privilege, however, of millionaires alone to work for or aid measures which are certain to benefit the community. Every one who has but a small surplus above his moderate wants may share this privilege with his richer brothers, and those without surplus can give at least a part of their time, which is usually as important as funds, and often more so.

It is not expected, neither is it desirable, that there should be general concurrence as to the best possible use of surplus wealth. For different men and different localities there are different uses. What commends itself most highly to the judgment of the administrator is the best use for him, for his heart should be in the work. It is as important in administering wealth as it is in any other branch of a man's work that he should be enthusiastically devoted to it and feel that in the field selected his work lies.

Besides this, there is room and need for all kinds of wise benefactions for the common weal. The man who builds a university, library, or laboratory performs no more useful work than he who elects to devote himself and his surplus means to the adornment of a park, the gathering together of a collection of pictures for the public, or the building of a memorial arch. These are all true laborers in the vineyard. The only point required by the gospel of wealth is that the surplus which accrues from time to time in the hands of a man should be administered by him in his own lifetime for that purpose which is seen by him, as trustee, to be best for the good of the people. To leave at death what he cannot take away, and place upon others the burden of the work which it was his own duty to perform, is to do nothing worthy. This requires no sacrifice, nor any sense of duty to his fellows.

Time was when the words concerning the rich man entering the kingdom of heaven were regarded as a hard saying. To-day, when all questions are probed to the bottom and the standards of faith receive the most liberal interpretations, the startling verse has been relegated to the rear, to await the next kindly revision as one of those things which cannot be quite understood, but which, meanwhile, it is carefully to be noted, are not to be understood literally. But is it so very improbable that the next stage of thought is to restore the doctrine in all its pristine purity and force, as being in perfect harmony with sound ideas upon the subject of wealth and poverty, the rich and the poor, and the contrasts everywhere seen and deplored? In Christ's day, it is evident, reformers were against the wealthy. It is none the less evident that we are fast recurring to that position to-day; and there will be nothing to surprise the student of sociological development if society should soon approve the text which has caused so much anxiety: "It is easier for a camel to enter the eye of a needle than for a rich man to enter the kingdom of heaven." Even if the needle were the small casement at the gates, the words betoken serious difficulty for the rich. It will be but a step for the theologian from the doctrine that he who dies rich dies disgraced, to that which brings upon the man punishment or deprivation hereafter.

The gospel of wealth but echoes Christ's words. It calls upon the millionaire to sell all that he hath and give it in the highest and best form to the poor by administering his estate himself for the good of his fellows, before he is called upon to lie down and rest upon the bosom of Mother Earth. So doing, he will approach his end no longer the ignoble hoarder of useless millions; poor, very poor indeed, in money, but rich, very rich, twenty times a millionaire still, in the affection, gratitude, and admiration of his fellow-men, and—sweeter far—soothed and sustained by the still, small voice within, which, whispering, tells him that, because he has lived, perhaps one small part of the great world has been bettered just a little. This much is sure: against such riches as these no bar will be found at the gates of Paradise.

III.6

"The Eleventh"

Henri Barbusse

In this story, Henri Barbusse (1873–1935), French journalist, editor, and author, starkly shows how arbitrary philanthropic decisions can be. On the first day of each month, at exactly eight o'clock, the luxurious palace-hospital opens its doors to the first ten vagabonds "of the file which, since the night before, had been washed up against the wall of the house." No more, no fewer are admitted. No questions are asked. Only one rule obtains: The ten must leave when the month expires and never come back again. During their month's stay, the vagabonds enjoy the life and privileges of archdukes and multimillionaires (the regular residents of this earthly paradise). Gradually, the young man whose job it is to admit the ten begins to notice, eventually exclusively to notice, the unlucky eleventh, who, only a step behind the rest, is the one on whom he must shut the door each month. "I glimpsed in a flash," he says, ". . . all the effort he had made to get there . . . and how much he too deserved to come in! . . . [H]e seemed to me the most pitiable case, and I felt that I was myself smitten in the person of the one condemned. . . . An idea beset me—that I was taking part in an abominable injustice." When he can stand it no longer, he resigns his position. Surely we can sympathize with the young man's concern, but does he draw the right conclusion? Is he an accomplice to an "abominable injustice"? What would you have advised him to do? Is the tradition of the luxury palace-hospital praiseworthy? If you were a member of its board, would you recommend a different way of targeting beneficiaries? A different sort of philanthropic effort altogether?

The Master, who had a pale head with long marble-like hair, and whose spectacles shone in solemnity, came to a standstill on his morning round opposite my little table at the door of Room 28, and condescended to announce to me that I was henceforth appointed to let in the ten poor people who every month were admitted to the hospitality of the House. Then he went on, so tall and so white among the assiduous flock of students that they seemed to be carrying a famous statuette from room to room.

From *We Others: Stories of Fate, Love and Pity*, by Henri Barbusse, translation by Fitzwater Wray, published by Weidenfeld & Nicolson. Reprinted with permission of Orion Publishing Group, Ltd.

I stammered the thanks which he did not hear. My 25-year-old heart felt a happy pride in reflecting that I had been chosen to preside in one of the noblest traditions of the House in which, a humble assistant, I was wandering lornly among wealthy invalids.

On the first day of every month the luxurious palace-hospital became the paradise of ten vagabonds. One of its outer doors was opened to admit the first ten who came, whoever they were, wherever they had fallen from or escaped. And for a whole month those ten human derelicts enjoyed the entire hospitality of the comfortable institution, just as much so as the Master's most valuable patients, as much as the arch-dukes and multi-millionaires. For them, too, were the lofty halls whose walls were not only white, but glistening, the huge corridors like covered streets, which in summer or in winter had the coolness or the mildness of spring. For them also, the immense garden beds set among green velvet, like bunches of flowers so enlarged by magic that one walked among them. For them equally, the outer walls, far off but impassable, which shield one against wide-open Space, against rambling roads, against the plains which come to an end no more than the sky. For thirty days the refugees busied themselves only with doing nothing, only worked when they ate, and were no longer afraid of the unknown or of the coming day. They who were remorseful learned to forget things, and they who were bereaved, to forget people.

When by chance they met each other, they simply had to turn their heads away hurriedly. There was not in all the House, by order of the Master, a mirror in which they would have found their bad dream again. At the day's end came the dormitory, peaceful as a cemetery, a nice cemetery, where one is not dead, where one waits—where one lives, but without knowing it.

At eight o'clock on the first day of the following month all ten of them went away, cast back into the world one by one, as into the sea. Immediately after, ten others entered, the first ten of the file which, since the night before, had been washed up against the wall of the house as upon the shores of an island. The first ten, no more, no less, no favours, no exceptions, no injustices; one rule only— they who had already been were never again admitted. The arrivals were asked nothing else—not even for the confession of their names.

And on the first day of the month, as soon as nine o'clock had sounded, exactly together from the Anglican church and the Catholic chapel of the House, I opened the little Poor-door.

A crowd of beings was massed against the door-wing and the wall. Hardly had the former turned in the shadow when the tattered heap rushed forward as though sucked in.

My helper had to throw himself forward to enforce a little order upon the greedy invasion. We had to detach by force, to tear away from the mass each one of the besiegers, who were pressed side by side and elbow to elbow, fastened to each other like fantastic friends. The eight entered, the ninth, the tenth.

And then the door was quickly closed, but not so quickly that it prevented me from seeing, only a step from me, him upon whom it closed, the eleventh, the unlucky one, the accursed.

He was a man of uncertain age; in his grey and withered face lack-lustre eyes floated. He looked at me so despairingly that he seemed to smile. The touch of that extraordinary disappointment made me start, of that face that was mute as a wound. I glimpsed in a flash—the time that the door took to shut—all the effort he had made to get there, even if too late, and how much he too deserved to come in!

Then I busied myself with the others; but a few minutes later, still affected by the distress I had read on the face of the outcast, I half opened the door to see if he were still there. No one. He and the three or four others—uncertain rags that had fluttered behind him—had gone to the four winds of heaven, carried away along the roads like dead leaves. A little shiver went through me, a shiver almost of mourning for the conquered.

At night, as I was falling asleep, my thoughts went again to them, and I wondered why they stayed there till the last moment, they who arrived only when ten had already taken their places at the door. What did they hope for? Nothing. Yet they were hoping all the same, and therein was a mean miracle of the heart.

We had reached the month of March. On the last day of the old month, towards nightfall, a rather frightened murmur crept from the side of the high road, close to the door. Leaning over a balcony, I could make men out there, stirring like insects. These were the suppliants.

The next morning we opened to these phantoms whom the magical story of the house had called across the world, who had awakened and unburied themselves from the lowest and most awful of depths to get there. We welcomed the ten who first came forward; we were obliged to drive back into life the eleventh.

He was standing, motionless, and offering himself from the other side of the door. I looked at him, and then lowered my eyes. He had a terrible look, with his hollow face and lashless eyelids. There breathed from him a reproach of unbearable artlessness.

When the door divided us for ever, I regretted him, and should have liked to see him again. I turned towards the others, swarming in gladness on the flagstones, almost with resignation, wondering at my own firm conviction that the other, sooner than these, ought to have come in with us.

And it was so every time. Every time I became more indifferent to the crowd of admitted and satisfied, and devoted my gaze still more to him who was refused salvation. And every time he seemed to me the most pitiable case, and I felt that I was myself smitten in the person of the one condemned.

In June, it was a woman. I saw her understand and begin to cry. I trembled as I furtively scanned her; to crown all, the weeper's eyelids were blood-red as wounds.

In July, the appointed victim was incomparably regrettable by reason of his great age; and no living being was so compassionable as he who was repulsed the month after, so young was he. Another time, he who had to be snatched from the group of the elect besought me with his poor hands, encircled with the remains of frayed linen, like lint. The one whom Fate sacrificed the following month showed me a menacing fist. The entreaty of the one made me afraid, and the threat of the other pitiful.

I could almost have begged his pardon, the "eleventh" of October. He drew himself up stiffly; his neck was wrapped high in a grayish tie that looked like a bandage; he was thin, and his coat fluttered in the wind like a flag. But what could I have said to the unfortunate who succeeded him thirty days later? He blushed, stammered a nervous apology, and withdrew after bowing with tragic politeness—piteous remnant of an earlier lot.

And thus a year passed. Twelve times I let in the vagrants whom the stones had worn out, the workmen for whom all work was hopeless, the criminals subdued. Twelve times I let in some of those who clung to the stones of the wall as on to reefs of the sea coast. Twelve times I turned others away, similar ones, whom I confusedly preferred.

An idea beset me—that I was taking part in an abominable injustice. Truly there was no sense in dividing all those poor folk like that into friends and enemies. There was only one arbitrary reason—abstract, not admissible; a matter of a figure, a sign. At bottom, this was neither just nor even logical.

Soon I could no longer continue in this series of errors. I went to the Master, and begged him to give me some other post, so that I should not have to do the same evil deed again every month.

III.7

"Mr. Plumter, B.A., Revisits the Old Shop"

Stephen Leacock

When was the last time you thought about dear old Alma Mater? In this short story, Stephen Butler Leacock (1869–1944), Canadian political economist and humorist, good-humoredly reminds us of our forgetfulness. Like many a college graduate, Archie Plumter took his B.A. and hasn't looked back. Not for twenty years. When he finally does so, the memories he summons—the "wizard" professors with whom he once studied, himself as an undergraduate—are distorted. He is certain that the campus itself is exactly as it once was. No change. Inspired by something he happened to see on a recent trip abroad (perhaps also by his own waywardness with respect to time?), and having become fairly prosperous in the interim, Plumter decides to give the "old shop" twenty-five thousand dollars for the purchase of a clock with chimes that will announce the hour and to build a tower to house it in. The reality of time's passage, however, hits him when he visits the campus to announce his intended benefaction. The chimes ringing from a newly constructed clock tower announce that another alumnus has beaten him to it. In the end, Archie, inspired by hearing a tiresome lecture by his old Professor Dim, endows an annual lecture series on the Crusades, to be inaugurated by his aptly named former teacher. Is Archie's gift simply laughable? Who is its beneficiary? Is there a better way for him—or anyone similarly situated—to honor Alma Mater? Does our own Alma Mater have a rightful claim on our philanthropy?

(Remember now thy college in the days of thy graduation.—Ecclesiastes—Improved).

Mr. Archie Plumter, college graduate, lives in one of those towns that lie fast asleep in the garden part of Western Ontario. You know the little places—all trees and grass and hedges and flowers, with the houses well back from the street and all boulevarded together. In Woodsdale you can't tell where the McLeans' lawn ends and Dr. Selby's begins. Somewhere concealed in the middle of the town is the main street with the shops on it, and away off at the side, down hill, is

From *Happy Stories Just to Laugh At* by Stephen Leacock (New York: Dodd, Mead and Co., 1944), pp. 90–107. Reprinted by permission of Nancy Kate Winthrop.

the railway station, which is really more of a lawn and a flower garden than a station. All the big through trains stop at Woodsdale (for water) and the passengers ask the porter what place this is and he looks out of the window and shakes his head.

But it's just the place for a college graduate. You see, a college graduate, as Plumter himself says, could hardly stand it in the country. His mind is too active. But here—again as Archie himself explains—you have everything, just as in the city. If you want to do any shopping you get anything you want right here on the main street; say you want a pair of boots—they have them; say you want a necktie, they'll have it, or they'll send for it. And, anyway, if you have any big shopping, any serious buying to do, you've only to hop on the train and even the slow train runs you into the City in three hours, and the flyer does it in two and three quarters. There's a picture house in town or if you want to go to the theatres you've only to step on the train and there you are, in Detroit. How long? About four hours. Or if you want music, well, what's the matter with taking a steamer across Lake Erie to Cleveland? That's what Archie Plumter does, or at least that's not what he does but it's what he could do if he did it. Or suppose you want a drink? Well, you can't get a drink in Woodsdale because it's local option and so they have no choice. But all you have to do is jump in the car, drive twelve miles and get all you want.

Mr. Plumter is in the milling business (flour and feed). That's his mill—as it was his father's—that huge stone grist mill, sunk down so deep in Woodsdale Creek that, big as it is, the trees have overgrown and overtopped it. A stone grist mill is one of the few of man's contrivances which, with a touch of time's hand, can even improve on nature. There it stands, with the water pounding over the dam beside it, and churning up white foam among the stones below; a roar of water outside, and inside a never ending trembling and vibration of the floors, as the great mill stones hum as drowsily and steadily as the earth upon its axis . . . The floors all a-tremble, and on them the millers, moving bags of flour on little hand trucks and talking with the incoming farmers with one hand to their ear. After work the millers go home, dusted all over with fine white—looking better men—right out of the Bible.

Thus roars and thunders Plumter's mill and it seems now that it is to start to grind grist for Mr. Plumter's old college. . . .

It has been my fortune at intervals to pass through Woodsdale on the through trains, and I often stop over between the flyer and the slow train, or contrariwise, and spend a few hours with Archie Plumter. He and I were at college together twenty years or more ago and so when we meet Archie's talk is all college—all about the "old shop" as he loves to call it. How is it getting on? Have I been round it at all lately?

Oddly enough, in the twenty years since our graduation Archie has never once been "back": and this, despite the fact that he's in and out of the city, as he himself says, practically all the time, certainly every two years or so. He means to go to the college! . . . always *means* to . . . every time he takes a trip to the city he tells Nell (that's his wife) that he means to have a look around the old joint. But he never does. You see he always has some business in the morning, and generally he takes "some feller" out to lunch, and is apt to meet "one or two fellers" on the street—when a man as genial and comfortable as Archie Plumter comes to the city, the whole street seems filled with accidental "good fellers" as genial as himself.

So he doesn't go. That's nothing. Most graduates are like that, even right in the city. They never go near the old college, unless it's in a bee line between their house and their office. Often they don't see it for ten years. That's nothing to do with their enthusiasm.

Plumter is keen on college. He tells me that they often talk, Dr. Selby and himself, of getting up a college dinner right there in Woodsdale. It seems they've quite a group of graduates. As Archie says, counting himself and Dr. Selby—and Dr. Selby and himself—and not counting the Methodist minister because you would hardly expect him to take anything, there'd be ten of the boys altogether, or eleven if you count the druggist. They often talk of a dinner. But there are difficulties. At a college dinner the boys would naturally like to wear dinner jackets. But there are two of the boys who haven't got dinner jackets. So that has held the thing up—just as it has for many college dinners from Halifax to Pasadena.

So I wasn't surprised when about a couple of weeks ago I got a letter from Archie which said, "If you are coming through here soon I'd be glad if you'd stay over and have dinner some evening. I have some college stuff to ask you about—important stuff—but I'd rather talk about it than explain it in a letter."

Naturally I took occasion as soon as I could stay from afternoon local to the night flyer.

It was one of those beautiful evenings in late September, everything soft and still and mellow; the water in the dam was lower and the water below the dam was quieter, and the main street drowsier and the trees heavier—and the gladioli and asters and late petunias and golden glow banked round the houses and all of Woodsdale hazy and soft with that touch of Indian summer that would have touched even an Indian.

Archie Plumter's house—but you know exactly what that would be like—large and low—sandstone and red brick, and half timber, with sweeping porches and verandahs and clipped grass and flowers, yet as if all in a woodland.

"There's the old college," Archie said as he led me into the library and pointed to a picture. "Nell will be down in a minute. Pretty good of the old joint, isn't it? Just take a good look at it while I shake up a cocktail."

The reader must make no mistake about that cocktail. I said above that you can't get drinks in Woodsdale. Neither can you. This was just some rye and vermouth that Archie had in the house. In fact that's the only way they can get it—to have it in the house.

"I've got some stuff to talk about," said Archie, "but I'd sooner let it keep till after dinner . . ."

We drank the cocktail and in came Nell. Archie Plumter has been as comfortable and fortunate in his marriage as in everything else. Nell's father was a lumberman; in fact, he was a big lumberman, one of the biggest, and there's something about that business of the forest almost as warm and natural as flour and feed, or big scale farming. Poets may talk as they like about a fisherman's daughter who lives on the water. But for matrimony, for comfortable companionship and financial strength, give me a lumberman's daughter every time. "Nell, you remember," said Archie as we shook hands, "was at college too. But she, of course, didn't go on to a degree."

No, of course she didn't. Anyone as pretty as she must have been twenty years ago didn't need a degree. She could pick up something easier at college than that.

"Nell," said Archie, "was a partial."

Was she really? You'd hardly think so now. She looks pretty complete. Still, the years have used her kindly.

"I was just showing this picture of the old circus," continued Archie. "That picture was taken the first year I played on the football team. You remember, Nell, the big game when the college moved up to second place but I couldn't play because of my wrist?"

No doubt Nell remembered it all right: but more likely as the game when he held her hand under the rug on the football benches, and she realized that perhaps she wouldn't need to go any further with mathematics. College girls have their own calendar. They don't remember the day the college gave an honorary degree to the British Ambassador. They remember the day they first wore their dark blue dress with the fur collar.

We went into dinner, one of those excellent and solid dinners, heavy with steak and light with claret and fragrant with coffee and cigars—the kind of real dinner only to be arranged by a lumberman's daughter who remembers feeding her father—just the thing to nourish the trained college brain. The claret, fortunately, was some that Archie had in the cellar; so was the Scotch whiskey that we had afterwards—just stuff out of the cellar.

All through dinner Archie was full of reminiscences and questions and filled with by-gone admiration.

"What became of Professor Crabbe, the Greek Professor?"

"He's still there, I think," I said.

"Some of the fellows didn't like him so much," said Archie, "and of course I never took Greek. But he was certainly a wizard. That man had the most remarkable and the most ready memory I ever came across. I asked him one day, for instance, what was the date of the foundation of Babylon."

"And did he answer?"

"Answered right off—not a moment's hesitation—said he didn't recall it. He certainly was a wonder."

Indeed from our dinner talk that evening the college in Plumter's days had been instructed by a set of "wizards," "wonders" and "wows," an illumination that never comes twice to a college.

"What became of old Professor Dim, the historian?" Archie asked.

"He's still right there," I said, "as far as I know. I haven't been actually inside the college for about a year but I'm sure he's there . . . Pretty old, of course."

"He must be. Do you remember the day I knocked him down in the corridor and the old fellow was nice about it? You remember the way we used to come rushing out of the First Year Latin lecture at twelve o'clock, all in a stampede, and I knocked the old fellow down and Bill, the janitor, picked him up. Where's Bill? When did he die?"

"He's not dead," I said, "he's there." Archie Plumter, like all stay-away graduates, imagined everybody had died since he went away.

After dinner Nell went upstairs to help their two little girls with their algebra. That's where Nell's education as a partial comes in, eh?—able to help the little girls (they're twelve and fourteen) with their algebra. That is, help them as far as simultaneous equations. They'll have to stop there. But they won't need quadratics—pretty little girls like those.

Archie unfolded his ideas over the Scotch and cigars. "What I feel is," he said, "I've been a pretty poor sort of graduate. What have I ever done for the old joint, except a casual subscription and things of that sort? Well—I've been doing pretty well lately—I want to give the college some money. I want to give it twenty-five thousand dollars. Now, here's the point. How do I go about it? What do I do? Where do I get the excuse?'

"Excuse?" I said.

"Yes. How do I start it?"

"Archie," I said, "you don't need any excuse when you give a college money. They'll find the excuse: you just find the money. What do you want to do, endow a set of lectures, or offer a fellowship—or just ask them what to do?"

"Oh, I know just what I want to give," Plumter said. "I want to give a clock— a clock set in a little tower so that students in the campus can see the time. Do you know, when I went to college I had no watch—at least I had an old silver watch of father's, but it wouldn't go."

"I know," I said, "all students used to have old silver watches that wouldn't go. Now they have new gunmetal watches that will."

"Well, this clock I want to give," said Archie, "does more than tell the time. I got the idea from one that Nell and I saw on our trip this summer to California, at one of those old missions. It has chimes inside it, and just before it strikes the hour it strikes a chime.

Bing! Bong! Bong!
Bong! Bing! Bing!

"The most melodious thing I ever heard," Archie said.

It seemed to me that I had heard things more melodious than Plumter's rendering of a chime. But his own opinion was different. He repeated his chimes.

Bing! Bong! Bong!
Bong! Bing! Bing!

And he added: "I've got all the data on the whole thing in a business way. It would cost twenty-five thousand and the contractor could hook the clock tower on at any spot on the roof they like. So what do I do next?"

"Why," I said, "go down to the city and go and see the president and tell him about it. That's all. That will give you a look round the place."

"That's so," he assented, "that's right. I'll have a look at the old shop. I'll come next week. You must meet me at the train."

So a week after that Plumter came up from Woodsdale to the city to make his benefaction.

I met him at the station. It was only half-past eight on a bright autumn morning, but he was nervous already. He began at once. "What I think I'll say, I'll say, 'Mr. President, I'm afraid I've been rather a delinquent graduate, but . . . ' Something like that, eh?"

I said that would be fine. At breakfast, and after, he was still rehearsing it; "'Mr. President, I'm afraid . . . ' I won't beat about the bush," he said. "I'll go right at it, eh?"

He had no notion how easy it is to give twenty-five thousand dollars to a college. You don't have to find the words; just the money.

So in the middle morning we started for the college. I hadn't realized till we came to the gates of the campus how much it has changed since Plumter had left it twenty years ago—the beautiful big Mines Building, all white stone, on one side of the campus and the new library, of white stone and slots of glass on the other.

Plumter stopped dead as we entered the campus.

"I'll be damned!" he said as he looked round it. "Is this all the size it was? No bigger than this? I thought it was twice the size."

Then he said, "What's that?"

"That's the new Mines building," I said.

"Where's the old one, the little old red brick building?"

"They knocked it down," I explained.

"Knocked it down!" repeated Plumter. "Good Lord, knocked it down! And what's the other building?"

"That's the new library," I said; "the old one was knocked down ten years ago."

"You mean they knocked down the library?" said Plumter. He sounded horrified. Then with evident relief, he exclaimed, "Say, there's the old museum, yes, sir, the same darned old museum! I'm certainly glad to see it again."

"You used to be in it much?" I asked.

"I never was in it," said Plumter. "There was ten cents admission, you remember?"

All this time little flocks of students, boys and girls, were overtaking and passing us, for this was the crowded time of the morning with the big lectures of the first and second year going on.

"Who are all these?" asked Plumter. "Is there partly a high school here now?"

"No," I said, "these are the students."

"Good Lord!" said Plumter and stood still to let a demure little group of seventeen-year-old girls go past. One of the demure little girls was saying as she went by, "I don't care what you call it, I call it a hell of a poor course . . ."

And just at that moment we ran into Professor Crabbe. Plumter hailed him with outstretched hand.

"How do you do, sir . . . you remember me . . . I hope . . . I'm Plumter."

"Oh, perfectly well, perfectly well," said the professor, "perfectly well." They shook hands.

"And what are you in now, Mr. Platter?" asked Professor Crabbe.

"I'm in the milling industry, sir," said Plumter.

"In the ministry!" said Professor Crabbe. "Dear me . . . well, you were always heading that way, heading that way! Your Greek must come very well for your sermons.

"I never took any," said Plumter.

"Of course," said the Professor.

"You're still lecturing, sir?" asked Plumter.

"All except my eyesight," answered Professor Crabbe. "My hearing is excellent, Mr. Plaster"—and he gave him a challenging look.

"You can still see for bookwriting, sir," said Plumter pleasantly.

"I never see him," said the professor. "In your class, wasn't he? But I never see him now, haven't for years. Time moves on, you know—well, good-bye, Mr. Blister."

But there was more cheer and consolation in meeting Bill, the janitor, as we went into the Arts Building, Bill who was timeless and ageless, and remembered everything.

"Well, Mr. Plumter, where you been all this time? We thought you was never coming back!"

"You remember me, eh?" said Plumter, much gratified.

"Remember you?" laughed Bill, "I should say so! You was a regular holy terror! More breakages to your name, Mr. Plumter, than any other student in college!"

Plumter joined in the laugh. He must tell them in Woodsdale about that "holy terror" stuff.

Just then there burst into the main hall through the opening class room door the full charge and onslaught of "Latin One Men" coming out after the lecture. It was like what we used to read of the stampede of Texas steers . . . Plumter was swept aside, pounded and jostled in the flooding pushing crowd; but all so polite, those boys. "Sorry, sir," they'd say as they ran into his stomach. "Excuse me, sir," as they got him in the small of his back . . .

"What's all this?" asked Plumter.

"First Year Latin coming out, sir . . . but Lord! That's nothing to what it was in your day. Remember when you knocked down Professor Dim?"

And as the flood subsided who should be standing there but Professor Dim, Professor of History and Archaeology. There he was just as ancient and as rosy and as cheery as ever—just as young at seventy as he had been old at fifty. There he was, gown and all, and his lectures, all in leather, under his arm. Being a professor of history he could remember anything up to three thousand years . . .

"Why, how do you, Mr. Plumter," he said, "how do you do. This is really a pleasure . . . "

"I'm very glad to see you, sir; I always wish I'd been fortunate enough to take your lectures."

"Ah, now, that's very kind of you! I wonder if you wouldn't care perhaps to come in and sit and listen now . . . oh no, these are not the old lectures of your time—this is a new course—it's only the sixth year I've given it—a course on the Crusades . . . But do come . . . I've just a small class . . . a dozen . . . I often have visitors drop in . . . only last month a young Chinaman came in . . . accidentally . . . but he was delighted . . . Please do."

So genial, so anxious, old Professor Dim, with that queer conceit a professor never loses—so what could we say?

"That's right," said Professor Dim. "William here will show you the room."

The class were already there, seated and decorously waiting—a professor's "dozen" of them, that is, seven. Anyone acquainted with a college register could have explained just who they were and why they were there: three divinity students who were taking the Crusades as a credit in Christianity, a football student taking it as a football qualification, a history student who was liable to the Crusades because he'd fallen down on the French Revolution, and two women Sociology students who had been compelled by a clash in the time-table to substitute the Crusades in place of a course in Motherhood which came at the wrong hour.

From the side door in came Professor Dim. He took his place behind his reading desk, unfolded and spread the blue fool's-cap sheets of the Crusades, bowed courteously to the class, and began:—

"Heliogabalus—" began Professor Dim.
"I beg your pardon, sir," said the football man.
"Heliogabalus, Mr. Munro—" repeated Professor Dim.
"Thank you, sir—"
"Heliogabalus," said Professor Dim, for the third time—and paused while all the class wrote down Heliogabalus . . .
"having now assumed the purple . . . " announced Professor Dim.
"purple" . . . wrote the class.

A college lecture is a queer thing, for people not accustomed to it. The Professor isn't exactly dictating the lecture, and he isn't exactly talking, and the class are not exactly taking dictation and they're not exactly listening. It's a system they both have grown so used to that it's second nature.

But for anyone to have to sit and listen to it, without writing down anything, not even "purple," is, of course, impossible. It's excruciating. I could watch Archie Plumter suffering; trying to look interested; trying to listen; trying to not listen. I knew just what he was thinking; he was wondering if it was really true that he had had four years of this! That he had gone not to one lecture in the morning but to two, three or even four of them!

So he sat agonizing. Then I found in my pocket a pencil and I took some sheets of paper "off" a divinity student behind us, and gave them to Plumter. Oh, my! what a change! What a transformation!

He happened to get the chance of a real start . . . Professor Dim had just opened up. "In the year A.D. 940, or, if you prefer it, the Arabian year 318 . . . " Oh, my! that was stuff! Mr. Plumter's pencil flew over the paper . . . In five minutes he was absorbed—in ten minutes lost to the world, in the fascination, the concentration of taking notes. Old habit and forgotten aptitude sprang again to life. He wrote and spelt such names Godroi de Bouillon and Saladin Ben Shirgah as easily as you jump a ditch in a van! Think what it would mean, how wonderful it would be, to spend four years like this, with perhaps two or three lectures every morning!

After the lecture we shook hands with Professor Dim—the Professor a little flushed, a little flurried but as happy over praise as a schoolboy.

"Certainly a wonderful lecture, sir," said Plumter, his notes all collected into a precious heap.

"I'm so glad you liked it," said Professor Dim. "It's one of four—as I say, a special course—when I get it into shape, in a year or two, my hope is to open the course to the public . . . if I had a large hall . . . "

"You'd certainly draw a big crowd," said Archie Plumter, and he meant it.

And then to see the President. Down the corridor and along and through and up, and so to the President's outer office, where we sent in Plumter's card and waited.

Archie, I saw, was all nervous again. I could hear him reciting.

The President's lady secretary, filing cards, said it was a fine day, and Plumter didn't hear her.

She filed some more and then asked him where he lived, and, he remembered and said, "Woodsdale." Then the buzzer buzzed and she said that the President would see us now, and so in we went.

The President rose and shook hands—with me, casually, as to someone known, but with Plumter, as evidently the main visitor, the person of the occasion.

"How do you do?" he said, "Mr.—" as he looked down at the little card—"Mr. Plumter, is it not?"

"Yes," Plumter said.

"Ah, yes," said the President, "Mr. Plumter of the class of . . . class of . . . "

"Yes," Plumter said.

"And you're now living in—"

"Woodsdale," Plumter said.

At that moment the lady secretary slipped into the room, said something into the President's ear to which he answered in a low voice, "Ask him kindly to wait—about five minutes."

"Woodsdale!" he said. "Woodsdale, oh, yes, that's out—out beyond . . . "

"Yes," said Plumter.

"And what profession are you following, Mr. Plumter?" asks the President.

"I'm not in a profession," Archie said. "I'm mostly in feed."

The President hadn't the least idea what he meant; it certainly sounded pretty hoggish but he answered as pleasantly as he could, "Ah, yes, you're in feed, eh!"

Just then the desk telephone on the table made a gurgling sound; the President picked it up, listened, and said, "Oh, yes, very pleased, indeed, yes, in about five minutes."

The brief pause had enabled Plumter to collect his courage for the effort he had to make. He determined to say what he had to and be done with it.

He rose and stood up—it seemed more formal and natural to say it in that attitude.

"Mr. President," he said, "I'm afraid I—" and he cleared his throat.

The President had risen also and put out his hand with a smile; he thought Plumter was leaving . . . He would have liked to speak of lunch, but with a man mostly in feed it seemed risky.

But just as he began to speak there fell upon our ears, from somewhere outside, the loud and melodious sound of a chime of bells:

Bing! Bong! Bong!

Bong! Bing! Bing!

"Ah"—said the President, his head on one side and an appreciative smile on his face—"Ah! Our new chimes! Beautiful, aren't they? The gift of one of our graduates, a clock tower with a chime! You may have noticed it on the left as you came up!"

As we walked away from the building I said, "I'm sorry, Archie, I didn't know about those chimes; I haven't been round here for a year; they are evidently just new."

"Oh, that's all right," he said, and he added, "To hell with them!"

And just then a little incident happened to cheer him up. For there was good old Bill, the janitor, running down the front steps . . . "Just to say good-bye, if you're off, sir," he called, and as he joined us, "Hope you'll come again before long, sir."

"Thanks very much Bill . . ."

"And here's a little note sir, that I was to give to you. The Bursar heard you was round, sir, and he said not to let you go without this. It's a bill for breakages he's had, sir, for years and years. He'd lost your address."

As we moved off down the avenue, we saw in the sideways distance Professor Dim starting off for home, his Crusades, all in leather, under his arm—he waved his hand in good-bye. "That old bird," said Plumter, "is worth the whole dam lot of them."

Depressed? You'd be surprised how fast that sort of thing wears off . . . By the time we'd had a cocktail at the club, Plumter was beginning to feel as if we'd had a pretty notable morning . . . By the time we'd had lunch, he was explaining to men at the club that he'd been having a look round the old shop . . . and that the new Mines Building was certainly all right . . .

For you see, after all, he hadn't bought the clock, he still had his twenty-five thousand dollars, and already a new idea was dawning on his mind . . . By the time he got to Woodsdale he was full of it all, more of a graduate than ever.

The Woodsdale *By-path* (Archie owned it) . . . printed in the next issue some interesting *Notes on the Third Crusade*, beginning "Heliogabalus, having assumed the purple . . ."

And a few weeks after that the "college boys" of Woodsdale pulled off their college dinner—put on their dinner jackets and pulled the dinner off. One of the two had bought one and the other one borrowed one—so it was all right. Archie Plumter made the speech of the evening, and he said that a college graduate who didn't from time to time, say at least once in twenty years, visit the old place was as low as a snake.

But just a little after that came the big thing, the announcement in all the city papers, of the foundation of an endowment at the college of a series of Four Lectures on the Crusades, to be given annually by the greatest scholars in the world. You'll see the lectures listed now right there in the front pages of the calendar among Endowments and Benefactions. They're called *The Dim Lectures on the Crusades, endowed by Archibald and Helen Plumter*—four of them endowed at five hundred dollars each. Professor Dim will give them the first ten years and after that they'll be thrown open to all the scholars of the world. My! Won't there be a scramble?

III.8

"The Men in the Storm"

Stephen Crane

In this story, American journalist, poet, and prolific author Stephen Crane (1871–1900) vividly conveys the relief that a "charitable house" (today, a "homeless shelter") can bring. As the freezing snow blows, men gather to await the opening of the charitable house, where for a nickel they can get a bed for the night and bread and coffee in the morning. As if the storm outside provides a license, these hordes of grim and desperate men quickly forget whatever self-restraint they may once have had. Invectives fly, and they nearly crush one another as they battle to position themselves as close as possible to the port of entry to the house. At long last the door is opened, and a miraculous change takes place in their behavior. Crane seems to suggest that charitable houses, however minimal their services, are absolutely necessary to perpetuate civilized ways. The hope that such houses offer instantly allays the truly threatening storm within, which lurks just beneath the surface, waiting to drag people back to the barbarisms of the state of nature. Is Crane's seemingly grim view of human nature correct? Does he exaggerate the difference a charitable house can make? Should there be more such places? Whom should they serve? Should the nickel that is required for entry to the charitable house in the story, or its current equivalent, be a requirement for attendance? Should there be any requirements? What services should such places provide?

The blizzard began to swirl great clouds of snow along the streets, sweeping it down from the roofs, and up from the pavements, until the faces of pedestrians tingled and burned as from a thousand needle-prickings. Those on the walks huddled their necks closely in the collars of their coats, and went along stooping like a race of aged people. The drivers of vehicles hurried their horses furiously on their way. They were made more cruel by the exposure of their position, aloft on high seats. The street cars, bound up-town, went slowly, the horses slipping and straining in the spongy brown mass that lay between the rails. The drivers, muffled to the eyes, stood erect, facing the wind, models of grim philosophy.

From *An Omnibus, Crane,* edited by Robert Wooster Stallman (New York: Alfred A. Knopf, 1952), pp. 23–30.

Overhead, trains rumbled and roared, and the dark structure of the elevated railroad, stretching over the avenue, dripped little streams and drops of water upon the mud and snow beneath.

All the clatter of the street was softened by the masses that lay upon the cobbles, until, even to one who looked from a window, it became important music, a melody of life made necessary to the ear by the dreariness of the pitiless beat and sweep of the storm. Occasionally one could see black figures of men busily shoveling the white drifts from the walks. The sounds from their labour created new recollections of rural experiences which every man manages to have in a measure. Later, the immense windows of the shops became aglow with light, throwing great beams of orange and yellow upon the pavement. They were infinitely cheerful, yet in a way they accentuated the force and discomfort of the storm, and gave a meaning to the pace of the people and the vehicles, scores of pedestrians and drivers, wretched with cold faces, necks, and feet, speeding for scores of unknown doors and entrances, scattering to an infinite variety of shelters, to places which the imagination made warm with the familiar colours of home.

There was an absolute expression of hot dinners in the pace of the people. If one dared to speculate upon the destination of those who came trooping, he lost himself in a maze of social calculation; he might fling a handful of sand and attempt to follow the flight of each particular grain. But as to the suggestion of hot dinners, he was in firm lines of thought, for it was upon every hurrying face. It is a matter of tradition; it is from the tales of childhood. It comes forth with every storm.

However, in a certain part of a dark west-side street, there was a collection of men to whom these things were as if they were not. In this street was located a charitable house where for five cents the homeless of the city could get a bed at night, and in the morning coffee and bread.

During the afternoon of the storm, the whirling snows acted as drivers, as men with whips, and at half-past three the walk before the closed doors of the house was covered with wanderers of the street, waiting. For some distance on either side of the place they could be seen lurking in the doorways and behind projecting parts of buildings, gathering in close bunches in an effort to get warm. A covered wagon drawn up near the curb sheltered a dozen of them. Under the stairs that led to the elevated railway station, there were six or eight, their hands stuffed deep in their pockets, their shoulders stooped, jiggling their feet. Others always could be seen coming, a strange procession, some slouching along with the characteristic hopeless gait of professional strays, some coming with hesitating steps, wearing the air of men to whom this sort of thing was new.

It was an afternoon of incredible length. The snow, blowing in twisting clouds, sought out the men in their meager hiding-places, and skillfully beat in among them, drenching their persons with showers of fine stinging flakes. They crowded together, muttering, and fumbling in their pockets to get their red inflamed wrists covered by the cloth.

New-comers usually halted at one end of the groups and addressed a question, perhaps much as a matter of form, "Is it open yet?"

Those who had been waiting inclined to take the questioner seriously and became contemptuous. "No; do yeh think we'd be standin' here?"

The gathering swelled in numbers steadily and persistently. One could always see them coming, trudging slowly through the storm.

Finally, the little snow plains in the street began to assume a leaden hue from the shadows of the evening. The buildings upreared gloomily save where various windows became brilliant figures of light, that made shimmers and splashes of yellow on the snow. A street lamp on the curb struggled to illuminate, but it was reduced to impotent blindness by the swift gusts of sleet crusting its panes.

In this half-darkness, the men began to come from their shelter-places and mass in front of the doors of charity. They were of all types, but the nationalities were mostly American, German, and Irish. Many were strong, healthy, clear-skinned fellows, with that stamp of countenance which is not frequently seen upon seekers after charity. There were men of undoubted patience, industry, and temperance, who, in time of ill-fortune, do not habitually turn to rail at the state of society, snarling at the arrogance of the rich, and bemoaning the cow- · ardice of the poor, but who at these times are apt to wear a sudden and singular meekness, as if they saw the world's progress marching from them, and were trying to perceive where they had failed, what they had lacked, to be thus vanquished in the race. Then there were others, of the shifting Bowery element, who were used to paying ten cents for a place to sleep, but who now came here because it was cheaper.

But they were all mixed in one mass so thoroughly that one could not have discerned the different elements, but for the fact that the labouring men, for the most part, remained silent and impassive in the blizzard, their eyes fixed on the windows of the house, statues of patience.

The sidewalk soon became completely blocked by the bodies of the men. They pressed close to one another like sheep in a winter's gale, keeping one another warm by the heat of their bodies. The snow came upon this compressed group of men until, directly from above, it might have appeared like a heap of snow-covered merchandise, if it were not for the fact that the crowd swayed gently with a unanimous rhythmical motion. It was wonderful to see how the snow lay upon the heads and shoulders of these men, in little ridges an inch thick perhaps in places, the flakes steadily adding drop and drop, precisely as they fall upon the unresisting grass of the fields. The feet of the men were all wet and cold, and the wish to warm them accounted for the slow, gentle rhythmical motion. Occasionally some man whose ear or nose tingled acutely from the cold winds would wriggle down until his head was protected by the shoulders of his companions.

There was a continuous murmuring discussion as to the probability of the doors being speedily opened. They persistently lifted their eyes toward the windows. One could hear little combats of opinion.

"There's a light in th' winder!"

"Naw; it's a reflection f'm across th' way."

"Well, didn't I see 'em light it?"

"You did?"

"I did!"

"Well, then, that settles it!"

As the time approached when they expected to be allowed to enter, the men crowded to the doors in an unspeakable crush, jamming and wedging in a way that, it seemed, would crack bones. They surged heavily against the building in a powerful wave of pushing shoulders. Once a rumour flitted among all the tossing heads.

"They can't open th' door! Th' fellers er smack up agin 'em."

Then a dull roar of rage came from the men on the outskirts; but all the time they strained and pushed until it appeared to be impossible for those that they cried out against to do anything but be crushed into pulp.

"Ah, git away f'm th' door!"

"Git outa that!"

"Throw 'em out!"

"Kill 'em!"

"Say, fellers, now, what th' 'ell? G've 'em a chance t' open th' door!"

"Yeh damn pigs, give 'em a chance t' open th' door!"

Men in the outskirts of the crowd occasionally yelled when a boot-heel of one of trampling feet crushed on their freezing extremities.

"Git off me feet, yeh clumsy tarrier!"

"Say, don't stand on me feet! Walk on th' ground!"

A man near the doors suddenly shouted: "O-o-oh! Le' me out—le' me out!" And another, a man of infinite valour, once twisted his head so as to half face those who were pushing behind him. "Quit yer shovin', yeh"—and he delivered a volley of the most powerful and singular invective, straight into the faces of the men behind him. It was as if he was hammering the noses of them with curses of triple brass. His face, red with rage, could be seen, upon it an expression of sublime disregard of consequences. But nobody cared to reply to his imprecations; it was too cold. Many of them snickered, and all continued to push.

In occasional pauses of the crowd's movement the men had opportunities to make jokes; usually grim things, and no doubt very uncouth. Nevertheless, they were notable—one does not expect to find the quality of humour in a heap of old clothes under a snowdrift.

The winds seemed to grow fiercer as time wore on. Some of the gusts of snow that came down on the close collection of heads cut like knives and needles, and the men huddled, and swore, not like dark assassins, but in a sort of American fashion, grimly and desperately, it is true, but yet with a wondrous under-effect, indefinable and mystic, as if there was some kind of humour in this catastrophe, in this situation in a night of snow-laden winds.

Once the window of the huge dry-goods shop across the street furnished material for a few moments of forgetfulness. In the brilliantly lighted space appeared the figure of a man. He was rather stout and very well clothed. His beard was fashioned charmingly after that of the Prince of Wales. He stood in an attitude of magnificent reflection. He slowly stroked his moustache with a certain grandeur of manner, and looked down at the snow-encrusted mob. From below, there was denoted a supreme complacence in him. It seemed that the sight operated inversely, and enabled him to more clearly regard his own delightful environment.

One of the mob chanced to turn his head, and perceived the figure in the window. "Hello, look-it 'is whiskers," he said genially.

Many of the men turned then, and a shout went up. They called to him in all strange keys. They addressed him in every manner, from familiar and cordial greetings to carefully worded advice concerning changes in his personal appearance. The man presently fled, and the mob chuckled ferociously, like ogres who had just devoured something.

They turned then to serious business. Often they addressed the stolid front of the house.

"Oh, let us in fer Gawd's sake!"

"Let us in, or we'll all drop dead!"

"Say, what's th' use o' keepin' us poor Indians out in th' cold?"

And always some one was saying, "Keep off my feet."

The crushing of the crowd grew terrific toward the last. The men, in keen pain from the blasts, began almost to fight. With the pitiless whirl of snow upon them, the battle for shelter was going to the strong. It became known that the basement door of the foot of a little steep flight of stairs was the one to be opened, and they jostled and heaved in this direction like labouring fiends. One could hear them panting and groaning in their fierce exertion.

Usually some one in the front ranks was protesting to those in the rear—"O-o-ow! Oh, say now, fellers, let up, will yeh? Do yeh wanta kill somebody?"

A policeman arrived and went into the midst of them, scolding and berating, occasionally threatening, but using no force but that of his hands and shoulders against these men who were only struggling to get in out of the storm. His decisive tones rang out sharply—"Stop that pushin' back there! Come, boys, don't push! Stop that! Here you, quit yer shovin'! Cheese that!"

When the door below was opened, a thick stream of men forced a way down the stairs, which were of an extraordinary narrowness, and seemed only wide enough for one at a time. Yet they somehow went down almost three abreast. It was a difficult and painful operation. The crowd was like a turbulent water forcing itself through one tiny outlet. The men in the rear, excited by the success of the others, made frantic exertions, for it seemed that this large band would more than fill the quarters, and that many would be left upon the pavements. It would be disastrous to be of the last, and accordingly men with the snow biting their faces writhed and twisted with their might. One expected that, from the tremendous pressure, the narrow passage to the basement door would be so choked and clogged with human limbs and bodies that movement would be impossible. Once indeed the crowd was forced to stop, and a cry went along that a man had been injured at the foot of the stairs. But presently the slow movement began again, and the policeman fought at the top of the flight to ease the pressure of those that were going down.

A reddish light from the window fell upon the faces of the men when they, in turn, arrived at the last three steps and were about to enter. One could then note a change of expression that had come over their features. As they stood thus upon the threshold of their hopes, they looked suddenly contented and complacent. The fire had passed from their eyes and the snarl had vanished from their lips. The very force of the crowd in the rear, which had previously vexed them, was regarded from another point of view, for it now made it inevitable that they should go through the little doors into the place that was cheery and warm with light.

The tossing crowd on the sidewalk grew smaller and smaller. The snow beat with merciless persistence upon the bowed heads of those who waited. The wind drove it up from the pavements in frantic forms of winding white, and it seethed in circles about the huddled forms passing in one by one, three by three, out of the storm.

III.9

"Charity and the Confines of Compassion"

Leon R. Kass

According to a recent (1996) survey, an estimated 93 million Americans do volunteer work each year, collectively clocking 20.3 billion hours. The vast majority of those hours are apparently spent doing work on behalf of the poor, the educationally disadvantaged, the sick, and the infirm. We have younger and younger people participating in tutoring programs, Habitat for Humanity, and the like. Indeed, many high schools have instituted community service requirements for graduation. Add to this the outpouring of concern, as well as the manifest readiness to give and to serve since September 11, 2001, and one might well conclude that we Americans are a most compassionate people. Deep down, we do regard ourselves as our brother's keeper. Is this an unqualifiedly good thing? What if those we serve bring their troubles on themselves? What if they deliberately put themselves in harm's way? What if they act irresponsibly?

In this essay, Leon R. Kass (born in 1939), a medically trained humanist, invites us to reflect on the limits or confines of our seemingly ever-ready compassion. Kass recalls us to the broader moral implications of the original meaning of the term "philanthropy"—*philanthropia,* the love of humankind, or practical goodwill toward human beings in general. Beside the banner of compassion, he would have us fly the banners of "decency, justice, liberty, reverence, and truth" and consider the importance of giving to those people and institutions most likely to cultivate the same. Though the explicit addressee of Kass's essay is organized philanthropy—the essay was originally a speech entitled "Am I My (Foolish) Brother's Keeper?", given to the Philanthropy Roundtable, a consortium of philanthropic foundations—both the questions Kass raises and the specific recommendations he makes drive home its relevance to each of us as individual would-be philanthropists. To what extent *am* I my foolish brother's keeper? How can I truly help him without compounding his foolishness with mine?

The brochure announcing The Philanthropy Roundtable's 1995 annual meeting observed that because of America's new political landscape, "the charitable sector is being asked not only to deliver services that government is casting off, but to deliver these services more efficiently and effectively." The brochure urged us to consider "whether philanthropy can meet this challenge." But, in my view, we should first consider a prior question: whether philanthropy *should* meet this challenge. In particular, should private philanthropy adopt for itself the goals of the Great Society and other social programs, programs that have not succeeded in the hands of Uncle Sam but that might succeed better in the nimbler hands of private philanthropy and its grantees?

Most of these programs, like them or not, sprang from a humane compassion for the less fortunate among us—the poor, the sick, and the needy; the ill-fed, the ill-housed, and the ill-educated; the deprived, the despised, and the disabled. Caring for the unfortunate has always been part of the mission of private charities, especially those connected to religious organizations. Thus, the adoption by the charitable sector of government's compassion-driven programs might seem to restore the *status quo ante* before the Great Society or even the New Deal. But times have changed, and we should think carefully before reaching this conclusion. Much depends on whether compassion is today the necessary and sufficient operating principle for philanthropic action.

For some people, especially on the left, the heart of the philanthropic spirit is compassion. One commentator even defines philanthropy as "compassionate action on behalf of other human beings." But this is a partial and narrowed view. In its root sense, philanthropy means the love of mankind, practical goodwill toward human beings in general, the disposition to promote the happiness and well-being of one's fellow men—not just the relief of their miseries.

This elementary definition raises some troubling questions. First, *toward whom* shall we practice philanthropy? Humankind is an abstraction, hard to love and certainly hard to love well. Even "one's fellow men" is rather an obscure object for good will and love. For which human beings should philanthropists exercise their benevolence and beneficence? In particular, should it matter if some of the proposed beneficiaries have brought their troubles on themselves? Should it matter if they are unwilling or unable to benefit from the philanthropist's offerings?

Second, *how* do we properly love those we seek to benefit? Philanthropy, strictly speaking, describes only a condition of our will or inclination or intention: having a good will toward one's fellow men. But does the *desire* to promote the good of others necessarily carry with it the *true knowledge* of that good, what it is, or how to obtain it? Are good intentions or goodwill sufficient? Is love or compassion enough?

Third, if philanthropy should be broader than charity, if the generous love of human beings goes beyond, and aims higher than, the alleviation of human suffering, how will the goals and works of philanthropy be confined should compassion increasingly command its ship? How should philanthropy seek to balance the competing claims of the high and the urgent, the promotion of excellence versus the demands of necessity? If the high is always being sacrificed to the urgent, what kind of a society will we be creating?

Let me address each of these three questions in turn.

WHOM SHOULD PHILANTHROPY SERVE?

First, whom to serve. Private philanthropy has always seen as part of its charge the care of those who are badly off through no fault of their own. But for several decades, we as a society have been increasingly asked, encouraged and sometimes even compelled to come to the aid of those who refuse to take care of themselves, who live dangerously, foolishly, and self-destructively, incurring great risks not only to life and limb, but also to the economic, psychic, and social well-being of those around them as well as themselves. I mean those engaged in heavy drinking, drug abuse, gangs, reckless driving, treacherous amusements, unsafe and irresponsible sexual activity, excessive gambling, excessive borrowing and spending, and refusal to make good on ordinary obligations in school or on the job.

In a free society, people will be free by and large to run these risks; the question is, to what extent should everyone—or anyone—else bear the cost of the resulting harms?

Our Judeo-Christian tradition teaches us that each of us is his brother's keeper. To deny responsibility for one's brother is, tacitly, to express indifference to his fate, and in this sense to be tacitly guilty of all harm that befalls him: in the extreme, to say yes even to his death.

But this moral lesson is both far from clear and far from complete. For who exactly is my brother—which is to say, for how many human beings do I bear such fraternal responsibility? More importantly, what does it mean to be someone's keeper? Does the duty to guard and protect against outside dangers extend also to dangers one's brother poses to himself? What if he chooses to court disaster, whether from vice, weakness of will, foolishness, or ignorance? Does guarding your brother mean picking up after his stupidity?

Consider an example. My entire liver has been damaged in an auto accident. My brother is the most suitable donor for a partial liver transplant. Have I claim on his liver? Not at all. But what does our brotherliness require of him? Should his decision to donate be influenced by the fact that I was responsible for the accident, that I had been speeding on icy roads, and not wearing a seat belt? Or what if my need of a liver transplant were due not to a one-time auto accident but to a lifetime of alcoholism? Should my brother be obliged to help? Does my promise to stop drinking and join Alcoholics Anonymous make a difference? Should our public policy regarding donation (or health insurance) be influenced by whether and how people have brought their troubles on themselves and whether they intend to reform?

There can, of course, be no simple or set rules for answering these questions. Much will depend upon the particulars. We will be more inclined and expected to alleviate harm caused by foolishness or weakness of will than by vice, by a singular or occasional episode of folly than by chronic foolhardiness, and so forth. These qualifications aside, any *prime facie* obligation to help will surely be limited and perhaps even overturned, first, when we do not know what real help is; second, when assistance will be useless because it is refused or squandered; or third, when there are better or more urgent outlets for one's beneficence including competing obligations to others.

For these reasons, among others, there are many times when it is surely foolish to come to the rescue of foolishness. Moral obligation cannot mean that the remedy for someone else's foolishness is to match or surpass it with our own. The obligation to be even our blood brother's keeper cannot be absolute.

Much as we may love our brothers, and much as we should endeavor to care for our neighbor, we also love and care for what is good and right. Indeed, the beginning of morality is the subordination of unqualified self-love and the love of one's own to the standards of good and bad, justice and injustice. We are taught to do what is right. We are taught not to make exceptions in our own case. We are taught to accept responsibility for our own lives and conduct, and to expect others to do the same.

Most Americans, in fact, believe in the importance of accepting and fostering personal moral responsibility. Most of us see that human action is based on human freedom, human freedom is manifested in choice, and human dignity in action resides in making our choices in full cognizance that we are the sources of our deeds and responsible for their effects. Self-conscious choice tacitly cheers for justice, for a world in which people get what they deserve. And while we all know that the world is far from wholly just, all societies and institutions and most human lives work on the premise that the world makes sense. Moreover, by our responsible practices and by our praise and blame we contrive to have the world make even more sense. We read children stories like "The Little Red Hen," to teach them that it is just that those who work for their food should get to eat and those who refuse to work should not. People are pleased when hard work and fair play are rewarded, and at least until recently we did not take kindly to whiners, complainers, and those who blamed others for their own failures. A man who pleaded drunkenness as an excuse for his violence was doubly punished; a woman who went to a man's bedroom and then got drunk with him could not escape bearing some responsibility for what happened next. America grew up strong because people acted in the spirit of the maxim, "By the time a man is 30, he is responsible even for his face."

But what then about compassion? The claims of compassion might seem to oppose the claims of justice and lead us always to our foolish brother's assistance. Yet if compassion is rightly understood, this turns out to be at best only partly true. In fact, compassion as experienced sentiment—rather than as ideological principle—is somewhat allied with justice. The point was noted by Aristotle in his account of pity: "Pity is a certain pain at manifest or apparent badness, destructive or painful, *hitting one who is undeserving,* which one might expect oneself or someone of one's own to suffer" (emphasis added).

Pity, or what we now call compassion, is not indiscriminate sympathy for suffering. A judgement of whether the badness suffered is deserved is implicit in the feeling of compassion.

This is not to say that everyone judges well whether the suffering is deserved, but most people, given half a chance and adequate information, will pity fittingly, which is to say justly. They feel more pity for crack babies than for their mothers, more pity for a man if his liver failure be caused by tainted blood transfusion than if it be the result of chronic alcoholism, more pity for the homeless person who is mentally ill than for the one who has for years refused to work.

Compassion as sentiment is not, in principle, at war with a concern for justice. Yet modern life and modern political thought have done much to distort the normal operation of compassion, even while elevating it to political principle. Powerful visual images of suffering—horror without context—are television's daily fare, tugging at our heartstrings, which are already overstretched far beyond the capacity for normal response. The media's exploitation of visual images of suffering corrupts compassion by demanding instant and unqualified sympathy, without knowledge or judgement. It moves us toward what one might call a merely medical view of the world, more precisely the emergency-room view of the world, with its amoral and no-fault approach to all troubles and its justice-neutral brand of compassion—a point to which I will return.

Add to this the political hegemony of compassion as the first proof of public virtue, and we see how we have created a world in which victims are more honored than heroes. Indeed, victims are lionized for their suffering—and, more to the point, despite their own culpability in coming to harm: Do more people think Magic Johnson is a fool for living dangerously than think he is a hero for going public as a victim? Sympathy and fellow-feeling are of course precious and praiseworthy, but an indiscriminate compassion that is deaf to judgement can hardly be the basis for a morally sound philanthropy.

Yet there are other reasons, beyond the inadequate claims of our new breed of compassion, why the principles of strict responsibility and giving to each his just deserts, however suitable as a starting point, cannot be the whole story. Given the unpredictabilities of life, it is presumptuous to believe that one can live with perfect forethought and planning, immune to bad results. Besides, there is frequently much virtue in risk-taking: many of society's greatest benefactors have gambled on their ability to make good in the absence of any guarantees. Needless to say, not all failure is the result of folly or vice. In recognition of this fact, society prepares partial safety nets to catch those who fall while trying to climb. We abolished debtor's prisons, permit people to declare bankruptcy, and in many other ways embody our sound belief in the rightness of second chances. America is internationally famous as the home of the second chance.

But for even more profound reasons, the principle of strict responsibility cannot be the sole standard for assessing the misfortunes of our foolish brethren. For not every one starts out with a full deck when it comes to living prudently. Differences in rearing and life experience create differences in each person's ability to choose, in the choices we make, and in our capacity to stick by our better choices. The mysterious yet nigh universal phenomenon of moral weakness—that is, knowing the good but not doing it—accounts for much of what we call foolish conduct, and, repeated, it is habit-forming.

Children are maimed for responsibility both by indulgent parents who shelter them from learning from the consequences of their mistakes and by negligent parents who fail to teach them the importance of avoiding them in the first place. Inborn influences, no less than environmental ones—neither of them of our own making—predispose to success or failure in the battle for self-command.

About these things science still knows very little, but enough to suspect that at least some aspects of intractable and self-harming behavior probably have a partly genetic foundation. And, perhaps most important, there are inborn differences in intelligence. One can say to one's child, "Be sensible," but one cannot say "Be intelligent." Yet if, in this increasingly complex world, it takes more and more intelligence to figure out what "being sensible" requires, lots of people are going to be playing the game of life with severe but invisible handicaps. And regarding their economic independence, it is sad but true that hard work and the best intentions will probably leave many people at the bottom of the heap, increasingly so in our hypertechnological age in which a strong back and a willingness to work are not enough to enable you to prosper.

On the basis of arguments like these, one might suggest that a decent community will try to care not only for those who are worse off than others through no fault of their own, but even to bear some of the costs of helping those who are partly responsible for their own troubles. This is not so much a matter of justice or rights or even compassion, but a matter of the common good. We care for our fellow citizens because we are all in this together. The fortunate and the less foolish among us have every reason not to be limited by strict proportionality. We can, not least for our own sakes, improve upon justice in the direction of generosity and care. Acts of beneficence not only contribute to the common good by the benefits they bestow; they contribute also because they are manifestation of virtue, and as such are central to the flourishing of the benefactors—and, indeed, of the whole society. Rightly understood, philanthropic deeds are not self-sacrificing but self-affirming and self-fulfilling, and a society that is generous beyond what is strictly owed must be counted amongst humanity's finest achievements. Thus, if our brothers need defense against themselves even more than against outsiders, we should be willing—in principle—to offer it, not least for our own goodness' sake.

HOW TO SERVE

This then brings me to the second dilemma: *How* should we care for them?

The difficulty for philanthropy turns out to be not one of intention, but of knowledge. What does it really mean to help and to keep? The present hegemony of no-fault compassion is to be blamed not so much for its implicit willingness to care, but for its failure to understand what care really means. For one does not really keep one's brother by helping him in ways likely to increase his foolishness. On the contrary, help aimed at undoing the harms caused by foolishness is insufficient if it is unaccompanied by help aimed at fostering the benefit of assuming moral and personal responsibility.

This is not easily done, not by anyone, certainly not by distant do-gooders. A desire to help does not translate readily into sensible policy or grant proposals. Compassionate measures aimed at preventing foolish behavior are often difficult to devise, for it is notoriously difficult to get people to do what is good for them without tyrannizing them. And measures aimed at remedying the harm afterwards may remove disincentives for prudent self-restraint. For example, we have compassionately spared illegitimate children the opprobrium that they once had to bear, but as a result, many more of them are sired out of wedlock and abandoned with impunity.

More generally, the availability of an ounce of cure drives out pounds of prevention. Worse, remedies can even change our view of whether risky behavior is in fact foolish. Not so long ago, a man who had contracted syphilis was, by and large, not an object of pity, and this quite apart from the question of his likely immorality. For he almost certainly consorted with the wrong sort of woman, and carelessly to boot; he knowingly brought his troubles on himself. Today, in our age of antibiotics, many sufferers from sexually transmitted diseases overlook their own responsibility; instead, they even blame their miseries on society's failure to provide a cure. Increasingly, the privileged status of suffering, of being a victim, makes it almost impossible to see this as a self-induced harm, one that clamors less for a miracle drug, more for decent and responsible conduct.

This points toward the forgotten crux of compassion. Most deserving of our sympathy and compassion is not our brother's bodily suffering but his inability or unwillingness to stand in the world with freedom and dignity, which is to say, as a responsible source of his own conduct ready and willing to be held accountable for himself and for his actions. Just as the sentiment of compassion rightly experienced is natively not immune to judgements of past responsibility, so the exercise of compassion rightly practiced is centrally concerned with enabling the recipient to become more willing and able to choose better and to accept responsibility in the future. True compassion, especially toward the remediably foolish, is synonymous in the current lingo with "tough love."

How this is to be accomplished is, of course, a tricky matter, varying case by case. There are no set rules; there is no single strategy. It is never easy to shift effectively from individualized strategies for interpersonal cases to the necessarily statistical approaches of public policy for larger populations. But the sound moral principle of tough-loving prudence is the same in every case, regardless of scale, and regardless of whether the benefactor is Uncle Sam or a private foundation: to foster personal responsibility and a world that approximates justice, in which people get what they deserve; and, at the same time, to foster fellow-feeling and a world in which people are inclined to be generous—and especially generous in helping people morally and spiritually so that they will eventually no longer need such generosity.

Unfortunately, institutionalized philanthropists, public and private, often enjoy nurturing dependency, for they too are needy creatures, with a great need to be needed. By labeling their beneficiaries as "victims," and by sometimes whipping up hostility toward non-victims and normal society, they degrade the objects of their compassion and encourage further dependence. They seem too often to forget that, as C. S. Lewis put it, "the proper aim of giving is to put the recipient in a state where he no longer needs our gift." This means attaching demands and inducements for change of behavior to offers of outright aid in relief of self-induced harm; it also means not destroying the public will to generosity with excessive and unreasonable demands upon our compassion or with unrealistic programs built on unreasonable hopes borrowed from utopian dreams.

THE CONFINES OF COMPASSION

Thus, finally to the third question: Should philanthropy sail increasingly under the flag of compassion? Compassionate humanitarianism, the guiding light of the welfare state, is arguably the most powerful idea of modernity. It is certainly at the root of the modern scientific-and-technological project, begun in the seventeenth century and growing, exponentially in our own, a project whose explicit purpose was from the start the conquest of nature for the relief of man's estate. Facing a world seemingly tragic for all human aspiration, our rationalist forebears —like Bacon and Descartes—set out to conquer fate and fortune on the basis of the scientific understanding of nature. They set the stage for the vast modern utopian project, in principle comprehensive and complete: by rational means, to banish all human misery and misfortune—perhaps even death—and to remake the world according to human aspirations.

We are all the grateful beneficiaries of science and technology, including its perhaps finest fruit, modern medicine. Yet these increasing benefits come at increasingly heavy costs. For one thing, we now suffer from a radically "medicalized" view of life: because illness is beyond guilt or innocence, because suffering is suffering, it demands attention. Even bad behavior often comes itself to be treated as illness (e.g., alcoholism or rage-behavior) or sometimes as an inborn, hard-wired predisposition that one must not judge in moral terms (such as a penchant for pederasty). The medical view of life not only focuses on the ills of the body to the neglect of the soul; it seeks bodily causes for all psychic and moral phenomena.

Drunk on its remarkable successes in analyzing and treating acute infectious disease, modern medicine is confident that its materialistic approach to life will unlock all the secrets of heart and mind and will permit for the first time a rational and successful approach to all the troubles of the human condition. The fault, dear Brutus, is not in ourselves, but in our genes, that we are underlings—which is to say, there is no fault or responsibility, only the misalignment of matter. Psychophysics, not praise and blame or moral self-command, is, as Descartes predicted, the wave of the future. It is no longer "God helps those who help themselves," but rather, "Mankind through a scientific medicine helps everyone regardless."

The successes of the modern project have materially improved our lives but they have not made us content. On the contrary, all residual failure and suffering now become increasingly unacceptable. We have come to expect technical solutions for all our ailments, and we demand that society provide them.

While science forges ahead toward the goal of complete mastery, the continuing presence of personal misery and misfortune becomes primarily the responsibility of society, often of the state. Compassion is "elevated" from natural human sentiment to necessary political principle. Society becomes one big hospital, government one big healer. The technological approach to life—rational mastery through methodical problem-solving—finds its political expression in bureaucracy and the welfare state. We go slowly but surely from "Uncle Sam Wants You" to "The Doctor Is In." No longer is the main goal of statesmanship to make the citizens good and obedient to the laws or to make secure against interference the natural rights of life, liberty, and the pursuit of happiness, but rather to guarantee universal day care, health care and hospice care.

Driven partly by guilt for its own good fortune, the utopian elite takes up the cudgels for the least fortunate, demanding a politics of compassion on behalf of society's victims. This is ironically a politics that blithely victimizes those hard-working and morally responsible Americans who do not have the margin to be very generous to strangers and who are not yet aboard the train to utopia.

Another irony of this project for the rational medical-cum-political conquest of fortune is that it leaves most of us less, rather than more, in command of our own attempt at a prudent life. Science's materialistic ideas about human life undermine human freedom and morality; our technologies (and their accompanying bureaucracies) in myriad ways make many of us actually more dependent and helpless in our daily lives. Even through its very successes, compassionate humanitarianism may pave the way to dehumanization, as Aldous Huxley brilliantly showed in his *Brave New World*.

The bureaucratic enforcement of compassion saps most of the impulse to care for another. For to look on every man as brother, and on every stranger-brother as guiltless victim for whom I am responsible, eventually produces a condition in which I feel myself victimized by the burdens of care, and therefore seek to excuse myself even from my primary duties to those who are nearest and dearest.

The utopian project for mastery of fortune through rationalization technique is thus in danger of bringing out the very tragedy it willfully sought to prevent. For to produce a herd of people who do not care for themselves and who consequently have to rely on unreliable and ineffective powers that are only capriciously responsive to their needs is to recreate that ill-fated and fatalistic world against which modern science first took up arms, a world that today is returning to our inner cities.

A HEALTHIER WORLDVIEW

Fortunately there is another worldview, between an irresponsible surrendering to indifferent fate and an unreasonable belief in human mastery, a view still within hailing distance of our collective memory. It was the reigning worldview of the West until the coming of the Enlightenment and its newer nihilistic descendants, and it remains the insufficiently defended view of most decent and hard-working Americans and the source of our residual moral good sense. It is the sensible, moderate but hope-filled worldview of human freedom and dignity under the rule of law, both encouraged and demanded by divine providence. It champions personal morality and responsibility, duties as well as rights, genuine neighborhoods and communities, hard work, fair play, and the pursuit of excellence.

Organized philanthropy, if it is truly to promote human flourishing, must come to the aid of this now beleaguered worldview. Concretely, this means supporting strong family life, rigorous schools, and all sorts of religious and other voluntary associations capable of renewing our moral and spiritual resources. It means flying the banners of decency, justice, liberty, reverence, and truth, as well as the banner of compassion. It means supporting those individuals and groups who can combat the relativism, cynicism, and decadence purveyed in our best colleges and universities and our worst popular culture, who can reinvigorate our belief in everything good, beautiful and holy. Anything less will be a betrayal of true philanthropy, of the wise love of humankind.

PART FOUR

What Should I Give?

Part IV: Table of Contents

Luke 15:11–32, The Parable of the Prodigal Son

Alexis de Tocqueville, *Democracy in America:* "Appendix U," The Pioneer Woman

Sholom Aleichem, "Epilogue: Reb Yozifl and the Contractor"

Rabindranath Tagore, "Gift"

O. Henry, "The Gift of the Magi"

Robert Frost, "The Death of the Hired Man"

Dorothy Parker, "Song of the Shirt, 1941"

John O'Hara, "Memorial Fund"

Eudora Welty, "Lily Daw and the Three Ladies"

Lewis Hyde, "Some Food We Could Not Eat"

Mitch Albom, *Tuesdays with Morrie:* "The Eighth Tuesday:
We Talk About Money"

IV.1

The Parable of the Prodigal Son

Luke 15:11–32

The famous parable of the prodigal son is most often studied for its teaching of forgiveness. But for our purposes, we are interested in the gifts that are given to the prodigal, at both the outset and the conclusion of his journey. As the parable begins, we learn that the younger son of "a certain man," for unspecified reasons, has asked his father to divide his "living," that is, his legacy, and that his father has readily obliged (15:12). He asks his father to act now as if he were already dead—literally, to give up his "living," and figuratively, to un-father himself. The father's willing accession enables the young man to leave home and to separate himself completely from his father and his ways—in effect, to un-son himself—and to turn into the prodigal he proceeds to become. In the many years that follow, we imagine the father, often at his window, looking out, straining to see whether his son is walking the long road of return. For despite his gift to his son, there is no reason to believe that *he* ever un-fathered himself. Thus, however miraculous the prodigal's return, however moving his embrace of his father, and however memorable his father's forgiveness, we are not really surprised that the father welcomes his son home with open arms. But what about the great gifts and the great feast he gives him in addition? Are such rewarding gifts appropriate, either for the father to give or for the son to accept? How do you understand—how would you answer—the complaints of the older brother? What do you think might have prompted the younger son to make his initial request? Was his father wise to be so obliging?

⌒∾⌒

15
11 ¶ And he said, A certain man had two sons:

12 And the younger of them said to *his* father, Father, give me the portion of goods that falleth *to me*. And he divided unto them *his* living.

13 And not many days after the younger son gathered all together, and took his journey into a far country, and there wasted his substance with riotous living.

From *The Holy Bible*, King James version (New York: American Bible Company).

14 And when he had spent all, there arose a mighty famine in that land; and he began to be in want.

15 And he went and joined himself to a citizen of that country; and he sent him into his fields to feed swine.

16 And he would fain have filled his belly with the husks that the swine did eat: and no man gave unto him.

17 And when he came to himself, he said, How many hired servants of my father's have bread enough and to spare, and I perish with hunger!

18 I will arise and go to my father, and will say unto him, Father, I have sinned against heaven, and before thee,

19 And am no more worthy to be called thy son: make me as one of thy hired servants.

20 And he arose, and came to his father. But when he was yet a great way off, his father saw him, and had compassion, and ran, and fell on his neck, and kissed him.

21 And the son said unto him, Father, I have sinned against heaven, and in thy sight, and am no more worthy to be called thy son.

22 But the father said to his servants, Bring forth the best robe, and put *it* on him; and put a ring on his hand, and shoes on *his* feet:

23 And bring hither the fatted calf, and kill *it*; and let us eat, and be merry:

24 For this my son was dead, and is alive again; he was lost, and is found. And they began to be merry.

25 Now his elder son was in the field: and as he came and drew nigh to the house, he heard musick and dancing.

26 And he called one of the servants, and asked what these things meant.

27 And he said unto him, Thy brother is come; and thy father hath killed the fatted calf, because he hath received him safe and sound.

28 And he was angry, and would not go in: therefore came his father out, and intreated him.

29 And he answering said to *his* father, Lo, these many years do I serve thee, neither transgressed I at any time thy commandment: and yet thou never gavest me a kid, that I might make merry with my friends:

30 But as soon as this thy son was come, which hath devoured thy living with harlots, thou hast killed for him the fatted calf.

31 And he said unto him, Son, though art ever with me, and all that I have is thine.

32 It was meet that we should make merry, and be glad: for this thy brother was dead, and is alive again; and was lost, and is found.

IV.2

Democracy in America: "Appendix U," The Pioneer Woman

Alexis de Tocqueville

In *Democracy in America*, Alexis de Tocqueville traces the influence of the equality of conditions on social customs and institutions, including the relations of men and women and the institution of marriage. Struck by the restlessness and turbulence of American public life, Tocqueville saw the need for a protected domestic sphere, where less individualistic and competitive, more moderate and generous habits of the heart could be cultivated, and he praises American women for anticipating and accepting the same necessity. He notes with appreciation the robust freedom in which girls in America are reared and educated equally with boys. But he notes with even greater appreciation how later, as wives, these same independent spirits freely choose to submit to their husbands, to confine their interests to the home, and to accept their own social inferiority. Indeed, he regards American women as superior precisely because they embrace these practices, and he ascribes the extraordinary prosperity and growing power of this nation to the superiority of its women. In this selection, Tocqueville paints a haunting portrait of the pioneer woman at her hearth, in which it is clear that he fully recognizes the high price women pay for their "superiority."

Few contemporary readers are likely to agree with Tocqueville's analysis of this matter, and fewer still will admire the pioneer woman or find her life attractive. But his portrait does make us realize that it is thanks to the sacrifices of the pioneer woman that life on the frontier became civilized and elevated; we realize the important role she played in safeguarding genuine human possibility against the wild and lonely forest. Do you find her admirable? Is she a woman for all seasons, or only for nineteenth-century pioneer America? Are the gifts she gives fundamentally different from those always given by mothers? Is there a fundamental difference between maternal giving and philanthropy? Is such self-sacrifice, whether on the frontier or in the midst of urban America, ever appropriate?

Pages 731–33 from *Democracy in America* By Alexis de Tocqueville. Edited by J. P. Mayer and Max Lerner. Translated by George Lawrence. English translation copyright © 1965 by Harper & Row, Publishers, Inc. Reprinted by permission of HarperCollins Publishers Inc.

I find the following passage in my travel diary, and it will serve to show what trials are faced by those American women who follow their husbands into the wilds. The description has nothing but its complete accuracy to recommend it.

" . . . From time to time we came to new clearings. As all these settlements are exactly like one another, I will describe the place at which we stopped tonight. It will provide a picture of all the others.

"The bells which the pioneer is careful to hang round his beasts' necks, so as to find them again in the forest, warned us from afar that we were getting near a clearing. Soon we heard the sound of an ax cutting down the forest trees. The closer we got, the more signs of destruction indicated the presence of civilized man. Our path was covered with severed branches; and tree trunks, scorched by fire or cut about by an ax, stood in our way. We went on farther and came to a part of the wood where all the trees seemed to have been suddenly struck dead. In full summer their withered branches seemed the image of winter. Looking at them close up, we saw that a deep circle had been cut through the bark, which by preventing the circulation of the sap had soon killed the trees. We were informed that this is commonly the first thing a pioneer does. As he cannot, in the first year, cut down all the trees that adorn his new property, he sows corn under their branches, and by striking them to death, prevents them from shading his crop. Beyond this field, itself an unfinished sketch, or first step toward civilization in the wilds, we suddenly saw the owner's cabin. It is generally placed in the middle of some land more carefully cultivated than the rest, but where man is yet sustaining an unequal fight against the forest. There the trees have been cut, but not grubbed up, and their trunks still cover and block the land they used to shade. Around these dry stumps wheat and oak seedlings and plants and weeds of all kinds are scattered pell-mell and grow together on rough and still half-wild ground. It is in the midst of this vigorous and variegated growth of vegetation that the planter's dwelling, or as it is called in this country, his log house, stands. Just like the field around it, this rustic dwelling shows every sign of recent and hasty work. It is seldom more that thirty feet long and fifteen high; the walls as well as the roof are fashioned from rough tree trunks, between which moss and earth have been rammed to keep out the cold and rain from the inside of the house.

"As the night was coming on, we decided to go and ask the owner of the log house to put us up.

"At the sound of our steps the children playing among the scattered branches got up and ran to the house, as if frightened at the sight of a man, while two large, half-wild dogs, with ears prickled up and outstretched muzzles, came growling out of the hut to cover the retreat of their young masters. Then the pioneer himself appeared at the door of his dwelling; he looked at us with a rapid, inquisitive glance, made a sign to the dogs to go indoors, and set them the example himself, without showing that our arrival aroused either his curiosity or apprehension.

"We went into the log house; the inside was quite unlike that of the cottages of European peasants; there was more that was superfluous and fewer necessities; a single window with a muslin curtain; on the hearth of beaten earth a great fire which illuminated the whole interior; above the hearth a good rifle, a deer-skin, and plumes of eagles' feathers; to the right of the chimney a map of the United States, raised and fluttering in the draft from the crannies in the wall; near it, on a shelf formed from a roughly hewn plank, a few books; a Bible, the first six cantos of Milton, and two plays of Shakespeare; there were trunks instead of cupboards along the wall; in the center of the room, a rough table with legs of green wood with the bark still on them, looking as if they grew out of the ground on which they stood; on the table was a teapot of English china, some silver spoons, a few cracked teacups, and newspapers.

"The master of this dwelling had the angular features and lank limbs characteristic of the inhabitants of New England. He was clearly not born in the solitude in which we found him. His physical constitution by itself showed that his earlier years were spent in a society that used its brains and that he belonged to that restless, calculating, and adventurous race of men who do with the utmost coolness things which can only be accounted for by the ardor of passion, and who endure for a time the life of a savage in order to conquer and civilize the backwoods.

"When the pioneer saw that we were crossing his threshold, he came to meet us and shake hands, as is their custom; but his face was quite unmoved. He opened the conversation by asking us what was going on in the world, and when his curiosity was satisfied, he held his peace, as if he was tired of the importunities and noise of the world. When we questioned him in our turn, he gave us all the information we asked and then turned, with no eagerness, but methodically, to see to our requirements. Why was it that, while he was thus kindly bent on aiding us, in spite of ourselves we felt our sense of gratitude frozen? It was because he himself, in showing his hospitality, seemed to be submitting to a tiresome necessity of his lot and saw in it a duty imposed by his position, and not a pleasure.

"A woman was sitting on the other side of the hearth, rocking a small child on her knees. She nodded to us without disturbing herself. Like the pioneer, this woman was in the prime of her life; her appearance seemed superior to her condition, and her apparel even betrayed a lingering taste for dress; but her delicate limbs were wasted, her features worn, and her eyes gentle and serious; her whole physiognomy bore marks of religious resignation, a deep peace free from passions, and some sort of natural, quiet determination which would face all the ills of life without fear and without defiance.

"Her children cluster around her, full of health, high spirits, and energy; they are true children of the wilds; their mother looks at them from time to time with mingled melancholy and joy; seeing their strength and her weariness, one might think that the life she has given them exhausted her own, and yet she does not regret what they have cost her.

"The dwelling in which these immigrants live had no internal division and no loft; its single room shelters the whole family in the evening. It is a little world of its own, an ark of civilization lost in a sea of leaves. A hundred paces away the everlasting forest spreads its shade, and solitude begins again."

IV.3

"Epilogue: Reb Yozifl and the Contractor"

Sholom Aleichem

Russian Yiddish writer Sholom Aleichem (1859–1916) wrote about the life he knew firsthand, living among poor and oppressed Jews in a small village in eastern Europe. But however parochial the culture that he describes, the human types and situations he depicts clearly endure, as do the questions they invite. In this story, he invites us to ponder whether the "worth" of a gift depends upon its being used. Reb Yozifl conceives a plan to erect a home for the poor and sick old folks of Kasrilevke, "a town of nothing but indigent, poverty-stricken, penniless, impoverished, destitute starvelings." He is moved to do so, instead of, say, building a hospital, because, he says, "People despise an infirm old man—there's no gainsaying that." Against all odds, he succeeds in raising the requisite funds from a visiting Muscovite contractor, and a luxurious Moshav Z'Kenim ("Home for the Aged") is built. Yet at the end of the story, we learn that to this day it stands unoccupied. Reb Yozifl has long since died, and there is no money with which to run it. How should we judge the gift or project of Reb Yozifl? Is it simply worthless? Is Reb Yozifl a philanthropic man?

Everything in the world is progressing and marching onward. So is our town of Kasrilevke.

Kasrilevke has taken a great stride ahead latterly. So much so, that you will be positively surprised if you go there now.

There is one sight in Kasrilevke especially that you will never tire of gazing at. You will see in the heart of the town, where the mud is at its deepest, a massive, yellow brick building—tall and wide—ornamented with iron, with a host of windows, a beautiful, high, carved door, and above it a marble slab bearing the following Hebrew inscription in golden letters:

Translated from the Yiddish by Isidore Goldstick

From *Inside Kasrilevke* by Sholom Aleichem, translated by Isidore Goldstick, copyright 1948, 1965 by Schocken Books. Copyright renewed 1976, 1993 by Schocken Books. Used by permission of Schocken Books, a division of Random House, Inc.

MOSHAV Z'KENIM

As you look at the building you can't help thinking of a gorgeous velvet patch atop a threadbare lustrine gaberdine, green with age. How comes this luxurious Home for the Aged in the midst of poverty-stricken Kasrilevke? you ask. Was it put up to spite anybody? Or just as a practical joke? Or did somebody make a mistake? Here is the story as it was told to me the last time I was there to visit my parents' grave.

It happened at the time when the railway was being put through Kasrilevke. All kinds of curious creatures came down from Moscow: engineers, surveyors, excavators and such like, and at the head of them all a contractor—a personage of importance and a Jew into the bargain. His name is unknown to this day. Maybe he was one of Poliakov's men, or maybe he was the great financier Poliakov himself, for all anybody knows. But even a child could see that he was worth a fortune—a veritable millionaire. For how else could he afford the luxury of occupying two rooms by himself, gorge himself with chicken, swill wine on weekdays, and dally with the hotel proprietor's young daughter-in-law, the hussy? (She wears no wig even in public and despises her husband, as everybody knows.)

In those days our old friend the rabbi, Reb Yozifl, conceived a plan to erect a *moshav z'kenim* in Kasrilevke—a home for the poor and sick old folk. But why a home for the aged? you might ask. Why not a hospital? There you are again with your questions! Supposing he had set his mind on a hospital; then you'd ask: Why not a home for the aged? I can assure you of one thing, however: he certainly had no personal motive; nothing was further from his mind than the thought of a refuge for his own old age. He simply concluded that a sick old man was to be pitied more than a sick young man. To be sure, an ailing young person was in a bad way too. But if you are ill and old into the bargain, you're simply a burden to the world. Just a loathed dead weight. People despise an infirm old man—there's no gainsaying that.

In short, he made up his mind once and for all: Kasrilevke simply must have a *moshav z'kenim*. A home for the aged must take precedence over everything else. And in order to bring home to everybody how necessary it was, Reb Yozifl delivered a sermon in the synagogue on Saturday afternoon, illustrating his talk with a parable: "Once upon a time there was a king who had an only son . . ." But since I am telling you a story, I'd rather not interrupt it with another one. So we'll just defer Reb Yozifl's parable for some other time. I might tell you, however, that although the parable may not have quite fitted the moral in question, nevertheless his audience was completely carried away by it, as they were by all the parables that Reb Yozifl used to tell them. One could only wish that he had been as good at earning his daily bread as he was talented in telling parables.

On hearing his parable, one of the prominent citizens spoke up—one of the most honored, it goes without saying, for who else would dare to contradict a rabbi before a congregation of Jews?

"Yes, indeed, rabbi, there's no denying that you are right. That was a beautiful parable. The only trouble is: where do we get the cash? A home for the aged costs a lot of money, and Kasrilevke is a town of nothing but indigent, poverty-stricken, penniless, impoverished, destitute starvelings."

"Pshaw! There is a parable that applies to this case too. Once upon a time there was a king who had an only son . . . "

Anyway, the fate of the king and his only son is of no importance. What is important is that on the following day, on a Sunday, our Reb Yozifl in company of two of the most prominent householders, with a kerchief in his hand, set out for the market square and started making the rounds, going from shop to shop and from house to house—the old Kasrilevke method of "raising funds." It goes without saying that no vast fortune can be amassed in this way. Reb Yozifl, however, had plenty of time. He could well afford to wait another week. Rome wasn't built in a day either. It just couldn't be helped: a townful of poor Jews! The only hope were the outsiders—merchants that come down to Kasrilevke, or other transients putting up at the local hotels.

In Kasrilevke, if ever they lay their hands on a bird of passage, they pluck it so bare that it'll warn all and sundry to shun the town: "If ever you have to pass through Kasrilevke, go miles out of your way to stay clear of it. The town beggars there are simply intolerable!"

On hearing that a Jewish contractor had come down from Moscow, one of Poliakov's men, or maybe Poliakov himself, a multi-millionaire—Reb Yozifl donned his Sabbath best, threw his cloak over it and put his fur hat on his head. Somehow the ceremonial hat didn't go well with the big weekday stick; and he had everybody puzzled. The people argued: it's either one thing or another. If it's the Sabbath, then why a stick; if it's a weekday, why a fur hat? The problem was not solved until Reb Yozifl was seen taking along with him the two most prominent citizens and making straight for the wealthy contractor in the hotel.

I don't know what other Moscow contractors are like. But this contractor who had come to Kasrilevke to put the railway through was a curious sort. Of low stature, limber, with chubby cheeks, fleshy lips, and short arms, he was a frisky little man, running more often than walking, shouting rather than talking and bursting now and then into an explosive little laugh: He-he-he! His little eyes were always moist with tears. All his movements were brisk, hurried, precipitate, and he was dangerously nervous! Not to satisfy his every whim or to irritate him with as much as a single remark was to invite disastrous consequences. His eyes immediately caught fire and he was ready to trample you underfoot or tear you to pieces. He was a very unusual contractor indeed.

He had given instructions at the hotel that no matter who came to see him, no matter who he might be, even if it should be the Governor himself (these were his very words), he was not to be admitted without the proprietor first rapping at his door and being told by the contractor to enter. Only then the proprietor was to report to him who the caller was. Then he would either see him at once or ask him to come the next day.

Needless to say, Kasrilevke had a good laugh at this odd person and his curious ways. Surely only a Moscow contractor could conceive such outlandish notions.

Isn't it enough when a man goes to all the trouble of calling on you—so they argued—must he also stand outside your door and wait till he gets your permission to enter, or else be told to come tomorrow? No, only a Moscow contractor could do a thing like that. There can be little doubt that there isn't a greater man than Reb Yozifl the rabbi, a man of learning and a God-fearing man. Nevertheless his door is open at all times for anybody who may need him. Surely this is an established Jewish custom.

On seeing Reb Yozifl in person and, what's more, wearing his Sabbath best, the hotel proprietor, a man with a good-sized paunch, unbuttoned coat and waistcoat, and a pipe in his mouth, became all flustered:

"I bid you welcome! Welcome indeed! Such a visitor! Just imagine, the rabbi in person in my house! Such a privilege! Do be seated, rabbi! What's that? Oh, you wish to see our guest? With the greatest pleasure!"

The proprietor in his confusion forgot all about the injunction "no matter who he might be" and "even if it should be the Governor," put away his pipe, buttoned his coat, showed the rabbi and the two most prominent citizens to the guest's door, and himself disappeared.

It is hard to say what the guest was busy doing at the moment. Perhaps he was in the very act of planning the railway, figuring where to lay the tracks and where to put up the station. Or maybe he was lying down in the adjoining room and dozing. Or maybe, for all one can tell, he was just sitting there and having a chat with the proprietor's young daughter-in-law, the hussy, who wears no wig and despises her husband, as everybody knows. Who is to say what a Jewish contractor from Moscow, a personage of importance and a Jew into the bargain, might be doing—a lone man occupying two rooms? In any event, when the deputation stepped into the first room, he wasn't there. The door to the adjoining room was open and there wasn't a sound. They didn't want to step any farther. That would be bad manners; he might be sleeping. So they had a brilliant idea: the three of them gave a cough (that's a Kasrilevke custom). Hearing the noise, the contractor bolted out of his room more dead than alive. When he saw the strangers, he flared up and burst out in the true Moscow manner:

"Who are you? What do you want, you so-and-so and so-and-so? Who let you in? Haven't I told them time and again to admit no one unannounced?"

Some say that he used the word *zhidy*, kikes, although it's hard to believe that a Jew would do that. All the same, when a man's wrath is kindled, and especially a millionaire's, there's no telling what he might do.

Our readers who are acquainted with the rabbi of Kasrilevke know full well what a humble man Reb Yozifl was. Why, he'd never dream of being forward. He always preferred to be last. For it was his idea that mortal man must not be in too great a hurry; he has nothing to lose and will never miss anything. But this time he had to step forward, because those "most prominent citizens" were plainly frightened by the millionaire, who was wildly waving his hands at them and emphasizing his fury by stamping his feet. Who could say who he was? Maybe he was one of Poliakov's men, and maybe even Poliakov himself. Such being the case, they naturally had to recede a bit, get a little closer to the door. For there was no telling what might happen. Only Reb Yozifl didn't get frightened this time. He argued this way. It's one of two things: he is either a *big* man or a *little* man. If he is a big man, I don't need to be afraid of him; if he is a little man, there surely can be no occasion for fear. So he spoke right up to him in these words:

"Pardon me, you are shouting at us. Maybe you are right. Forgive us for disturbing you. But we are engaged in the performance of a good deed, and the messengers of a good deed—so our sages tell us—can suffer no injury. You see, we are collecting contributions for a great cause, a home for the aged."

The Moscow contractor stood speechless. The intrusion of the three men into his room, unannounced, like a bolt from the blue, and the conduct of this old man (the fellow with the fur hat) which struck him as both foolish and impudent, so enraged our Muscovite, so infuriated him, that he felt a tickling sensation in his nose, a sense of pressure against his brain, and all his blood rushed to his face. He was simply frantic and so completely lost control of himself that he just didn't know what he was doing. His hand was raised, as if against his own will, he swung it with all his might and dealt the old man a resounding, flaming slap.

"Take this! This is for your old folks' home!"

The slap sent the old man's fur hat and skullcap flying off his head together, and for a moment the rabbi of Kasrilevke stood with uncovered head—perhaps for the first time in his life. But this lasted no more than a second. Reb Yozifl quickly bent down, snatched up the fur hat and covered his bared head. Then he cautiously felt his cheek and looked at his hand to see if there was any blood. At the same time he said to the guest, speaking softly, sweetly, and with a curious smile on his deathly pale face:

"That's that. I take it that this was meant for me. Now, my dear man, what are you going to give for the sick old folk—I mean the home for the aged?"

What happened next can't be told. No one knows, for "the most prominent citizens," on hearing the language of Moscow from the lips of the contractor, had beaten a hasty retreat. And Reb Yozifl just wouldn't talk about the affair. This is known, however: on leaving the hotel, the old rabbi's face beamed strangely. One of his cheeks—the left—beamed even more than the other. He said with a sweet smile:

"*Mazl tov,* congratulations, fellow Jews, I have good news for you: we are going to have now, with the aid of the Almighty, a home for the aged—a home that will be a delight to God and man."

The "little folk" might have had some doubts about the rabbi's statement, if they hadn't heard with their own ears the contractor himself say, while tapping his shirt-front with his pudgy fingers:

"Men, I'm putting up a home for the aged in your town. I, I . . . "

Not only did they hear this with their own ears, but they soon saw with their own eyes the contractor walking about the town with the rabbi, then stopping to measure a plot with his stick and saying:

"This is where the building is going to stand; it'll have this frontage and this depth . . . "

Before they knew it, loads of brick, lumber, and other building materials arrived. The structure was under way.

To be sure, there were the curious who tried to question the rabbi, sound him out, get him to talk:

"Rabbi, just what did happen? Just how did this man make it up to you for his harsh words? . . . What did *you* say to *him* and what did he answer *you*? . . . "

Reb Yozifl, however, took no notice of what was said and avoided the subject, merely saying with his ever sweet smile:

"All the same, we are going to have a home for the aged, God willing. I'm telling you, it will be a delight to God and man."

Too bad—the home for the aged is unoccupied to this day. Reb Yozifl departed from this world long ago—there is no money to run the institution with.

This has ever been the fate of the little folk of Kasrilevke: when they dream of good things to eat—they haven't a spoon; when they have a spoon—they don't dream of good things to eat.

IV.4

"Gift"

Rabindranath Tagore

India's most eminent modern writer, Rabindranath Tagore (1861–1941) was a man of prodigious literary and artistic accomplishments, as well as a social and political activist. In addition to winning the Nobel Prize for literature (1913)—the first such award given to a man of his nationality—he was honored as an actor, producer, director, musician, and founder of various institutions, including a university. In a speech Tagore made on the occasion of his seventieth birthday, he said, "I have, it is true, engaged myself in a series of activities. But the innermost me is not to be found in any of these. At the end of the journey I am able to see, a little more clearly, the orb of my life. Looking back, the only thing of which I feel certain is that I am a poet (*ami kavi*)."

In this lyric poem, Tagore distinguishes between two sorts of gifts: those that are deliberately chosen and pointedly presented, such as flowers or gems, and those that are delightful, wondrous surprises, such as discoveries or insights that occur, as he puts it, in a "displaced moment." The former, he suggests, are "trifling"; the latter, though clearly more dependent on the readiness and openness of the recipient than the giver, he calls "truest treasure." In the light of the distinction he draws in his poem, as well as his own reported self-understanding, what sort of gift might Tagore regard his own "Gift" to be? In which of his categories would you place it? Is Tagore right to call those nameless, fleeting moments, however wondrous, "*truest* treasure"? Can a gift be both deliberate and, in Tagore's sense, surprising at the same time?

O my love, what gift of mine
Shall I give you this dawn?
A morning song?
But morning does not last long—
The heat of the sun
Wilts it like a flower

Translated from the Bengali by William Radice
"Gift" from *Rabindranath Tagore: Selected Poems*, translated by William Radice, published by Penguin Books, copyright © William Radice, 1985. Reproduced by permission of Penguin Books, Ltd.

And songs that tire
Are done.

O friend, when you come to my gate
At dusk
What is it you ask?
What shall I bring you?
A light?
A lamp from a secret corner of my silent house?
But will you want to take it with you
Down the crowded street?
Alas,
The wind will blow it out.

Whatever gifts are in my power to give you,
Be they flowers,
Be they gems for your neck,
How can they please you
If in time they must surely wither,
Crack,
Lose lustre?
All that my hands can place in yours
Will slip through your fingers
And fall forgotten to the dust
To turn into dust.

Rather,
When you have leisure,
Wander idly though my garden in spring
And let an unknown, hidden flower's scent startle you
Into sudden wondering—
Let that displaced moment
Be my gift.
Or if, as you peer your way down a shady avenue,
Suddenly, spilled
From the thick gathered tresses of evening
A single shivering fleck of sunset-light stops you,
Turns your daydreams to gold,
Let that light be an innocent
Gift.

Truest treasure is fleeting;
It sparkles for a moment, then goes.
It does not tell its name; its tune
Stops us in our tracks, its dance disappears

At the toss of an anklet.
I know no way to it—
No hand, nor word can reach it.
Friend, whatever you take of it,
On your own,
Without asking, without knowing, let that
Be yours.
Anything I can give you is trifling—
Be it a flower, or a song.

IV.5

"The Gift of the Magi"

O. Henry

Is there a peculiar wisdom that attaches to giving and receiving gifts, especially when the gifts themselves, however heartfelt, are ultimately futile? O. Henry's short story "The Gift of the Magi" seems to suggest that there is. The James Dillingham Youngs—Jim and Della—have two prized possessions, Jim's gold heirloom watch and Della's long, cascading brown hair. Yet he sells his treasure, and she hers, each for the sake of buying a Christmas present for the other. The combs Jim buys in exchange for his watch will never adorn Della's hair; nor will the carefully chosen chain that Della purchases in exchange for her hair ever carry Jim's watch. At the end of the story, the narrator speaks of Jim and Della as "two foolish children . . . who most unwisely sacrificed for each other the greatest treasures of their house." But he adds, "Of all who give and receive gifts, such as they are wisest. Everywhere they are wisest. They are the magi." Why does he call them the magi (traditionally understood to be the wise men from the East who came to pay homage to the infant Jesus)? Are the gifts themselves, despite their ultimate futility, redemptive? What makes a gift—or giver—wise or foolish? Can one measure the worth of these gifts? Should one even try?

One dollar and eighty-seven cents. That was all. And sixty cents of it was in pennies. Pennies saved one and two at a time by bulldozing the grocer and the vegetable man and the butcher until one's cheeks burned with the silent imputation of parsimony that such close dealing implied. Three times Della counted it. One dollar and eighty-seven cents. And the next day would be Christmas.

There was clearly nothing to do but flop down on the shabby little couch and howl. So Della did it. Which instigates the moral reflection that life is made up of sobs, sniffles, and smiles, with sniffles predominating.

While the mistress of the home is gradually subsiding from the first stage to the second, take a look at the home. A furnished flat at $8 per week. It did not exactly beggar description, but it certainly had that word on the lookout for the mendicancy squad.

From *The Complete Works of O. Henry* (Garden City, NY: Doubleday & Co., 1953).

In the vestibule below was a letter-box into which no letter would go, and an electric button from which no mortal finger could coax a ring. Also appertaining thereunto was a card bearing the name "Mr. James Dillingham Young."

The "Dillingham" had been flung to the breeze during a former period of prosperity when its possessor was being paid $30 per week. Now, when the income was shrunk to $20, the letters of "Dillingham" looked blurred, as though they were thinking seriously of contracting to a modest and unassuming D. But whenever Mr. James Dillingham Young came home and reached his flat above he was called "Jim" and greatly hugged by Mrs. James Dillingham Young, already introduced to you as Della. Which is all very good.

Della finished her cry and attended to her cheeks with the powder rag. She stood by the window and looked out dully at a gray cat walking a gray fence in a gray backyard. Tomorrow would be Christmas Day and she had only $1.87 with which to buy Jim a present. She had been saving every penny she could for months, with this result. Twenty dollars a week doesn't go far. Expenses had been greater than she had calculated. They always are. Only $1.87 to buy a present for Jim. Her Jim. Many a happy hour she had spent planning for something nice for him. Something fine and rare and sterling—something just a little bit near to being worthy of the honor of being owned by Jim.

There was a pier-glass between the windows of the room. Perhaps you have seen a pier-glass in an $8 flat. A very thin and very agile person may, by observing his reflection in a rapid sequence of longitudinal strips, obtain a fairly accurate conception of his looks. Della, being slender, had mastered the art.

Suddenly she whirled from the window and stood before the glass. Her eyes were shining brilliantly, but her face had lost its color within twenty seconds. Rapidly she pulled down her hair and let it fall to its full length.

Now, there were two possessions of the James Dillingham Youngs in which they both took a mighty pride. One was Jim's gold watch that had been his father's and his grandfather's. The other was Della's hair. Had the Queen of Sheba lived in the flat across the airshaft, Della would have let her hair hang out the window some day to dry just to depreciate Her Majesty's jewels and gifts. Had King Solomon been the janitor, with all his treasures piled up in the basement, Jim would have pulled out his watch every time he passed, just to see him pluck at his beard from envy.

So now Della's beautiful hair fell about her rippling and shining like a cascade of brown waters. It reached below her knee and made itself almost a garment for her. And then she did it up again nervously and quickly. Once she faltered for a minute and stood still while a tear or two splashed on the worn red carpet.

On went her old brown jacket; on went her old brown hat. With a whirl of skirts and with the brilliant sparkle still in her eyes, she fluttered out the door and down the stairs to the street.

Where she stopped the sign read: "Mme. Sofronie. Hair Goods of All Kinds." One flight up Della ran, and collected herself, panting. Madame, large, too white, chilly, hardly looked the "Sofronie."

"Will you buy my hair?" asked Della.

"I buy hair," said Madame. "Take yer hat off and let's have a sight at the looks of it."

Down rippled the brown cascade.

"Twenty dollars," said Madame, lifting the mass with a practised hand.

"Give it to me quick," said Della.

Oh, and the next two hours tripped by on rosy wings. Forget the hashed metaphor. She was ransacking the stores for Jim's present.

She found it at last. It surely had been made for Jim and no one else. There was no other like it in any of the stores, and she had turned all of them inside out. It was a platinum fob chain simple and chaste in design, properly proclaiming its value by substance alone and not by meretricious ornamentation—as all good things should do. It was even worthy of The Watch. As soon as she saw it she knew that it must be Jim's. It was like him. Quietness and value—the description applied to both. Twenty-one dollars they took from her for it, and she hurried home with the 87 cents. With that chain on his watch Jim might be properly anxious about the time in any company. Grand as the watch was, he sometimes looked at it on the sly on account of the old leather strap that he used in place of a chain.

When Della reached home her intoxication gave way a little to prudence and reason. She got out her curling irons and lighted the gas and went to work repairing the ravages made by generosity added to love. Which is always a tremendous task, dear friends—a mammoth task.

Within forty minutes her head was covered with tiny, close-lying curls that made her look wonderfully like a truant schoolboy. She looked at her reflection in the mirror long, carefully, and critically.

"If Jim doesn't kill me," she said to herself, "before he takes a second look at me, he'll say I look like a Coney Island chorus girl. But what could I do—oh! what could I do with a dollar and eighty-seven cents?"

At 7 o'clock the coffee was made and the frying-pan was on the back of the stove hot and ready to cook the chops.

Jim was never late. Della doubled the fob chain in her hand and sat on the corner of the table near the door that he always entered. Then she heard his step on the stair away down on the first flight, and she turned white for just a moment. She had a habit of saying little silent prayers about the simplest everyday things, and now she whispered: "Please God, make him think I am still pretty."

The door opened and Jim stepped in and closed it. He looked thin and very serious. Poor fellow, he was only twenty-two and to be burdened with a family! He needed a new overcoat and he was without gloves.

Jim stepped inside the door, as immovable as a setter at the scent of quail. His eyes were fixed upon Della, and there was an expression in them that she could not read, and it terrified her. It was not anger, nor surprise, nor disapproval, nor horror, nor any of the sentiments that she had been prepared for. He simply stared at her fixedly with that peculiar expression on his face.

Della wriggled off the table and went for him.

"Jim, darling," she cried, "don't look at me that way. I had my hair cut off and sold it because I couldn't have lived through Christmas without giving you a present. It'll grow out again—you won't mind, will you? I just had to do it. My hair grows awfully fast. Say 'Merry Christmas!' Jim, and let's be happy. You don't know what a nice—what a beautiful, nice gift I've got for you."

"You've cut off your hair?" asked Jim, laboriously, as if he had not arrived at that patent fact yet even after the hardest mental labor.

"Cut if off and sold it," said Della. "Don't you like me just as well, anyhow? I'm me without my hair, ain't I?"

Jim looked about the room curiously.

"You say your hair is gone?" he said, with an air almost of idiocy.

"You needn't look for it," said Della. "It's sold, I tell you—sold and gone, too. It's Christmas Eve, boy. Be good to me, for it went for you. Maybe the hairs on my head were numbered," she went on with a sudden serious sweetness, "but nobody could ever count my love for you. Shall I put the chops on, Jim?"

Out of his trance Jim seemed quickly to wake. He enfolded his Della. For ten seconds let us regard with discreet scrutiny some inconsequential object in the other direction. Eight dollars a week or a million a year—what is the difference? A mathematician or a wit would give you the wrong answer. The magi brought valuable gifts, but that was not among them. This dark assertion will be illuminated later on.

Jim drew a package from his overcoat pocket and threw it upon the table.

"Don't make any mistake, Dell," he said, "about me. I don't think there's anything in the way of a haircut or a shave or a shampoo that could make me like my girl any less. But if you'll unwrap that package you may see why you had me going a while at first."

White fingers and nimble tore at the string and paper. And then an ecstatic scream of joy; and then, alas! a quick feminine change to hysterical tears and wails, necessitating the immediate employment of all the comforting powers of the lord of the flat.

For there lay The Combs—the set of combs, side and back, that Della had worshipped for long in a Broadway window. Beautiful combs, pure tortoise shell, with jewelled rims—just the shade to wear in the beautiful vanished hair. They were expensive combs, she knew, and her heart had simply craved and yearned over them without the least hope of possession. And now, they were hers, but the tresses that should have adorned the coveted adornments were gone.

But she hugged them to her bosom, and at length she was able to look up with dim eyes and a smile and say: "My hair grows so fast, Jim!"

And then Della leaped up like a little singed cat and cried, "Oh, oh!"

Jim had not yet seen his beautiful present. She held it out to him eagerly upon her open palm. The dull precious metal seemed to flash with a reflection of her bright and ardent spirit.

"Isn't it a dandy, Jim? I hunted all over town to find it. You'll have to look at the time a hundred times a day now. Give me your watch. I want to see how it looks on it."

Instead of obeying, Jim tumbled down on the couch and put his hands under the back of his head and smiled.

"Dell," said he, "let's put our Christmas presents away and keep 'em a while. They're too nice to use just at present. I sold the watch to get the money to buy your combs. And now suppose you put the chops on."

The magi, as you know, were wise men—wonderfully wise men—who brought gifts to the Babe in the manger. They invented the art of giving Christmas presents. Being wise, their gifts were no doubt wise ones, possibly bearing the privilege of exchange in case of duplication. And here I have lamely related to you the uneventful chronicle of two foolish children in a flat who most unwisely sacrificed for each other the greatest treasures of their house. But in a last word to the wise of these days let it be said that of all who give gifts these two were the wisest. Of all who give and receive gifts, such as they are wisest. Everywhere they are wisest. They are the magi.

IV.6

"The Death of the Hired Man"

Robert Frost

What makes a home a home? To whom does one's home belong? In this
poem, Robert Frost (1874–1963), one of twentieth-century America's
most distinguished and popular poets, addresses these concerns. A
farmer and his wife converse on the farmhouse porch about the shiftless
hired man, Silas, who has come back to their home to die. Warren is re-
sentful because Silas deserted him in the middle of the last haying season,
when he needed him most. Mary insists that theirs is the only home Silas
has. The core of their disagreement surfaces when they try to articulate
what makes a home a home. Warren says, "Home is the place where,
when you have to go there, / They have to take you in." His wife sees
things differently. "I should have called it / Something you somehow
haven't to deserve," she says. Few readers doubt that Mary was right to
take Silas in. But is Warren simply hard-hearted and petty? Is Mary's view
of home unqualifiedly right? Ought we to see our homes as she does, in
effect, as "charitable houses"? In general, is a home an unmerited, no-
strings-attached gift? If so, to whom? Is it ever inappropriate to open
your home to needy strangers?

◦◦◦◦◦

Mary sat musing on the lamp-flame at the table,
Waiting for Warren. When she heard his step,
She ran on tiptoe down the darkened passage
To meet him in the doorway with the news
And put him on his guard. "Silas is back."
She pushed him outward with her through the door
And shut it after her. "Be kind," she said.
She took the market things from Warren's arms
And set them on the porch, then drew him down
To sit beside her on the wooden steps.

"When was I ever anything but kind to him?
But I'll not have the fellow back," he said.
"I told him so last haying, didn't I?
If he left then, I said, that ended it.

What good is he? Who else will harbor him
At his age for the little he can do?
What help he is there's no depending on.
Off he goes always when I need him most.
He thinks he ought to earn a little pay,
Enough at least to buy tobacco with,
So he won't have to beg and be beholden.
'All right,' I say, 'I can't afford to pay
Any fixed wages, though I wish I could.'
'Someone else can.' 'Then someone else will have to.'
I shouldn't mind his bettering himself
If that was what it was. You can be certain,
When he begins like that, there's someone at him
Trying to coax him off with pocket money—
In haying time, when any help is scarce.
In winter he comes back to us. I'm done."

"Sh! not so loud: he'll hear you," Mary said.

"I want him to: he'll have to soon or late."

"He's worn out. He's asleep beside the stove.
When I came up from Rowe's I found him here,
Huddled against the barn door fast asleep,
A miserable sight, and frightening, too—
You needn't smile—I didn't recognize him—
I wasn't looking for him—and he's changed.
Wait till you see."

                        "Where did you say he'd been?"

"He didn't say. I dragged him to the house,
And gave him tea and tried to make him smoke.
I tried to make him talk about his travels.
Nothing would do: he just kept nodding off."

"What did he say? Did he say anything?"

"But little."

            Anything? Mary, confess
He said he'd come to ditch the meadow for me."

"Warren!"

            "But did he? I just want to know."

"Of course he did. What would you have him say?
Surely you wouldn't grudge the poor old man
Some humble way to save his self-respect.

He added, if you really care to know,
He meant to clear the upper pasture, too.
That sounds like something you have heard before?
Warren, I wish you could have heard the way
He jumbled everything. I stopped to look
Two or three times—he made me feel so queer—
To see if he was talking in his sleep.
He ran on Harold Wilson—you remember—
The boy you had in haying four years since.
He's finished school, and teaching in his college.
Silas declares you'll have to get him back.
He says they two will make a team for work:
Between them they will lay this farm as smooth!
The way he mixed that in with other things.
He thinks young Wilson a likely lad, though daft
On education—you know how they fought
All through July under the blazing sun,
Silas up on the cart to build the load,
Harold along beside to pitch it on."

"Yes, I took care to keep well out of earshot."

"Well, those days trouble Silas like a dream.
You wouldn't think they would. How some things linger!
Harold's young college-boy's assurance piqued him.
After so many years he still keeps finding
Good arguments he sees he might have used.
I sympathize. I know just how it feels
To think of the right thing to say too late.
Harold's associated in his mind with Latin.
He asked me what I thought of Harold's saying
He studied Latin, like the violin,
Because he liked it—that an argument!
He said he couldn't make the boy believe
He could find water with a hazel prong—
Which showed how much good school had ever done him.
He wanted to go over that. But most of all
He thinks if he could have another chance
To teach him how to build a load of hay——"

"I know, that's Silas' one accomplishment.
He bundles every forkful in its place,
And tags and numbers it for future reference,
So he can find and easily dislodge it
In the unloading. Silas does that well.
He takes it out in bunches like big birds' nests.

You never see him standing on the hay
He's trying to lift, straining to lift himself."

"He thinks if he could teach him that, he'd be
Some good perhaps to someone in the world.
He hates to see a boy the fool of books.
Poor Silas, so concerned for other folk,
And nothing to look backward to with pride,
And nothing to look forward to with hope,
So now and never any different."

Part of a moon was falling down the west,
Dragging the whole sky with it to the hills.
Its light poured softly in her lap. She saw it
And spread her apron to it. She put out her hand
Among the harplike morning-glory strings,
Taut with the dew from garden bed to eaves,
As if she played unheard some tenderness
That wrought on him beside her in the night.
"Warren," she said, "he has come home to die:
You needn't be afraid he'll leave you this time."

"Home," he mocked gently.

                              "Yes, what else but home?
It all depends on what you mean by home.
Of course he's nothing to us, any more
Than was the hound that came a stranger to us
Out of the woods, worn out upon the trail."

"Home is the place where, when you have to go there,
They have to take you in."

                              "I should have called it
Something you somehow haven't to deserve."

Warren leaned out and took a step or two,
Picked up a little stick, and brought it back
And broke it in his hand and tossed it by.
"Silas has better claim on us you think
Than on his brother? Thirteen little miles
As the road winds would bring him to his door.
Silas has walked that far no doubt today.
Why doesn't he go there? His brother's rich,
A somebody—director in the bank."

"He never told us that."

                              "We know it, though."

"I think his brother ought to help, of course.
I'll see to that if there is need. He ought of right
To take him in, and might be willing to—
He may be better than appearances.
But have some pity on Silas. Do you think
If he had any pride in claiming kin
Or anything he looked for from his brother,
He'd keep so still about him all this time?"

"I wonder what's between them."

                       "I can tell you.
Silas is what he is—we wouldn't mind him—
But just the kind that kinsfolk can't abide.
He never did a thing so very bad.
He don't know why he isn't quite as good
As anybody. Worthless though he is,
He won't be made ashamed to please his brother."

"*I* can't think Si ever hurt anyone."

"No, but he hurt my heart the way he lay
And rolled his old head on that sharp-edged chair-back.
He wouldn't let me put him on the lounge.
You must go in and see what you can do.
I made the bed up for him there tonight.
You'll be surprised at him—how much he's broken.
His working days are done; I'm sure of it."

"I'd not be in a hurry to say that."

"I haven't been. Go, look, see for yourself.
But, Warren, please remember how it is:
He's come to help you ditch the meadow.
He has a plan. You mustn't laugh at him.
He may not speak of it, and then he may.
I'll sit and see if that small sailing cloud
Will hit or miss the moon."

                       It hit the moon.
Then there were three there, making a dim row,
The moon, the little silver cloud, and she.

Warren returned—too soon, it seemed to her—
Slipped to her side, caught up her hand and waited.

"Warren?" she questioned.

                       "Dead," was all he answered.

IV.7

"Song of the Shirt, 1941"

Dorothy Parker

Dorothy Rothschild Parker (1893–1967), American humorist and journalist, is legendary for her instant wit and satirical verses. But in this
short story her tone is more serious than light, as is her subject—the
plight of a well-intentioned wartime volunteer. Mrs. Martindale is
known among her friends for the size of her heart. The war is on, and like
many of her public-spirited compatriots, Mrs. Martindale, a woman of
some means, volunteers at "Headquarters" to sew hospital shirts for the
wounded and weary soldiers. But she works longer hours than most—a
full five afternoons a week and then some—and the work itself is doubly
hard for her, for she is not at all skilled at what she does. No one can
doubt that the work she volunteers to do is necessary and urgent. But
neither can one doubt, as one watches Mrs. Martindale, that the work is
wearing her down, physically and psychically. Should she continue? Is
there another form of service that you think more appropriate or more
important for her to do? To what extent should we regard her as a latter-
day pioneer woman? (See Tocqueville selection in this part.)

It was one of those extraordinarily bright days that make things look somehow
bigger. The Avenue seemed to stretch wider and longer, and the buildings to
leap higher into the skies. The window-box blooms were not just a mass and a
blur; it was as if they had been enlarged, so that you could see the design of the
blossoms and even their separate petals. Indeed you could sharply see all sorts of
pleasant things that were usually too small for your notice—the lean figurines
on radiator caps, and the nice round gold knobs on flag poles, the flowers and
fruits on ladies' hats and the creamy dew applied to the eyelids beneath them.
There should be more of such days.

The exceptional brightness must have had its effect upon unseen objects,
too, for Mrs. Martindale, as she paused to look up the Avenue, seemed actually

to feel her heart grow bigger than ever within her. The size of Mrs. Martindale's heart was renowned among her friends, and they, as friends will, had gone around babbling about it. And so Mrs. Martindale's name was high on the lists of all those organizations that send out appeals to buy tickets and she was frequently obliged to be photographed seated at a table, listening eagerly to her neighbor, at some function for the good of charity. Her big heart did not, as is so sadly often the case, inhabit a big bosom. Mrs. Martindale's breasts were admirable, delicate yet firm, pointing one to the right, one to the left; angry at each other, as the Russians have it.

Her heart was the warmer, now, for the fine sight of the Avenue. All the flags looked brand-new. The red and the white and the blue were so vivid they fairly vibrated, and the crisp stars seemed to dance on their points. Mrs. Martindale had a flag, too, clipped to the lapel of her jacket. She had had quantities of rubies and diamonds and sapphires just knocking about, set in floral designs on evening bags and vanity boxes and cigarette-cases; she had taken the lot of them to her jeweller, and he had assembled them into a charming little Old Glory. There had been enough of them for him to devise a rippled flag, and that was fortunate, for those flat flags looked sharp and stiff. There were numbers of emeralds, formerly figuring as leaves and stems in the floral designs, which were of course of no use to the present scheme and so were left over, in an embossed leather case. Some day, perhaps, Mrs. Martindale would confer with her jeweller about an arrangement to employ them. But there was no time for such matters now.

There were many men in uniform walking along the Avenue under the bright banners. The soldiers strode quickly and surely, each on to a destination. The sailors, two by two, ambled, paused at a corner and looked down a street, gave it up and went slower along their unknown way. Mrs. Martindale's heart grew again as she looked at them. She had a friend who made a practice of stopping uniformed men on the street and thanking them, individually, for what they were doing for *her*. Mrs. Martindale felt that this was going unnecessarily far. Still, she did see, a little bit, what her friend meant.

And surely no soldier or sailor would have objected to being addressed by Mrs. Martindale. For she was lovely, and no other woman was lovely like her. She was tall, and her body streamed like a sonnet. Her face was formed all of triangles, as a cat's is, and her eyes and her hair were blue-gray. Her hair did not taper in its growth about her forehead and temples; it sprang suddenly, in great thick waves, from a straight line across her brow. Its blue-gray was not premature. Mrs. Martindale lingered in her fragrant forties. Has not afternoon been adjudged the fairest time of the day?

To see her, so delicately done, so finely finished, so softly sheltered by her very loveliness, you might have laughed to hear that she was a working-woman. "Go on!" you might have said, had such been your unfortunate manner of expressing disbelief. But you would have been worse than coarse; you would have been wrong. Mrs. Martindale worked, and worked hard. She worked doubly hard, for she was unskilled at what she did, and she disliked the doing of it. But for two months she had worked every afternoon five afternoons of every week, and had shirked no moment. She received no remuneration for her steady services. She gave them because she felt she should do so. She felt that you should do what you could, hard and humbly. She practiced what she felt.

The special office of the war-relief organization where Mrs. Martindale served was known to her and her co-workers as Headquarters; some of them had come to call it H.Q. These last were of the group that kept agitating for the adoption of a uniform—the design had not been thoroughly worked out, but the idea was of something nurselike, only with a fuller skirt and a long blue cape and white gauntlets. Mrs. Martindale was not in agreement with this faction. It had always been hard for her to raise her voice in opposition, but she did, although softly. She said that while of course there was nothing *wrong* about a uniform, certainly nobody could possibly say there was anything *wrong* with the idea, still it seemed—well, it seemed not quite right to make the work an excuse, well, for fancy dress, if they didn't mind her saying so. Naturally, they wore their coifs at Headquarters, and if anybody wanted to take your photograph in your coif, you should go through with it, because it was good for the organization and publicized its work. But please, not whole uniforms, said Mrs. Martindale. Really, *please,* Mrs. Martindale said.

Headquarters was, many said, the stiffest office of all the offices of all the war-relief organizations in the city. It was not a place where you dropped in and knitted. Knitting, once you have caught the hang of it, is agreeable work, a relaxation from what strains life may be putting upon you. When you knit, save when you are at those bits where you must count stitches, there is enough of your mind left over for you to take part in conversations, and for you to be receptive of news and generous with it. But at Headquarters they sewed. They did a particularly difficult and tedious form of sewing. They made those short, shirtlike coats, fastened in back with tapes, that are put on patients in hospitals. Each garment must have two sleeves, and all the edges must be securely bound. The material was harsh to the touch and the smell, and impatient of the needle of the novice. Mrs. Martindale had made three and had another almost half done. She had thought that after the first one the others would be easier and quicker of manufacture. They had not been.

There were sewing machines at Headquarters, but few of the workers understood the running of them. Mrs. Martindale herself was secretly afraid of a machine; there had been a nasty story, never traced to its source, of somebody who put her thumb in the wrong place, and down came the needle, right through nail and all. Besides, there was something—you didn't know quite how to say it—something more of sacrifice, of service, in making things by hand. She kept on at the task that never grew lighter. It was wished that there were more of her caliber.

For many of the workers had given up the whole thing long before their first garment was finished. And many others, pledged to daily attendance, came only now and then. There was but a handful like Mrs. Martindale.

All gave their services, although there were certain doubts about Mrs. Corning, who managed Headquarters. It was she who oversaw the work, who cut out the garments, and explained to the workers what pieces went next to what other pieces. (It did not always come out as intended. One amateur seamstress toiled all the way to the completion of a coat that had one sleeve depending from the middle of the front. It was impossible to keep from laughing; and a sharp tongue suggested that it might be sent in as it was, in case an elephant was brought to bed. Mrs. Martindale was the first to say "Ah, don't! She worked so hard over it.") Mrs. Corning was a cross woman, hated by all. The high standards of Headquarters were important to the feelings of the workers, but it was agreed that there was no need for Mrs. Corning to scold so shrilly when one of them moistened the end of her thread between her lips before thrusting it into her needle.

"Well, really," one of the most spirited among the rebuked had answered her. "If a little clean spit's the worst they're ever going to get on them . . ."

The spirited one had returned no more to Headquarters, and there were those who felt that she was right. The episode drew new members into the school of thought that insisted Mrs. Corning was paid for what she did.

When Mrs. Martindale paused in the clear light and looked along the Avenue, it was at a moment of earned leisure. She had just left Headquarters. She was not to go back to it for many weeks, nor were any of the other workers. Somewhere the cuckoo had doubtless sung, for summer was coming in. And what with everybody leaving town, it was only sensible to shut Headquarters until autumn. Mrs. Martindale, and with no guilt about it, had looked forward to a holiday from all that sewing.

Well, she was to have none, it turned out. While the workers were gaily bidding farewells and calling out appointments for the autumn, Mrs. Corning had cleared her throat hard to induce quiet and had made a short speech. She stood beside a table piled with cut-out sections of hospital coats not yet sewn together. She was a graceless woman, and though it may be assumed that she meant to be appealing, she sounded only disagreeable. There was, she said, a desperate need, a dreadful need, for hospital garments. More were wanted right away, hundreds and thousands of them; the organization had had a cable that morning, urging and pleading. Headquarters was closing until September—that meant all work would stop. Certainly they had all earned a vacation. And yet, in the face of the terrible need, she could not help asking—she would like to call for volunteers to take coats with them, to work on at home.

There was a little silence, and then a murmur of voices, gaining in volume and in assurance as the owner of each realized that it was not the only one. Most of the workers, it seemed, would have been perfectly willing, but they felt that they absolutely must give their entire time to their children, whom they had scarcely *seen* because of being at Headquarters so constantly. Others said they were just plain too worn out, and that was all there was to it. It must be admitted that for some moments Mrs. Martindale felt with this latter group. Then shame waved over her like a blush, and swiftly, quietly, with the blue-gray head held high, she went to Mrs. Corning.

"Mrs. Corning," she said. "I should like to take twelve, please."

Mrs. Corning was nicer than Mrs. Martindale had ever seen her. She put out her hand and grasped Mrs. Martindale's.

"Thank you," she said, and her shrill voice was gentle.

But then she had to go and be the way she always had been before. She snatched her hand from Mrs. Martindale's and turned to the table, starting to assemble garments.

"And please, Mrs. Martindale," she said, shrilly, "kindly try and remember to keep the seams straight. Wounded people can be made terribly uncomfortable by crooked seams, you know. And if you could manage to get your stitches even, the coat would look much more professional and give our organization a higher standing. And time is terribly important. They're in an awful hurry for these. So if you could just manage to be a little quicker, it would help a lot."

Really, if Mrs. Martindale hadn't offered to take the things, she would have . . .

The twelve coats still in sections, together with the coat that was half finished, made a formidable bundle. Mrs. Martindale had to send down for her chauffeur to come and carry it to her car for her. While she waited for him, several of the workers came up, rather slowly, and volunteered to sew at home. Four was the highest number of garments promised.

Mrs. Martindale did say good-by to Mrs. Corning, but she expressed no pleasure at the hope of seeing her again in the autumn. You do what you can, and you do it because you should. But all you can do is all you can do.

Out on the Avenue, Mrs. Martindale was herself again. She kept her eyes from the great package the chauffeur had placed in the car. After all, she might, and honorably, allow herself a recess. She need not go home and start sewing again immediately. She would send the chauffeur home with the bundle, and walk in the pretty air, and not think of unfinished coats.

But the men in uniform went along the Avenue under the snapping flags, and in the sharp, true light you could see all their faces; their clean bones and their firm skin and their eyes, the confident eyes of the soldiers and the wistful eyes of the sailors. They were so young, all of them, and all of them doing what they could, doing everything they could, doing it hard and humbly, without question and without credit. Mrs. Martindale put her hand to her heart. Some day, maybe, some day some of them might be lying on hospital cots . . .

Mrs. Martindale squared her delicate shoulders and entered her car.

"Home, please," she told her chauffeur. "And I'm in rather a hurry."

At home, Mrs. Martindale had her maid unpack the clumsy bundle and lay the contents in her up-stairs sitting-room. Mrs. Martindale took off her outdoor garments and bound her head, just back of the first great blue-gray wave, in the soft linen coif she had habitually worn at Headquarters. She entered her sitting-room, which had recently been redone in the color of her hair and her eyes; it had taken a deal of mixing and matching, but it was a success. There were touches, splashes rather, of magenta about, for Mrs. Martindale complemented brilliant colors and made them and herself glow sweeter. She looked at the ugly, high pile of unmade coats, and there was a second when her famous heart shrank. But it swelled to its norm again as she felt what she must do. There was no good thinking about those twelve damned new ones. Her job immediately was to get on with the coat she had half made.

She sat down on quilted blue-gray satin and set herself to her task. She was at the most hateful stretch of the garment—the binding of the rounded neck. Every thing pulled out of place, and nothing came out even and a horrid starchy smell rose from the thick material, and the stitches that she struggled to put so prettily appeared all different sizes and all faintly gray. Over and over, she had to rip them out for their imperfection, and load her needle again without moistening the thread between her lips, and see them wild and straggling once more. She felt almost ill from the tussle with the hard, monotonous work.

Her maid came in, mincingly, and told her that Mrs. Wyman wished to speak to her on the telephone; Mrs. Wyman wanted to ask a favor of her. Those were two of the penalties attached to the possession of a heart the size of Mrs. Martindale's—people were constantly telephoning to ask her favors and she was constantly granting them. She put down her sewing, with a sigh that might have been of one thing or of another, and went to the telephone.

Mrs. Wyman, too, had a big heart, but it was not well set. She was a great, hulking, stupidly dressed woman, with flapping cheeks and bee-stung eyes. She spoke with rapid diffidence, inserting apologies before she needed to make them, and so was a bore and invited avoidance.

"Oh, my dear," she said now to Mrs. Martindale, "I'm so sorry to bother you. Please do forgive me. But I do want to ask you to do me the most tremendous favor. Please do excuse me. But I want to ask you, do you possibly happen to know of anybody who could possibly use my little Mrs. Christie?"

"Your Mrs. Christie?" Mrs. Martindale asked. "Now, I don't think—or do I?"

"You know," Mrs. Wyman said. "I wouldn't have bothered you for the world, with all you do and all, but you know my little Mrs. Christie. She has that daughter that had infantile, and she has to support her, and I just don't know *what* she's going to do. I wouldn't have bothered you for the world, only I've been sort of thinking up jobs for her to do for me right along, but next week we're going to the ranch, and I really don't know *what* will become of her. And the crippled daughter and all. They just won't be able to *live!*"

Mrs. Martindale made a soft little moan. "Oh, how awful," she said. "How perfectly awful. Oh, I wish I could—tell me, what can I do?"

"Well, if you could just think of somebody that could use her," Mrs. Wyman said. "I wouldn't have bothered you, honestly I wouldn't, but I just didn't know who to turn to. And Mrs. Christie's really a wonderful little woman—she can do anything. Of course, the thing is, she has to work at home, because she wants to take care of the crippled child—well, you can't blame her, really. But she'll call for things and bring them back. And she's so quick, and so good. Please do forgive me for bothering you, but if you could just think—"

"Oh, there must be somebody!" Mrs. Martindale cried. "I'll think of somebody. I'll rack my brains, truly I will. I'll call you up as soon as I think."

Mrs. Martindale went back to her blue-gray quilted satin. Again she took up the unfinished coat. A shaft of the exceptionally bright sunlight shot past a vase of butterfly orchids and settled upon the waiving hair under the gracious coif. But Mrs. Martindale did not turn to meet it. Her blue-gray eyes were bent on the drudgery of her fingers. This coat, and then the twelve others beyond it. The need, the desperate, dreadful need, and the terrible importance of time. She took a stitch and another stitch and another stitch and another stitch; she looked at their wavering line, pulled the thread from her needle, ripped out three of the stitches, rethreaded her needle, and stitched again. And as she stitched, faithful to her promise and to her heart, she racked her brains.

IV.8

"Memorial Fund"

John O'Hara

What is a fitting way to honor someone's memory? Who should decide? These are questions invited by this story, written by American author John O'Hara (1905–1970). When war hero Duke Brady is killed, several of his closest college friends propose that a scholarship fund be established in his memory. But Jarwin, also a former classmate of "the Duke's," though never a close friend, challenges the proposal, and suggests instead that something permanent be erected, like a marble pillar. He offers matching funds to accomplish his plan, but his effort is scorned. Russell, spokesman for the committee of friends, agrees to take Jarwin's proposal to the committee, but with the recommendation that it be turned down, for two reasons: first, because Jarwin ought not to be allowed to "overwhelm" them with his money; and second, because large gifts of the sort proposed ought to come only from close friends. Jarwin nevertheless presents Russell with a sizable check, telling him to do as he pleases with it. Duke Brady, he explains, "was an inspiration to me. I wanted to be like him, and if I couldn't be like him in college at least I could keep punching when I got out of college. I consider him to a great extent responsible for whatever success I've had in business." Is Russell right to sneer at Jarwin's advice or his money? Are his reasons defensible? Should Jarwin have taken his money elsewhere? In general, should memorial gifts come within the purview of philanthropy?

Miss Ames came in and stood silently in front of the desk in an annoying way she had, waiting for him to speak.

"Yes, Miss Ames?" said Russell.

"There's a Mr. Jarwin outside to see you," she said.

"What about?" said Russell. "Who is he, and what does he want? You know how busy I am, Miss Ames."

"I do know how busy you are, Mr. Russell, but this man said he was a classmate of yours and wanted to see you about the Duke Brady Fund."

"Jarwin? . . . Oh, Lord, Jarwin," said Russell. "All right, I'll see him in five minutes."

Miss Ames went out, and Russell got up and took down his college yearbook from one of the crowded shelves. "J. Jarwin. Economics Club. Candidate for track in sophomore year. Played in band in junior and senior years." That was all, that was the recorded collegiate history of J. Jarwin. It was the opposite extreme from Russell's own and Duke Brady's lists of campus achievement, with their fashionable clubs, prom committees, athletic endeavors. Russell studied the picture of Jarwin, who had a thick pompadour and thick glasses and a high stiff collar, and he remembered the one time he had seen Jarwin away from college. That had been the summer vacation between junior and senior years. Russell had gone to visit some friends in the White Mountains, and in the intermission at the hotel dance Jarwin had come over to him: "Hello, Russell, do you remember me? I'm Jarwin. In your class."

"Oh, yes. How are you?"

"Fine. This is my band playing here. We're here all summer. How's Duke Brady?"

"Duke's fine. He's working as a lumberjack, keeping in shape for football." In September, back at college, Russell had kidded Duke Brady about running into his friend Jarwin, and the Duke hadn't had the faintest idea who Jarwin was. But there was one thing about Brady that Russell never quite liked: the Duke was by way of being a campus politician, and for the remainder of his days in college Brady had made a point of speaking to Jarwin. That was from September to April. Brady had quit college in April 1917, joined the Army, and matched his football and hockey reputation with a D.S.C. and a Croix de Guerre with a couple of palms. And now, in another war, the Duke was dead, killed in the crash of an Army transport plane.

Russell signaled to Miss Ames, and presently Jarwin bustled in. Russell rose and the two men shook hands. Jarwin's unfortunate pompadour was gone, and the glasses were perhaps a trifle thicker, but it was recognizably Jarwin, a curiously pushy little man whose pushiness had not got him anywhere in college. It was going to be just like that time in the White Mountains and the so-familiar mention of Duke Brady.

"You've got a nice office here," said Jarwin. "It's more like the kind of offices you see in England. I mean, the books all over the place and so on."

"Well, we're in the book business," said Russell.

"Yes, but not only the books. I mean the old furniture, the pictures. I almost expect you to serve tea."

"We do serve tea," said Russell. "We're not terribly high-powered, I suppose."

"Oh, don't get me wrong. I like it," said Jarwin.

Russell refrained from commenting that that was nice of him. "What are you doing these days?" he asked.

"I have my own business now. Jarwin Manufacturing. We make certain parts for guns, and that brings me around to the Fund, the Duke's Memorial Fund. I got your letter, the committee's letter, and I was wondering if you had the right idea, establishing a scholarship in his memory."

"Why, yes. I think it's a very good idea. We all thrashed it out pretty thoroughly and a scholarship seemed like the best idea."

"I don't," said Jarwin.

"No? That's interesting. Why not?"

"I'll tell you why not," said Jarwin. "First of all, from a purely business point of view, if you start a fund now you aren't going to know how to invest it to yield a uniform sum every year, therefore you don't know how much the scholarship will be worth from one year to another, and that isn't even taking into consideration inflation."

"How about war bonds?"

"Oh, don't think you have me there, Russell. I buy plenty of them for myself, but in this case I don't think it's a good idea. You certainly don't want to cash your war bonds, you want to hold on to them, so that means you wouldn't have what you might call a 'live' fund for some years to come, and in my opinion the memorial to the Duke ought to start right away. Have you thought of a marble shaft?"

"Naturally that came up."

"That's what I'm in favor of. Something permanent and something we can see in a few months' time. That's the kind of memorial the Duke ought to have. An inspiration, just as he was an inspiration to me."

"I see. Well, I think the committee have already made up their minds, Jarwin."

"Yes, probably have. That's why I came to see you, to see if I could get you to change their minds."

"I'm afraid not," said Russell.

"I didn't think you'd agree with me, but I have a counter-proposition. How much did you plan to put in the scholarship fund?"

"Three thousand dollars."

"Uh-huh. You call that enough for the memory of Duke Brady, with all the money there is in our class?"

"You sound as if you had some pretty big ideas," said Russell.

Jarwin smiled. "Not too big. You see, Russell, I was very fond of Duke."

"He was my best friend," said Russell. "I, uh—"

"Go ahead, say it. You didn't know he knew me. Well, he didn't. He merely spoke to me, but he was an inspiration to me. I wanted to be like him, and if I couldn't be like him in college at least I could keep punching when I got out of college. I consider him to a great extent responsible for whatever success I've had in business."

"Is that so?"

"Yes, that's so, Russell, and that's why I want to make this proposition: you fellows on the committee can have your scholarship, but will you let me match the three thousand with another three thousand of my own so that you can build something permanent as a memorial to the Duke?"

Russell hesitated before answering, and then he spoke deliberately: "Jarwin, I think you ought to be reminded that I am only a member of the committee and not the whole committee, but I'll tell you now, quite frankly, that I'll take your proposition to the committee, but with the recommendation that they turn it down. You see, my dear fellow, I don't think you ought to be allowed to overwhelm us with your money. And I'll tell you something else, if there were to be any really large gifts to the fund, I think they ought to come from people who were close friends of the Duke's, not from someone that he didn't even know existed for three years. If it hadn't been for me, Duke Brady never would have known you existed."

"Do you think I don't know that?"

"Oh? How did you know it?"

"In senior year he started speaking to me and one day I asked him why, and he said you told him I considered him a friend of mine."

"He did?" said Russell.

"Oh, I guessed how it happened, Russell. That time in the White Mountains when I asked about him, you probably went back to college and you probably laughed about it and said you didn't know he was such a great friend of Jarwin's. That's true, isn't it? Isn't that about the size of it? It's all right Russell, it was so long ago you wouldn't be hurting my feelings."

"To tell you the truth, it was," said Russell, ashamed.

"Yes, I was a sort of joke in college, but Duke Brady was nice to me, so here's a cheque, and you can do as you please with it." He took out a chequebook and wrote quickly while the two of them sat in silence. Jarwin tossed the cheque to Russell, and rose.

"And you know, Russell," said Jarwin. "If it had been you instead of Duke Brady, I think I'd have done the same thing. In a funny way you were good for me too. So long, Classmate."

IV.9

"Lily Daw and the Three Ladies"

Eudora Welty

What should we do for handicapped and/or abused children? In "Lily Daw and the Three Ladies," Eudora Welty (1909–2001), American novelist and short-story writer, turns our attention to this important matter. The three leading ladies of Victory, Mississippi, have been looking after Lily Daw ever since her mother died. They have given her food and clothing, sent her to Sunday school, had her baptized a Baptist, and found a place for her to live, away from her abusive father. But now that she has "gotten so she is very mature for her age," they plan to send her, at their expense, to the "Ellisville Institute for the Feeble-Minded of Mississippi," even though she is only slightly mentally impaired. Lily, however, has another plan. She has met a young man who allegedly has proposed marriage to her, and she has already set about starting her own hope chest. When the three ladies get wind of her plan, they are horrified. Assuming the worst, they instantly try to change her course, and after a little prodding, they succeed. But as the train carrying Lily to Ellisville is about to leave, the young courtier materializes and confirms Lily's report. The ladies, once again, instantly move into action, this time arranging for the marriage they earlier thought unthinkable. In the end, do they do what is appropriate? Have they done so all along?

Mrs. Watts and Mrs. Carson were both in the post office in Victory when the letter came from the Ellisville Institute for the Feeble-Minded of Mississippi. Aimee Slocum, with her hand still full of mail, ran out in front and handed it straight to Mrs. Watts, and they all three read it together. Mrs. Watts held it taut between her pink hands, and Mrs. Carson underscored each line slowly with her thimbled finger. Everybody else in the post office wondered what was up now.

"What will Lily say," beamed Mrs. Carson at last, "when we tell her we're sending her to Ellisville!"

"She'll be tickled to death," said Mrs. Watts, and added in a guttural voice to a deaf lady, "Lily Daw's getting in at Ellisville!"

"Don't you all dare go off and tell Lily without me!" called Aimee Slocum, trotting back to finish putting up the mail.

"Do you suppose they'll look after her down there?" Mrs. Carson began to carry on a conversation with a group of Baptist ladies waiting in the post office. She was the Baptist preacher's wife.

"I've always heard it was lovely down there, but crowded," said one.

"Lily lets people walk over her so," said another.

"Last night at the tent show—" said another, and then popped her hand over her mouth.

"Don't mind me, I know there are such things in the world," said Mrs. Carson, looking down and fingering the tape measure which hung over her bosom.

"Oh, Mrs. Carson. Well, anyway, last night at the tent show, why, the man was just before making Lily buy a ticket to get in."

"A ticket!"

"Till my husband went up and explained she wasn't bright, and so did everybody else."

The ladies all clucked their tongues.

"Oh, it was a very nice show," said the lady who had gone. "And Lily acted so nice. She was a perfect lady—just set in her seat and stared."

"Oh, she can be a lady—she can be," said Mrs. Carson, shaking her head and turning her eyes up. "That's just what breaks your heart."

"Yes'm, she kept her eyes on—what's that thing makes all the commotion?— the xylophone," said the lady. "Didn't turn her head to the right or to the left the whole time. Set in front of me."

"The point is, what did she do after the show?" asked Mrs. Watts practically. "Lily has gotten so she is very mature for her age."

"Oh, Etta!" protested Mrs. Carson, looking at her wildly for a moment.

"And that's how come we are sending her to Ellisville," finished Mrs. Watts.

"I'm ready, you all," said Aimee Slocum, running out with white powder all over her face. "Mail's up. I don't know how good it's up."

"Well, of course, I do hope it's for the best," said several of the other ladies. They did not go at once to take their mail out of their boxes; they felt a little left out.

The three women stood at the foot of the water tank.

"To find Lily is a different thing," said Aimee Slocum.

"Where in the wide world do you suppose she'd be?" It was Mrs. Watts who was carrying the letter.

"I don't see a sign of her either on this side of the street or on the other side," Mrs. Carson declared as they walked along.

Ed Newton was stringing Redbird school tablets on the wire across the store.

"If you're after Lily, she come in here while ago and tole me she was fixin' to git married," he said.

"Ed Newton!" cried the ladies all together, clutching one another. Mrs. Watts began to fan herself at once with the letter from Ellisville. She wore widow's black, and the least thing made her hot.

"Why she is not. She's going to Ellisville, Ed," said Mrs. Carson gently. "Mrs. Watts and I and Aimee Slocum are paying her way out of our own pockets. Besides, the boys of Victory are on their honor. Lily's not going to get married, that's just an idea she's got in her head."

"More power to you, ladies," said Ed Newton, spanking himself with a tablet.

When they came to the bridge over the railroad tracks, there was Estelle Mabers, sitting on a rail. She was slowly drinking an orange Ne-Hi.

"Have you seen Lily?" they asked her.

"I'm supposed to be out here watching for her now," said the Mabers girl, as though she weren't there yet. "But for Jewel—Jewel says Lily come in the store while ago and picked out a two-ninety-eight hat and wore it off. Jewel wants to swap her something else for it."

"Oh, Estelle, Lily says she's going to get married!" cried Aimee Slocum.

"Well, I declare," said Estelle; she never understood anything.

Loralee Adkins came riding by in her Willys-Knight, tooting the horn to find out what they were talking about.

Aimee threw up her hands and ran out into the street. "Loralee, Loralee, you got to ride us up to Lily Daws'. She's up yonder fixing to get married!"

"Hop in, my land!"

"Well, that just goes to show you right now," said Mrs. Watts, groaning as she was helped into the back seat. "What we've got to do is persuade Lily it will be nicer to go to Ellisville."

"Just to think!"

While they rode around the corner Mrs. Carson was going on in her sad voice, sad as the soft noises in the hen house at twilight. "We buried Lily's poor defenseless mother. We gave Lily all her food and kindling and every stitch she had on. Sent her to Sunday school to learn the Lord's teachings, had her baptized a Baptist. And when her old father commenced beating her and tried to cut her head off with the butcher knife, why, we went and took her away from him and gave her a place to stay."

The paintless frame house with all the weather vanes was three stories high in places and had yellow and violet stained-glass windows in front and gingerbread around the porch. It leaned steeply to one side, toward the railroad, and the front steps were gone. The car full of ladies drew up under the cedar tree.

"Now Lily's almost grown up," Mrs. Carson continued. "In fact, she's grown," she concluded, getting out.

"Talking about getting married," said Mrs. Watts disgustedly. "Thanks, Lora-lee, you run on home."

They climbed over the dusty zinnias onto the porch and walked through the open door without knocking.

"There certainly is always a funny smell in this house. I say it every time I come," said Aimee Slocum.

Lily was there, in the dark of the hall, kneeling on the floor by a small open trunk.

When she saw them she put a zinnia in her mouth, and held still.

"Hello, Lily," said Mrs. Carson reproachfully.

"Hello," said Lily. In a minute she gave a suck on the zinnia stem that sounded exactly like a jay bird. There she sat, wearing a petticoat for a dress, one of the things Mrs. Carson kept after her about. Her milky-yellow hair streamed freely down from under a new hat. You could see the wavy scar on her throat if you knew it was there.

Mrs. Carson and Mrs. Watts, the two fattest, sat in the double rocker. Aimee Slocum sat on the wire chair donated from the drugstore that burned.

"Well, what are you doing, Lily?" asked Mrs. Watts, who led the rocking.

Lily smiled.

The trunk was old and lined with yellow and brown paper, with an asterisk pattern showing darker circles and rings. Mutely the ladies indicated to each other that they did not know where in the world it had come from. It was empty except for two bars of soap and a green washcloth, which Lily was now trying to arrange in the bottom.

"Go on and tell us what you're doing, Lily," said Aimee Slocum.

"Packing, silly," said Lilly.

"Where are you going?"

"Going to get married, and I bet you wish you was me now," said Lily. But shyness overcame her suddenly, and she popped the zinnia back into her mouth.

"Talk to me, dear," said Mrs. Carson. "Tell old Mrs. Carson why you want to get married."

"No," said Lily, after a moment's hesitation.

"Well, we've thought of something that will be so much nicer," said Mrs. Carson. "Why don't you go to Ellisville!"

"Won't that be lovely?" said Mrs. Watts. "Goodness, yes."

"It's a lovely place," said Aimee Slocum uncertainly.

"You've got bumps on your face," said Lily.

"Aimee, dear, you stay out of this, if you don't mind," said Mrs. Carson anxiously. "I don't know what it is comes over Lily when you come around her."

Lily stared at Aimee Slocum meditatively.

"There! Wouldn't you like to go to Ellisville now?" asked Mrs. Carson.

"No'm," said Lily.

"Why not?" All the ladies leaned down toward her in impressive astonishment.

"'Cause I'm goin' to get married," said Lily.

"Well, and who are you going to marry, dear?" asked Mrs. Watts. She knew how to pin people down and make them deny what they'd already said.

Lily bit her lip and began to smile. She reached into the trunk and held up both cakes of soap and wagged them.

"Tell us," challenged Mrs. Watts. "Who you're going to marry, now."

"A man last night."

There was a gasp from each lady. The possible reality of a lover descended suddenly like a summer hail over their heads. Mrs. Watts stood up and balanced herself.

"One of those show fellows! A musician!" she cried.

Lily looked up in admiration.

"Did he—did he do anything to you?" In the long run, it was still only Mrs. Watts who could take charge.

"Oh, yes'm," said Lily. She patted the cakes of soap fastidiously with the tips of her small fingers and tucked them in with the washcloth.

"What?" demanded Aimee Slocum, rising up and tottering before her scream. "What?" she called out in the hall.

"Don't ask her what," said Mrs. Carson, coming up behind. "Tell me, Lily— just yes or no—are you the same as you were?"

"He had a red coat," said Lily graciously. "He took little sticks and went *ping-pong! ding-dong!*"

"Oh, I think I'm going to faint," said Aimee Slocum, but they said, "No, you're not."

"The xylophone!" cried Mrs. Watts. "The xylophone player! Why, the coward, he ought to be run out of town on a rail!"

"Out of town? He is out of town, by now," cried Aimee. "Can't you read?— the sign in the café—Victory on the ninth, Como on the tenth? He's in Como. Como!"

"All right! We'll bring him back!" cried Mrs. Watts. "He can't get away from me!"

"Hush," said Mrs. Carson. "I don't think it's any use following that line of reasoning at all. It's better in the long run for him to be gone out of our lives for good and all. That kind of a man. He was after Lily's body alone and he wouldn't ever in this world make the poor little thing happy, even if we went out and forced him to marry her like he ought—at the point of a gun."

"Still—" began Aimee, her eyes widening.

"Shut up," said Mrs. Watts. "Mrs. Carson, you're right, I expect."

"This is my hope chest—see?" said Lily politely in the pause that followed. "You haven't even looked at it. I've already got soap and a washrag. And I have my hat—on. What are you all going to give me?"

"Lily," said Mrs. Watts, starting over, "we'll give you lots of gorgeous things if you'll only go to Ellisville instead of getting married."

"What will you give me?" asked Lily.

"I'll give you a pair of hemstitched pillowcases," said Mrs. Carson.

"I'll give you a big caramel cake," said Mrs. Watts.

"I'll give you a souvenir from Jackson—a little toy bank," said Aimee Slocum. "Now will you go?"

"No," said Lily.

"I'll give you a pretty little Bible with your name on it in real gold," said Mrs. Carson.

"What if I was to give you a pink crêpe de Chine brassière with adjustable shoulder straps?" asked Mrs. Watts grimly.

"Oh, Etta."

"Well, she needs it," said Mrs. Watts. "What would they think if she ran all over Ellisville in a petticoat looking like a Fiji?"

"I wish *I* could go to Ellisville," said Aimee Slocum luringly.

"What will they have for me down there?" asked Lily softly.

"Oh! lots of things. You'll have baskets to weave, I expect. . . ." Mrs. Carson looked vaguely at the others.

"Oh, yes indeed, they will let you make all sorts of baskets," said Mrs. Watts; then her voice too trailed off.

"No'm, I'd rather get married," said Lily.

"Lily Daw! Now that's just plain stubbornness!" cried Mrs. Watts. "You almost said you'd go and then you took it back!"

"We've all asked God, Lily," said Mrs. Carson finally, "and God seemed to tell us—Mr. Carson, too—that the place where you ought to be, so as to be happy, was Ellisville."

Lily looked reverent, but still stubborn.

"We've really just got to get her there—now!" screamed Aimee Slocum all at once. "Suppose—! She can't stay here!"

"Oh, no, no, no," said Mrs. Carson hurriedly. "We mustn't think that."

They sat sunken in despair.

"Could I take my hope chest—to go to Ellisville?" asked Lily shyly, looking at them sidewise.

"Why, yes," said Mrs. Carson blankly.

Silently they rose once more to their feet.

"Oh, if I could just take my hope chest!"

"All the time it was just her hope chest," Aimee whispered.

Mrs. Watts struck her palms together. "It's settled!"

"Praise the fathers," murmured Mrs. Carson.

Lily looked up at them, and her eyes gleamed. She cocked her head and spoke out in a proud imitation of someone—someone utterly unknown.

"O.K.—Toots!"

The ladies had been nodding and smiling and backing away toward the door.

"I think I'd better stay," said Mrs. Carson, stopping in her tracks. "Where—where could she have learned that terrible expression?"

"Pack up," said Mrs. Watts. "Lily Daw is leaving for Ellisville on Number One."

In the station the train was puffing. Nearly everyone in Victory was hanging around waiting for it to leave. The Victory Civic Band had assembled without any orders and was scattered through the crowd. Ed Newton gave false signals to start on his bass horn. A crate full of baby chickens got loose on the platform. Everybody wanted to see Lily all dressed up, but Mrs. Carson and Mrs. Watts had sneaked her into the train from the other side of the tracks.

The two ladies were going to travel as far as Jackson to help Lily change trains and be sure she went in the right direction.

Lily sat between them on the plush seat with her hair combed and pinned up into a knot under a small blue hat which was Jewel's exchange for the pretty one. She wore a traveling dress made out of part of Mrs. Watts's last summer's mourning. Pink straps glowed through. She had a purse and a Bible and a warm cake in a box, all in her lap.

Aimee Slocum had been getting the outgoing mail stamped and bundled. She stood in the aisle of the coach now, tears shaking from her eyes.

"Good-bye, Lily," she said. She was the one who felt things.

"Good-bye, silly," said Lily.

"Oh, dear, I hope they get our telegram to meet her in Ellisville!" Aimee cried sorrowfully, as she thought how far away it was. "And it was so hard to get it all in ten words, too."

"Get off, Aimee, before the train starts and you break your neck," said Mrs. Watts, all settled and waving her dressy fan gaily. "I declare, it's so hot, as soon as we get a few miles out of town I'm going to slip my corset down."

"Oh, Lily, don't cry down there. Just be good, and do what they tell you—it's all because they love you." Aimee drew her mouth down. She was backing away, down the aisle.

Lily laughed. She pointed across Mrs. Carson's bosom out the window toward a man. He had stepped off the train and just stood there, by himself. He was a stranger and wore a cap.

"Look," she said, laughing softly through her fingers.

"Don't—look," said Mrs. Carson very distinctly, as if, out of all she had ever spoken, she would impress these two solemn words upon Lily's soft little brain. She added, "Don't look at anything till you get to Ellisville."

Outside, Aimee Slocum was crying so hard she almost ran into the stranger. He wore a cap and was short and seemed to have on perfume, if such a thing could be.

"Could you tell me, madam," he said, "where a little lady lives in this burg name of Miss Lily Daw?" He lifted his cap—and he had red hair.

"What do you want to know for?" Aimee asked before she knew it.

"Talk louder," said the stranger. He almost whispered, himself.

"She's gone away—she's gone to Ellisville!"

"Gone?"

"Gone to Ellisville!"

"Well, I like that!" The man stuck out his bottom lip and puffed till his hair jumped.

"What business did you have with Lily?" cried Aimee suddenly.

"We was only going to get married, that's all," said the man.

Aimee Slocum started to scream in front of all those people. She almost pointed to the long black box she saw lying on the ground at the man's feet. Then she jumped back in fright.

"The xylophone! The xylophone!" she cried, looking back and forth from the man to the hissing train. Which was more terrible? The bell began to ring hollowly, and the man was talking.

"Did you say Ellisville? That in the state of Mississippi?" Like lightning he had pulled out a red notebook entitled, "Permanent Facts & Data." He wrote down something. "I don't hear well."

Aimee nodded her head up and down, and circled around him.

Under "Ellis-Ville Miss" he was drawing a line; now he was flicking it with two little marks.

"Maybe she didn't say she would. Maybe she said she wouldn't." He suddenly laughed very loudly, after the way he had whispered. Aimee jumped back. "Women!—Well, if we play anywheres near Ellisville, Miss., in the future I may look her up and I may not," he said.

The bass horn sounded the true signal for the band to begin. White steam rushed out of the engine. Usually the train stopped for only a minute in Victory, but the engineer knew Lily from waving at her, and he knew this was her big day.

"Wait!" Aimee Slocum did scream. "Wait, mister! I can get her for you. Wait, Mister Engineer! Don't go!"

Then there she was back on the train, screaming in Mrs. Carson's and Mrs. Watt's faces.

"The xylophone player! The xylophone player to marry her! Yonder he is!"

"Nonsense," murmured Mrs. Watts, peering over the others to look where Aimee pointed. "If he's there I don't see him. Where is he? You're looking at One-Eye Beasley."

"The little man with the cap—no, with the red hair! Hurry!"

"Is that really him?" Mrs. Carson asked Mrs. Watts in wonder. "Mercy! He's small, isn't he?"

"Never saw him before in my life!" cried Mrs. Watts. But suddenly she shut up her fan.

"Come on! This is a train we're on!" cried Aimee Slocum. Her nerves were all unstrung.

"All right, don't have a conniption fit, girl," said Mrs. Watts. "Come on," she said thickly to Mrs. Carson.

"Where are we going now?" asked Lily as they struggled down the aisle.

"We're taking you to get married," said Mrs. Watts. "Mrs. Carson, you'd better phone up your husband right there in the station."

"But I don't want to git married," said Lily, beginning to whimper. "I'm going to Ellisville."

"Hush, and we'll all have some ice-cream cones later," whispered Mrs. Carson.

Just as they climbed down the steps at the back end of the train, the band went into "Independence March."

The xylophone player was still there, patting his foot. He came up and said, "Hello, Toots. What's up—tricks?" and kissed Lily with a smack, after which she hung her head.

"So you're the young man we've heard so much about," said Mrs. Watts. Her smile was brilliant. "Here's your little Lily."

"What say?" asked the xylophone player.

"My husband happens to be the Baptist preacher of Victory," said Mrs. Carson in a loud, clear voice. "Isn't that lucky? I can get him here in five minutes: I know exactly where he is."

They were in a circle around the xylophone player, all going into the white waiting room.

"Oh, I feel just like crying, at a time like this," said Aimee Slocum. She looked back and saw the train moving slowly away, going under the bridge at Main Street. Then it disappeared around the curve.

"Oh, the hope chest!" Aimee cried in a stricken voice.

"And whom have we the pleasure of addressing?" Mrs. Watts was shouting, while Mrs. Carson was ringing up the telephone.

The band went on playing. Some of the people thought Lily was on the train, and some swore she wasn't. Everybody cheered, though, and a straw hat was thrown into the telephone wires.

IV.10

"Some Food We Could Not Eat"

Lewis Hyde

In this selection, excerpted from the first chapter of his longer study *The Gift: Imagination and the Erotic Life of Property,* American poet and literary critic Lewis Hyde (born in 1945) discusses what makes a gift a gift. He emphasizes in particular the fundamental differences between gifts and commodities, and the difference such differences make. Two essential features of a gift are elaborated: Unlike other property, "the gift must always move," and "the gift is property that perishes." Hyde draws on ethnographic evidence from the work of prominent social anthropologists to ground his claims, which he then develops and illustrates by expounding folktales. Readers who treasure their heirlooms should have little difficulty with what Hyde says. But does Hyde's analysis apply equally well to all gifts, be they gifts of time, talent, or treasure? If the philanthropist is one who initiates the giving of a gift, in Hyde's understanding can anyone really be a philanthropist? In the light of Hyde's analysis, which, if any, of the many sorts of gifts considered in this section are true gifts?

I. THE MOTION

When the Puritans first landed in Massachusetts, they discovered a thing so curious about the Indians' feelings for property that they felt called upon to give it a name. In 1764, when Thomas Hutchinson wrote his history of the colony, the term was already an old saying: "An Indian gift," he told his readers, "is a proverbial expression signifying a present for which an equivalent return is expected." We still use this, of course, and in an even broader sense, calling that friend an Indian giver who is so uncivilized as to ask us to return a gift he has given.

Imagine a scene. An Englishman comes into an Indian lodge, and his hosts, wishing to make their guest feel welcome, ask him to share a pipe of tobacco. Carved from a soft red stone, the pipe itself is a peace offering that has traditionally circulated among the local tribes, staying in each lodge for a time but always given away again sooner or later. And so the Indians, as is only polite among their people, give the pipe to their guest when he leaves. The Englishman is tickled pink. What a nice thing to send back to the British Museum! He takes it home and sets it on the mantelpiece. A time passes and the leaders of a neighboring tribe come to visit the colonist's home. To his surprise he finds his guests have some expectation in regard to his pipe, and his translator finally explains to him that if he wishes to show his goodwill he should offer them a smoke and give them the pipe. In consternation the Englishman invents a phrase to describe these people with such a limited sense of private property. The opposite of "Indian giver" would be something like "white man keeper" (or maybe "capitalist"), that is, a person whose instinct is to remove property from circulation, to put it in a warehouse or museum (or, more to the point for capitalism, to lay it aside to be used for production).

The Indian giver (or the original one, at any rate) understood a cardinal property of the gift: whatever we have been given is supposed to be given away again, not kept. Or, if it is kept, something of similar value should move on in its stead, the way a billiard ball may stop when it sends another scurrying across the felt, its momentum transferred. You may keep your Christmas present, but it ceases to be a gift in the true sense unless you have given something else away. As it is passed along, the gift may be given back to the original donor, but this is not essential. In fact, it is better if the gift is not returned but is given instead to some new, third party. The only essential is this: *the gift must always move.* There are other forms of property that stand still, that mark a boundary or resist momentum, but the gift keeps going.

Tribal peoples usually distinguish between gifts and capital. Commonly they have a law that repeats the sensibility implicit in the idea of an Indian gift. "One man's gift," they say, "must not be another man's capital." Wendy James, a British social anthropologist, tells us that among the Uduk in northeast Africa, "any wealth transferred from one subclan to another, whether animals, grain or money, is in the nature of a gift, and should be consumed, and not invested for growth. If such transferred wealth is added to the subclan's capital [cattle in this case] and kept for growth and investment, the subclan is regarded as being in an immoral relation of debt to the donors of the original gift." If a pair of goats received as a gift from another subclan is kept to breed or to buy cattle, "there will be general complaint that the so-and-so's are getting rich at someone else's expense, behaving immorally by hoarding and investing gifts, and therefore being in a state of severe debt. It will be expected that they will soon suffer storm damage...."

The goats in this example move from one clan to another just as the stone pipe moved from person to person in my imaginary scene. And what happens then? If the object is a gift, it keeps moving, which in this case means that the man who received the goats throws a big party and everyone gets fed. The goats needn't be given back, but they surely can't be set aside to produce milk or more goats. And a new note has been added: the feeling that if a gift is not treated as such, if one form of property is converted into another, something horrible will happen. In folk tales the person who tries to hold onto a gift usually dies; in this anecdote the risk is "storm damage." (What happens in fact to most tribal groups is worse than storm damage. Where someone manages to commercialize a tribe's gift relationships the social fabric of the group is invariably destroyed.)

If we turn now to a folk tale, we will be able to see all of this from a different angle. Folk tales are like collective dreams; they are told in the kind of voice we hear at the edge of sleep, mingling the facts of our lives with their images in the psyche. The first tale I have chosen was collected from a Scottish woman in the middle of the nineteenth century.

The Girl and the Dead Man

Once upon a time there was an old woman and she had a leash of daughters. One day the eldest daughter said to her mother, "It is time for me to go out into the world and seek my fortune." "I shall bake a loaf of bread for you to carry with you," said the mother. When the bread came from the oven the mother asked her daughter, "Would you rather have a small piece and my blessing or a large piece and my curse?" "I would rather have the large piece and your curse," replied the daughter.

Off she went down the road and when the night came wreathing around her she sat at the foot of a wall to eat her bread. A ground quail and her twelve puppies gathered near, and the little birds of the air. "Wilt thou give us a part of thy bread," they asked. "I won't, you ugly brutes," she replied. "I haven't enough for myself." "My curse on thee," said the quail, "and the curse of my twelve birds, and thy mother's curse which is the worst of all." The girl arose and went on her way, and the piece of bread had not been half enough.

She had not traveled far before she saw a little house, and though it seemed a long way off she soon found herself before its door. She knocked and heard a voice cry out, "Who is there?" "A good maid seeking a master." "We need that," said the voice, and the door swung open.

The girl's task was to stay awake every night and watch over a dead man, the brother of the housewife, whose corpse was restless. As her reward she was to receive a peck of gold and a peck of silver. And while she stayed she was to have as many nuts as she broke, as many needles as she lost, as many thimbles as she pierced, as much thread as she used, as many candles as she burned, a bed of green silk over her and a bed of green silk under her, sleeping by day and watching by night.

On the very first night, however, she fell asleep in her chair. The housewife came in, struck her with a magic club, killed her dead, and threw her out back on the pile of kitchen garbage.

Soon thereafter the middle daughter said to her mother, "It is time for me to follow my sister and seek my fortune." Her mother baked her a loaf of bread and she too chose the larger piece and her mother's curse. And what had happened to her sister happened to her.

Soon thereafter the youngest daughter said to her mother, "It is time for me to follow my sisters and seek my fortune." "I had better bake you a loaf of bread," said her mother, "and which would you rather have, a small piece and my blessing or a large piece and my curse?" "I would rather," said the daughter, "have the smaller piece and your blessing."

And so she set off down the road and when the night came wreathing around her she sat at the foot of a wall to eat her bread. The ground quail and her twelve puppies and the little birds of the air gathered about. "Wilt thou give us some of that?" they asked. "I will, you pretty creatures, if you will keep me company." She shared her bread, all of them ate their fill, and the birds clapped their wings about her 'til she was snug with the warmth.

The next morning she saw a house a long way off. . . . [here the task and the wages are repeated].

She sat up at night to watch the corpse, sewing to pass the time. About midnight the dead man sat up and screwed up a grin. "If you do not lie down properly I will give you one good leathering with a stick," she cried. He lay down. After a while he rose up on one elbow and screwed up a grin; and a third time he sat and screwed up a grin.

When he rose the third time she walloped him with the stick. The stick stuck to the dead man and her hand stuck to the stick and off they went! He dragged her through the woods, and when it was high for him it was low for her, and when it was low for him it was high for her. The nuts were knocking at their eyes and the wild plums beat at their ears until they both got through the wood. Then they returned home.

The girl was given the peck of gold, the peck of silver, and a vessel of cordial. She found her two sisters and rubbed them with the cordial and brought them back to life. And they left me sitting here, and if they were well, 'tis well; if they were not, let them be.

There are at least four gifts in this story. The first, of course, is the bread, which the mother gives to her daughters as a going-away present. This becomes the second gift when the youngest daughter shares her bread with the birds. She keeps the gift in motion—the moral point of the tale. Several benefits, in addition to her survival, come to her as a result of treating the gift correctly. These are the fruits of the gift. First, she and the birds are relieved of their hunger; second, the birds befriend her; and third, she's able to stay awake all night and accomplish her task. (As we shall see, these results are not accidental, they are typical fruits of the gift.)

In the morning the third gift, the vessel of cordial, appears. "Cordial" used to mean a liqueur taken to stimulate the heart. In the original Gaelic of this tale the phrase is *ballen íocshlaint,* which translated more literally as "teat of ichor" or "teat of health" ("ichor" being the fluid that flows instead of blood in the veins of the gods). So what the girl is given is a vial of healing liquid, not unlike the "water of life," which appears in folk tales from all over the world. It has power: with it she is able to revive her sisters.

This liquid is thrown in as a reward for the successful completion of her task. It's a gift, mentioned nowhere in the wonderful litany of wages offered to each daughter. We will leave for later the question of where it comes from; for now, we are looking at what happens to the gift after it is given, and again we find that this girl is no dummy—she moves it right along, giving it to her sisters to bring them back to life. That is the fourth and final gift in the tale.*

This story also gives us a chance to see what happens if the gift is not allowed to move on. A gift that cannot move loses its gift properties. Traditional belief in Wales holds that when the fairies give bread to the poor, the loaves must be eaten on the day they are given or they will turn to toadstools. If we think of the gift as a constantly flowing river, we may say that the girl in the tale who treats it correctly does so by allowing herself to become a channel for its current. When someone tries to dam up the river, one of two things will happen: either it will stagnate or it will fill the person up until he bursts. In this folk tale, it is not just the mother's curse that gets the first two girls. The night birds give them a second chance, and one imagines the mother bird would not have repeated the curse had she met with generosity. But instead the girls try to dam the flow, thinking that what counts is ownership and size. The effect is clear: by keeping the gift they get no more. They are no longer channels for the stream and they no longer enjoy its fruits, one of which seems to be their own lives. Their mother's bread has turned to toadstools inside them.

---

*This story illustrates almost all the main characteristics of a gift, so I shall be referring back to it. As an aside, therefore, I want to take a stab at its meaning. It says, I think, that if a girl without a father is going to get along in the world, she'd better have a good connection to her mother. The birds are the mother's spirit, what we'd now call the girls' psychological mother. The girl who gives the gift back to the spirit-mother has, as a result, her mother-wits about her for the rest of the tale.

Nothing in the tale links the dead man with the girls' father, but the mother seems to be a widow, or at any rate the absence of a father at the start of the story is a hint that the problem may have to do with men. It's not clear, but when the first man she meets is not only dead but difficult, we are permitted to raise our eyebrows.

The man is dead, but not dead enough. When she hits him with the stick, we see that she is in fact attached to him. So here's the issue: when a fatherless woman leaves home, she'll have to deal with the fact that she's stuck on a dead man. It's a risky situation—the two elder daughters end up dead.

Not much happens in the wild run through the forest, except that both parties get bruised. The girl manages to stay awake the whole time, however. This is a power she probably got from the birds, for they are night birds. The connection to the mother cannot spare her the ordeal, but it allows her to survive. When it's all over she's unstuck, and we may assume that the problem won't arise again.

Though the dilemma of the story is not related to gift, all the psychological work is accomplished through gift exchange.

Another way to describe the motion of the gift is to say that a gift must always be used up, consumed, eaten. *The gift is property that perishes.* It is no accident that the gifts in two of our stories so far have been food. Food is one of the most common images for the gift because it is so obviously consumed. Even when the gift is not food, when it is something we would think of as a durable good, it is often referred to as a thing to be eaten. Shell necklaces and armbands are the ritual gifts in the Trobriand Islands, and when they are passed from one group to the next, protocol demands that the man who gives them away toss them on the ground and say, "Here, some food we could not eat." Or, again, a man in another tribe that Wendy James has studied says, in speaking of the money he was given at the marriage of his daughter, that he will pass it on rather than spend it on himself. Only, he puts it this way: "If I receive money for the children God has given me, I cannot eat it. I must give it to others."

Many of the most famous of the gift systems we know about center on food and treat durable goods as if they were food. The potlatch of the American Indians along the North Pacific coast was originally a "big feed." At its simplest a potlatch was a feast lasting several days given by a member of a tribe who wanted his rank in the group to be publicly recognized. Marcel Mauss translates the verb "potlatch" as "to nourish" or "to consume." Used as a noun, a "potlatch" is a "feeder" or "place to be satiated." Potlatches included durable goods, but the point of the festival was to have these perish as if they were food. Houses were burned; ceremonial objects were broken and thrown into the sea. One of the potlatch tribes, the Haida, called their feasting "killing wealth."

To say that the gift is used up, consumed and eaten sometimes means that it is truly destroyed as in these last examples, but more simply and accurately it means that the gift perishes *for the person who gives it away.* In gift exchange the transaction itself consumes the object. Now, it is true that something often comes back when a gift is given, but if this were made an explicit condition of the exchange, it wouldn't be a gift. If the girl in our story had offered to sell the bread to the birds, the whole tone would have been different. But instead she sacrifices it: her mother's gift is dead and gone when it leaves her hand. She no longer controls it, nor has she any contract about repayment. For her, the gift has perished. This, then, is how I use "consume" to speak of a gift—a gift is consumed when it moves from one hand to another with no assurance of anything in return. There is little difference, therefore, between its consumption and its movement. A market exchange has an equilibrium or stasis: you pay to balance the scale. But when you give a gift there is momentum, and the weight shifts from body to body.

I must add one more word on what it is to consume, because the Western industrial world is famous for its "consumer goods" and they are not at all what I mean. Again, the difference is in the form of the exchange, a thing we can feel most concretely in the form of the goods themselves. I remember the time I went to my first rare-book fair and saw how the first editions of Thoreau and Whitman and Crane had been carefully packaged in heat-shrunk plastic with the price tags on the inside. Somehow the simple addition of airtight plastic bags had transformed the books from vehicles of liveliness into commodities, like bread made with chemicals to keep it from perishing. In commodity exchange it's as if the buyer and the seller were both in plastic bags; there's none of the contact of a gift exchange. There is neither motion nor emotion because the whole point is to keep the balance, to make sure the exchange itself doesn't consume anything or involve one person with another. Consumer goods are consumed by their owners, not by their exchange.

The desire to consume is a kind of lust. We long to have the world flow through us like air or food. We are thirsty and hungry for something that can only be carried inside bodies. But consumer goods merely bait this lust, they do not satisfy it. The consumer of commodities is invited to a meal without passion, a consumption that leads to neither satiation nor fire. He is a stranger seduced into feeding on the drippings of someone else's capital without benefit of its inner nourishment, and he is hungry at the end of the meal, depressed and weary as we all feel when lust has dragged us from the house and led us to nothing.

Gift exchange has many fruits, as we shall see, and to the degree that the fruits of the gift can satisfy our needs there will always be pressure for property to be treated as a gift. This pressure, in a sense, is what keeps the gift in motion. When the Uduk warn that a storm will ruin the crops if someone tries to stop the gift from moving, it is really their desire for the gift that will bring the storm. A restless hunger springs up when the gift is not being eaten. The brothers Grimm found a folk tale they called "The Ungrateful Son":

> Once a man and his wife were sitting outside the front door with a roast chicken before them which they were going to eat between them. Then the man saw his old father coming along and quickly took the chicken and hid it, for he begrudged him any of it. The old man came, had a drink, and went away.
>
> Now the son was about to put the roast chicken back on the table, but when he reached for it, it had turned into a big toad that jumped in his face and stayed there and didn't go away again.
>
> And if anybody tried to take it away, it would give them a poisonous look, as if about to jump in their faces, so that no one dared touch it. And the ungrateful son had to feed the toad every day, otherwise it would eat part of his face. And thus he went ceaselessly hither and yon about in the world.

This toad is the hunger that appears when the gift stops moving, whenever one man's gift becomes another man's capital. To the degree that we desire the fruits of the gift, teeth appear when it is hidden away. When property is hoarded, thieves and beggars begin to be born to rich men's wives. A story like this says that there is a force seeking to keep the gift in motion. Some property must perish—its preservation is beyond us. We have no choice. Or rather, our choice is whether to keep the gift moving or to be eaten with it. We choose between the toad's dumb-lust and that other, more graceful perishing in which our hunger disappears as our gifts are consumed.

IV.11

Tuesdays with Morrie: "The Eighth Tuesday: We Talk About Money"

Mitch Albom

Mitch Albom (born in 1958) was fifteen years out of college and rapidly achieving a name for himself in the world of sports journalism when he suddenly learned of Morrie's plight. As an undergraduate at Brandeis University, he had taken every course his favorite professor, Morrie Schwartz, had offered. But as with so many others bent on success after college, despite his intentions to keep in touch, as time passed, Morrie became an ever more distant memory, his teachings all but forgotten. "It would have stayed that way," Albom explains, "had I not been flicking through the TV channels late one night, when something caught my ear. . . . Ted Koppel, from behind his desk in Washington, asked, 'Who is Morrie Schwartz and why, by the end of the night, are so many of you going to care about him?'" Morrie was dying of a brutal degenerative neurological disease (commonly known as Lou Gehrig's disease), and he had granted Koppel an interview about the topic of his "final course": his own death.

Like the millions of other viewers, Albom was deeply moved by Morrie's candor, courage, and wisdom. But most of all, listening to his old professor made him take stock of himself: his life, his accomplishments, his hopes, and his regrets. Albom flew to Boston to be with Morrie, to take one last class. And as if he had been expecting him all along, Morrie resumed their conversation that had been interrupted fifteen years earlier. Albom's recent bestseller, *Tuesdays with Morrie: An Old Man, a Young Man and Life's Greatest Lesson,* was the final paper—a recap of their "class"—which he wrote, by agreement, after Morrie's death. The nearness of death gave urgency and poignancy to their conversations. On the eighth Tuesday, in the conversation reported below, they speak about money: what it can and cannot buy, and what really is worth giving. Morrie's answer: "my time." Does Morrie have it right?

"Fate succumbs
many a species: one alone
jeopardises itself."

—W. H. Auden, Morrie's Favorite Poet

I held up the newspaper so that Morrie could see it:

I DON'T WANT MY TOMBSTONE TO READ
"I NEVER OWNED A NETWORK."

Morrie laughed, then shook his head. The morning sun was coming through the window behind him, falling on the pink flowers of the hibiscus plant that sat on the sill. The quote was from Ted Turner, the billionaire media mogul, founder of CNN, who had been lamenting his inability to snatch up the CBS network in a corporate megadeal. I had brought the story to Morrie this morning because I wondered if Turner ever found himself in my old professor's position, his breath disappearing, his body turning to stone, his days being crossed off the calendar one by one—would he really be crying over owning a network?

"It's all part of the same problem, Mitch," Morrie said. "We put our values in the wrong things. And it leads to very disillusioned lives. I think we should talk about that."

Morrie was focused. There were good days and bad days now. He was having a good day. The night before, he had been entertained by a local a cappella group that had come to the house to perform, and he relayed the story excitedly, as if the Ink Spots themselves had dropped by for a visit. Morrie's love for music was strong even before he got sick, but now it was so intense, it moved him to tears. He would listen to opera sometimes at night, closing his eyes, riding along with the magnificent voices as they dipped and soared.

"You should have heard this group last night, Mitch. Such a sound!"

Morrie had always been taken with simple pleasures, singing, laughing, dancing. Now, more than ever, material things held little or no significance. When people die, you always hear the expression "You can't take it with you." Morrie seemed to know that a long time ago.

"We've got a form of brainwashing going on in our country," Morrie sighed. "Do you know how they brainwash people? They repeat something over and over. And that's what we do in this country. Owning things is good. More money is good. More property is good. More commercialism is good. *More is good. More is good.* We repeat it—and have it repeated to us—over and over until nobody bothers to even think otherwise. The average person is so fogged up by all this, he has no perspective on what's really important anymore.

"Wherever I went in my life, I met people wanting to gobble up something new. Gobble up a new car. Gobble up a new piece of property. Gobble up the latest toy. And then they wanted to tell you about it. 'Guess what I got? Guess what I got?'

"You know how I always interpreted that? These were people so hungry for love that they were accepting substitutes. They were embracing material things and expecting a sort of hug back. But it never works. You can't substitute material things for love or for gentleness or for tenderness or for a sense of comradeship.

"Money is not a substitute for tenderness, and power is not a substitute for tenderness. I can tell you, as I'm sitting here dying, when you most need it, neither money nor power will give you the feeling you're looking for, no matter how much of them you have."

I glanced around Morrie's study. It was the same today as it had been the first day I arrived. The books held their same places on the shelves. The papers cluttered the same old desk. The outside rooms had not been improved or upgraded. In fact, Morrie really hadn't bought anything new—except medical equipment—in a long, long time, maybe years. The day he learned that he was terminally ill was the day he lost interest in his purchasing power.

So the TV was the same old model, the car that Charlotte drove was the same old model, the dishes and the silverware and the towels—all the same. And yet the house had changed so drastically. It had filled with love and teaching and communication. It had filled with friendship and family and honesty and tears. It had filled with colleagues and students and meditation teachers and therapists and nurses and a cappella groups. It had become, in a very real way, a wealthy home, even though Morrie's bank account was rapidly depleting.

"There's a big confusion in this country over what we want versus what we need," Morrie said. "You need food, you *want* a chocolate sundae. You have to be honest with yourself. You don't *need* the latest sports car, you don't *need* the biggest house.

"The truth is, you don't get satisfaction from those things. You know what really gives you satisfaction?"

What?

"Offering others what you have to give."

You sound like a Boy Scout.

"I don't mean money, Mitch. I mean your time. Your concern. Your storytelling. It's not so hard. There's a senior center that opened near here. Dozens of elderly people come there every day. If you're a young man or young woman and you have a skill, you are asked to come and teach it. Say you know computers. You come there and teach them computers. You are very welcome there. And they are very grateful. This is how you start to get respect, by offering something that you have.

"There are plenty of places to do this. You don't need to have a big talent. There are lonely people in hospitals and shelters who only want some companionship. You play cards with a lonely older man and you find new respect for yourself, because you are needed.

"Remember what I said about finding a meaningful life? I wrote it down, but now I can recite it: Devote yourself to loving others, devote yourself to your community around you, and devote yourself to creating something that gives you purpose and meaning.

"You notice," he added, grinning, "there's nothing in there about a salary."

I jotted some of the things Morrie was saying on a yellow pad. I did this mostly because I didn't want him to see my eyes, to know what I was thinking, that I had been, for much of my life since graduation, pursuing these very things he had been railing against—bigger toys, nicer house. Because I worked among the rich and famous athletes, I convinced myself that my needs were realistic, my greed inconsequential compared to theirs.

This was a smokescreen. Morrie made that obvious.

"Mitch, if you're trying to show off for people at the top, forget it. They will look down at you anyhow. And if you're trying to show off for people at the bottom, forget it. They will only envy you. Status will get you nowhere. Only an open heart will allow you to float equally between everyone."

He paused, then looked at me. "I'm dying, right?"

Yes.

"Why do you think it's so important for me to hear other people's problems? Don't I have enough pain and suffering of my own?

"Of course I do. But giving to other people is what makes me feel alive. Not my car or my house. Not what I look like in the mirror. When I give my time, when I can make someone smile after they were feeling sad, it's as close to healthy as I ever feel.

"Do the kinds of things that come from the heart. When you do, you won't be dissatisfied, you won't be envious, you won't be longing for somebody else's things. On the contrary, you'll be overwhelmed with what comes back."

He coughed and reached for the small bell that lay on the chair. He had to poke a few times at it, and I finally picked it up and put it in his hand.

"Thank you," he whispered. He shook it weakly, trying to get Connie's attention.

"This Ted Turner guy," Morrie said, "he couldn't think of anything else for his tombstone?"

"Each night, when I go to sleep, I die. And the next morning, when I wake up, I am reborn."

—MAHATMA GANDHI

PART FIVE

Can Giving Be Taught?

PART V: TABLE OF CONTENTS

Aristotle, *Nichomachean Ethics:* "Moral Virtue as the Result of Habits"

Benjamin Franklin, *The Autobiography of Benjamin Franklin:*
Practice Makes Perfect?

Woodrow Wilson, "Princeton for the Nation's Service"

Pierre Mac Orlan, "The Philanthropist"

Kenneth E. Kirk, Worship, Humility and Service

Stephen Vincent Benet, "The Bishop's Beggar"

Edward Holmes, "Town Office"

His Holiness the XIV Dalai Lama, "Giving and Receiving:
A Practical Way of Directing Love and Compassion"

Elizabeth M. Lynn and D. Susan Wisely, "Only Reflect:
A Philanthropic Education for Our Time"

V.1

Nichomachean Ethics:
"Moral Virtue as the Result of Habits"

Aristotle

Not by accident does Aristotle call his treatise on ethics *Nichomachean Ethics*. Nichomachus was the name both of his father and of his son, and as he explains in the selection excerpted below, our parents are primordially responsible for the habits we acquire and, in turn, cultivate in our children. We are not, as Aristotle notes in this selection (excerpted from Book II, Chapters 1 and 2), virtuous by nature, that is to say, by birth, but we are by nature capable of cultivating the habits that enable us to become virtuous (or vicious). Well before we are capable of reasoning and deciding for ourselves, our parents (and, more generally, the customs and laws under which we live) shape the habits we acquire, by directing our desires to certain ends, through directing our deeds in certain paths, and through praise and blame for our conduct. For Aristotle, then, moral virtue is acquired by practice, that is, by doing good or virtuous deeds. As Aristotle warns, since "the same causes and the same means that produce any excellence or virtue can also destroy it," it makes no small difference what sort of activities we do or what habits we acquire as children. Assuming that one's purpose is to cultivate the habit of giving—for Aristotle, generosity (see selection in Part I)—how would a good Aristotelian go about doing it? What sort of deeds should be practiced? At what age should one begin? Is Aristotle correct in thinking that how one has been reared from childhood makes *all* the difference? Is it, as Aristotle implies, nearly impossible for a person who was not blessed with generous parents or who lives in a corrupt or impoverished community to become generous? What is the difference between the sort of habituation that Aristotle is speaking of and animal training?

Virtue, as we have seen, consists of two kinds, intellectual virtue and moral virtue. Intellectual virtue or excellence owes its origin and development chiefly to teaching, and for that reason requires experience and time. Moral virtue, on the other hand, is formed by habit . . . This shows, too, that none of the moral virtues is implanted in us by nature, for nothing which exists by nature can be changed by habit. For example, it is impossible for a stone, which has a natural downward movement, to become habituated to moving upward, even if one should try ten thousand times to inculcate the habit by throwing it in the air; nor can fire be made to move downward, nor can the direction of any nature-given tendency be changed by habituation. Thus, the virtues are implanted in us neither by nature nor contrary to nature: we are by nature equipped with the ability to receive them, and habit brings this ability to completion and fulfillment.

Furthermore, of all the qualities with which we are endowed by nature, we are provided with the capacity [in Greek, *dynamis,* which can also mean "ability" or "potentiality"] first, and display the activity [in Greek, *energeia,* which can also mean "actuality"] afterward. That this is true is shown by the senses: it is not by frequent seeing or frequent hearing that we acquired our senses, but on the contrary we first possess and then use them; we do not acquire them by use. The virtues, on the other hand, we acquire by first having put them into action, and the same is also true of the arts [in Greek, *techné,* i.e., "skill," "art," or "know-how," the possession of which enables one to produce a certain product, e.g., the skill needed to produce shoes, or music, or health]. For the things which we have to learn before we can do them we learn by doing: men become builders by building houses, and harpists by playing the harp. Similarly, we become just by the practice of just actions, self-controlled by exercising self-control, and courageous by performing acts of courage.

This is corroborated by what happens in states. Lawgivers make the citizens good by inculcating (good) habits in them, and this is the aim of every lawgiver; if he does not succeed in doing that, his legislation is a failure. It is in this that a good constitution differs from a bad one.

Moreover, the same causes and the same means that produce any excellence or virtue can also destroy it, and this is also true of every art. It is by playing the harp that men become both good and bad harpists, and correspondingly with builders and all the other craftsmen: a man who builds well will be a good builder, one who builds badly a bad one. For if this were not so, there would be no need for an instructor, but everybody would be born as a good or bad craftsman. The same holds true of the virtues: in our transactions with other men it is by action that some become just and others unjust, and it is by acting in the face of danger and by developing the habit of feeling fear or confidence that some become brave men and others cowards. The same applies to the appetites and feelings of anger: by reacting in one way or in another to given circumstances some people become self-controlled and gentle, and others self-indulgent and short-tempered. In a word, characteristics [in Greek, *hexis,* also translated "habit"] develop from corresponding activities. For that reason, we must see to it that our activities are of a certain kind, since any variations in them will be reflected in our characteristics/habits. Hence it is no small matter whether one habit or another is inculcated in us from early childhood; on the contrary, it makes a considerable difference, or, rather, all the difference.

V.2

The Autobiography of Benjamin Franklin: Practice Makes Perfect?

Benjamin Franklin

Benjamin Franklin's life spanned the eighteenth century (1706–1790), and he saw and participated firsthand in much that it had to offer. Reared in Boston, young Franklin struck out on his own, at age 17, in order to escape the yoke of authority. Alone and without any visible means of support, he wandered to Philadelphia, where by age 24 he established his own printing business. Thereafter, in fairly short order, he entered public life and established his indispensability, first to his city, then to his country, and then to the world. He became known worldwide for his writings and statesmanship, his scientific discoveries and inventions, and his philanthropy (in Franklin's terms, his usefulness as a citizen). By all accounts, Benjamin Franklin was no ordinary man. Not in his own time, not in any time. And yet when he sat down at the age of 65 to write his autobiography, he crafted an account consciously intended to be a model for everyone.

The "bold and arduous Project of arriving at moral Perfection," Franklin's plan, rehearsed below, is meant to point the way for us, as it did—or so he claims—for him. To each of the thirteen virtues he chose to cultivate, he attaches a brief explanatory self-injunction. He then arranges the virtues in an order designed to promote easy acquisition. For example, "temperance," regarded by Franklin as essential for acquiring the "Coolness and Clearness of Head" needed for studying, comes before "silence." Leaving nothing to chance, Franklin also devised a careful method for systematically acquiring his carefully ordered virtues. Are the virtues Franklin regarded as requisite for a flourishing life adequate for us today? Are we really as free to remake ourselves as Franklin implies? If we adopt Franklin's regimen, are we likely to become Franklins—that is, free, useful, and philanthropic citizens?

It was about this time [c.1728] that I conceiv'd the bold and arduous Project of arriving at moral Perfection. I wish'd to live without committing any Fault at any time; I would conquer all that either Natural Inclination, Custom, or Company might lead me into. As I knew, or thought I knew, what was right and wrong, I did not see why I might not *always* do the one and avoid the other. But I soon found I had undertaken a Task of more Difficulty than I had imagined. While my *Attention was taken up* in guarding against one Fault, I was often sur-priz'd by another. Habit took the Advantage of Inattention. Inclination was sometimes too strong for Reason. I concluded at length, that the mere specula-tive Conviction that it was our Interest to be compleatly virtuous, was not suffi-cient to prevent our Slipping, and that the contrary Habits must be broken and good ones acquired and established, before we can have any Dependance on a steady uniform Rectitude of Conduct. For this purpose I therefore contriv'd the following Method.

In the various Enumerations of the moral Virtues I had met with in my Reading, I found the Catalogue more or less numerous, as different Writers in-cluded more or fewer ideas under the same Name. Temperance, for Example, was by some confin'd to Eating and Drinking, while by others it was extended to mean the moderating every other Pleasure, Appetite, Inclination or Passion, bodily or mental, even to our Avarice and Ambition. I propos'd to myself, for the sake of Clearness, to use rather more Names with fewer Ideas annex'd to each, than a few Names with more Ideas; and I included under Thirteen Names of Virtues all that at that time occurr'd to me as necessary or desirable, and annex'd to each a short Precept, which fully express'd the Extent I gave to its Meaning.

These Names of Virtues with their Precepts were

1. Temperance.

Eat not to Dulness.
Drink not to Elevation.

2. Silence.

Speak not but what may benefit others or yourself. Avoid trifling Conversation.

3. Order.

Let all your Things have their Places. Let each Part of your Business have its Time.

4. Resolution.

Resolve to perform what you ought. Perform without fail what you resolve.

5. Frugality.

Make no Expence but to do good to others or yourself: i.e. Waste nothing.

6. Industry.

Lose no Time. Be always employ'd in something useful. Cut off all unnecessary Actions.

7. Sincerity.

Use no hurtful Deceit.
Think innocently and justly; and, if you speak, speak accordingly.

8. Justice.

Wrong none, by doing Injuries or omitting the Benefits that are your Duty.

9. Moderation.

Avoid Extreams. Forbear resenting Injuries so much as you think they deserve.

10. Cleanliness

Tolerate no Uncleanness in Body, Cloaths or Habitation.

11. Tranquility

Be not disturbed at Trifles, or at Accidents common or unavoidable.

12. Chastity

Rarely use Venery but for Health or Offspring; Never to Dulness, Weakness, or the Injury of your own or another's Peace or Reputation.

13. Humility

Imitate Jesus and Socrates.

My Intention being to acquire the *Habitude* of all these Virtues, I judg'd it would be well not to distract my Attention by attempting the whole at once, but to fix it on one of them at a time, and when I should be Master of that, then to proceed to another, and so on till I should have gone thro' the thirteen. And as the previous Acquisition of some might facilitate the Acquisition of certain others, I arrang'd them with that View as they stand above. *Temperance* first, as it tends to procure that Coolness and Clearness of Head, which is so necessary where constant Vigilance was to be kept up, and Guard maintained, against the unremitting Attraction of ancient Habits, and the Force of perpetual Temptations. This being acquir'd and establish'd, *Silence* would be more easy, and my Desire being to gain Knowledge at the same time that I improv'd in Virtue, and considering that in Conversation it was obtain'd rather by the use of the Ears than of the Tongue, and therefore wishing to break a Habit I was getting into of Prattling, Punning and Joking, which only made me acceptable to trifling Company, I gave *Silence* the second Place. This, and the next, *Order*, I expected would allow me more Time for attending to my Project and my Studies; RESOLUTION, once become habitual, would keep me firm in my Endeavours to obtain all the subsequent Virtues; *Frugality* and *Industry*, by freeing me from my remaining Debt, and producing Affluence and Independence, would make more easy the Practice of *Sincerity* and *Justice*, &c. &c. Conceiving then that agreable [*sic*] to the Advice of Pythagoras in his Golden Verses daily Examination would be necessary, I contriv'd the following Method for conducting that Examination.

I made a little Book in which I allotted a Page for each of the Virtues. I rul'd each Page with red Ink, so as to have seven Columns, one for each Day of the Week, marking each Column with a Letter for the Day. I cross'd these Columns with thirteen red Lines, marking the Beginning of each Line with the first Letter of one of the Virtues, on which Line and in its proper Column I might mark by a little black Spot every Fault I found upon Examination to have been committed respecting that Virtue upon the Day.

I determined to give a Week's strict Attention to each of the Virtues successively. Thus in the first Week my great Guard was to avoid every the least Offence against Temperance, leaving the other Virtues to their ordinary Chance, only marking every Evening the Faults of the Day. Thus if in the first Week I could keep my first Line marked T clear of Spots, I suppos'd the Habit of that Virtue so much strengthen'd and its opposite weaken'd, that I might venture extending my Attention to include the next, and for the following Week keep both Lines clear of Spots. Proceeding thus to the last, I could go thro' a Course compleat in Thirteen Weeks, and four Courses in a Year. And like him who having a Garden to weed, does not attempt to eradicate all the bad Herbs at once, which would exceed his Reach and his Strength, but works on one of the Beds at a time, and having accomplish'd the first proceeds to a Second; so I should have, (I hoped) the encouraging Pleasure of seeing on my Pages the Progress I made in Virtue, by clearing successively my Lines of their Spots, till in the End by a Number of Courses, I should be happy in viewing a clean Book after a thirteen Weeks daily Examination.

Form of the Pages

Temperance.						
Eat not to Dulness. *Drink not to Elevation.*						
	S	M	T	W	T	F	S

	S	M	T	W	T	F	S
T							
S	••	•		•		•	
O	•	•	•		•	•	•
R			•			•	
F		•			•		
I			•				
S							
J							
M							
Cl							
T							
Ch							
H							

... The Precept of *Order* requiring that *every Part of my Business should have its allotted Time,* one Page in my little Book contain'd the following Scheme of Employment for the Twenty-four Hours of a natural Day,

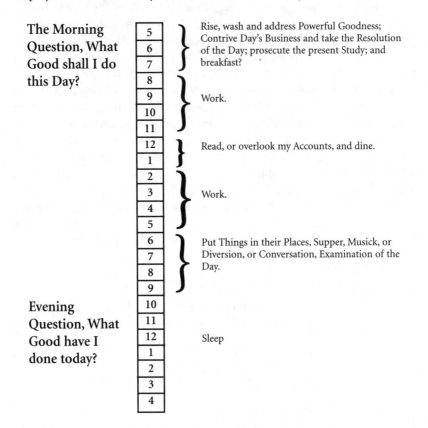

The Morning Question, What Good shall I do this Day?	5	}	Rise, wash and address Powerful Goodness; Contrive Day's Business and take the Resolution of the Day; prosecute the present Study; and breakfast?
	6		
	7		
	8	}	Work.
	9		
	10		
	11		
	12	}	Read, or overlook my Accounts, and dine.
	1		
	2	}	Work.
	3		
	4		
	5		
	6	}	Put Things in their Places, Supper, Musick, or Diversion, or Conversation, Examination of the Day.
	7		
	8		
	9		
Evening Question, What Good have I done today?	10		
	11		
	12		Sleep
	1		
	2		
	3		
	4		

I enter'd upon the Execution of this Plan for Self Examination, and continu'd it with occasional Intermissions for some time. I was surpriz'd to find myself so much fuller of Faults than I had imagined, but I had the Satisfaction of seeing them diminish. To avoid the Trouble of renewing now and then my little Book, which by scraping out the Marks on the Paper of old Faults to make room for new Ones in a new Course, became full of Holes: I transferr'd my Tables and Precepts to the Ivory Leaves of a Memorandum Book, on which the Lines were drawn with red Ink that made a durable Stain, and on those Lines I mark'd my Faults with a black Lead Pencil, which Marks I could easily wipe out with a wet Sponge. After a while I went thro' one Course only in a Year, and afterwards only one in several Years, till at length I omitted them entirely, being employ'd in Voyages and Business abroad with a Multiplicity of Affairs, that interfered, but I always carried my little Book with me.

My Scheme of ORDER, gave me the most Trouble, and I found, that tho' it might be practicable where a Man's Business was such as to leave him the Disposition of his Time, that of a Journey-man Printer for instance, it was not possible to be exactly observ'd by a Master, who must mix with the World, and often receive People of Business at their own Hours. *Order* too, with regard to Places for Things, Papers, &c. I found extreamely difficult to acquire. I had not been early accustomed to *Method,* and having an exceeding good Memory, I was not so sensible of the Inconvenience attending Want of Method. This Article therefore cost me so much painful Attention and my Faults in it vex'd me so much, and I made so little Progress in Amendment, and had such frequent Relapses, that I was almost ready to give up the Attempt, and content my self with a faulty Character in that respect. Like the Man who in buying an Ax of a Smith my neighbour, desired to have the whole of its Surface as bright as the Edge; the Smith consented to grind it bright for him if he would turn the Wheel. He turn'd while the Smith press'd the broad Face of the Ax hard and heavily on the Stone, which made the Turning of it very fatiguing. The Man came every now and then from the Wheel to see how the Work went on; and at length would take his Ax as it was without farther Grinding. No, says the Smith, Turn on, turn on; we shall have it bright by and by; as yet 'tis only speckled. Yes, says the Man; but—*I think I like a speckled Ax best.* And I believe this may have been the Case with many who having for want of some such Means as I employ'd found the Difficulty of obtaining good, and breaking bad Habits, in other Points of Vice and Virtue, have given up the Struggle, and concluded that *a speckled Ax was best.* For something that pretended to be Reason was every now and then suggesting to me, that such extream Nicety as I exacted of my self might be a kind of Foppery in Morals, which if it were known would make me ridiculous; that a perfect Character might be attended with the Inconvenience of being envied and hated; and that a benevolent Man should allow a few Faults in himself, to keep his Friends in Countenance.

In Truth I found myself incorrigible with respect to *Order;* and now I am grown old, and my Memory bad, I feel very sensibly the want of it. But on the whole, tho' I never arrived at the Perfection I had been so ambitious of obtaining, but fell far short of it, yet I was by the Endeavour a better and happier Man than I otherwise should have been, if I had not attempted it; As those who aim at perfect Writing by imitating the engraved Copies, tho' they never reach the wish'd for Excellence of those Copies, their Hand is mended by the Endeavour, and is tolerable while it continues fair and legible.

And it may be well my Posterity should be informed, that to this little Artifice, with the Blessing of God, their Ancestor ow'd the constant Felicity of his Life down to his 79th Year in which this is written. What Reverses may attend the Remainder is in the Hand of Providence: But if they arrive the Reflection on past Happiness enjoy'd ought to help his bearing them with more Resignation.

To *Temperance* he ascribes his long-continu'd Health, and what is still left to him of a good Constitution. To *Industry* and *Frugality* the early Easiness of his Circumstances, and Acquisition of his Fortune, with all that Knowledge which enabled him to be an useful Citizen, and obtain'd for him some Degree of Reputation among the Learned. To *Sincerity* and *Justice* the Confidence of his Country, and the honourable Employs it conferr'd upon him. And to the joint Influence of the whole Mass of the Virtues, even in the imperfect State he was able to acquire them, all that Evenness of Temper, and that Chearfulness in Conversation which makes his Company still sought for, and agreable even to his younger Acquaintance. I hope therefore that some of my Descendants may follow the Example and reap the Benefit. . . .

My List of Virtues contain'd at first but twelve: But a Quaker Friend having kindly inform'd me that I was generally thought proud; that my Pride show'd itself frequently in Conversation; that I was not content with being in the right when discussing any Point, but was overbearing and rather insolent; of which he convinc'd me by mentioning several Instances; I determined endeavouring to cure myself if I could of this Vice or Folly among the rest, and I added *Humility* to my List, giving an extensive Meaning to the Word. I cannot boast of much Success in acquiring the *Reality* of this Virtue; but I had a good deal with regard to the *Appearance* of it. I made it a Rule to forbear all direct Contradiction to the Sentiments of others, and all positive Assertion of my own. I even forbid myself agreable to the old Laws of our Junto, the Use of every Word or Expression in the Language that imported a fix'd Opinion; such as *certainly, undoubtedly,* &c. and I adopted instead of them, *I conceive, I apprehend,* or *I imagine* a thing to be so or so, or it so appears to me at present. When another asserted something, that I thought an Error, I deny'd my self the Pleasure of contradicting him abruptly, and of showing immediately some Absurdity in his Proposition; and in answering I began by observing that in certain Cases or Circumstances his Opinion would be right, but that in the present case there *appear'd* or *seem'd* to me some Difference, &c. I soon found the Advantage of this change in my Manners. The Conversations I engag'd in went on more pleasantly. The modest way in which I propos'd my Opinions, procur'd them a readier Reception and less Contradiction; I had less Mortification when I was found to be in the wrong, and I more easily prevail'd with others to give up their Mistakes and join with me when I happen'd to be in the right. And this mode, which I at first put on, with some violence to natural Inclination, became at length so easy and so habitual to me, that perhaps for these Fifty Years past no one has ever heard a dogmatical Expression escape me. And to this Habit (after my Character of Integrity) I think it principally owing, that I had early so much Weight with my Fellow Citizens, when I proposed new Institutions, or Alterations in the old; and so much Influence in public Councils when I became a Member. For I was but a bad Speaker, never eloquent, subject to much Hesitation in my choice of Words, hardly correct in Language, and yet I generally carried my Points.

In reality there is perhaps no one of our natural Passions so hard to subdue as *Pride.* Disguise it, struggle with it, beat it down, stifle it, mortify it as much as one pleases, it is still alive, and will every now and then peep out and show itself. You will see it perhaps often in this History. For even if I could conceive that I had compleatly overcome it, I should probably by [be] proud of my Humility.

V.3

"Princeton for the Nation's Service"

Woodrow Wilson

Woodrow Wilson (1856–1924), the twenty-eighth president of the United States (1913–1921), also served as president of Princeton University. In both offices, he vigorously promoted the same high-minded idealism, well illustrated in his inaugural address at Princeton (October 1902), reprinted here in its entirety. In opposition to the then-new (and still existing) emphasis on diversification, professionalization, and specialty training, Wilson urges institutions of higher learning to reclaim their lost coherence and to emphasize instead systems of instruction that address the spirit, enlarge the scope, and prepare men to be ready citizens of the world. "We are here not merely to release the faculties of men for their own use," he explains, "but also to quicken their social understanding, instruct their consciences, and give them the catholic vision of those who know their just relations to their fellow men. Here in America, for every man touched . . . with the spirit of our institutions, social service is the high law of duty, and every American university must square its standards by that law or lack its national title." The university is not a refuge to dream in, Wilson argues, but a place "for a thoughtful poring upon the map of life; and the boundaries which should emerge to the mind's eye are not more the intellectual than the moral boundaries of thought and action." For Wilson, this requires universities not only to make liberal learning their very heart and essence, but also to inform their curriculum with the spirit and energy of positive faith.

Contrary to Aristotle and to Pierre Mac Orlan's philanthropist (see the next selection in this part), Wilson thinks that the virtue requisite for social service is acquired neither by practice nor by birth, but by teaching informed by religion. Is Wilson too idealistic? Does the fact that so many more people, men *and* women, attend university today make him seem more or less idealistic? Can liberal learning, pursued according to Wilson's plan, achieve the practical results he advocates? Can it do so regardless of how students have been reared before college? Does it necessarily require religious belief to succeed?

From *An Address Delivered on the Occasion of His Inauguration as President of Princeton University,* October 25, 1902. Printed (not published) by Gilliss Press.

Six years ago I had the honor of standing in this place to speak of the memories with which Princeton men heartened themselves as they looked back a century and a half to the founding of their college. To-day my task is more difficult, more delicate. Standing here in the light of those older days, we must now assess our present purposes and powers and sketch the creed by which we shall be willing to live in the days to come. We are but men of a single generation in the long life of an institution which will still be young when we are dead, but while we live her life is in us. What we conceive she conceives. In planning for Princeton, moreover, we are planning for the country. The service of institutions of learning is not private but public. It is plain what the nation needs as its affairs grow more and more complex and its interests begin to touch the ends of the earth. It needs efficient and enlightened men. The universities of the country must take part in supplying them.

American universities serve a free nation whose progress, whose power, whose prosperity, whose happiness, whose integrity depend upon individual initiative and the sound sense and equipment of the rank and file. Their history, moreover, has set them apart to a character and service of their own. They are not mere seminaries of scholars. They never can be. Most of them, the greatest of them and the most distinguished, were first of all great colleges before they became universities; and their task is two-fold: the production of a great body of informed and thoughtful men and the production of a small body of trained scholars and investigators. It is one of their functions to take large bodies of young men up to the places of outlook whence the world of thought and affairs is to be viewed; it is another of their functions to take some men, a little more mature, a little more studious, men self-selected by aptitude and industry, into the quiet libraries and laboratories where the close contacts of study are learned which yield the world new insight into the processes of nature, of reason, and of the human spirit. These two functions are not to be performed separately, but side by side, and are to be informed with one spirit, the spirit of enlightenment, a spirit of learning which is neither superficial nor pedantic, which values life more than it values the mere acquisitions of the mind.

Universities, we have learned to think, include within their scope, when complete, schools of law, of medicine, of theology, and of those more recondite mechanic arts, such as the use of electricity, upon which the skilled industry of the modern world is built up; and, though in dwelling upon such an association of schools as of the gist of the matter in our definitions of a university, we are relying upon historical accidents rather than upon essential principles for our conceptions, they are accidents which show the happy order and system with which things often come to pass. Though the university may dispense with professional schools, professional schools may not dispense with the university. Professional schools have nowhere their right atmosphere and association except where they are parts of a university and share its spirit and method. They must love learning as well as professional success in order to have their perfect usefulness. This is not the verdict of the universities merely but of the professional men themselves, spoken out of hard experience of the facts of business. It was but the other day that the Society for the Promotion of Engineering Education indorsed the opinion of their president, Mr. Eddy, that the crying need of the engineering profession was men whose technical knowledge and proficiency should rest upon a broad basis of general culture which should make them free of the wider worlds of learning and experience, which should give them largeness of view, judgment, and easy knowledge of men. The modern world nowhere shows a closeted profession shut in to a narrow round of technical functions to which no knowledge of the outside world need ever penetrate. Whatever our calling, our thoughts must often be afield among men of many kinds, amidst interests as various as the phases of modern life. The managing minds of the world, even the efficient working minds of the world, must be equipped for a mastery whose chief characteristic is adaptability, play, and initiative which transcends the bounds of mere technical training. Technical schools whose training is not built up on the foundations of a broad and general discipline cannot impart this. The stuff they work upon must be prepared for them by processes which produce fibre and elasticity, and their own methods must be shot through with the impulses of the university.

It is this that makes our age and our task so interesting: this complex interdependence and interrelationship of all the processes which prepare the mind for effectual service: this necessity that the merchant and the financier should have travelled minds, the engineer a knowledge of books and men, the lawyer a wide view of affairs, the physician a familiar acquaintance with the abstract data of science, and that the closeted scholar should throw his windows open to the four quarters of the world. Every considerable undertaking has come to be based on knowledge, on thoughtfulness, on the masterful handling of men and facts. The university must stand in the midst, where the roads of thought and knowledge interlace and cross, and, building upon some coign of vantage, command them all.

It has happened that throughout two long generations,—long because filled with the industrial and social transformation of the world,—the thought of studious men has been bent upon devising methods by which special aptitudes could be developed, detailed investigations carried forward, inquiry broadened and deepened to meet the scientific needs of the age, knowledge extended and made various and yet exact by the minute and particular researches of men who devoted all the energies of their minds to a single task. And so we have gained much, though we have also lost much which must be recovered. We have gained immensely in knowledge but we have lost system. We have acquired an admirable, sober passion for accuracy. Our pulses have been quickened, moreover, by discovery. The world of learning has been transformed. No study has stood still. Scholars have won their fame, not by erudition, but by exploration, the conquest of new territory, the addition of infinite detail to the map of knowledge. And so we have gained a splendid proficiency in investigation. We know the right methods of advanced study. We have made exhaustive records of the questions waiting to be answered, the doubts waiting to be resolved, in every domain of inquiry; thousands of problems once unsolved, apparently insoluble, we have reduced to their elements and settled, and their answers have been added to the commonplaces of knowledge. But, meanwhile, what of the preliminary training of specialists, what of the general foundations of knowledge, what of the general equipment of mind which all men must have who are to serve this busy, this sophisticated generation?

Probably no one is to blame for the neglect of the general into which we have been led by our eager pursuit of the particular. Every age has lain under the reproach of doing but one thing at a time, of having some one signal object for the sake of which other things were slighted or ignored. But the plain fact is, that we have so spread and diversified the scheme of knowledge in our day that it has lost coherence. We have dropped the threads of system in our teaching. And system begins at the beginning. We must find the common term for college and university; and those who have great colleges at the heart of the universities they are trying to develop are under a special compulsion to find it. Learning is not divided. Its kingdom and government are centered, unitary, single. The processes of instruction which fit a large body of young men to serve their generation with powers released and fit for great tasks ought also to serve as the initial processes by which scholars and investigators are made. They ought to be but the first parts of the method by which the crude force of untrained men is reduced to the expert uses of civilization. There may come a day when general study will be no part of the function of a university, when it shall have been handed over, as some now talk of handing it over, to the secondary schools, after the German fashion; but that day will not be ours, and I, for one, do not wish to see it come. The masters who guide the youngsters engaged in general studies are very useful neighbors for those who prosecute detailed inquiries and devote themselves to special tasks. No investigator can afford to keep his door shut against the comradeships of the wide world of effort and of thought.

To have a great body of undergraduates crowding our class-rooms and setting the pace of our lives must always be a very wholesome thing. These young fellows, who do not mean to make finished scholars of themselves, but who do mean to learn from their elders, now at the outset of their lives, what the thoughts of the world have been and its processes of progress, in order that they may start with light about them, and not doubt or darkness, learning in the brief span of four years what it would else take them half a lifetime to discover by mere contact with men, must teach us the real destiny with which knowledge came into the world. Its mission is enlightenment and edification, and these young gentlemen shall keep us in mind of this.

The age has hurried us, has shouldered us out of the old ways, has bidden us be moving and look to the cares of a practical generation; and we have suffered ourselves to be a little disconcerted. No doubt we were once pedants. It is a happy thing that the days have gone by when the texts we studied loomed bigger to our view than the human spirit which underlay them. But there are some principles of which we must not let go. We must not lose sight of that fine conception of a general training which led our fathers, in the days when men knew how to build great states, to build great colleges also to sustain them. No man who knows the world has ever supposed that a day would come when every young man would seek a college training. The college is not for the majority who carry forward the common labor of the world, nor even for those who work at the skilled handicrafts which multiply the conveniences and the luxuries of the complex modern life. It is for the minority who plan, who conceive, who superintend, who mediate between group and group, and who must see the wide stage as a whole. Democratic nations must be served in this wise no less than those whose leaders are chosen by birth and privilege; and the college is no less democratic because it is for those who play a special part. I know that there are men of genius who play these parts of captaincy and yet have never been in the classrooms of a college, whose only school has been the world itself. The world is an excellent school for those who have vision and self-discipline enough to use it. It works in this wise, in part, upon us all. Raw lads are made men of by the mere sweep of their lives through the various school of experience. It is this very sweep of life that we wish to bring to the consciousness of young men by the shorter processes of the college. We have seen the adaptation take place; we have seen crude boys made fit in four years to become men of the world.

Every man who plays a leading or conceiving part in any affair must somehow get this schooling of his spirit, this quickening and adaptation of his perceptions. He must either spread the process through his lifetime and get it by an extraordinary gift of insight and upon his own initiative, or else he must get it by the alchemy of mind practiced in college halls. We ought distinctly to set forth in our philosophy of this matter the difference between a man's preparation for the specific and definite tasks he is to perform in the world and that general enlargement of spirit and release of powers which he shall need if his task is not to crush and belittle him. When we insist that a certain general education shall precede all special training which is not merely mechanical in its scope and purpose, we mean simply that every mind needs for its highest serviceability a certain preliminary orientation, that it may get its bearings and release its perceptions for a wide and catholic view. We must deal in college with the spirits of men, not with their fortunes. Here, in history and philosophy and literature and science, are the experiences of the world summed up. These are but so many names which we give to the records of what men have done and thought and comprehended. If we be not pedants, if we be able to get at the spirit of the matter, we shall extract from them the edification and enlightenment as of those who have gone the long journey of experience with the race.

There are two ways of preparing a young man for his life work. One is to give him the skill and special knowledge which shall make a good tool, an excellent bread-winning tool, of him; and for thousands of young men that way must be followed. It is a good way. It is honorable. It is indispensable. But it is not for the college, and it never can be. The college should seek to make the men whom it receives something more than excellent servants of a trade or skilled practitioners of a profession. It should give them elasticity of faculty and breadth of vision, so that they shall have a surplus of mind to expend, not upon their profession only, for its liberalization and enlargement, but also upon the broader interests which lie about them, in the spheres in which they are to be, not breadwinners merely, but citizens as well, and in their own hearts, where they are to grow to the stature of real nobility. It is this free capital of mind the world most stands in need of,—this free capital that awaits investment in undertakings, spiritual as well as material, which advance the race and help all men to a better life.

And are we to do this great thing by the old discipline of Greek, Latin, mathematics, and English? The day has gone by when that is possible. The circle of liberal studies is too much enlarged, the area of general learning is too much extended, to make it any longer possible to make these few things stand for all. Science has opened a new world of learning, as great as the old. The influence of science has broadened and transformed old themes of study and created new, and all the boundaries of knowledge are altered. In the days of our grandfathers all learning was literary, was of the book; the phenomena of nature were brought together under the general terms of an encyclopædic Natural Philosophy. Now the quiet rooms where once a few students sat agaze before a long table at which, with a little apparatus in front of him, a lecturer discoursed of the laws of matter and of force, are replaced by great laboratories, physical, chemical, biological, in which the pupil's own direct observation and experiment take the place of the conning of mere theory and generalization, and men handle the immediate stuff of which nature is made. Museums of natural history, of geology, of paleontology, stretch themselves amidst our lecture rooms, for demonstration of what we say of the life and structure of the globe. The telescope, the spectroscope, not the text-book merely, are our means of teaching the laws and movements of the sky. An age of science has transmuted speculation into knowledge and doubled the dominion of the mind. Heavens and earth swing together in a new universe of knowledge. And so it is impossible that the old discipline should stand alone, to serve us as an education. With it alone we should get no introduction into the modern world either of thought or affairs. The mind of the modern student must be carried through a wide range of studies in which science shall have a place not less distinguished than that accorded literature, philosophy, or politics.

But we must observe proportion and remember what it is that we seek. We seek in our general education, not universal knowledge, but the opening up of the mind to a catholic appreciation of the best achievements of men and the best processes of thought since days of thought set in. We seek to apprise young men of what has been settled and made sure of, of the thinking that has been carried through and made an end of. We seek to set them securely forward at the point at which the mind of the race has definitively arrived, and save them the trouble of attempting the journey over again, so that they may know from the outset what relation their own thought and effort bear to what the world has already done. We speak of the "disciplinary" studies through which a boy is put in his school days and during the period of his introduction into the full privileges of college work, having in our thought the mathematics of arithmetic, elementary algebra, and geometry, the Greek and Latin texts and grammars, the elements of English and of French or German; but a better, truer name for them were to be desired. They are indeed disciplinary. The mind takes fibre, facility, strength, adaptability, certainty of touch from handling them, when the teacher knows his art and their power. But they are disciplinary only because of their definiteness and their established method: and they take their determinateness from their age and perfection. It is their age and completeness that render them so serviceable and so suitable for the first processes of education. By their means the boy is informed of the bodies of knowledge which are not experimental but settled, definitive, fundamental. This is the stock upon which time out of mind all the thoughtful world has traded. These have been food of the mind for long generations.

It is in this view of the matter that we get an explanation of the fact that the classical languages of antiquity afford better discipline and are a more indispensable means of culture than any language of our own day except of the language, the intimate language, of our own thought, which is for us universal coin of exchange in the intellectual world and must have its values determined to a nicety before we pay it out. No modern language is definitive, classically made up. Modern tongues, moreover, carry the modern babel of voices. The thoughts they utter fluctuate and change; the phrases they speak alter and are dissolved with every change of current in modern thought or impulse. They have had, first or last, the same saturations of thought that our own language has had; they carry the same atmosphere; in traversing their pleasant territory, we see only different phases of our own familiar world, the world of our own experience; and, valuable as it is to have this various view of the world we live in and send our minds upon their travels up and down the modern age, it is not fundamental, it is not an indispensable first process of training. It can be postponed. The classical literatures give us, in tones and with an authentic accent we can nowhere else hear, the thoughts of an age we cannot visit. They contain airs of a time not our own, unlike our own, and yet its foster parent. To these things was the modern thinking world first bred. In them speaks a time naïve, pagan, an early morning day when men looked upon the earth while it was fresh, untrodden by crowding thought, an age when the mind moved, as it were, without prepossessions and with an unsophisticated, childlike curiosity, a season apart during which those seats upon the Mediterranean seem the first seats of thoughtful men. We shall not anywhere else get a substitute for it. The modern mind has been built upon that culture and there is no authentic equivalent.

Drill in the mathematics stands in the same category with familiar knowledge of the thought and speech of classical antiquity, because in them also we get the life-long accepted discipline of the race, the processes of pure reasoning which lie at once at the basis of science and at the basis of philosophy, grounded upon observation and physical fact and yet abstract and of the very stuff of the essential processes of the mind, a bridge between reason and nature. Here, too, as in the classics, is a definitive body of knowledge and of reason, a discipline which has been made test of through long generations, a method of thought which has in all ages steadied, perfected, enlarged, strengthened, and given precision to the powers of the mind. Mathematical drill is an introduction of the boy's mind to the most definitely settled rational experiences of the world.

I shall attempt no proof that English also is of the fundamental group of studies. You will not require me to argue that no man has been made free of the world of thought who does not know the literature, the idiomatic flavor, the discriminative and masterful use of his own tongue.

But, if we cannot doubt that these great studies are fundamental, neither can we doubt that the circle of fundamental studies has widened in our day; and that education, even general education, has been extended to new boundaries. And that chiefly because science has had its credentials accepted as of the true patriciate of learning. It is as necessary that the lad should be inducted into the thinking of the modern time as it is that he should be carefully grounded in the old, accepted thought which has stood test from age to age; and the thought of the modern time is based upon science. It is only a question of choice in a vast field. Special developments of science, the parts which lie in controversy, the parts which are as yet but half built up by experiment and hypothesis, do not constitute the proper subject matter of general education. For that you need, in the field of science as in every other field, the bodies of knowledge which are most definitively determined and which are most fundamental. Undoubtedly the fundamental sciences are physics, chemistry, and biology. Physics and chemistry afford a systematic body of knowledge as abundant for instruction, as definitive almost, as mathematics itself; and biology, young as it is, has already supplied us with a scheme of physical life which lifts its study to the place of a distinctive discipline. These great bodies of knowledge claim their place at the foundation of liberal training not merely for our information, but because they afford us direct introduction into the most essential analytical and rational processes of scientific study, impart penetration, precision, candor, openness of mind, and afford the close contacts of concrete thinking. And there stand alongside of these geology and astronomy, whose part in general culture, aside from their connection with physics, mechanics, and chemistry, is to apply to the mind the stimulation which comes from being brought into the presence and in some sort into the comprehension of stupendous, systematized physical fact,—from seeing nature in the mass and system of her might and structure. These, too, are essential parts of the wide scheme which the college must plot out. And when we have added to these the manifold discipline of philosophy, the indispensable instructions of history, and the enlightenments of economic and political study, and to these the modern languages which are the tools of scholarship, we stand confused. How are we to marshal this host of studies within a common plan which shall not put the pupil out of breath?

No doubt we must make choice among them, and suffer the pupil himself to make choice. But the choice that we make must be the chief choice, the choice the pupil makes the subordinate choice. Since he cannot in the time at his disposal go the grand tour of accepted modern knowledge, we who have studied the geography of learning and who have observed several generations of men attempt the journey, must instruct him how in a brief space he may see most of the world, and he must choose only which one of several tours that we may map out he will take. Else there is no difference between young men and old, between the novice and the man of experience, in fundamental matters of choice. We must supply the synthesis and must see to it that, whatever group of studies the student selects, it shall at least represent the round whole, contain all the elements of modern knowledge, and be itself a complete circle of general subjects. Princeton can never have any uncertainty of view on that point.

And that not only because we conceive it to be our business to give a general, liberalizing, enlightening training to men who do not mean to go on to any special work by which they may make men of science or scholars of themselves or skilled practitioners of a learned profession, but also because we would create a right atmosphere for special study. Critics of education have recently given themselves great concern about over-specialization. The only specialists about whom, I think, the thoughtful critic need give himself serious anxiety are the specialists who have never had any general education in which to give their special studies wide rootage and nourishment. The true American university seems to me to get its best characteristic, its surest guarantee of sane and catholic learning, from the presence at its very heart of a college of liberal arts. Its vital union with the college gives it, it seems to me, the true university atmosphere, a pervading sense of the unity and unbroken circle of learning,— not so much because of the presence of a great body of undergraduates in search of general training (because until these youngsters get what they seek they create ideals more by their lack than by their achievement), as because of the presence of a great body of teachers whose life-work it is to find the general outlooks of knowledge and give vision of them every day from quiet rooms which, while they talk, shall seem to command all the prospects of the wide world.

I should dread to see those who guide special study and research altogether excused from undergraduate instruction, should dread to see them withdraw themselves altogether from the broad and general survey of the subjects of which they have sought to make themselves masters. I should equally despair of seeing any student made a truly serviceable specialist who had not turned to his specialty in the spirit of a broad and catholic learning,—unless, indeed, he were one of those rare spirits who once and again appear amongst us, whose peculiar, individual privilege it is to have safe vision of but a little segment of truth and yet keep his poise and reason. It is not the education that concentrates that is to be dreaded, but the education that narrows,—that is narrow from the first. I should wish to see every student made, not a man of his task, but a man of the world, whatever his world may be. If it be the world of learning, then he should be a conscious and a broad-minded citizen of it. If it be the world of letters, his thought should run free upon the whole field of it. If it be the world of affairs, he should move amidst affairs like a man of thought. What we seek in education is full liberation of the faculties, and the man who has not some surplus of thought and energy to expend outside the narrow circle of his own task and interest is a dwarfed, uneducated man. We judge the range and excellence of every man's abilities by their play outside the task by which he earns his livelihood. Does he merely work, or does he also look abroad and plan? Does he, at the least, enlarge the thing he handles? No task, rightly done, is truly private. It is part of the world's work. The subtle and yet universal connections of things are what the truly educated man, be he man of science, man of letters, or statesman, must keep always in his thought, if he would fit his work to the work of the world. His adjustment is as important as his energy.

We mean, so soon as our generous friends have arranged their private finances in such a way as to enable them to release for our use enough money for the purpose, to build a notable graduate college. I say "build" because it will be not only a body of teachers and students but also a college of residence, where men shall live together in the close and wholesome comradeships of learning. We shall build it, not apart, but as nearly as may be at the very heart, the geographical heart, of the university; and its comradeships shall be for young men and old, for the novice as well as for the graduate. It will constitute but a single term in the scheme of coördination which is our ideal. The windows of the graduate college must open straight upon the walks and quadrangles and lecture halls of the *studium generale*.

In our attempt to escape the pedantry and narrowness of the old fixed curriculum we have, no doubt, gone so far as to be in danger of losing the old ideals. Our utilitarianism has carried us so far afield that we are in a fair way to forget the real utilities of the mind. No doubt the old, purely literary training made too much of the development of mere taste, mere delicacy of perception, but our modern training makes too little. We pity the young child who, ere its physical life has come to maturity, is put to some task which will dwarf and narrow it into a mere mechanic tool. We know that it needs first its free years in the sunlight and fresh air, its irresponsible youth. And yet we do not hesitate to deny to the young mind its irresponsible years of mere development in the free air of general studies. We have too ignorantly served the spirit of the age,—have made no bold and sanguine attempt to instruct and lead it. Its call is for efficiency, but not for narrow, purblind efficiency. Surely no other age ever had tasks which made so shrewdly for the testing of the general powers of the mind. No sort of knowledge, no sort of training of the perceptions and the facility of the mind could come amiss to the modern man of affairs or the modern student. A general awakening of the faculties, and then a close and careful adaptation to some special task is the programme of mere prudence for every man who would succeed.

And there are other things besides material success with which we must supply our generation. It must be supplied with men who care more for principles than for money, for the right adjustments of life than for the gross accumulations of profit. The problems that call for sober thoughtfulness and mere devotion are as pressing as those which call for practical efficiency. We are here not merely to release the faculties of men for their own use, but also to quicken their social understanding, instruct their consciences, and give them the catholic vision of those who know their just relations to their fellow men. Here in America, for every man touched with nobility, for every man touched with the spirit of our institutions, social service is the high law of duty, and every American university must square its standards by that law or lack its national title. It is serving the nation to give men the enlightenments of a general training; it is serving the nation to equip fit men for thorough scientific investigation and for the tasks of exact scholarship, for science and scholarship carry the truth forward from generation to generation and give the certain touch of knowledge to the processes of life. But the whole service demanded is not rendered until something is added to the mere training of the undergraduate and the mere equipment of the investigator, something ideal and of the very spirit of all action. The final synthesis of learning is in philosophy. You shall most clearly judge the spirit of a university if you judge it by the philosophy it teaches; and the philosophy of conduct is what every wise man should wish to derive from his knowledge of the thoughts and the affairs of the generations that have gone before him. We are not put into this world to sit still and know; we are put into it to act.

It is true that in order to learn men must for a little while withdraw from action, must seek some quiet place of remove from the bustle of affairs, where their thoughts may run clear and tranquil, and the heats of business be for the time put off; but that cloistered refuge is no place to dream in. It is a place for the first conspectus of the mind, for a thoughtful poring upon the map of life; and the boundaries which should emerge to the mind's eye are not more the intellectual than the moral boundaries of thought and action. I do not see how any university can afford such an outlook if its teachings be not informed with the spirit of religion, and that the religion of Christ, and with the energy of a positive faith. The argument for efficiency in education can have no permanent validity if the efficiency sought be not moral as well as intellectual. The ages of strong and definite moral impulse have been the ages of achievement; and the moral impulses which have lifted highest have come from Christian peoples,— the moving history of our own nation were proof enough of that. Moral efficiency is, in the last analysis, the fundamental argument for liberal culture. A merely literary education, got out of books and old literatures, is a poor thing enough if the teacher stick at grammatical and syntactical drill; but if it be indeed an introduction into the thoughtful labors of men of all generations it may be made a prologue to the mind's emancipation; its emancipation from narrowness,—from narrowness of sympathy, of perception, of motive, of purpose, and of hope. And the deep fountains of Christian teaching are its most refreshing springs.

I have said already, let me say again, that in such a place as this we have charge, not of men's fortunes, but of their spirits. This is not the place in which to teach men their specific tasks, except their tasks be those of scholarship and investigation; it is the place in which to teach them the relations which all tasks bear to the work of the world. Some men there are who are condemned to learn only the technical skill by which they are to live; but these are not the men whose privilege it is to come to a university. University men ought to hold themselves bound to walk the upper roads of usefulness which run along the ridges and command views of the general fields of life. This is why I believe general training, with no particular occupation in view, to be the very heart and essence of university training, and the indispensable foundation of every special development of knowledge or of aptitude that is to lift a man to his profession or a scholar to his function of investigation.

I have studied the history of America; I have seen her grow great in the paths of liberty and of progress by following after great ideals. Every concrete thing that she has done has seemed to rise out of some abstract principle, some vision of the mind. Her greatest victories have been the victories of peace and of humanity. And in days quiet and troubled alike Princeton has stood for the nation's service, to produce men and patriots. Her national tradition began with John Witherspoon, the master, and James Madison, the pupil, and has not been broken until this day. I do not know what the friends of this sound and tested foundation may have in store to build upon it; but whatever they add shall be added in that spirit and with that conception of duty. There is no better way to build up learning and increase power. A new age is before us, in which, it would seem, we must lead the world. No doubt we shall set it an example unprecedented not only in the magnitude and telling perfection of our industries and arts, but also in the splendid scale and studied detail of our university establishments: the spirit of the age will lift us to every great enterprise. But the ancient spirit of sound learning will also rule us; we shall demonstrate in our lecture rooms again and again, with increasing volume of proof, the old principles that have made us free and great; reading men shall read here the chastened thoughts that have kept us young and shall make us pure; the school of learning shall be the school of memory and of ideal hope; and the men who spring from our loins shall take their lineage from the founders of the republic.

V.4

"The Philanthropist"

Pierre Mac Orlan

Can the virtue of generosity, as Aristotle and Franklin suggest (see their selections in this part), be acquired by everyone, given enough time and enough practice? Aren't there some people who are, simply by birth, more disposed than others to be generous and philanthropic? Consider the protagonist in "The Philanthropist," by French poet and novelist Pierre Mac Orlan (1882–1970; a.k.a. Pierre Dumarchais). Monsieur de Tire-Moulure has, we are told at the start of the story, "constitutional benevolence." A man of leisure, Monsieur de Tire-Moulure resettles himself in a place that allows him to give free rein to his benevolence and proceeds, quickly, to acquire a vast retinue of reliable beggars. One in particular, the "artiste" Bijou, becomes his "protégé." Every day, at exactly the same time and place, Bijou presents himself, hand held out, to Monsieur de Tire-Moulure, and the latter reaches into his pocket and gives him two sous. But in the end Monsieur de Tire-Moulure, bound by his own good nature, is sunk by his own benevolence. It seems that he could not help himself. Or could he? Could—should—Monsieur de Tire-Moulure have tried to change his own nature? Had he wanted to, how might he have tried to do so? Would Aristotle regard this philanthropist as a truly generous man? Do you? Should we regard him as the archetypal philanthropist that Mac Orlan's title suggests he is?

<hr />

Before settling down to live on his income in a house arranged according to his taste, M. de Tire-Moulure sought out in the first place a district where the inhabitants were poor enough to enable him to give a free rein to his constitutional benevolence.

On the coast of Brittany he found the Land of Promise that had filled his dreams, in the shape of a little god-forsaken town bordering on a heath about as fertile as the shell of a turtle.

The place was suitable in all respects. M. de Tire-Moulure took a comfortable house, and when his furniture had been moved into it, he began to make anxious inquiries concerning the distressful population of the neighborhood.

From *Twenty-Nine Tales from the French*, selected and translated by Alys Eyre Macklin (New York: Harcourt, Brace and Co., 1922), pp. 191–195.

He could not help feeling the pleasurable thrill of a pig when its back is scratched on learning that cadgers and mumpers of every description, of every size, sex and age, infested the vicinity, giving this lost corner of the world the seductive appearance of being peopled by the crowd that frequents places where miraculous cures are expected.

The best traditions of the race of beggars were preserved in this Breton Thebaid as perfectly as pickles are in vinegar or flies in syrup. No inhuman notice to the effect that begging was prohibited interposed to stop the development of their curious industry. The master-beggars of bygone days, those who, with mouth spluttering foam as a result of chewing ground-ivy, imitated the convulsions of epilepsy, or those who manufactured hideous tumors by fastening to their legs a raw ox-spleen distended with blood and milk—such types of past greatness seemed to live again amid the appropriate surroundings of this abominable locality. M. de Tire-Moulure rubbed his hands; then put them in his pocket, and distributed *largesse* right and left to the extent of ten centimes or four sous.

When the worthy man went to the station to catch the train to Nantes, an occasional visit there being the only form of amusement the locality afforded, his gratification oozed from every pore as he found himself escorted by all the blind, crippled, deformed, cretinous, plague-stricken, one-armed, besotted, bone-lazy wrecks whom his philanthropy attracted to his breeches-pockets as valerian attracts cats.

Among these picturesque creatures, M. de Tire-Moulure had taken a special liking to a certain unfinished piece of humanity, whose screw-like construction suggested a dirty wet cloth that had been wrung out, but who was the only one who did not invoke God and the Saints, using instead something of a Parisian patter that was very agreeable to the smiling benefactor.

If Yahn, the blind man, hymned his miseries in the Breton of Quimper, if Yorick psalmed his distresses in the dialect of Vannes, Bijou—that was the name of M. de Tire-Moulure's protégé—Bijou brought into this fraternity the personal note of his natural tone and the up-to-date audacity of his ballads.

From ten to twelve, Bijou perambulated the High Street arrayed in a deplorable sailor suit of canvas that was once blue, but now was as spotted as the patched dress of harlequin. His cap in his hand, his legs crooked like those of a basset, he howled before well-to-do houses the song for which he had a particular affection, and which always proved productive.

> With treacherous smile and words of guile
> He led astray the ga-a-mine,
> But left her dead on truckle bed,
> Devoured by fleas and fa-a-mine.

M. de Tire-Moulure never omitted to give two sous to the artiste, who after a "Thank you, gents and ladies!" renewed his vocal efforts under a sun strong enough to melt the nails in boards.

As time went on, a friendship grew between the man of leisure and the busy vocalist. Every day Bijou came and held out his hand to M. de Tire-Moulure, and the latter, feeling his pocket, gave him two sous.

This event was as certain in the life of the philanthropist as the arrival of the morning paper, announced at his door by the joyous blast of the horn of Goazec, the newspaper-man.

As a rule, Bijou exercised his talents under the balcony of the Café Mittonne on the market-place. Always in the same position, his back against a lime-tree, he awaited complacently the arrival of his patron. The meeting always took place at the same hour with astronomical exactitude. Hand held out by Bijou, hand seeking pocket by gentleman.

This daily action became such a habit in the existence of these two beings that one morning M. de Tire-Moulure, finding himself at Bijou's tree, dropped two sous into space unconscious of the fact that the actual Bijou was not present.

It is thus with many habits; they seem innocent enough when first they are formed, but in the end they may have a fatal importance. And so it happened with M. de Tire-Moulure.

It chanced that on a certain day the good man went out to take a walk on the banks of a small, but somewhat deep stream. His mind elsewhere, his eyes unobservant, the philanthropist unconsciously adopted the locomotive method of the crab, and this had the effect of precipitating him into the water, not, however, without permitting him to describe a graceful parabola.

As soon as the protector of the poor found himself in the water, and could therefore have no doubt as to the nature of his misfortune, he began to raise cries even more piercing than those of enthusiasm, doubtless with the intention of letting some charitable soul know of his misfortune.

The charitable soul appeared in the person of Bijou, who, seeing the sad plight of his patron, hastened to his assistance, hoping by saving his life to discharge the debt of all the ten-centime pieces he had received. Happy, in short, to get quit of his many obligations at so cheap a rate, he ran to the bank, stooped down and, with the old instinctive gesture held out his hand to M. de Tire-Moulure.

That gesture caused the death of the philanthropist. Before that extended hand, broad as a tennis-racquet, which appeared to be offering itself in the habitual manner, instinctively he put his hand in his pocket and placed two sous in the animated begging-bowl presented by Bijou.

It was his last effort. Exhausted, and already three-quarters full of water, M. de Tire-Moulure went down to explore the bottom of the river, leaving to other philanthropists, equipped with poles and grappling-irons, the delicate business of getting him out after a search of twenty-four hours.

V.5

Worship, Humility and Service

Kenneth E. Kirk

For those who have long recognized the importance of religious activity for spurring civic engagement, success is often attributed to the authority of the church or the energy of its clergy. But English theologian and moral philosopher Kenneth E. Kirk (1886–1954) argues that the ground for their success may well lie elsewhere, namely, in the activity of worship itself. In this selection, excerpted from his lecture on "Law and Promise," Kirk expounds the "spirit of worship," in the light of which he then discusses the relation between worship and service. Like the volume of lectures *The Vision of God,* from which this lecture is taken, Kirk's argument here specifically targets two sorts of critics: first, those who claim that the life devoted to God is essentially selfish, and second, those who maintain that such a life, as compared with the life of service, "has all the appearance of a barren, limited and anti-social aspiration," even if it can be shown to be unselfish. Though he readily admits that worship as such is not altogether exempt from the dangers of pride and despair, Kirk argues that service absent the spirit of humility is far more prone to such vices. In order to acquire the requisite spirit of humility to serve well, he concludes, one must first cultivate the spirit of worship. How important is humility for service? Are worship, humility, and service as mutually dependent as Kirk argues? (For further reflection on the ground of the close relation between worship and serving, see the selection by William F. May in Part I.)

Is the quest for the Vision of God a Selfish Ideal?

It would be foolish to deny that the desire to see God in pre-Christian religious thought appealed often enough to motives rightly deserving the adjectives 'selfish' or 'interested.' In the main it seems to have been animated by a passion for a personal experience—for the attaining of a particular state of consciousness, or indeed, in some cases, of unconsciousness. The special characteristics of this

From "The Vision of God: The Christian Doctrine of the Summum Bonum," *The Bampton Lectures for 1928,* by Kenneth E. Kirk, pp. 180–186. Used by permission of James Clarke and Co., Ltd. The Lutterworth Press.

state, as conceived or experienced by different persons or groups, do not affect the question of principle—whether God was 'seen' in ecstasy, or in dreams, or in a calm untroubled communion with nature, matters nothing. At heart, in all these aspirations, the believer was in pursuit of something *for himself*—regardless, it may almost be said, of the interests of any other, whether God or his neighbour.

Large parts of Christendom, again, in every generation have adopted this same ideal, and can without hesitation be accused of selfishness for that reason. But here the accusation holds at best only within certain limits. The Christian seeker after God was rarely content with solitary enjoyment of the vision. To S. Paul and S. John it could have no other context than that of the Church—now militant, but in eternity triumphant. Clement's gnostic—a person at first sight wholly self-contained—longs for a city like Plato's 'set up as a pattern in heaven'—an 'ordered multitude' of the blessed; to Augustine the vision of God in the city of God was an ideal from which the one member could no more be subtracted than the other.

Christian poetry tells the same tale. No account of the vision of God and its influence upon the history of Christian ideals could be complete without some allusion to the 'Divina Commedia.' But the reference is specially appropriate at this point. In the final cantos of the 'Purgatorio' the animated crowds which hitherto have marked the poet's journey have gradually been withdrawn, and on the threshold of the 'Paradiso' he stands alone with Beatrice in the terrestrial Paradise. As they rise towards the empyrean, heaven grows radiant around them with the spirits of the blest—the 'myriad splendors, living and victorious'; the 'jewels dear and fair' of the celestial court. The final vision portrays the great Rose of God and His innumerable saints, word-painted as no other poet has ever found it possible to depict them:—

> 'Thus in the form of a white rose revealed itself to me that saintly host, which Christ espoused in His own blood. Therewith that other host—the angels—which as it soars, contemplates and chants the glory of Him Who fills it with love, and the goodness which made it so great—like as a swarm of bees, which one while settles within the flowers and anon returns to the hive where its work is stored in sweetness—now lighted down upon the great flower with its coronal of many petals; now again soared aloft to the place where its love doth for ever dwell. And all their faces were of living flame, and of gold their wings; and for the rest they were all white beyond the whiteness of snow.... This realm of security and joy, peopled by folk alike of old time and of new, centred its looks and its love upon one mark alone. O threefold light, whose bright radiance, shed in a single beam upon their eyes, doth so content them, look hither down upon our storm-tossed lives.'

The vision then is to be a corporate one; and this makes the quest for it, in any case, something less than wholly selfish. But this is only half the truth. The greatest saints have always recognized that to make enjoyment, even though it be a communal enjoyment, the goal of life, is to import a motive less than the purest into ethics. The emphatic protests against 'panhedonism' in any one of its different forms, which we have noticed at different stages, are evidence that Christianity was alive to the danger; and that however much lesser minds succumbed to it, the greatest figures in the history of the Church knew that it represented something in essence at once immoral and un-Christian.

The doctrine that the 'end of man is the vision of God,' as a practical maxim for life, implies that the Christian should set himself first of all to focus his thought upon God in the spirit of worship. It implies this of necessity, and of necessity it implies nothing more—nothing whatever as to the achieving of pleasures, rapture, exaltation in the act of worship. The only achievement man has the right to hope for is that of greater Christian saintliness—greater zeal for service—coming from this direction of the heart and mind to God. It can hardly be denied that in so far as unselfishness is possible in this life at all (to anticipate for a moment another question), this is an unselfish ideal. To look towards God, and from that 'look' to acquire insight both into the follies of one's own heart and the needs of one's neighbours, with power to correct the one no less than to serve the other—this is something very remote from any quest for 'religious experience' for its own sake. Yet this, and nothing else, is what the vision of God has meant in the fully developed thought of historic Christianity.

Is 'Worship' a Higher Ideal than 'Service'?

The second question prompted by this review of Christian thought has many aspects. Granted that 'worship' is unselfish, it may be said, surely 'service' may be unselfish too? And further, a comparison of worship and service, viewed in relation to the world's deepest needs, both spiritual and temporal, suggests that service—the unremitting service of God and man—is the more urgently needed of the two. The most, then, that can be allowed to worship is that it is a means, and only a means, to better service. It has no independent value. The true Christian must set before himself as the goal of his efforts the realization of the kingdom of God or the brotherhood of man; must form his thought and centre his activity upon these ideals. Prayer and meditation, if they are to have a place in life at all, must make no such claim as will seriously detract from the time available for action. Every hour they monopolize must show fruit in enhanced efficiency if it is to be accounted anything but wasted. This is the plea of the champion of 'service.' Virile, philanthropic, restless in his zeal to do good, he is jealous of every moment given to prayer; he tolerates it simply as a tonic or stimulant to fit him for new ventures of heroic activity. That in its own nature worship is a service no less heroic than any other, is a sentiment from which his whole being recoils.

If this conclusion of the apostles of energy is accepted, the whole development of Christian thought about the vision of God must be adjudged a wasteful, if not a tragic, mistake. Selfish the ideal of seeing God may not be; erroneous it is. It mistakes the means for the end, and in so doing veils the true end from men's eyes. It diverts them from the king's highway of loving energy into a maze of contemplative prayer wholly remote from God's purposes. Unless I am wholly at fault, that is how robust common sense, even among Christians, has always regarded, and to-day more than ever regards, those who insist that worship or contemplation has the primary place in the ideal life. Its test is wholly pragmatic. If it uplifts, then, but only then, is worship commendable; if it strengthens and purifies, so far, but only so far, has it a place. But it has no value for its own sake, or apart from these possible influences which it may exert. And in any case, a little of it goes a long way; it must never be allowed to oust positive benevolence from its position as the Christian's first, final, and only genuine duty.

This is a serious criticism: but even so the Christian tradition of the vision of God seems to have a message for the restless energizers of the modern world, with their problems, programmes, and calls to discipleship. The concept of service embraces two very different ideas. Only one of these is Christian—indeed, only one of them realizes the ideal of service at all; for service of the other kind is self-destructive and nugatory. For the purposes of the present discussion, they may be called the *service of humility,* and the *service of patronage.* It should not be difficult to see that only the former of these two has real worth. Once this is recognized, it becomes not unreasonable to suggest that worship alone guarantees to service that quality of humility without which it is no service at all; and therefore that worship may claim and must be allowed a substantive position in the Christian ideal once more. So far from being a selfish goal, worship is the only way to unselfishness which the Christian has at his command.

To serve humanity in the spirit of patronage—as a genius condescending to stupidity, as an expert coming to the help of the inefficient, as a millionaire lavishing gifts upon the destitute—is there anything in the world which breeds more dissension, discontent, just resentment and open revolt than this? The question has only to be asked to be answered; every generation has writhed under the well-meant patronage of Ladies Bountiful. Yet apart from an atmosphere of worship, every act of service avails only to inflate the agent's sense of patronage. He is the doctor, humanity is his patient: he is the Samaritan, his neighbour the crippled wayfarer: he is the instructor, others are merely his pupils. Gratitude (if they show gratitude) only confirms his conviction of his own importance; resentment (if they resent his services) only ministers to the glow of self-esteem with which he comforts himself in secret. The phenomenon has been the commonplace of satirists since the world began. Not only so—we recognize in it as well a principal cause of the divisions of Christendom, of the stultifying of effort, of the disillusionment of enthusiasts. The experts quarrel over rival panaceas; the hierophants jostle each other at the altar; and the more there is of such 'service,' the less the cause of humanity is in truth served at all.

A man must be blind not to recognize something of himself in this picture; he must be no less callous if he fails to long for the spirit of humility. But humility cannot be acquired by taking thought for oneself; that way, as S. Paul's condemnation of the law has once for all made clear, lie only the alternatives of pride and despair. The way of worship is the only way left open. Even worship is not altogether exempt from the dangers of pride and despair. But in so far as contemplation, or worship, is to be distinguished from service—and the distinction is one which the world has agreed to make—it is surely true to say that contemplation ministers to humility just as service ministers to patronage. The man who 'serves'—who plans, and organizes, and issues instructions, advice or exhortations—is doing so from the vantage ground of independence. He thinks of himself as a free agent, dowered with talents to be employed for the benefit of others. In worship, on the contrary, the worshipper puts himself in an attitude of dependence. In looking towards God, who is All in All, he sees himself to be nothing; in worshipping his Redeemer, he knows himself incapable of redeeming even the least of God's creatures. The most he can hope for is that God will deign to use him for the forwarding of His high designs. Worship tells us much good of God, but little good of ourselves, except that we are the work of God's hands. For that we may praise Him, but it leaves us nothing upon which to pride ourselves.

Thus the danger of 'service,' as an ideal, is that it fosters the spirit of patronage: the glory of worship is to elicit the grace of humility. Without humility there can be no service worth the name; patronizing service is self-destructive—it may be the greatest of all disservices. Hence to serve his fellows *at all*—to avoid doing them harm greater even than the good he proposed to confer on them—a man must find a place for worship in his life. The truth is not that worship (as the advocate of action allowed us to assert) will help him to serve *better*. The alternative lies not between service of a better and a worse kind; it lies between service and no service at all. If we would attempt to do good with any sure hope that it will prove good and not evil, we must act in the spirit of humility; and worship alone can make us humble. There is no other course.

This is no more than to carry to its conclusion what we have noticed already on more than one occasion, that a system of thought which is primarily moralistic, in so far as it sets before men a rule of conduct by which it is their first duty to measure themselves, is in essence egocentric. It is only one of the many forms which selfishness can take, even though its rule appear superficially altruistic. The ultimate purpose which its devotee has in view is not the well-being of others, but the vindication of his own personal worth. This gives us material for a conclusion. 'Your ideal of service,'—so we may imagine traditional Christianity answering robust common sense—'necessarily leads up to the ideal of worship as its consummation. Without the latter you cannot achieve the former; and, if worship languishes, service will once more degenerate into mere self-assertion. The two are, at least, co-ordinate parts of the same ideal whole.'

Disinterested service, then, is the only service that is serviceable; and disinterestedness comes by the life of worship alone. . . .

V.6

"The Bishop's Beggar"

Stephen Vincent Benet

As many of us can no doubt testify, we sometimes learn the most important things in unlikely ways, at unlikely times, and from unlikely people.
But what makes those lessons take? In "The Bishop's Beggar," American
poet and writer Stephen Vincent Benet (1898–1943) depicts the transformation of the attitudes and ambitions of the bishop of Remo, pre-
cipitated by accident and brought about with the help of a beggar. The
bishop's skillful coachman could not help running over the "tall, gangling boy" who darted across the path right under the nose of his horses.
Yet the incident forever changed not only the life of Luigi, who lost the
use of his legs, but also the life of the bishop. Despite the bishop's multiple efforts to care for the youth and to find him a suitable trade, Luigi
deliberately chooses to follow the "trade" of his father before him, becoming a beggar—the bishop's beggar. Every bit as proud as the bishop,
Luigi is nobody's fool and will not be duped. From the start of their acquaintance, he correctly sees, despite his anger and self-pity, what lurks
in the bishop's heart. By voluntarily degrading himself, he hopes also to
disgrace the bishop, to tempt him to act out his thinly veiled evil inclina-
tions, to lose his soul.

But Luigi's plot does not work. Instead, the bishop of Remo, the once
proud young nobleman who took the cloth merely to satisfy his ambition for power and honor, finds his true vocation: he becomes a "beggars'
bishop." Even Luigi acknowledges the change, and in the end he asks the
bishop in earnest for the blessing he previously asked for in mockery.
What is responsible for the transformation of the bishop? How—why—
does his change come about? What is responsible for the change in Luigi?
Is the "education" of the bishop or that of Luigi generalizable? Can reading and pondering "The Bishop's Beggar" do for us what the beggar and
the bishop do for each other? Might it have more or less a chance of succeeding if we are already part of a religious community?

It seems that in the old days there was a bishop of Remo, and he was a heedless
and proud young man, though of good intentions. Now, that was possible in

those days, when the fire and light of the new learning had spread through Italy, and men drank, as if intoxicated, at a new spring. There were bishops who cared less for the Word of God than for their own splendor, and cardinals who were rather men of the world—and of no good world—than sons of the Church. I do not say that our bishop was as idle and self-seeking as some of these; I do say that he was a child of his time. He would have liked to be a lord, but his eldest brother was the lord; he would have liked to be a soldier, but his second brother was the soldier. So he went into the Church, for there, too, a man who bore a great name could rise. He was clever, he was ambitious, he had great connections. Now and then, to be sure, he asked a disquieting question, but the Baldis had always been original. The path that is rugged for many was made smooth for him from the first. When he was made bishop of Remo at an early age, the fact did not surprise him. Since he was to be neither lord nor soldier, he found that pleasant enough.

All went well for him, at first. They were glad to have a young and handsome bishop at Remo, for the bishop before him had been old and ill-favored. It was a pleasure to no one to kiss his ring, and he frightened the children with his peering eyes. With the coming of our bishop all this was changed. There was a great to-do and refurbishing of the bishop's palace; the smells of good cooking drifted again from the bishop's kitchens; when the bishop drove through the city, men threw their caps in the air. There were fine new frescoes in the cathedral, a new way of chanting in the choir. As for sin and suffering—well, they are always with us. The people of Remo liked to sin pleasantly and be reminded of it as little as possible.

Nevertheless, at times, a grayness would come over our bishop's spirit. He could not understand why it came. His life was both full and busy. He was a friend to art, a host to the gay and the learned, a ruler of men. He did not meddle in things which did not concern him; he felt in his heart that there was no prize in the Church which might not be within his grasp. And yet, at times, there was a grayness within him. It was singular.

He could not show that grayness before the world, he could not show it to his secretary or the witty company that gathered at his table. He could wrestle with it in prayer, and so he did. But he found it no easy task. Had the Devil appeared before him with horns and a tail, he would have known what to do. But a grayness of spirit—a cool little voice in the mind which said to him now and then, "What do you in these robes, at this place, Gianfrancesco Baldi?"—that was another matter.

He came to find by experience that motion in the open air helped him as much as anything. When the grayness oppressed him too severely, he would summon his coach and drive about the countryside. So one day, as he drove through a small country village in the hills beyond Remo, it happened. It was nobody's fault; the bishop's least of all. He saw to it that he had a skillful coachman and good horses as he saw to all such matters. But when a tall, gangling boy darts across the street right under the nose of the horses, the most skillful coachman cannot always save him. There was a cry and a scream and a soft jar. Then, where the coach had passed, the boy lay writhing in the street.

The bishop always showed at his best in emergency. When he got out of the coach, the angry shouts of the crowd died away to a respectful murmur. He lifted the boy into the coach with his strong arms and drove back with him to Remo. On the way he talked to him soothingly, though the boy was in too much pain to pay much attention to this graciousness. When they got to Remo, he had the boy carried to a servant's room in the palace and doctors summoned for him. Later on he gave instructions about cleaning the coach.

At dinner his secretary recounted the little incident, and all men praised the kindliness of the bishop. The bishop passed it off pleasantly, but, at heart, he felt a trifle irritated. He had not felt particularly drawn toward the boy; on the other hand, he could not have left him lying in the road.

By the next day, as such things do, the story had gone all over Remo, and there were unusual demonstrations of good will as the bishop passed to the cathedral. The bishop received them with dignity, but his irritation remained. He disliked ostentatious shows of virtue and distrusted the fickleness of crowds. Nevertheless, it was his duty to see the boy, and he did so.

Washed, combed, and rid of his vermin, the boy looked ordinary enough, though somewhat older than the bishop had thought him. His body was slight and emaciated, but he had a well-shaped head and large liquid eyes. These stared at the bishop with some intensity; indeed, with such intensity that the bishop wondered, at first, if the boy might not be an idiot. But a little conversation proved him sound of mind, though rustic in speech.

His name was Luigi and he was an orphan, living as best he could. In the summer he tended goats; in the winter he lived with his uncle and aunt, the tavern-keepers, who fed him and beat him. His age was about nineteen. He had made his Easter duty as a Christian. He would never walk again.

Such were the facts of the case, and the bishop thought them over clearheadedly. He wondered what to do with the boy.

"Luigi," he said "would you like to go back to your village?"

"Oh, no," said the boy. "It is a very good village, but now that I can no longer herd goats, there is no place in it for me. Besides, one eats better in Remo—I have had white cheese twice already." And he smacked his lips. His voice was remarkably strong and cheerful, the bishop noticed with surprise.

"Very well," said the bishop patiently. "You need not go back if you do not choose. You are now, in some sense, a ward of the Church, and the wings of the Church are sheltering." He looked at the boy's legs, lying limp and motionless under the covers, and felt, though against his will, the natural distaste of the hale man for the maimed. "You might learn some useful trade," he said thoughtfully. "There are many trades where the hands do all—a cobbler's, a tailor's, a basket-weaver's."

The boy shook his head joyfully. "Oh, no, your lordship," he said. "Trades take so long to learn and I am very stupid. It would not be worth the expense; your lordship would be embarrassed."

"My lordship, perhaps, is the best judge of that," said the bishop a trifle grimly. He kept thinking of the boy's remark about white cheese; it must be a spare life indeed where white cheese was such a treat. "But we are reasonable," he said. "Come, what would you be?"

"A beggar!" said the boy, and his dark eyes shone with delight.

"A beggar?" said the bishop, astonished and somewhat revolted.

"Why, yes," said the boy, as if it were the most natural thing in the world. "For ten years my father begged on the cathedral steps. That was before your lordship's time, but he was an excellent beggar and a master of his craft. True, he was subject to continual persecutions and jealousies from the honorable corporation of the beggars of Remo, coming, as he did, from outside the city. It was that which caused the ruin of our fortunes, for, in the end, when he had begun to fail, they threw him down a well, where he caught a bad cold and died of it. But in his good days he could outbeg any two of them. If your lordship would care to have me demonstrate his celebrated fainting fit, when his eyeballs rolled backward in his head—"

"I can think of nothing I should like less," said the bishop, shocked and disgusted, for it seemed to him an unworthy thing that a sturdy young man, though a cripple, should think of nothing better than beggary. "Besides," he said, "these other beggars you speak of—if they persecuted your father, no doubt they would persecute you."

"Me?" said the boy, and laughed. "Oh, once they understood, they would not dare touch me—not even Giuseppe, the Hook. I would be your lordship's beggar—the bishop's beggar!" And a light as of great peace and contentment spread over his countenance.

The bishop stared at him for a long time in silence. "That is what you wish?" he said, and his voice was dry.

"That is what I wish, your lordship," said the boy, nodding his head.

"So be it," said the bishop with a sigh, and left him. But when his coachman came to him the next morning for orders, it was all he could do to keep from reviling the man.

The bishop was not the sort of man who liked beggars. Indeed, were it not for custom and Christian charity, he would long since have cleared them from the steps of his cathedral. He could not very well do that; he knew what an impression such a move would make. Nevertheless, when he passed among them, as he must at times, he saw to it that his almoner made a suitable distribution of small coins, but he himself did his best to see and smell them as little as possible. Their whines and their supplications, their simulated sores, and their noisome rags—these were a fret and a burden to him.

Now, it seemed, he was to have a beggar of his own. He would have taken it as a suitable humiliation for pride, but he did not feel himself to be a proud man. Nor could he think of the accident as anything but an accident. Had he deliberately trodden the lad beneath the hoofs of his horses—but he had not. He was well liked, able, decisive, a rising son of the Church. Nevertheless, he was to have a beggar—every day he must see his beggar on the steps of the cathedral, living reproach, a living lesson in idleness and heedlessness. It was a small thing, to be sure, but it darkened his dinner and made him sore at heart.

Therefore, being the man he was, he put a mask upon his face. He meant to speak of the thing, so it should be known—at least *that* might ward off ridicule. He spoke of it to his secretary; the secretary agreed that it was a very seemly and Christian idea of his lordship's, while the bishop wondered if the man laughed at him in his sleeve. He spoke of it to others; there were compliments, of course. Each time he spoke of it, it turned a small knife in his breast. But that did not keep him from speaking of it, nor from seeing that every care was given Luigi.

Nevertheless, he dreaded the day when Luigi would take up his post on the steps of the cathedral. He dreaded and yearned for it, both. For then, at last, the thing would be done. After that, like many things, it would become a custom, and in time Luigi himself would fade into the mass of whining beggary that haunted the steps of the cathedral. But things were not to be quite that way.

He admired, while he detested, the thoroughness with which Luigi prepared himself for his profession. He heard the whine ring out from the servants' quarters—"Ten scudi for Luigi!"—he saw the little cart and the crutches Luigi had made for himself. Now and then he heard his own servants laugh at the beggar's stories. This was hard enough to bear. But at last the day of parting came.

To his disgust, the bishop found the boy neither clean nor well-clad, as he had been since his accident, but dirty and dressed in tatters. He opened his mouth to reprove the boy, then he shut it again, for it seemed pitifully true that a beggar must dress his part. Nevertheless, the bishop did not like it. He asked Luigi, coolly, how he meant to live.

"Oh, your lordship's secretary has found me a very suitable chamber," said Luigi eagerly. "It is on the ground floor of a rookery by the river and it has room for crutches, my gear, and my cart. He will move me there tonight. Tomorrow I will be at my post on the steps of the cathedral." And he smiled gratefully at the bishop. "That will be a great day," he said.

"So," said the bishop, who could not trust himself to say anything further.

"Yet before I go," said Luigi, "I must thank your lordship for his kindness, and ask your lordship's blessing on my work. That is only suitable."

The bishop stiffened. "I may bless you, Luigi," he said, "but your work I cannot bless. I cannot give the blessing of the Church to the work of a man who lives by beggary when he might live otherwise."

"Well, then, I must go unblessed," said Luigi cheerfully. "After all, your lordship has already done so much for me! The bishop's beggar! How my uncle and aunt will stare!"

Now, of all the vainglorious, self-seeking, worthless, rascally sons of iniquity— and to think that I stand your sponsor, said the bishop, but, fortunately, he did not say it aloud. Silently he extended his ring and Luigi kissed it with such innocent reverence that the bishop was sorely moved to give him his blessing after all. But he summoned up his principles and departed in silence.

The bishop slept ill that night, tormented by dreams of Luigi. He dreamed that, for his sins, he must carry Luigi on his back all the way up the steps of the cathedral. And as he mounted each step, the weight upon his back became more crushing, till at last he woke, unrefreshed.

The next day he went to the cathedral in great state, though it was an ordinary Sunday. Yet he felt the state to be, in some measure, a protection. When he passed by the steps of the cathedral, the beggars set up their usual supplications. He sent his almoner among them; it was over quicker than he thought. He did not look for Luigi and yet he felt Luigi's eyes upon him as he stood there for a moment, splendid in robe and miter. Then the thing was finished.

In the cathedral that same day, he preached passionately against the sins of idleness and heedlessness. Seldom had he been so moving—he could feel that from his congregation. When Mass was over he retired to his palace, exhausted. Yet it was pleasant for him to walk about the palace and know that Luigi was not there.

It was just after vespers when his secretary came to him and told him that a man called Giuseppe, self-styled provost of the company of the beggars of Remo, requested an audience. The bishop sighed wearily and ordered the man brought before him. He was a squat fellow of great strength and an evil cast of countenance, for one side of his face had been so burned in a fire that it was as if he had two faces, one of them inhuman. Also, his left arm terminated in an iron hook.

"This is Giuseppe, the beggar, your lordship," said the secretary with repugnance.

"Giuseppe, called Double-Face, also called the Hook, provost of the honorable company of the beggars of Remo," said Giuseppe in a rusty voice, and plumped on his knees.

The bishop raised him and asked his business.

"Well, your lordship, it's this new fellow, Luigi Lamelegs," said Giuseppe. "I've got nothing against him personal—I wouldn't hurt a fly myself in a personal way"—and he grinned horribly—"but there he is in a good place on the steps, and your lordship's servants put him there. Well, now, if he's your lordship's beggar, that's one thing—though, even so, there's fees and vails to be paid, for that's the custom. But if he isn't your lordship's beggar—and your lordship paid him no attention this morning—"

"Stop!" said the bishop with anger. "Do you mean to tell me that the very steps of the cathedral are bartered and sold among you? Why, this is simony— this is the sin of simony!"

"Your lordship can call it hard words," said Giuseppe stolidly, "but that's been the way it's been done ever since there were beggars in Remo. I paid twenty crowns for my own place, and fought old Marco too. But that's beside the point. Your lordship has a right to a beggar if your lordship wants one—we're all agreed on that. But the question is: Is this man your lordship's beggar or isn't he?"

"And supposing I said he was not my beggar?" said the bishop, trembling.

"Well, that's all we'd want to know," said Giuseppe. "And thank your lordship kindly. I had my own suspicions of the man from the first. But we've got him down by the river now—Carlo and Benito and old blind Marta; she's a tough one, old blind Marta—and once we're through with him, he'll trouble your lordship no more." And sketching a clumsy salute, the man turned to go.

"Stop!" said the bishop again. "Would you have the guilt of murder upon your conscience?"

"Oh, your lordship takes it too hard," said Giuseppe, shuffling his feet. "What's one beggar more or less? We're not rich folk or learned folk to bother a mind like your lordship's. We breed and we die, and there's an end. And even at the best, it's no bed of roses on the steps of the cathedral."

The bishop wished to say many things, but he could think of only one.

"I declare to you that this man is my beggar," he said. "I stretch my hand over him."

"Well, that's very nicely spoken of your lordship," said Giuseppe in a grumbling voice, "and I dare say we can make room for him. But if the man's to keep a whole skin, your lordship had best come with me—old Marta was talking of ear-slitting when I left her."

So they found Luigi, bound but cheerful, in his first-floor chamber by the river, guarded by the persons Giuseppe had described—a hunchback, a dwarf, and a blind woman. The window which gave upon the river was open, and a large sack, weighted with stones, lay in one corner of the room. The bishop's arrival produced a certain consternation on the part of all but Luigi, who seemed to take it as a matter of course. After the boy had been unbound, the bishop addressed the beggars with some vivacity, declared that Luigi was his beggar, and gave him a piece of silver before them all, in token. This seemed to satisfy the company, who then crept away in silence.

"And yet have I done right? Have I done right?" said the bishop, striding up and down the chamber. "I greatly fear I have condoned the sin of simony! I have spent Mother Church's substance among the unworthy! And yet, even so, your blood may be upon my head," and he looked at Luigi doubtfully.

"Oh, your lordship need not take it so hard," said Luigi, rubbing his arms. "All is safe enough now. I arranged about the dues and vails with Giuseppe while your lordship was discussing her state of grace with Marta. He's an honest fellow enough, and his point is reasonable. One should not take a good place without money to keep it up. Had your lordship given me alms with your own hand this morning, our little difficulty would never have arisen. That was my fault—I assumed that your lordship knew."

"Knew?" said the bishop. "What should I know of such things? And yet, God forgive me, I am a priest and I should have knowledge of evil."

"It is merely a difference in knowledge," said Luigi gently. "Now, your lordship, doubtless, has never been in a room quite like this before."

The bishop stared at the damp walls and the mean chamber. He smelled the smell that cannot be aired from a room, the smell of poverty itself. He had never doubted his own experience before—when he had been first made a priest, he had gone on certain works of charity. Now it seemed to him that those works must have been rather carefully selected.

"No," he said, "I have never been in a room just like this one."

"And yet there are many of us who live in such rooms—and not all beggars," said Luigi. He changed his tone. "That was a fine rousing sermon your lordship gave us on idleness and heedlessness this morning," he said. "Hey, it brought the scudi forth from the good folks' pockets! An admirable sermon!"

"I am grateful for your encomiums," said the bishop bitterly. He glanced around the room again. "Is there nought else I can do?" he asked unwillingly.

"No, thank your lordship," said Luigi, and his eyes were smiling. "I have a woman to cook my dinner—it is true she is a thief, but she will not steal from a cripple—and soon, with your lordship's patronage, I shall be able to afford a charcoal brazier. Moreover, my friends seem to have left me a sack. So, after dinner I shall say my prayers and go to bed to refresh myself for tomorrow's labor."

I shall say mine, too, for I need them, said the bishop, though he did not say it to Luigi.

So that was how it began. Soon enough, the bishop's beggar was a familiar figure on the steps of the cathedral—one of the admitted curiosities of the town. He was well-liked in his trade, for he always had a merry word or a sharp one for his clients—and it passed around until "Luigi says" became a byword. The bishop became used to him as one becomes used to a touch of rheumatism. Other men had their difficulties; he had his beggar. Now and then it seemed odd to the bishop that he had ever thought of the beggars on the steps as a vague and indistinguishable heap of misery and rags. He knew them all by now—blind Marta and Carlo, the dwarf, Giuseppe Double-Face, and Benito, the hunchback. He knew their ways and their thoughts. He knew the hovels where they lived and the bread they ate. For every week or so he would slip from his palace to visit Luigi's chamber.

It was necessary for him to do so, for to him Luigi represented the gravest problem of the soul that he had yet encountered. Was the man even a Christian? The bishop was not sure. He professed religion, he followed the rites of the Church. Yet sometimes when he confessed him, the bishop was appalled. Every sin that could ravage the human heart was there—if not in act, then in desire—and all told so gaily! Sometimes the bishop, angrily, would tax him with willful exaggeration, and Luigi, with a smile, would admit the charge and ask for still another penance. This left the bishop confused.

Yet through the years there grew up between the two men a singular bond. The bishop may have been heedless, he was not stupid. Very soon he began to realize that there was another Remo than the city he had come to first—a city not of lords and scholars and tradesmen and pious ladies, but a city of the poor and the ignorant, the maimed and the oppressed. For, as Luigi said, when one lay all day on the steps of the cathedral one heard stories, and anyone will talk to a beggar. Some of the stories struck the bishop to the heart. He could hardly believe them at first, yet, when he investigated them, they were true. When he was convinced they were true, he set himself stubbornly to remedy them. He was not always successful—pleasant sinners like the Church to keep its own place. Now and then he discussed his efforts with Luigi, who listened, it seemed to the bishop, with an air of perfect cynicism. His attitude seemed to be that it was all very well for a man like the bishop to concern himself about these things and, if other folk starved and died, it was none of his concern. This irritated the bishop inordinately and made him more determined than ever.

Gradually, he noticed, the composition of his table changed. There were fewer courtiers and scholars; there were more priests from the country, smelling of poverty and chestnut bread. They came in their tattered cassocks, with their big red wrists; at first they were strange and ill at ease at his table. But the bishop was able to talk to them. After all, were they not like the old parish priest that Luigi talked of so often? When the ceremony of his table disturbed them he saw to it that there was less ceremony. Luigi mocked him for this and told him bluntly what his richer clients were saying. The bishop rebuked him for impertinence to his spiritual director and persisted.

It is strange how time flies when the heart is occupied. In no time at all, it seemed to the bishop, he was a middle-aged man with gray at his temples, and Luigi a man in his thirties. That seemed odd to the bishop; he did not know where the time had gone. He thought of it, one morning, with a sense of loss. He had meant to do many things—he was still ambitious. Now, when night came, he was often too tired to think. The troubles of many people weighed upon his heart—the troubles of the peasants in the hills, who lived from hand to mouth;

the troubles of Domenico, the shoemaker, who had too pretty a daughter; the troubles of Tessa, the flower-seller, whose son was a thief. When he had first come to Remo, he had not had all these troubles. He picked up a letter on his desk—a letter that had lain there for days—and, having read it, sat staring.

The dreams of his youth came back to him, doubly hot, doubly dear. While he idled his life away in Remo, his brother and his friends had been busy. They had not forgotten him, after all. Cardinal Malaverni, the great, sage statesman whose hand was ever upon the strings of policy, meant to pass by Remo on his way to Rome. The bishop knew the cardinal—once, long ago, he had been one of the cardinal's promising young men. There was a letter also from the bishop's brother, the lord—a letter that hinted of grave and important matters. The bishop almost sobbed when he thought how long both letters had lain unanswered. He summoned his secretary and set himself about an unaccustomed bustle of preparation.

It often occurred to him, sorrowfully, within the next few days, how foolish it was to leave one's letters unopened. The preparations went forward for the cardinal's visit, yet it seemed to him that they went forward ill, though he could not put his finger upon the cause. Somehow he had got out of the way of the world where such things go forward smoothly; he was more used to his country priests than to entertaining distinguished visitors. Nevertheless, he botched together a few Latin verses, saw to it that the hangings in the guestchambers were cleaned and mended, drove his choirmaster nearly frantic, and got in the way of his servants. He noticed that these were no longer afraid of him, but treated him with tolerant patience, more like a friend than a master, and this irked him oddly. What irked him even more, perhaps, was Luigi's shameless and undisguised self-interest in the whole affair.

"Ah, your lordship, we've waited a long time for this," he said, "but it's come at last. And everyone knows that a great man like Cardinal Malaverni doesn't come to a place like Remo for nothing. So all we have to do is to play our cards well, and then, when we move on, as we doubtless shall—well, I, for one, won't be sorry."

"Move on?" said the bishop, astonished.

The beggar yawned.

"But how else?" he said. "I have been the bishop's beggar. When your lordship is made a cardinal I will be the cardinal's beggar. The post will entail new responsibilities, no doubt, but I have confidence in my abilities. Perhaps I shall even employ an assistant for my actual begging—after all, it is often drafty on the steps of the cathedral."

The bishop turned and left him without a word. Yet what Luigi had said caused trouble and disquiet in his heart, for he knew that Luigi often had news of things to come before even the Count of Remo had an inkling of them.

At last the great day of the cardinal's visit came.

Like all such days, it passed as a dream passes, with heat and ceremony and worry about small things. The Latin verses of welcome were unexpectedly well read; on the other hand, the choristers were nervous and did not sing their best. Two gentlemen of the cardinal's suite had to be lodged over the stables, much to the bishop's distress, and the crayfish for dinner had been served without sauce.

The bishop hoped that all had gone well, but he did not know. As he sat, at last, alone with his old friend in his study that overlooked the garden, he felt at once wrought-up and drowsy.

This should be the real pleasure of the day, to sit with his old friend in the cool of the evening and renew contact with the great world. But the bishop was used to country hours by now, and the feast had broken up late. He should be listening to the cardinal with the greatest attention, and yet those accursed crayfish kept coming into his mind.

"Well, Gianfrancesco," said the cardinal, sipping delicately at his wine, "you have given your old tutor a most charming welcome. Your wine, your people, your guests—it reminds me somehow of one of those fine Virgilian Eclogues we used to parse together. '*Tityre, tu patulae recubans*—'"

"The choir," said the bishop—"the choir usually is—"

"Why, they sang very well!" said the cardinal. "And what good, honest, plain-spoken priests you have in your charge!" He shook his head sadly. "I fear that we do not always get their like in Rome. And yet, each man to his task."

"They have a hard charge in these hills," said the bishop wearily. "It was a great honor for them to see Your Eminence."

"Oh, honor!" said the cardinal. "To see an old man with the gout—yes, I have the gout these days, Gianfrancesco—I fear we both are not so young as we were." He leaned forward and regarded the bishop attentively. "You, too, have altered, my old friend," he said softly.

"Your Eminence means that I have rusticated," said the bishop a trifle bitterly. "Well, it is true."

"Oh, not rusticated," said the cardinal, with a charming gesture. "Not at all. But there has been a change—a perceptible one—from the Gianfrancesco I knew." He took a walnut and began to crack it. "That Gianfrancesco was a charming and able young man," he said. "Yet I doubt if he would have made the Count of his city do penance in his shirt, for his sins, before the doors of his cathedral!"

"I can explain about that," said the bishop hurriedly. "The shirt was a silk one and the weather by no means inclement. Moreover, the Count's new tax would have ruined my poor. It is true we have not always seen eye to eye since then, yet I think he respects me more than he did before."

"That is just what I said to your brother, Piero," said the cardinal comfortably. "I said, 'You are wrong to be perturbed about this, Piero; it will have a good effect.' Yes, even as regards the beggar."

"My beggar?" said the bishop, and sighed.

"Oh, you know how small things get about," said the cardinal. "Some small thing is seized upon; it even travels to Rome. The bishop's beggar—the beggars' bishop—the bishop who humbles his soul to protect the poor."

"But it was not like that at all," said the bishop. "I—"

The cardinal waved him aside. "Do not hide your good works beneath a bushel, Gianfrancesco," he said. "The Church herself has need of them. These are troubled times we live in. The French king may march any day. There is heresy and dissension abroad. You have no idea what difficult days may lie ahead." He watched the bishop intently. "Our Holy Father leans much upon my unworthy shoulder," he said, "and our Holy Father is beginning to age."

"That is sore news for us all," said the bishop.

"Sore indeed," said the cardinal. "And yet, one must face realities. Should our Holy Father die, it will be necessary for those of us who truly love the Church to stand together—more especially in the college of cardinals." He paused and with a silver nutpick extracted the last meat from the walnut. "I believe that our Holy Father is disposed to reward your own labors with the see of Albano," he said.

"The see of Albano?" said the bishop as if in a dream, for, as all men knew, Albano was an old and famous diocese outside the walls of Rome, and he who was bishop of Albano wore a cardinal's hat.

"It might have a most excellent affect," said the cardinal. "I myself think it might. We have clever and able men who are sons of the Church. Indeed. And yet, just at this moment, with both the French and the German parties so active—well, there is perhaps need for another sort of man—at least as regards the people." He smiled delightfully. "You would be very close to me as cardinal-bishop of Albano—very close to us all," he said. "I should lean upon you, Gianfrancesco."

"There is nought that would please me more!" cried the bishop, like a boy. He thought for a moment of the power and the glory, of the great, crowded streets of Rome and the Church that humbles kings. "I would have to leave Remo?" he said.

"Well, yes, naturally, it would mean your having to leave Remo," said the cardinal. "Your new duties would demand it."

"That would be hard," said the bishop. "I would have to leave Luigi and all my people." He thought of them suddenly—the lame, the halt, the oppressed.

"Your people, perhaps," said the cardinal, "but certainly not Luigi. He should come with you by all means, as a living example."

"Oh, no, no, that would never do," said the bishop. "Your Eminence does not understand. Luigi is difficult enough as a bishop's beggar. As a cardinal's beggar, he would be overweening. You have no idea how overweening he would be."

The cardinal regarded him with a puzzled stare.

"Am I dreaming, Gianfrancesco?" he said. "Or are you declining the see of Albano and a cardinal's hat for no more reason than that you are attached to a beggar?"

"Oh, no, no, no!" cried the bishop, in an agony. "I am not in the least attached to him—he is my cross and my thorn. But you see, it would be so bad for him if I were to be made a cardinal. I tremble to think what would happen to his soul. And then there are all his companions—Giuseppe, the Hook, is dead, but there is still blind Marta, and Benito, the hunchback, and the new ones. No, I must stay in Remo."

The cardinal smiled—a smile of exasperation. "I think you have forgotten something, Gianfrancesco," he said. "I think you have forgotten that obedience is the first law of the Church."

"I am five times obedient," said the bishop. "Let our Holy Father do with me as he wills. Let him send me as a missionary to savages; let him strip me of my bishopric and set me to work in the hills. I shall be content. But while I have been given Remo, I have work to do in Remo. I did not expect it to be so when I first came here," he said in a low voice, "and yet, somehow, I find that it is so."

The cardinal said nothing at all for a long time.

Then at last he rose, and, pressing the bishop's hand, he retired to his own quarters. The bishop hoped that he was comfortable in them, though it occurred to him, in the uneasy sleep before dawn, that the chimney smoked.

Next morning the cardinal departed on his journey toward Rome without speaking of these matters further. The bishop felt sorry to see him go, and yet relieved. He had been very glad to see his old friend again—he told himself that. Yet from the moment of the cardinal's arrival there had been an unfamiliar grayness upon his spirit, and now that grayness was gone. Nevertheless, he knew that he must face Luigi—and that thought was hard for him.

Yet it went well enough, on the whole.

The bishop explained to him, as one explains to a child, that it did not seem as if God had intended him to be a cardinal, only bishop of Remo, and with that Luigi had to be content. Luigi grumbled about it frequently and remarked that if he had known all this in the first place, he might never have accepted the position of bishop's beggar. But he was not any more overweening than before, and with that the bishop had to be satisfied.

Then came the war with the French, and that was hard upon the bishop. He did not like wars, he did not like the thought of his people being killed. Yet, when the Count of Remo fled with most of his soldiery, and the mayor locked himself in his house and stayed there, shaking, there was no one to take over the rule of the town but the bishop. The very beggars in the streets cried out for him; he could not escape the task.

He took it with a heavy heart, under the mocking eyes of Luigi. With Luigi in his cart, he inspected the walls and defenses.

"Well, your lordship has a very pretty problem," said Luigi. "Half a dozen good cannon shot and the city will be taken by storm."

"I thought so, I feared so," said the bishop, sighing. "And yet my people are my people."

"Your lordship might easily compromise with the enemy," said Luigi. "They are angry with the Count, it is true—they thought they had him bought over. Yet it would mean but two score hangings or so, and a tribute, properly assessed."

"I cannot permit my flock to be harried and persecuted," said the bishop.

"Well, if your lordship must die, I will die with your lordship," said Luigi. "Meanwhile, we might set the townsfolk to work on the walls—at least it will give them something to do. And yet, there may be another way."

So it was done, and the bishop worked day and night, enheartening and encouraging his people. For once, all Remo was one, and the spirit and will that burned within it were the bishop's. Yet it seemed no time at all before the French sat down before Remo.

They sent a trumpet and a flag to demand the surrender of the city. The bishop received the young officer who came with the trumpet—a dark-faced man he was, with a humorous twist to his mouth. The bishop even took him on a tour of the walls, which seemed to surprise him a little.

"You are well defended," said the Frenchman politely.

"Oh, no, we are very ill defended," said the bishop. "My good children have been trying to strengthen the wall with sandbags, but, as you perceive, it is rotten and needs rebuilding. Moreover, the Count was badly cheated on his powder. I must speak to him of it sometime, for hardly a gun we have is fit to fire."

The Frenchman's astonishment grew. "I do not wish to doubt your lordship's word," he said, "but if those things are so, how does your lordship propose to defend Remo?"

"By the will of God," said the bishop very simply. "I do not wish my poor people killed; neither do I wish them oppressed. If needs must, I shall die in their stead, but they shall go scatheless. Ere you hang one man of Remo, I shall take the noose from around his neck and put it around my own."

"Your lordship makes things very difficult," said the Frenchman, thoughtfully. "My King has no desire to attack the Church—and, indeed, the walls of Remo seem stronger than your lordship reckons."

Then he was conscious of a plucking at his sleeve. It was Luigi, the beggar, in his little cart, who, by signs and grimaces, seemed to wish the Frenchman to follow him.

"What is it, Luigi?" said the bishop wearily. "Ah, yes, you wish to show our friend the room where we store the powder. Very well. Then he may see how little we have."

When the Frenchman rejoined the bishop, he was wiping sweat from his forehead, and his face was white. The bishop pressed him to stay for a glass of wine, but he said he must return to his camp, and departed, muttering something incoherent about it being indeed the will of God that defended Remo.

When he had gone, the bishop looked severely upon Luigi. "Luigi," he said sternly, "I fear you have been up to some of your tricks."

"How your lordship mistakes me," said the beggar. "It is true I showed him three of my fellow-beggars—and they did not seem to him in the best of health. But I did not say they had plague; I let him draw his own conclusions. It took me four days to school them in their parts, but that I did not tell him either."

"That was hardly honest, Luigi," said the bishop. "We know there is no plague in the town."

"We know also that our walls are rotten," said Luigi, "but the French will not believe that, either. Men of war are extremely suspicious—it is their weakness. We shall wait and see."

They waited and saw, for that night a council of war was held in the French camp and the officer who had come with the trumpet reported (a) that Remo was held in great force and strongly defended; (b) that its bishop was resolved to die in the breach, and (c) that there was plague in the city. Taking all these factors into account, the French wisely decided, after some forty-eight hours' delay, to strike camp and fall back on their main army—which they did just in time to take part in the historic defeat of the whole French invasion a week later. This defeat sealed for all time the heroic defense of Remo; for, had the part of the French army occupied before Remo rejoined their main body before, the historic defeat might have been as historic a victory for the French. As it was, all Italy rang with the name of the bishop of Remo.

But of all this the bishop knew nothing, for his beggar, Luigi, was dying.

As the French moved away they had loosed off a few cannon shot, more in irritation than for any real military purpose. However, one of the cannon shot, heedlessly aimed, struck the steps of the cathedral, and you may still see the scars. It also struck the cart wherein Luigi lay directing his beggars at one task of defense or another. When the bishop first heard that his beggar was hurt, he went to him at once. But there was little that a man could do but wait, and the waiting was long. It was not until seven weeks later that Luigi passed from this earth. He endured, indeed till the messengers came from Rome.

After they had talked with the bishop, the bishop went alone to his cathedral and prayed. Then he went to see Luigi.

"Well?" said the dying man eagerly, staring at him with limpid eyes.

"His Holiness has been graciously pleased to make of me the first archbishop of Remo, placing under my staff, as well, the dioceses of Ugri and Soneto," said the bishop slowly. "But I have the news from Cardinal Malaverni, and I may remain here till I die." He stared at Luigi. "I do not understand," he said.

"It is well done. You have stood by the poor in their poverty and the wretched in their hour of trial," said Luigi, and for once there was no trace of mockery in his voice.

"I do not understand. I do not understand at all," said the bishop again. "And yet I think you deserve recompense rather than I, Luigi."

"No," said Luigi, "that I do not."

The bishop passed his hand across his brow. "I am not a fool," he said. "It was well done, to humble my spirit. And yet, why did you do so, Luigi?"

"Why, that was my great sin," said Luigi. "I have confessed many vain and imaginary sins, but never the real one till now." He paused, as if the words hurt him. "When your lordship's coach rolled over my legs, I was very bitter," he said. "A poor man has little. To lose that little—to lose the air on the hills and the springing step, to lie like a log forever because a bishop's coachman was careless—that made me very bitter. I had rather your lordship had driven over me again than taken me back to your palace and treated me with kindness. I hated your lordship for your indifferent kindness—I hated you for everything."

"Did you so, Luigi?" said the bishop.

"Yes," said Luigi. "And I could see that your lordship hated me—or, if not hated, loathed, like a crippled dog that one must be kind to without liking. So I set myself out to tease and torment your lordship—at first by being your beggar, then in other ways. I could not believe in goodness; I could not believe there would not come a moment when your lordship would turn upon me and drive me forth."

He paused a moment and wiped his mouth with a cloth.

"Yes, I could not believe that at all," he said. "But you were not to be broken, Gianfrancesco, my brother. The evil I showed you daily was like a knife in your heart and a burden on your back, but you bore the knife and the burden. I took delight in showing you how ill things went in your city—how, below the fair surface, there was misery and pain. And had you once turned aside from that misery and pain, I would have been satisfied, for then, bishop or no bishop, you would have lost your soul. Was that evil of me, Gianfrancesco?"

"Very evil in intent," said the bishop steadily, "for, while it is permitted to be tempted, it is evil to tempt. And yet proceed."

"Well," said Luigi, with a sudden and childlike stare, "it did not work. The more I tried to make you a bad man, the better man you became. You would not do what was ill; you would not depart from your poor, once you had known them—not even for a red hat or a count's favor. You would not do ill at all. So now we have defended Remo, the two of us, and I am dying." He stirred uneasily in his bed. "It is just as well," he said, with a trace of his old mockery. "I told my uncle I would live to be a cardinal's beggar, but I am not sure that I would have liked it. I have been the bishop's beggar so long. And yet, from the first I have loved you also, Gianfrancesco. Will you give me your blessing now, on me and my work—the blessing you denied me once?"

The bishop's face was wrung. Yet he lifted his hand and absolved and blessed Luigi. He blessed Luigi and his work in the name of the Father and of the Son and of the Holy Ghost. When that had been done, a smile appeared on Luigi's face.

"A very fine blessing," he said. "I must tell that to the Hook when I see him; he will be envious. I wonder is it drafty on the steps of heaven? A very fine blessing, your lordship . . . ten . . . scudi . . . for . . . Luigi." And with that his jaw dropped, and it was over. But the bishop knelt beside the bed with streaming eyes.

And all that, to be sure, was a long time ago. But they still tell the story in Remo when they show the bishop's tomb. He lies upon it, fairly carven in marble. But carved all around the tomb are a multitude of beggars, lame, halt, and misshapen, yet all praising God. And there are words in Latin which say, "It is not enough to have knowledge—these also are my sheep." Of the tomb of Luigi, the beggar—that no man knows. They say it is beside the bishop's but, in one war or another, it was destroyed and there is no trace of it now. Yet Luigi was an arrogant spirit; perhaps he would have liked that best.

V.7

"Town Office"

Edward Holmes

Edward Holmes (born in 1910), professor emeritus of English at the University of Maine, is a prolific writer of scholarly and popular articles, as well as of short stories. Like his protagonist in this story, Phil Ackerman, Holmes served as second selectman in his town in Maine and may well have faced Phil's dilemma. For many years, the town has turned over the interest on one of its funds to Frieda Roberts and the "Ladies' Aid" to distribute to the "worthy poor." When Phil learns just who the "worthy poor" are, and that to be "worthy" one must pass the test of "respectability" as locally defined, he tries to make some changes. Is he right to try to do so? Are Frieda and her cohorts misguided? What does Phil learn from his experience? Should we be as confident as the narrator seems to be that he will remain in office for a long time to come? If so, do we have grounds for thinking that he will be a better and wiser selectman in the future? Though most of us will never hold office, we may face similar issues. In general, how can we learn to negotiate between our principles and our desire not to offend? Between our rational convictions and established custom?

"Which are the worthy poor?" Phil Ackerman asked.

He wasn't looking at me; he was staring out the dust-crusted window of the town office, though there wasn't nothing out there to look at but a scrubby old black spruce already fading into the December dusk.

I drew a deep breath and stretched my legs out under the desk. This was the thing I had been waiting for, with mixed feelings, ever since the town had elected Phil second selectman last March. Because I knew in my bones there would be something. Not that there was any reason why they shouldn't have elected Phil, any more than they shouldn't have elected Aaron Abram third selectman either. The truth was, nobody much wanted to run, and I was old and these two lobsterfishermen were young, so people thought I could break them in and that would be it. Well, I more or less had: we had had our differences as assessors, but

"Town Office" from *A Part of the Main: Short Stories of the Maine Coast* (Orono, Maine: University of Maine Press, 1973), pp. 168–172. Used by permission of the University of Maine and Edward Holmes.

nothing we couldn't go halfway to each other and meet. At the same time, I had come to know Phil and how he thought, and I could see that, for him, how we done things last year, or the last fifty years for that matter, was not much of an argument. He had been away for a few years, and had come back with a wife and two small children, and was book-educated. He knew I knew town law, and enough town history, or maybe gossip, to fill volumes, but he didn't put more than a little stock in custom just because it was custom.

"Which are the worthy poor?" he said.

"I don't know. It's legal phrasing, the way them lawyers write it."

"And you say each year the Town's turned the interest on the Thompson Fund—all twenty-five dollars of it—over to Frieda Roberts and the Ladies' Aid to give to the worthy poor?"

"That's right."

"And last year they showered clothes, food, and nobody knows what else, on George and Anna Dexter and their kids?"

"Ayeah."

"You call them poor?"

"They ain't rich," I said.

"You can say that about anybody in Oak Harbor."

Aaron just sat there in the corner, grinning and saying nothing.

"And how did George and Anna like that?" Phil asked.

"Thought 'twas funny," I said.

"But they took the stuff."

"Sure. Why not?"

Phil swung his chair around a bit and put one foot on the bottom part of the stove. "I can think of lots poorer people than that: Al Hamor and his bunch, half-clothed and half-fed both, and living in that cowshed."

"Al is a drunk," I said. "He ain't sobered up in eighteen months."

"And the Clintock bunch and Amy Blake's family—"

"They don't live right," I told him. "They ain't one of Amy's kids knows which neighbor to call Daddy, nor anyone else neither."

Phil jumped to his feet and brought one fist against the wall ka-wham-oh!

Aaron kind of snorted.

"Don't get mad at me," I said. "I'm just saying how Frieda Roberts and doubtless her friends see it. The document reads, 'worthy poor.' She figures if they ain't respectable, they ain't worthy. Besides, if she gives food to Al's kids, she's as good as buying him another quart. And if she helps support Amy, she's encouraging more fatherless kids."

"Christ on a mountain! What's so respectable about Frieda Roberts? What was she like in her youth?"

"Best not ask," I said.

"There. You see!"

"But them is the ones that lace things the straitest for everyone else, once they've cooled off a bit."

"Hypocrites!"

"There's no news in that," I said.

"And she's the one keeps the key to the church so there can't no one get into it except for prayer service."

"What do you want? Somebody to bust it up? Desecrate it?" I said.

"Even God couldn't get into it."

"Maybe He never tried," I said.

"Be damned if I'll vote to turn that money over to Frieda and her bunch."

"Then who's going to buy the gifts and deliver them?"

"I will," Phil said.

I turned to Aaron Abram: "How do you vote?"

"I vote with Phil," Aaron said.

"All right." I reached for my pen and the Town checkbook.

"And how do you vote, Mace?" Phil asked.

"Me? I vote to do it the way we done before."

"Why?"

"Because I'm old, and I like things quiet."

For a wonder, too, we had things quiet. I simply said nothing to Frieda Roberts about it. And Phil and Aaron and Phil's wife—who had decided, they told me, that any child that was poor was worthy—they drove a deal with Carl Abbott over to the store to supply them with clothing and children's goodies to brighten things up somewhat for the Blake and Hamor kids. They also delivered the gifts.

Word got around, of course, but there was no explosion. The thing wasn't scandalous; it was just new and different, a revolution perhaps, but of the quiet sort.

And then in January Phil Ackerman came into the Town Office one Wednesday, the day we keep it open, with a strange look on his face.

"Well?" I asked.

Phil sat down and loosened his jacket. "She come to the house," he said.

"She?"

"Frieda Roberts."

"Oh, did she? That sounds interesting."

"She brought a box," Phil said, "a box full of scarves and mittens and stuff she and the Ladies' Aid had made for kids. She said where it was being handled a different way now, she would turn all that over to us."

I kind of grinned to myself; I could imagine it. "Well, you can still distribute the clothes," I said.

"It ain't that."

"No? Was she nasty? She's got a sharp tongue."

Phil shook his head. "It ain't that. I wish to hell she had been."

"Oh, I see: she was nice."

"Too damned nice. She looked and sounded and walked like she'd prayed over it for a week. Forgiveness stuck out of her like pins and needles out of a cushion."

I chuckled. "You're an oppressor, Phil."

"It was enough to turn a man's stomach."

"How do you like being on the receiving end of Christianity?" I asked.

"God damn it, it's not Christian," he said. "She'd have been kinder if she'd lost her temper and thrown the stuff in my face. She just wants to make me squirm."

"Well, she has, hasn't she? She figured out what you were like."

He didn't pound the wall this time, but his fist went up and down quietly, firmly, in rhythm, on the edge of my desk. "Aaron and I weren't wrong," he said.

"No, you weren't wrong."

"But we've hurt some others."

"That's right."

"So perhaps we weren't right. Do we always have to hurt others?"

"Could you have gone to her and worked it out?"

"God no! We'd have snapped like catfish."

"Well, then—"

He wasn't listening; he had that far-away look again. "Mace, how do you do it, year after year?"

"Do what?"

"Be first selectman. Run things," he said.

"I won't much longer."

"How did you learn?"

"Doing what you did, when I had the courage. What I thought was right."

"And people were hurt."

"Sure," I said. "But somebody has to run the town. You're learning."

He shook his head in doubt, got up, buttoned his jacket, and walked slowly out. But his head was up; his spine was straight; and I never doubted that he'd be back in the town office, long after I had left.

V.8

"Giving and Receiving: A Practical Way of Directing Love and Compassion"

His Holiness the XIV Dalai Lama

Tenzi Gyatso (born in 1935), enthroned in 1940 as His Holiness the XIV Dalai Lama of Tibet, is especially devoted to promulgating the ideas and practices of Buddhism. In this selection, his emphasis is on the Buddhist way of directing love and compassion. But the grounds of his appeal are far from parochial. "I see compassion, love and forgiveness as common ground for all different religions," he asserts, "irrespective of tradition or philosophy." And he makes clear why all human beings as human beings need all three. In his lecture, His Holiness speaks, first, about the general faults of a self-centered way of thinking and life; second, about the positive consequences of being mindful of the well-being of all other sentient beings and working for their benefit; and finally, about the particular training in Buddhism that is designed to enhance the power of compassion and love toward other beings. Though the language he uses for effecting change is, much like Aristotle's (see selection in this part), that of training or practice, His Holiness's training consists primarily of meditating, not the doing of deeds; the change he is looking for is primarily mental, not characterological. Such training may very well, he says, "bring about a transformation in your mind so effectively that your feeling of love and compassion is much more enhanced." Might mental and spiritual training be sufficient to alter one's actual practice? His Holiness insists that one need not be a Buddhist to profit from the training he recommends, but is he right? Can this Buddhist remedy be effective if we do not also embrace the beliefs and many other ways of Buddhism?

Compassion is the most wonderful and precious thing. When we talk about compassion, it is encouraging to note that basic human nature is, I believe, compassionate and gentle. Sometimes I argue with friends who believe that human

From *The Power of Compassion* by His Holiness, the Dalai Lama, published by HarperCollins Publishers, Ltd., pp. 58–82. Used by permission of HarperCollins Publishers, Ltd.

nature is more negative and aggressive. I argue that if you study the structure of the human body you will see that it is akin to those species of mammals whose way of life is more gentle or peaceful. Sometimes I half joke that our hands are arranged in such a manner that they are good for hugging, rather than hitting. If our hands were mainly meant for hitting, then these beautiful fingers would not be necessary. For example, if the fingers remain extended, boxers cannot hit forcefully, so they have to make fists. So I think that means that our basic physical structure creates a compassionate or gentle kind of nature.

If we look at relationships, marriage and conception are very important. As I said earlier, marriage should not be based on blind love or an extreme sort of mad love; it should be based on a knowledge of one another and an understanding that you are suitable to live together. Marriage is not for temporary satisfaction, but for some kind of sense of responsibility. That is the genuine love which is the basis of marriage.

The proper conception of a child takes place in that kind of moral or mental attitude. While the child is in the mother's womb, the mother's calmness of mind has a very positive effect on the unborn child, according to some scientists. If the mother's mental state is negative, for instance if she is frustrated or angry, then it is very harmful to the healthy development of the unborn child. One scientist has told me that the first few weeks after birth is the most important period, for during that time the child's brain is enlarging. During that period, the mother's touch or that of someone who is acting like a mother is crucial. This shows that even though the child may not realize who is who, it somehow physically needs someone else's affection. Without that, it is very damaging for the healthy development of the brain.

After birth, the first act by the mother is to give the child nourishing milk. If the mother lacks affection or kind feelings for the child, then the milk will not flow. If the mother feeds her baby with gentle feelings towards the child, in spite of her own illness or pain, as a result the milk flows freely. This kind of attitude is like a precious jewel. Moreover, from the other side, if the child lacks some kind of close feeling towards the mother, it may not suckle. This shows how wonderful the act of affection from both sides is. That is the beginning of our lives.

Similarly with education, it is my experience that those lessons which we learn from teachers who are not just good, but who also show affection for the student, go deep into our minds. Lessons from other sorts of teachers may not. Although you may be compelled to study and may fear the teacher, the lessons may not sink in. Much depends on the affection from the teacher.

Likewise, when we go to a hospital, irrespective of the doctor's quality, if the doctor shows genuine feeling and deep concern for us, and if he or she smiles, then we feel OK. But if the doctor shows little human affection, then even though he or she may be a very great expert, we may feel unsure and nervous. This is human nature.

Lastly, we can reflect on our lives. When we are young and again when we are old, we depend heavily on the affection of others. Between these stages we usually feel that we can do everything without help from others and that other people's affection is simply not important. But at this stage I think it is very important to keep deep human affection. When people in a big town or city feel lonely, this does not mean that they lack human companions, but rather that they lack human affection. As a result of this, their mental health eventually becomes very poor. On the other hand, those people who grow up in an atmosphere of human affection have a much more positive and gentle development of their bodies, their minds and their behaviour. Children who have grown up lacking that atmosphere usually have more negative attitudes. This very clearly shows the basic human nature. Also, as I have mentioned, the human body appreciates peace of mind. Things that are disturbing to us have a very bad effect upon our health. This shows that the whole structure of our health is such that it is suited to an atmosphere of human affection. Therefore, our potential for compassion is there. The only issue is whether or not we realize this and utilize it.

The basic aim of my explanation is to show that by nature we are compassionate, that compassion is something very necessary and something which we can develop. It is important to know the exact meaning of compassion. Different philosophies and traditions have different interpretations of the meaning of love and compassion. Some of my Christian friends believe that love cannot develop without God's grace; in other words, to develop love and compassion you need faith. The Buddhist interpretation is that genuine compassion is based on a clear acceptance or recognition that others, like oneself, want happiness and have the right to overcome suffering. On that basis one develops some kind of concern about the welfare of others, irrespective of one's attitude to oneself. That is compassion.

Your love and compassion towards your friends is in many cases actually attachment. This feeling is not based on the realization that all beings have an equal right to be happy and to overcome suffering. Instead, it is based on the idea that something is 'mine', 'my friend' or something good for 'me'. That is attachment. Thus, when that person's attitude towards you changes, your feeling of closeness immediately disappears. With the other way, you develop some kind of concern irrespective of the other person's attitude to you, simply because that person is a fellow human being and has every right to overcome suffering. Whether that person remains neutral to you or even becomes your enemy, your concern should remain because of his or her right. That is the main difference. Genuine compassion is much healthier; it is unbiased and it is based on reason. By contrast, attachment is narrow-minded and biased.

Actually, genuine compassion and attachment are contradictory. According to Buddhist practice, to develop genuine compassion you must first practice the meditation of equalization and equanimity, detaching oneself from those people who are very close to you. Then, you must remove negative feelings towards your enemies. All sentient beings should be looked on as equal. On that basis, you can gradually develop genuine compassion for all of them. It must be said that genuine compassion is not like pity or a feeling that others are somehow lower than yourself. Rather, with genuine compassion you view others as more important than yourself.

As I pointed out earlier, in order to generate genuine compassion, first of all one must go through the training of equanimity. This becomes very important because without a sense of equanimity towards all, one's feelings towards others will be biased. So now I will give you a brief example of a Buddhist meditative training on developing equanimity. You should think about, first, a small group of people whom you know, such as your friends and relatives, towards whom you have an attachment. Second, you should think about some people to whom you feel totally indifferent. And third, think about some people whom you dislike. Once you have imagined these different people, you should try to let your mind go into its natural state and see how it would normally respond to an encounter with these people. You will notice that your natural reaction would be that of attachment towards your friends, that of dislike towards the people whom you consider enemies and that of total indifference towards those whom you consider neutral. Then you should try to question yourself. You should compare the effects of the two opposing attitudes you have towards your friends and your enemies, and see why you should have such fluctuating states of mind towards these two different groups of people. You should see what effects such reactions have on your mind and try to see the futility of relating to them in such an extreme manner. I have already discussed the pros and cons of harbouring hatred and generating anger towards enemies, and I have also spoken a little about the defects of being extremely attached towards friends and so on. You should reflect upon this and then try to minimize your strong emotions towards these two opposing groups of people. Then, most importantly, you should reflect on the fundamental equality between yourself and all other sentient beings. Just as you have the instinctive natural desire to be happy and overcome suffering, so do all sentient beings; just as you have the right to fulfil this innate aspiration, so do all sentient beings. So on what exact grounds do you discriminate?

If we look at humanity as a whole, we are social animals. Moreover, the structures of the modern economy, education and so on, illustrate that the world has become a smaller place and that we heavily depend on one another. Under such circumstances, I think the only option is to live and work together harmoniously and keep in our minds the interest of the whole of humanity. That is the only outlook and way we must adopt for our survival.

By nature, especially as a human being, my interests are not independent of others. My happiness depends on others' happiness. So when I see happy people, automatically I also feel a little bit happier than when I see people in a difficult situation. For example, when we see pictures on television which show people starving in Somalia, including old people and young children, then we automatically feel sad, regardless of whether that sadness can lead to some kind of active help or not.

Moreover, in our daily lives we are now utilizing many good facilities, including things like air-conditioned houses. All these things or facilities became possible, not because of ourselves, but because of many other people's direct or indirect involvement. Everything comes together. It is impossible to return to the way of life of a few centuries ago, when we depended on simple instruments, not all these machines. It is very clear to us that the facilities that we are enjoying now are the products of the activities of many people. In 24 hours you sleep on a bed—many people have been involved in that—and in the preparation of your food, too, especially for the non-vegetarian. Fame is definitely a product of other people—without the presence of other people the concept of fame would not even make sense. Also, the interest of Europe depends on America's interest and Western Europe's interest depends on the Eastern European economic situation. Each continent is heavily dependent on the others; that is the reality. Thus many of the things that we desire, such as wealth, fame and so forth, could not come into being without the active or indirect participation and co-operation of many other people.

Therefore, since we all have an equal right to be happy and since we are all linked to one another, no matter how important an individual is, logically the interest of the other five billion people on the planet is more important than that of one single person. By thinking along these lines, you can eventually develop a sense of global responsibility. Modern environmental problems, such as the depletion of the ozone layer, also clearly show us the need for world co-operation. It seems that with development, the whole world has become much smaller, but the human consciousness is still lagging behind.

This is not a question of religious practice, but a question of the future of humanity. This kind of wider or more altruistic attitude is very relevant in today's world. If we look at the situation from various angles, such as the complexity and inter-connectedness of the nature of modern existence, then we will gradually notice a change in our outlook, so that when we say 'others' and when we think of others, we will no longer dismiss them as something that is irrelevant to us. We will no longer feel indifferent.

If you think only of yourself, if you forget the rights and well-being of others, or, worse still, if you exploit others, ultimately you will lose. You will have no friends who will show concern for your well-being. Moreover, if a tragedy befalls you, instead of feeling concerned, others might even secretly rejoice. By contrast, if an individual is compassionate and altruistic, and has the interests of others in mind, then irrespective of whether that person knows a lot of people, wherever that person moves, he or she will immediately make friends. And when that person faces a tragedy, there will be plenty of people who will come to help.

A true friendship develops on the basis of genuine human affection, not money or power. Of course, due to your power or wealth, more people may approach you with big smiles or gifts. But deep down these are not real friends of yours; these are friends of your wealth or power. As long as your fortune remains, then these people will often approach you. But when your fortunes decline, they will no longer be there. With this type of friend, nobody will make a sincere effort to help you if you need it. That is the reality.

Genuine human friendship is on the basis of human affection, irrespective of your position. Therefore, the more you show concern about the welfare and rights of others, the more you are a genuine friend. The more you remain open and sincere, then ultimately more benefits will come to you. If you forget or do not bother about others, then eventually you will lose your own benefit. So sometimes I tell people, if we really are selfish, then wise selfishness is much better than the selfishness of ignorance and narrow-mindedness.

For Buddhist practitioners, the development of wisdom is also very important—and here I mean wisdom which realizes *Shunya,* the ultimate nature of reality. The realization of *Shunya* gives you at least some kind of positive sense about cessation. Once you have some kind of feeling for the possibility of cessation, then it becomes clear that suffering is not final and that there is an alternative. If there is alternative then it is worth making an effort. If only two of the Buddha's Four Noble Truths exist, suffering and the cause of suffering, then there is not much meaning. But the other two Noble Truths, including cessation, point towards an alternative way of existence. There is possibility of ending suffering. So it is worthwhile to realize the nature of suffering. Therefore wisdom is extremely important in increasing compassion infinitely.

So that is how one engages in the practice of Buddhism: there is an application of the faculty of wisdom, using intelligence, and an understanding of the nature of reality, together with the skillful means of generating compassion. I think that in your daily lives and in all sorts of your professional work, you can use this compassionate motivation.

Of course, in the field of education, there is no doubt that compassionate motivation is important and relevant. Irrespective of whether you are a believer or non-believer, compassion for the students' lives or futures, not only for their examinations, makes your work as a teacher much more effective. With that motivation, I think your students will remember you for the whole of their lives.

Similarly, in the field of health, there is an expression in Tibetan which says that the effectiveness of the treatment depends on how warm-hearted the physician is. Because of this expression, when treatments from a certain doctor do not work, people blame the doctor's character, speculating that perhaps that he or she was not a kind person. The poor doctor sometimes gets a very bad name!

So in the medical field there is no doubt that compassionate motivation is something very relevant.

I think this is also the case with lawyers and politicians. If politicians and lawyers had more compassionate motivation then there would be less scandal. And as a result the whole community would get more peace. I think the work of politics would become more effective and more respected.

Finally, in my view, the worst thing is warfare. But even warfare with human affection and with human compassion is much less destructive. The completely mechanized warfare that is without human feeling is worse.

Also, I think compassion and a sense of responsibility can also enter into the fields of science and engineering. Of course, from a purely scientific point of view, awful weapons such as nuclear bombs are remarkable achievements. But we can say that these are negative because they bring immense suffering to the world. Therefore, if we do not take into account human pain, human feelings and human compassion, there is no demarcation between right and wrong. Therefore, human compassion can reach everywhere.

I find it a little bit difficult to apply this principle of compassion to the field of economics. But economists are human beings and of course they also need human affection, without which they would suffer. However, if you think only of profit, irrespective of the consequences, then drug dealers are not wrong, because, from the economic viewpoint, they are also making tremendous profits. But because this is very harmful for society and for the community, we call this wrong and name these people criminals. If that is the case, then I think arms dealers are in the same category. The arms trade is equally dangerous and irresponsible.

So I think for these reasons, human compassion, or what I sometimes call 'human affection', is the key factor for all human business. Just as you see that with the palm of our hand all five fingers become useful, if these fingers were not connected to the palm they would be useless. Similarly, every human action that is without human feeling becomes dangerous. With human feeling and an appreciation of human values, all human activities become constructive.

Even religion, which is supposedly good for humanity, without that basic human compassionate attitude can become foul. Unfortunately even now there are problems which are entirely down to different religions. So human compassion is something fundamental. If that is there, then all other human activities become more useful.

Generally speaking, I have the impression that in education and some other areas there is some negligence of the issue of human motivation. Perhaps in ancient times religion was supposed to carry this responsibility. But now in the community, religion generally seems a little bit old-fashioned, so people are losing interest in it and in deeper human values. However, I think these should be two separate things. If you have respect for or interest in religion, that is good.

But even if you have no interest in religion, you should not forget the importance of these deeper human values.

There are various positive side-effects of enhancing one's feeling of compassion. One of them is that the greater the force of your compassion, the greater your resilience in confronting hardships and your ability to transform them into more positive conditions. One form of practice that seems to be quite effective is found in *A Guide to the Bodhisattva Way of Life,* a classic Buddhist text. In this practice you visualize your old self, the embodiment of self-centredness, selfishness and so on, and then visualize a group of people who represent the masses of other sentient beings. Then you adopt a third person's point of view as a neutral, unbiased observer and make a comparative assessment of the value, the interests and then the importance of these two groups. Also try to reflect upon the faults of being totally oblivious to the well-being of other sentient beings and so on, and what this old self has really achieved as a result of leading such a way of life. Then reflect on the other sentient beings and see how important their well-being is, the need to serve them and so forth, and see what you, as a third neutral observer, would conclude as to whose interests and well-being are more important. You would naturally begin to feel more inclined towards the countless others.

I also think that the greater the force of your altruistic attitude towards sentient beings, the more courageous you become. The greater your courage, the less you feel prone to discouragement and loss of hope. Therefore, compassion is also a source of inner strength. With increased inner strength it is possible to develop firm determination and with determination there is a greater chance of success, no matter what obstacles there may be. On the other hand, if you feel hesitation, fear and a lack of self-confidence, then often you will develop a pessimistic attitude. I consider that to be the real seed of failure. With a pessimistic attitude you cannot accomplish even something you could easily achieve. Whereas even if something is difficult to achieve, if you have an unshakeable determination there is eventually the possibility of achievement. Therefore, even in the conventional sense, compassion is very important for a successful future.

As I pointed out earlier, depending on the level of your wisdom, there are different levels of compassion, such as compassion which is motivated by genuine insight into the ultimate nature of reality, compassion which is motivated by the appreciation of the impermanent nature of existence and compassion which is motivated by awareness of the suffering of other sentient beings. The level of your wisdom, or the depth of your insight into the nature of reality, determines the level of compassion that you will experience. From the Buddhist viewpoint, compassion with wisdom is very essential. It is as if compassion is like a very honest person and wisdom is like a very able person—if you join these two, then the result is something very effective.

I see compassion, love and forgiveness as common ground for all different religions, irrespective of tradition or philosophy. Although there are fundamental differences between different religious ideas, such as the acceptance of an Almighty Creator, every religion teaches us the same message: be a warm-hearted person. All of them emphasize the importance of compassion and forgiveness. Now in ancient times when the various religions were based in different places and there was less communication between them, there was no need for pluralism among the various religious traditions. But today, the world has become much smaller, so communication between different religious faiths has become very strong. Under such circumstances, I think pluralism among religious believers is very essential. Once you see the value to humanity through the centuries of these different religions through unbiased, objective study then there is plenty of reason to accept or to respect all these different religions. After all, in humanity there are so many different mental dispositions, so simply one religion, no matter how profound, cannot satisfy all the variety of people.

For instance, now, in spite of such a diversity of religious traditions, the majority of people still remain unattracted by religion. Of the five billion people, I believe only around one billion are true religious believers. While many people say, 'My family background is Christian, Muslim or Buddhist, so I'm a Christian, Muslim or Buddhist,' true believers, in their daily lives and particularly when some difficult situation arises, realize that they are followers of a particular religion. For example, I mean those who say, 'I am Christian,' and during that moment remember God, pray to God and do not let out negative emotions. Of these true believers, I think there are perhaps less than one billion. The rest of humanity, four billion people, remain in the true sense non-believers. So one religion obviously cannot satisfy all of humanity. Under such circumstances, a variety of religions is actually necessary and useful, and therefore the only sensible thing is that all different religions work together and live harmoniously, helping one another. There have been positive developments recently and I have noticed closer relations forming between various religions.

So, having reflected upon the faults of a self-centred way of thinking and life, and also having reflected upon the positive consequences of being mindful of the well-being of other sentient beings and working for their benefit, and being convinced of this, then in Buddhist meditation there is a special training which is known as 'the practice of Giving and Taking'. This is especially designed to enhance your power of compassion and love towards other sentient beings. It basically involves visualizing taking upon yourself all the suffering, pain, negativity and undesirable experiences of other sentient beings. You imagine taking these upon yourself and then giving away or sharing with others your own positive qualities, such as your virtuous states of mind, your positive energy, your wealth, your happiness and so forth. Such a form of training, though it cannot actually result in a reduction of suffering by other sentient beings or a production of your own positive qualities, psychologically brings about a transformation in your mind so effectively that your feeling of love and compassion is much more enhanced.

Trying to implement this practice in your daily life is quite powerful and can be a very positive influence on your mind and on your health. If you feel that it seems worthwhile to practice, then irrespective of whether you are a believer or a non-believer, you should try to promote these basic human good qualities.

One thing you should remember is that these mental transformations take time and are not easy. I think some people from the West, where technology is so good, think that everything is automatic. You should not expect this spiritual transformation to take place within a short period; that is impossible. Keep it in your mind and make a constant effort, then after 1 year, 5 years, 10 years, 15 years, you will eventually find some change. I still sometimes find it very difficult to practice these things. However, I really do believe that these practices are extremely useful.

My favourite quotation from Shantideva's book is: 'So long as sentient beings remain, so long as space remains, I will remain in order to serve, or in order to make some small contribution for the benefit of others.'

V.9

"Only Reflect: A Philanthropic Education for Our Time"

Elizabeth M. Lynn and D. Susan Wisely

The other readings in this part address ways of sowing and cultivating seeds of the philanthropic spirit in individual givers. This final selection considers ways of helping those already philanthropically inclined to give and serve more wisely. Elizabeth M. Lynn and D. Susan Wisely are pioneers in the Project on Civic Reflection, which seeks to help people educate themselves regarding the why and wherefore of their own civic and philanthropic activities. In their understanding, not the least purpose of philanthropic activity is to foster greater civic participation and public spiritedness in those who give and serve.

We are today on the brink of many changes in philanthropy. Thanks to a decade-long period of prosperity, there is more wealth in our nation than ever before. As a result, the philanthropic landscape is dotted with new financial vehicles and a greater variety of mechanisms to encourage giving not only by the wealthiest among us but also by people of more ordinary means. Donor-advised funds, now a mainstay of community foundations and Jewish federations across the country, have multiplied, as have mutual fund companies which offer charitable gift funds to the public. Indeed, the competition among such companies has itself broadened and improved options for donors. In addition, givers may choose from a proliferating array of non-profit organizations and, thanks to the internet, information about these organizations is at their fingertips. Ours is in short a time of many givers, many causes, and many ways of connecting the one with the other.

As we survey the philanthropic landscape, we notice two prevalent ways in which people have responded to this world of choice: by turning to experts or professionals for guidance and assistance, and by turning to standard-setters and regulators to establish and enforce the rules of the enterprise.

Original contribution by Elizabeth M. Lynn and D. Susan Wisely.

The first path is a logical extension of well-worn patterns. In certain areas of our lives, including health, legal arrangements, and finances, many of us have come to rely on expert advice and trust the judgments of professionals. Even if we are sometimes uncomfortable, puzzled, or frustrated in our dealings with doctors, lawyers, accountants, or financial planners, such reliance makes eminently good sense in dealing with matters that call for specialized knowledge. The world is too complex for the "Renaissance man," much less the ordinary man (or woman), to navigate without expert assistance. As the slogan of a local law firm warns: "It's a complex world, be advised."

In money matters, as in much else, we have become used to seeking and relying upon expert advice. Giving is no exception. It is now commonplace for individuals or families to seek advice (and sooner rather than later) on estate planning from an accountant or lawyer and to incorporate decisions about giving into their larger financial plan. In response, increasing numbers of financial planners and institutions are expanding services to include advice about giving. A growing cadre of "philanthropic advisors" has hung out shingles to offer professional advice about giving.

Seeking professional advice is a natural and reasonable response to the proliferation of options in charitable giving. Seeking accountability by setting standards and regulating practices is equally reasonable. Like claims of special expertise, the pursuit of accountability is not a recent innovation. For example, since its birth in 1918, the National Charities Information Bureau has been setting standards for charitable practice and assessing adherence, in order to help donors make better choices. The public has come to count on its help, as well as the help of the Attorney Generals' Offices and the Charity Offices of their respective states, both of which assist donors and guard against fraud and abuse.

These two responses—professionalism and regulation—meet real and pressing needs in philanthropy today. Professional advisors help givers with the "how" of giving: they instruct us in how to manage our money wisely and conscientiously, so that it goes as far as possible. So too, the regulators: they help us with the "whom" of giving, by assessing the credibility of potential recipients.

But in our experience those who are interested in giving need something more. They hunger for help with the "why" and "wherefore" of giving. Why give to one cause, or institution, or individual rather than another? What are we hoping will happen as a result of our giving? What should we expect from those we help with our gifts?

As these questions suggest, decisions about giving entail more than a choice among donor-advised funds. Such decisions press us to say what we value and how we believe the world works. Set in motion, our gifts establish—and sometimes transform—our relationships to others in our world, not always in expected or pleasant ways. Giving well requires not just technique but reflection, not just expertise but wisdom.

But where can Americans turn for wisdom about giving? Here, money managers and charity watchdogs have little guidance to offer. Some of us may turn to religious traditions or family traditions as a source of wisdom. Yet on the whole, Americans are disinclined to rely on tradition. As Alexis de Tocqueville observed more than 150 years ago, because we Americans believe that no one person is better than another, we seek the reasons for things largely in ourselves, not in tradition, nor in the wisdom of singular individuals. "Not only does democracy make every man forget his ancestors, but it hides his descendants and separates his contemporaries from him; it throws him back forever upon himself alone, and threatens in the end to confine him entirely within the solitude of his own heart." The result, in our own time, is unprecedented freedom—and loneliness—especially when it comes to choosing how to give.

But, as Tocqueville also observed, Americans regularly associate with one another to achieve common goals, and we have as a consequence developed "a taste for giving and serving" that can counter the isolating tendencies of individualism. This "art of association" is evident in the proliferation of philanthropic organizations and causes mentioned earlier. Indeed, we Americans often congratulate ourselves on our gift for association, quoting Tocqueville as we go. We pay less attention to his equally perceptive observations about our moral loneliness. Both, however, make up the reality of American philanthropy. The result is bittersweet. In a world of many choices, we have few sources of guidance to help us make those choices wisely.

We also have few people with whom we can comfortably talk about our giving choices. As sociologist Robert Wuthnow has noted, talking about money is one of the great American taboos. Businesses routinely suppress salary information in order not to fuel anger or envy in the workplace; parents resist telling their children how much they earn, give or save in order to protect the children from worry or pride; friends avoid asking each other how much they earn or how much they spent on their house. When it comes to giving, this taboo gains new intensity, fueled by fears that others will judge us or, worse yet, try to manipulate us for their own purposes.

There may be good reasons for American taboos on talking about money. But the result, as Wuthnow suggests, is that we do not speak about money with one another in terms of our values (it is "only" economics, after all) and become increasingly isolated in our dealings with and feelings about money.

Ours is, in short, a time of *unprecedented freedom*—and *loneliness*—in choosing how to give. For all these reasons, today's givers need special help in reflecting on the choices available to them. They need access to wisdom about giving, and conversation partners with whom they can explore their questions in a candid and unpressured way. They need a philanthropic education for our time.

The hunger for education, as well as for expert advice, is evident in the variety of donor education efforts that have been cropping up in recent years. From programs to reach the newly wealthy in high-technology companies to efforts focused on farmers, small-business owners, members of minority groups, and young people, many of these efforts hope to encourage more effective giving. Many of these programs are close cousins to efforts to promote a more professional, or expert, approach to giving—stressing knowledge of the techniques by which to give or advocating a particular style of giving, such as so-called "strategic philanthropy" or "venture philanthropy."

Others, such as "giving circles" and study groups, are less prescriptive, aiming to open up conversations among peers about giving. They invite reflection on personal experience and allow givers to learn from friends, neighbors, and family members. Here, the aim is not to produce experts or professionals. It is rather to help ordinary individuals reflect on their giving in the company of others. Giving circles offer participants the company of their peers, and open up a space for conversation about giving in a world of dizzying choices. They allow us to articulate our beliefs, describe our experience, and hear the beliefs and experiences of others. But without additional resources, such activities may not go far enough. Like any support group, they rely heavily upon the collective wisdom of the participants, and they are therefore circumscribed by the inevitable limits of that wisdom.

For the last five years, we have been trying to develop a program that would provide the needed additional resources. We have been experimenting with a particular kind of philanthropic education called "civic reflection." Like giving circles, civic reflection acknowledges the desire of people to decide for themselves about giving as an aspect of the good life. Like giving circles, it invites attention to personal experience. But it also seeks to enlarge the circle of wisdom by connecting contemporary givers with larger traditions of understanding about giving and serving, through group reading and discussion of selected texts from literature, religion, and history.

Through a University of Chicago project called the Tocqueville Seminars and two successor efforts (the Project on Civic Reflection at Valparaiso University and the Art of Association Project of the Federation of State Humanities Councils), small groups of civic leaders have been meeting on a regular basis to discuss their questions about "the why and wherefore of giving," in light of selected readings, and with the aid of facilitators. Some examples of civic reflection activities include the following:

> In Portland, Maine, staff and trustees of the Maine Community Foundation and state grantmakers' associations came together over a six month period in 1998–1999 to explore "Perspectives on Philanthropy," with special attention to New England traditions of giving. Readings included works by Andrew Carnegie, Sarah Orne Jewett, Moses Maimonides, and

Michael Sandel. This seminar has given birth in turn to philanthropy seminars for foundation staff and individual givers in each of the New England states, coordinated by state humanities councils with support from the National Endowment for the Humanities.

In South Bend, Indiana, members of a voluntary association for women interested in philanthropy met in 1997–1998 to discuss "Generosity of Spirit and the American Tradition," with special attention to giving by American women. Readings included selections by Catherine Beecher, Ralph Waldo Emerson, Henri Nouwen, and Eudora Welty. When the seminar concluded, the group continued to meet to explore opportunities for giving and serving in South Bend.

In Fort Wayne, Indiana, civic leaders gathered for a seminar on "Giving in America: Tradition, Challenge and Choice." These leaders, all actively involved in giving through volunteering, fundraising, institutional development, foundation leadership, trusteeship, and individual giving, wanted an opportunity to explore fundamental questions, like: What does it mean to give well? How can we give more effectively? How can we encourage others to give? Participants discussed these questions in light of short texts by writers such as Alexis de Tocqueville, Robert Wuthnow, and Jane Addams. They also created their own "giving autobiography" and drafted a giving plan for personal use. This seminar, too, spawned several other study circles, including an inter-generational effort that brought together parents and children of several families for reading and conversation about giving.

These seminars vary in certain respects. Some have been supported by foundation dollars, others by participant subscriptions. They may meet in a church basement or a country club, a living room or a health center. They differ widely in the type, length and density of the assigned readings (although, as a general rule, readings have gotten shorter with each successive seminar). They are facilitated variously by historians, college instructors, foundation executives and adult educators.

Notwithstanding these minor differences, civic reflection seminars share five essential features: First, they are for civic leaders—men and women who are actively engaged in giving and serving. These conversations are *not* designed to engage the disengaged. Instead, civic reflection seminars are designed to offer the many men and women who are *already engaged* in civic life a rare opportunity to understand and deepen their giving and service.

Second, they offer these leaders opportunities for candid conversation with peers, unconstrained by the prospect of a pledge card marking the conclusion of the process. Donors and other civic leaders seldom have unpressured space for conversation where they are neither "targets" nor "prospects" but people with convictions, experiences and questions of their own. Civic reflection seminars provide these leaders with an opportunity to talk with one another candidly about the challenges, choices, questions, and doubts arising out of their philanthropy. These seminars are not lectures or "visits with a prospective donor" but facilitated conversations.

Third, these seminars start with the participants' own questions about giving. Some of the most troubling questions civic leaders encounter in their work are enduring human questions—questions not unique to one organization or profession, time or place, but arising in a variety of times, places, and circumstances—questions like, What is a good gift? Who is my neighbor? What should we expect from those we serve? Seminar facilitators listen carefully to participants and help them articulate the fundamental human questions that arise naturally out of their giving activity. Indeed, in our experience, one of the greatest gifts of these occasions is the gift of one's own questions—and the discovery that those questions have been asked by other persons in other times and places.

Fourth, participants read and discuss texts with other givers. Starting from participants' questions, facilitators assign readings that address their questions in an accessible yet thought-provoking way. In our experience, the use of readings is important for two reasons, one substantive and the other practical. Substantively, texts enlarge understanding and deepen imagination, connecting participants with larger traditions of thought and imagination and other times and places. But readings have practical benefits as well for enhancing discussion. They provide a fresh and shared point of reference for participants, and so help to move the conversation beyond personal experience and hardened opinion. There is no set canon of readings for philanthropic education. All sorts of texts, from classic works of literature or philosophy to movies and children's books have been found useful. The key to successful reflection seems to be less the nature of the text itself and more the asking of interesting and personally important questions about the texts.

Finally, civic reflection seminars include opportunities for civic leaders to look back on how they learned to give and to perceive and describe their own familial, religious and regional traditions of giving. For instance, facilitators might ask participants to write down their earliest impressions of service to others. Or they might invite philanthropists to fill out a giving autobiography or timeline, plotting key memories and experiences that have shaped (for better or worse) their ideas about giving, and then to reflect upon striking patterns or themes. These exercises have proven useful in starting group conversation about individual values and larger traditions of giving, and in helping participants think about how they can in turn teach others to give.

Though the number of these seminars continues to multiply, we are well aware that they are only a start, a small start at an attempt to deepen the thoughtfulness and commitment of those who already give. The volume to which this article has been donated invites many more givers, now unknown to us, to participate in civic reflection. Indeed, you, the readers of *The Perfect Gift,* are perhaps in the best of all possible positions to bear witness to the merits of such an education. Have any of the readings helped to enlighten, deepen, or possibly even to change the way in which you now think about your own philanthropic deeds and intentions? Has your own willingness to "reflect, only reflect," improved your philanthropic understanding and encouraged your philanthropic intentions? We hope so.

Acknowledgments

I wish to acknowledge, with deep gratitude, the help of those individuals who supported and contributed to the preparation of this volume. Probably unbeknownst to himself, Mark Schwehn initiated it by urging the Lilly Endowment to invite me to serve as a consultant to their leadership education program. Little did I know when I visited the Endowment, in summer 1996, how much more they would do for me than I for them: Craig Dykstra, Director of Lilly's Religion division, took an immediate interest in my concerns and ideas and has been a steady advocate ever since. D. Susan Wisely, Director of Lilly's Program Evaluation division, helped transform my fledgling ideas into the "Tocqueville Seminars for Civic Leadership" program, which the Lilly Endowment generously supported and promoted, and which, in turn, was the seedbed of this collection.

I was introduced to the fundamental importance of the many issues raised herein by the questions and concerns addressed by the twelve seminars that were implemented by the "Tocqueville Seminars" program. I am, in particular, grateful for the time and efforts of their able leaders: Ruth Nadelhaft and Marlie Weiner, who led a seminar for staff and trustees of the Eastern Maine Medical Center; Richard Heinemann and Laura McClure, who led a seminar for members of the Government Lawyers Division of the State Bar of Wisconsin; Adam Schulman and Robert Goldberg, who conducted a seminar on law and justice for judges, public defenders, prosecutors, and attorneys in Maryland; Charles Biebel and Charles Calhoun, who led a seminar for community leaders in Skowhegan, Maine; Joseph Conforti and Robert Lynn, who led a seminar for the Maine philanthropic community; Elizabeth Lynn and Katherine Tillman, who led a seminar for members of a voluntary association for women interested in philanthropy in Indiana; Jan Blits and Robert Goldberg, who led a seminar for museum leaders in the Annapolis area; William Kuhn, who co-directed with me a seminar for faculty, administrators, trustees, and students at Carthage College in Kenosha, Wisconsin; Kathleen Ashley and Charles Biebel, who led a seminar in Maine for educational leaders—school board members, teachers, principals, and superintendents at the K–12 level, and faculty and administrators from university schools of education; Henry Higuera and Chris Kelly, who led a seminar with service-providers for new citizens at the Office of New Americans in Maryland; Sanford Kessler and Kim Curtis, who conducted a seminar for staff and trustees from two literacy organizations in North Carolina; and finally, Mark Schwehn and Albert Trost, who led a seminar for staff and trustees of a northwest Indiana youth-serving organization. Special thanks, too, to the Maryland Humanities Council, which assisted in the organization of the seminars in Maryland; and, most especially, to Dorothy Schwartz, whose enthusiasm for the "Tocqueville Seminars" program from its inception in no small part helped sustain it nationwide, and whose leadership of the Maine Humanities Council was responsible for all of the seminars in Maine.

Of the many wonderful gifts Susan Wisely bestowed upon me, the very best was introducing me to Elizabeth Lynn, whose friendship, prudent advice, and optimism about the worthiness of this volume were indispensable for its completion. Thanks also to Elizabeth Lynn for making available to me her own very able administrative staff at the Project on Civic Reflection at Valparaiso University: Gloria Ruff arranged for the typing of the manuscript and helped to proofread it. Pat Dwyer provided able assistance securing permissions to reprint the various selections. Mary Kennedy helped secure permissions and, along with Elizabeth Lynn, offered invaluable suggestions for inclusion and organization, as well as critical comments on my own introductory materials.

My bibliographical research was made far easier than it otherwise would have been by Joseph C. Harmon's "Philanthropy in Short Fiction: An Annotated Bibliography and Subject Index" (published in the Essays on Philanthropy series by the Indiana University Center on Philanthropy), as well as by Jan Harbaugh's considerable efforts.

Jane Lyle at Indiana University Press rendered excellent help with copyediting. My sponsoring editor, Marilyn Grobschmidt, skillfully and very diligently shepherded the volume through production.

Last but most, I am grateful to Leon, who has been, from beginning to end, as intimately a part of this project as he has been of everything else most dear to me these past two score and more years.

Index

Addams, Jane,
  "Charitable Effort," 140
Albom, Mitch,
  "The Eighth Tuesday: We Talk About
  Money," 336
Aleichem, Sholom,
  "Epilogue: Reb Yozifl and the
  Contractor," 289
Alumni giving. *See* Higher education and
  giving
Aristotle,
  "Generosity, Extravagance, and
  Stinginess," 15
  "Moral Virtue as the Result of Habits,"
  345
Art and giving,
  Wharton, "The Rembrandt," 161
Associations,
  Lynn and Wisely, "Only Reflect," 411
  Tocqueville, Freedom and Utility, 21

Barbusse, Henri,
  "The Eleventh," 245
Benefactor. *See* Giver, hopes and
  expectations of
Beneficiary. *See* Recipient, criteria for
Brooks, Gwendolyn,
  "The Lovers of the Poor," 200

Carnegie, Andrew,
  "The Gospel of Wealth," 230
Charity, fictive examples of,
  Barbusse, "The Eleventh," 245
  Benet, "The Bishop's Beggar," 378
  Brooks, "The Lovers of the Poor,"
  200
  Crane, "The Men in the Storm," 261
  Frost, "The Death of the Hired Man,"
  303
  Henry, "Two Thanksgiving Day
  Gentlemen," 42
  Holmes, "Town Office," 395
  Homer, The Meeting of Nausikaa and
  Odysseus, 119
  Jewett, "The Spur of the Moment," 127

Kipling, "The Record of Badalia
  Herodsfoot," 174
Peretz, "Motl Prince," 135
Reed, "Another Case of Ingratitude,"
  197
Shakespeare, *Timon of Athens,* 215
Warner, "A Work of Art," 191
Welty, "Lily Daw and the Three Ladies,"
  319
Wharton, "The Rembrandt," 161
Charity, meaning of,
  Addams, "Charitable Effort," 140
  Carnegie, "The Gospel of Wealth," 230
  Kass, L., "Charity and the Confines of
  Compassion," 267
  Lewis, "Charity," 47
  Lynn and Wisely, "Toward a Fourth
  Philanthropic Response," 103
  Maimonides, "The Book of Seeds," 125
  Orwin, "Princess Diana and Mother
  Teresa," 88
Church liturgy,
  Kirk, "Worship, Humility and Service,"
  378
  May, "The Prayers of Thanksgiving,"
  75
Churches, giving to,
  Carnegie, "The Gospel of Wealth," 242
Citizenship,
  Eliot, "An Arresting Voice," 37
  Franklin, "Practice Makes Perfect?," 348
  Tocqueville, Freedom and Utility, 21
  Wilson, "Princeton for the Nation's
  Service," 356
Civic reflection, practice of,
  Kass, A., Introduction, 6
  Lynn and Wisely, "Only Reflect," 409
Compassion, history of,
  Orwin, "Princess Diana and Mother
  Teresa," 88
Compassion, meaning and limits of,
  XIV Dalai Lama, "Giving and
  Receiving" 399
  Kass, L., "Charity and the Confines of
  Compassion," 267

Crane, Stephen,
  "The Men in the Storm," 261
Cynicism about giving,
  Reed, "Another Case of Ingratitude,"
    197
  Schwartz, "The Social Psychology of the
    Gift," 77
  Shakespeare, *Timon of Athens,*
    222–226

Democracy and philanthropy,
  Addams, "Charitable Effort," 140
  Tocqueville, Freedom and Utility, 21
Developmentally disabled persons, care
    for,
  Welty, "Lily Daw and the Three Ladies,"
    319
Domestic violence, relief of,
  Kipling, "The Record of Badalia
    Herodsfoot," 174
Duty,
  Carnegie, "The Gospel of Wealth," 230
  Eliot, "An Arresting Voice," 34
  Wilson, "Princeton for a Nation's
    Service," 356

Eliot, George,
  "An Arresting Voice," 34
Estate-planning,
  Carnegie, "The Gospel of Wealth,"
    230–234
  Luke, The Parable of the Prodigal Son,
    283
Evaluating giving,
  Aristotle, "Generosity, Extravagance,
    and Stinginess," 15
  Barbusse, "The Eleventh," 245
  Carnegie, "The Gospel of Wealth," 236
  Jewett, "The Spur of the Moment," 127
  Matthew, Three Parables, 115
  Schwartz, "The Social Psychology of the
    Gift," 77
Extravagance,
  Aristotle, "Generosity, Extravagance,
    and Stinginess," 15
  Carnegie, "The Gospel of Wealth," 236

Faith and giving (*see also* Churches,
    giving to),
  Maimonides, "The Book of Seeds," 125
  May, "The Prayers of Thanksgiving," 75
Faith and philanthropic leadership,

Aleichem, "Reb Yozifl and the
    Contractor," 289
Peretz, "Motl Prince," 135
Faith and service,
  Benet, "The Bishop's Beggar," 378
  XIV Dalai Lama, "Giving and
    Receiving," 399
  Kirk, Worship, Humility and Service,
    372–375
  Lewis, "Charity," 47
  Orwin, "Princess Diana and Mother
    Teresa," 88
Foolish giving (*see also* Wisdom),
  Aleichem, "Reb Yozifl and the
    Contractor," 289
  Henry, "Two Thanksgiving Day
    Gentlemen," 42
  Leacock, "Mr. Plumter, B.A., Revisits the
    Old Shop," 249
  Mac Orlan, "The Philanthropist," 369
  Shakespeare, *Timon of Athens,* 215
Foundations, private,
  Lynn and Wisely, "Toward a Fourth
    Philanthropic Response," 102
XIV Dalai Lama,
  "Giving and Receiving: A Practical Way
    of Directing Love and Compassion,"
    399
Franklin, Benjamin,
  "Practice Makes Perfect?," 348
Freedom,
  Eliot, "An Arresting Voice," 36
  Tocqueville, Freedom and Utility, 22
Frost, Robert,
  "The Death of the Hired Man," 303
Fundraising,
  Aleichem, "Reb Yozifl and the
    Contractor," 289
  Henry, "The Chair of
    Philanthromathematics," 155
  O'Hara, "Memorial Fund," 315

Generosity,
  Aristotle, "Generosity, Extravagance,
    and Stinginess," 15
  Jewett, "The Spur of the Moment," 127
  Mac Orlan, "The Philanthropist," 369
Genesis,
  4, The Offering of Cain, 13
  25:19–34, 27–28:9, Parents and
    Children: The Case of Jacob and Esau,
    207

Gift-love,
  Lewis, "Charity," 47
Gifts, assessing worth of,
  Hyde, "Some Food We Could Not Eat,"
    328
  Jewett, "The Spur of the Moment,"
    127
  Schwartz, "The Social Psychology of the
    Gift," 77
  Shakespeare, *Timon of Athens,* 215
  Wharton, "The Rembrandt," 161
Gifts, good,
  Albom, "The Eighth Tuesday," 336
  Homer, The Meeting of Nausikaa and
    Odysseus, 119
  Maimonides, "The Book of Seeds,"
    125
  Tagore, "Gift," 295
Giver and recipient, relationship of,
  Addams, "Charitable Effort," 140
  Benet, "The Bishop's Beggar," 378
  Brooks, "The Lovers of the Poor," 200
  Henry, "Two Thanksgiving Day
    Gentlemen," 42
  Hyde, "Some Food We Could Not Eat,"
    328
  Lynn and Wisely, "Toward a Fourth
    Philanthropic Response," 102
  Matthew, Three Parables, 115
  May, "The Prayers of Thanksgiving,"
    75
  Peretz, "Motl Prince," 135
  Reed, "Another Case of Ingratitude,"
    197
  Schwartz, "The Social Psychology of the
    Gift," 77
  Warner, "A Work of Art," 191
  Wodehouse, "Jeeves Takes Charge," 57
Giver, hopes and expectations of,
  Addams, "Charitable Effort," 140
  Crane, "The Men in the Storm," 261
  Kass, L., "Charity and the Confines of
    Compassion," 267
  Warner, "A Work of Art," 191
Giving in wartime,
  Benet, "The Bishop's Beggar," 378
  Eliot, "An Arresting Voice," 34
  Parker, "Song of the Shirt, 1941," 308
Gratitude and ingratitude,
  Brooks, "The Lovers of the Poor," 200
  May, "The Prayers of Thanksgiving,"
    75

  Reed, "Another Case of Ingratitude,"
    197
  Shakespeare, *Timon of Athens,* 215

Henry, O.,
  "The Chair of Philanthromathematics,"
    155
  "The Gift of the Magi," 298
  "Two Thanksgiving Day Gentlemen," 42
Higher education and giving,
  Henry, "The Chair of
    Philanthromathematics," 155
  Leacock, "Mr. Plumter, B.A., Revisits the
    Old Shop," 249
  O'Hara, "Memorial Fund," 315
  Wilson, "Princeton for the Nation's
    Service," 356
Holiday giving,
  Henry, "The Gift of the Magi," 298
  Henry, "Two Thanksgiving Day
    Gentlemen," 42
  Schwartz, "The Social Psychology of the
    Gift," 81
Holmes, Edward,
  "Town Office," 395
Homelessness, relief of,
  Crane, "The Men in The Storm," 261
  Frost, "The Death of the Hired Man,"
    303
Homer,
  The Meeting of Nausikaa and Odysseus,
    119
Hunger, relief of,
  Henry, "Two Thanksgiving Day
    Gentlemen," 42
  Reed, "Another Case of Ingratitude,"
    197
Hyde, Lewis,
  "Some Food We Could Not Eat," 328

Indian-giving, concept of,
  Hyde, "Some Food We Could Not Eat,"
    328
Ingratitude. *See* Gratitude and
    ingratitude
Inheritance,
  Genesis, Parents and Children, 207
  Luke, The Parable of the Prodigal Son,
    283

Jewett, Sarah Orne,
  "The Spur of the Moment," 127

Kass, Leon R.,
  "Charity and the Confines of
  Compassion," 267
Kipling, Rudyard,
  "The Record of Badalia Herodsfoot,"
  174
Kirk, Kenneth E.,
  Worship, Humility and Service, 372

Leacock, Stephen,
  "Mr. Plumter, B.A., Revisits the Old
  Shop," 249
Legacy. *See* Inheritance
Lewis, C. S.,
  "Charity," 47
Love,
  Addams, "Charitable Effort," 140
  Albom, "The Eighth Tuesday," 336
  Brooks, "The Lovers of the Poor," 200
  Henry, "The Gift of the Magi," 298
  Lewis, "Charity," 47
  Luke, The Parable of the Prodigal Son,
  283
  Lynn and Wisely, "Toward a Fourth
  Philanthropic Response," 104
  May, "The Prayers of Thanksgiving,"
  75
  Orwin, "Princess Diana and Mother
  Teresa," 88
  Tagore, "The Gift," 295
  Tocqueville, "Appendix U," The Pioneer
  Woman, 285
Luke,
  15:11–32, The Parable of the Prodigal
  Son, 283
Lynn, Elizabeth M., with D. Susan Wisely,
  "Only Reflect: A Philanthropic
  Education for our Time," 409
  "Toward a Fourth Philanthropic
  Response: American Philanthropy and
  Its Public," 102

Mac Orlan, Pierre
  "The Philanthropist," 369
Maimonides, Moses,
  "The Book of Seeds," 125
Matthew,
  25:1–46, Three Parables, 115
  25:14–30, The Parable of the Talents,
  213
May, William F.,
  "The Prayers of Thanksgiving," 75

McGuffey, William H.,
  "True and False Philanthropy," 227
Memorial giving,
  O'Hara, "Memorial Fund," 315
Museums. *See* Art and giving

Need-love,
  Lewis, "Charity," 47
Neighborliness,
  Addams, "Charitable Effort," 142–144
  Eliot, "An Arresting Voice," 34

Offering, making an (*see also* Sacrifice),
  Albom, "The Eighth Tuesday," 336
  Eliot, "An Arresting Voice," 34
  Genesis, The Offering of Cain, 13
  Mac Orlan, "The Philanthropist," 369
Office Pollyanna, tradition of
  Schwartz, "The Social Psychology of the
  Gift," 78
O'Hara, John,
  "Memorial Fund," 315
Orwin, Clifford,
  "Princess Diana and Mother Teresa:
  Compassion and Christian Charity,"
  88

Parental giving,
  Luke, The Parable of the Prodigal Son,
  283
  Schwartz, "The Social Psychology of the
  Gift," 78
  Tocqueville, "Appendix U," The Pioneer
  Woman, 285
Parker, Dorothy,
  "Song of the Shirt, 1941," 308
Parks and recreation, giving for,
  Carnegie, "The Gospel of Wealth,"
  241–242
Peretz, Isaac,
  "Motl Prince," 135
Philanthropy as civic engagement,
  Addams, "Charitable Effort," 140
  Eliot, "An Arresting Voice," 34
  Lynn and Wisely, "Toward a Fourth
  Philanthropic Response," 108
  Tocqueville, Freedom and Utility, 27–31
Philanthropy as improvement,
  Carnegie, "The Gospel of Wealth," 230
  Franklin, "Practice Makes Perfect?," 348
  Kass, L., "Charity and the Confines of
  Compassion," 267

Lynn and Wisely, "Toward a Fourth Philanthropic Response," 105

Wilson, "Princeton for the Nation's Service," 356

Philanthropy as relief (*see also* Charity, fictive examples of; Charity, meaning of),

Barbusse, "The Eleventh," 245

Carnegie, "The Gospel of Wealth," 230

Crane, "The Men in the Storm," 261

Frost, "The Death of the Hired Man," 303

Kass, L., "Charity and the Confines of Compassion," 267

Lynn and Wisely, "Toward a Fourth Philanthropic Response," 103

McGuffey, "True and False Philanthropy," 227

Philanthropy as social control,

Addams, "Charitable Effort," 140

Crane, "The Men in the Storm," 261

Hyde, "Some Food We Could Not Eat," 328

Schwartz, "The Social Psychology of the Gift," 77

Welty, "Lily Daw and the Three Ladies," 319

Philanthropy as social reform,

Addams, "Charitable Effort," 140

Lynn and Wisely, "Toward a Fourth Philanthropic Response," 106

McGuffey, "True and False Philanthropy," 227

Philanthropy, perils of,

Crane, "The Men in the Storm," 261

Henry, "Two Thanksgiving Day Gentlemen," 42

Holmes, "Town Office," 395

Kass, L., "Charity and the Confines of Compassion," 267

Kipling, "The Record of Badalia Herodsfoot," 174

Mac Orlan, "The Philanthropist," 369

Peretz, "Motl Prince," 135

Reed, "Another Case of Ingratitude," 197

Welty, "Lily Daw and the Three Ladies," 319

Philanthropy, traditions of,

Lynn and Wisely, "Toward a Fourth Philanthropic Response," 102

Poverty, relief of,

Addams, "Charitable Effort," 140

Aleichem, "Reb Yozifl and the Contractor," 289

Barbusse, "The Eleventh," 245

Brooks, "The Lovers of the Poor," 200

Crane, "The Men in the Storm," 261

Holmes, "Town Office," 395

Kipling, "The Record of Badalia Herodsfoot," 174

Shakespeare, *Timon of Athens,* 215

Warner, "A Work of Art," 191

Wharton, "The Rembrandt," 161

Recipient, criteria for,

Carnegie, "The Gospel of Wealth," 230

Frost, "The Death of the Hired Man," 303

Genesis, Parents and Children, 207

Holmes, "Town Office," 395

Kipling, "The Record of Badalia Herodsfoot," 174

Luke, The Parable of the Prodigal Son, 283

Matthew, The Parable of the Talents, 213

McGuffey, "True and False Philanthropy," 227

Shakespeare, *Timon of Athens,* 215

Recipient, hopes and expectations of,

Addams, "Charitable Effort," 140

Benet, "The Bishop's Beggar," 378

Shakespeare, *Timon of Athens,* 215

Warner, "A Work of Art," 191

Reed, John,

"Another Case of Ingratitude," 197

Sacrifice (*see also* Offering, making an),

Benet, "The Bishop's Beggar," 378

Eliot, "An Arresting Voice," 34

Genesis, The Offering of Cain, 13

Henry, "The Gift of the Magi," 298

Kipling, "The Record of Badalia Herodsfoot," 174

Parker, "Song of the Shirt, 1941," 308

Tocqueville, "Appendix U," The Pioneer Woman, 285

Schwartz, Barry,

"The Social Psychology of the Gift," 77

Self-interest,

Franklin, "Practice Makes Perfect?," 348

Hyde, "Some Food We Could Not Eat,"
328
Schwartz, "The Social Psychology of the
Gift," 77
Tocqueville, Freedom and Utility,
31–33
Service and servants,
Benet, "The Bishop's Beggar," 378
Eliot, "An Arresting Voice," 34
Kass, L., "Charity and the Confines of
Compassion," 267
Kipling, "The Record of Badalia
Herodsfoot," 174
Kirk, Worship, Humility and Service,
372
Parker, "Song of the Shirt, 1941," 308
Wilson, "Princeton for the Nation's
Service," 356
Wodehouse, "Jeeves Takes Charge," 57
Service-learning (*see also* Higher
education and giving),
Wilson, "Princeton for the Nation's
Service," 356
Shakespeare, William,
Timon of Athens, Act I, Scene I, 215
Social anthropology,
Hyde, "Some Food We Could Not Eat,"
328
Social control. *See* Philanthropy as social
control
Social psychology,
Schwartz, "The Social Psychology of the
Gift," 77
Stinginess,
Aristotle, "Generosity, Extravagance,
and Stinginess," 15

Tagore, Rabindranath,
"Gift," 295
Tainted money,
Kass, A., Introduction, 3
Henry, "The Chair of
Philanthromathematics," 155
Thanksgiving, holiday of,
Henry, "Two Thanksgiving Day
Gentlemen," 42
Thanksgiving, prayer of,
May, "The Prayers of Thanksgiving," 75
Tocqueville, Alexis de,
"Appendix U," The Pioneer Woman, 285
Freedom and Utility, 21
Traditions of giving,

Henry, "Two Thanksgiving Day
Gentlemen," 42
Hyde, "Some Food We Could Not Eat,"
328
Lynn and Wisely, "Toward a Fourth
Philanthropic Response," 102
Schwartz, "The Social Psychology of the
Gift," 77

Vocation,
Benet, "The Bishop's Beggar," 378
Eliot, "An Arresting Voice," 34
Orwin, "Princess Diana and Mother
Teresa," 88
Wodehouse, "Jeeves Takes Charge," 57
Volunteerism,
Brooks, "The Lovers of the Poor," 200
Holmes, "Town Office," 395
Kass, L., "Charity and the Confines of
Compassion," 267
Parker, "Song of the Shirt, 1941," 308
Tocqueville, Freedom and Utility, 21
Welty, "Lily Daw and the Three Ladies,"
319

Warner, Sylvia,
"A Work of Art," 191
War-relief. *See* Giving in wartime
Wealth,
Aristotle, "Generosity, Extravagance and
Stinginess," 16
Carnegie, "The Gospel of Wealth," 230
Hyde, "Some Food We Could Not Eat,"
328
Lynn and Wisely, "Only Reflect," 409
Welty, Eudora,
"Lily Daw and the Three Ladies," 319
Wharton, Edith,
"The Rembrandt," 161
Wilson, Woodrow,
"Princeton for the Nation's Service," 356
Wisdom (*see also* Foolish giving),
Henry, "The Gift of the Magi," 298
Wisely, D. Susan, with Elizabeth M. Lynn,
"Only Reflect: A Philanthropic
Education for Our Time," 409
"Toward a Fourth Philanthropic
Response: American Philanthropy and
Its Public," 102
Wodehouse, P. G.,
"Jeeves Takes Charge," 57
Worship. *See* Church liturgy

Women and giving,
  Addams, "Charitable Effort," 140
  Brooks, "The Lovers of the Poor,"
    200
  Eliot, "An Arresting Voice," 34
  Henry, "The Gift of the Magi," 298
  Holmes, "Town Office," 395
  Homer, The Meeting of Nausikaa and
    Odysseus, 119
  Jewett, "The Spur of the Moment,"
    127
  Kipling, "The Record of Badalia
    Herodsfoot," 174

Orwin, "Princess Diana and Mother
  Teresa," 88
Parker, "Song of the Shirt, 1941," 308
Tocqueville, "Appendix U," The Pioneer
  Woman, 285
Warner, "A Work of Art," 191
Welty, "Lily Daw and the Three Ladies,"
  319

XIV Dalai Lama,
  "Giving and Receiving: A Practical Way
    of Directing Love and Compassion,"
    399

Amy A. Kass is Senior Lecturer in the Humanities Collegiate Division at the University of Chicago. An award-winning teacher, she has for more than twenty-five years taught classic texts of literature and philosophy to college students. Looking beyond the academy, she has directed seminars nationwide to help people think about the whys and wherefores of their own civic and philanthropic activities. She is the author of two other anthologies: *American Lives: Cultural Differences, Individual Distinction* and *Wing to Wing, Oar to Oar: Readings on Courting and Marrying* (with Leon Kass).